Wesley's Bunch

Written by Amy Swapp
Told by Alton Miller

In remembrance of

Hoyt Lynn Miller, Sr.

Harry Milton Miller

And for the lost memories of

Louie Edward Miller

My daddy is Alton Miller. I grew up hearing wonderful stories of him and his brothers and sisters. They travelled from South to West and back again living in sawmill shacks, roadside camps and train cars. It wasn't until I was grown that I realized that no one had experiences like him and his family. No one I knew had ever driven to Alaska in December, or actually saved puppies from being drown in a creek.

As we sat down to get these stories on paper, even though many years had passed, he remembered so much detail. I felt I was there. I could feel the cold, the hot, the hunger. I also felt the joy, the love and the adventure.

When I put these stories together for this book, I could only write them in the first person. These are Alton's memories and I hope you hear his voice as you head down the road with Wesley's Bunch.

Amy Swapp

Good Timber

The tree that never had to fight
For sun and sky and air and light,
But stood out in the open plain
And always got its share of rain,
Never became a forest king
But lived and died a scrubby thing.

The man who never had to toil
To gain and farm his patch of soil,
Who never had to win his share
Of sun and sky and light and air,
Never became a manly man
But lived and died as he began.

Good timber does not grow with ease:
The stronger wind, the stronger trees;
The further sky, the greater length;
The more the storm, the more the strength.
By sun and cold, by rain and snow,
In trees and men good timbers grow.

Where thickest lies the forest growth,
We find the patriarchs of both.
And they hold counsel with the stars
Whose broken branches show the scars
Of many winds and much of strife.
This is the common law of life.

Douglas Malloch

ALCAN HIGHWAY 1961

The car sputtered... and choked... and died.

"We're out of gas," Daddy said. All of us sat up in the '51 Ford. Mama was in the middle and I was by the passenger door. We looked at him as he pumped the pedal. The five younger kids got quiet in the back, not wanting to make a fuss. The cold was already creeping in.

Daddy pumped the pedal again trying to start her up, just in case he was wrong. But the engine wouldn't turn over. The car was quiet and we were silent as we coasted down the road. Daddy steered to a wide spot on the right and we came to a dead stop.

Out of gas, out of money, out of food.

Daddy was upset and banged his hand on the steering wheel, "Confound it!"

We had left Alamosa, Colorado on the seventeenth day of December, just a few days before. It was hard to tell how many since we hadn't seen much of the sun. Of all the trips we had made, the dark and cold road to Alaska was the longest. Daddy had spent the last of his money on gas. We had hoped it would get us to Anchorage.

I sat there trying to think; I was sixteen and ought to be able to find a way to help. Mama got busy, "All of you children wrap up tight, right away. It's gonna get colder fast. Esther hand us a couple of blankets from those y'all are layin' on. You wrap up together to share warmth. We'll all just rest and wait for someone to come." Mama was calm as she told us what to do.

"I'm gonna leave these lights on, it'll help somebody see us if they come up the road," Daddy said.

The car groaned and creaked as it lost what little heat it had held. The fogged windows froze until we couldn't see out. Time ticked by. Darkness surrounded us. Even though we strained to look out the window, no car came around the curve to find us. We were quiet as we huddled together for warmth. None of us kids wanted to sound like we were scared so we didn't say anything. The silence was broken only by Mama's whispers as she prayed non-stop.

Nine year old Mary whispered to Sheron, "Surely the Lord's heard Mama, she's said the same prayer enough times." Sheron shushed her, being older, she knew better than Mary not to complain.

Daddy patted Mama on the leg every once in a while and told her somebody'd come for us. Days and nights of driving and lack of sleep made it easy for him to doze off. He fell asleep with his head against the door, using his felt hat as a cushion. We all tried to sleep or pretended to. Every time I opened my eyes, Mama was looking through a spot in the window she had rubbed, hoping to see lights coming.

As the night wore on, the cold kept creeping in. At first, it was mostly my feet that were so cold, then my legs, until my whole body seemed frozen. I couldn't stop the shivers that snuck up on me every so often. I tried to ignore the cold, but the ache in my hands from using them to shovel snow earlier wouldn't let me forget. The headlights on our car got dimmer, the beam of lights got smaller and lower until they were gone. The colder it got, the easier it was to sleep.

"Try to think of somethin' warm," Mama told us. I closed my eyes and my thoughts slowed down as I imagined hot coffee and wood fire. Something warm? There wasn't anything much hotter than back in Louisiana in the summer. I saw myself running, red faced and sweaty in the humid heat, trying to find shade under the pines. The smell of cut timber drifted up from the sawmill as I listened to Daddy cut the logs. The song of the saw echoing through the woods...

RW and Fonceal,
Harry, Elaine, Rubin, Louie
Sheron, Esther and Alton
1949

LOUISIANA 1949

Song of the Saw

We lived in a little house off a white, dusty road in a clear spot under the pines. The house was made from rough lumber that had grown dark over time. The windows were wide open to catch a cool breeze which let in all the gnats, flies and mosquitoes. They were probably looking for a cool spot themselves.

My older brothers, Louie and Rubin, drew our water from the well for Mama and brought her the wood for the cook stove. Louie was ten and Rubin eight, but they were almost the same size. Mama was frying an old hen she had decided to kill for the noonday meal. She'd wrung its neck fast with just a few jerks of her wrist and off came the head. The chicken's body jumped around the yard flapping its wings like it was still alive, head or no head. I wouldn't ever let on that it was scary but I couldn't keep my eyes off it, making sure it didn't get near me.

Mama and my older sister, Elaine, were cooking. I didn't pay much attention to those older than me, but folks sure thought it was something that Louie and Elaine were both born in the same year, Louie in February and Elaine in December of 1939. Elaine was the only help Mama had since my others sisters Sheron, was just two, and Esther, was just a baby.

Mama scalded the dead chicken in a pot of hot water outside and had Elaine help her scrape the feathers. They cut it up, floured and fried it. Mama took the last pieces out of the pan of grease. Today there would be meat to go with potatoes and cornbread. There might be enough chicken left for us kids, too.

I was just about five and just younger than my brother Harry. I had been born right after a big war ended. I knew about it because Mama's brother, Uncle Milton, fought in it.

Grandma and Grandpa Mac's house.

When he came back from France, Grandpa and Grandma Mac were so excited they painted the house. They didn't have enough money to paint it all so they painted the front and the side he would see when he drove up. It still looked good from that side.

"Harry! Alton! Come help us tote this to the mill," hollered Mama. Mama was coming down the back steps of the house. She told Elaine to watch Sheron and Esther while we fed Daddy and the men at the mill. Mama had long reddish brown hair that she put in two braids and pinned to the top of her head. She didn't ever get too upset no matter how much trouble anybody gave her. She was mild and sweet, but we had better mind or she would take a switch to us.

Harry was about the only one of us able to get out of trouble with Mama. It seemed like he could just grin his way out of a whippin'. Elaine told a story about Mama whippin' Harry. When he was old enough to talk good he came in the house and told Mama, "I bookied in my britches." She was fit to be tied as she stood there with her hands on her hips. "A boy old enough to talk, still going in his britches!"

She'd had enough. She got a stick from the kindling pile and took it to his backside. He wailed and she whipped. When she got done she saw that the stick had a nail in it that

2

had poked Harry. She felt so bad about it she just about cried. From then on it took a lot for her to whip Harry. He knew it too. I didn't know how to wink and laugh myself out of trouble so I just learned to take it.

A whippin' from Mama wasn't too bad anyway, but if it was from Daddy that was something else. He'd hold your arm and whip you till you danced. Mama might have to holler and holler to get us to do something, but if Daddy cleared his throat, that was it, we jumped. We didn't push Daddy far.

Mama walked down the path towards the woods. Harry and me were half running along to keep up with her. I could hear the sound of a motor running and as we got closer to the mill it got louder. As regular as the tick of a clock the motor was drowned out by the sharp whistle of the saw cutting through a log to make lumber.

I watched as the big flywheel spun a hundred times a minute. The wheel was taller than me and when it spun, a leather strap on the outside turned a pulley that spun even faster and that powered the saw to cut logs. Once it got to turning, the flywheel was so big it almost kept itself turning. That's what I heard Daddy say, anyway. Daddy worked as a sawmiller. That's what he had always done and his daddy before him.

When Daddy spotted us coming he signaled the men to stop working. They were colored men from the same family named Gay who lived in New Town. They found spots to rest either on the ground or sitting on stumps out of the sun. There wasn't any place to get out of the heat. Mama fed everybody at the mill, and Harry and me made sure we didn't get in the way of the grown men.

"Afternoon, Miz Fonceal, that chicken shore do smell good," Bob Gay greeted Mama. Mama answered him with a smile and a thank you and found a place to put all the food.

3

Bob Gay was a big man, the biggest of the brothers and the oldest. He was like us kids and didn't wear shoes in the summer either. I wasn't sure I'd ever seen him wear shoes any time.

"How you chilluns today?" Crit asked us. We answered but knew we weren't to talk too much. Children couldn't be a bother to grownups. We scampered around handing out plates to the men. We took the water bucket around and handed the dipper full of water for them to drink.

"Mister Wesley, y'all shouldn't have these young'uns runnin' to get water for us," Little Jimmy told Daddy.

"These boys ain't got nothin' better to do than to get water. It's good for 'em," Daddy said to the colored men. Daddy thought that's just how it should be. They thanked us before putting the dipper of water to their mouth and getting a long drink.

The men were sweaty from working in the heat. It ran down Daddy's face and neck from his hair. He was a dark headed man or he had been when he was younger, now he had quite a bit of gray that he kept covered with a small brimmed hat. Up against other men he was somewhere in the middle of them in size. He wore tan pants and a shirt buttoned to his neck and the sleeves buttoned to his wrists. He always wore an undershirt or sometimes long underwear under his clothes. When his underclothes would get soaked with sweat it would help cool him down. You had to find tricks to get cool in Louisiana.

Daddy sat right alongside the colored men as they ate their dinner. It didn't make any difference to him to dip water out of the same bucket. I had heard some at the store in town talking about how to treat colored men, especially how Daddy ought to do it. From what I saw Daddy always treated them the same as everyone, white or colored. No matter what folks told Daddy, he always went his own way.

4

"Thank ye, Miz Miller," every one of them said to Mama. We cleaned up and headed back to the house while the men rested in the heat of the day. I heard Daddy's big laugh as he told them all about his days riding the train with his brother, my Uncle Ted. I stopped walking back and sat by a tree and listened to Daddy tell stories of his loafing days before Mama.

"Me and ol' Ted were in Texas in '31, didn't know which way to go, east or west. We sat on the railroad tracks and let the next train decide us. Here it came and west it was. We jumped on and rode. Now boys, you got to jump on from the front of the car. If you miss you'll fall into the train and hit the side of the car, keeping you from going under. If you jump from the back and miss you can swing in between the cars and go under the wheels real easy." I made sure to remember how to jump a freight car. I planned on being just like Daddy and knew I needed to know how to get around.

"Sometimes there'd be thirty or forty of us fellas on a car. If you had any money you never could put all of it in the same pocket, in case you got jumped. Nobody had nothin' then, boys. Ted would go up to people's doors and act crippled so we could get something to eat. We'd work in a place and when the work run out we'd jump a railcar and head to the next town."

Daddy was living fast in those days. He knew about all kinds of places from his days before Mama. I didn't know anybody else who had stories like Daddy. The family always said Wesley sure did like to ramble. The men laughed at the stories Daddy told and said, "Come on now, Mister Wesley," acting like the story couldn't be true. I don't think any of them had ever been out of Natchitoches Parish.

They started back up the motor and got the flywheel turning. The log was rolled down into the carriage which held it in place. Crit rode on the carriage as the ratchet setter, that

5

set how thick to cut the board. Daddy moved the log in the carriage with Crit riding it towards the saw blade. I watched Crit on that carriage and it sure looked like fun, but I didn't dare ask Daddy to ride it. He probably wouldn't let me that close to the saw, but more than that I'd be in the way. Jesse threw the bark strips in the slab pile, Little Jimmy and Ed put the bundles together.

Daddy listened to the saw like it was singing a song. If the sound changed he would slow down how fast he pulled the lever so he wouldn't jam up the saw. If the saw sang different, he pushed the log faster to keep the cut straight and true. They cut a hundred railroad ties a day. Bigger ones were made of hickory, sweet gum and post oak, smaller ties were made of pine. I was learning, I could already tell hardwood from softwood like pine. When I carried wood for Mama, pine was lighter. The cross ties were carried up a gangplank to be stacked. Some men carried one tie, Daddy and Bob Gay carried two. Daddy didn't have the size of Bob Gay, but he had the strength.

After I'd gone back to the house I heard the song from the saw change. They were shutting down the mill. The work day was over. One of the men took a two by four and pried it against the flywheel to stop it from spinning. The two by four turned black on the end and if you were close by you could smell the burning wood. The men walked towards their houses at New Town where the colored folks lived.

It was said Daddy was a hard man to work for because he bossed his crew pretty heavy. A lot of the white men wouldn't work for RW Miller because he used so much colored labor. Daddy was kind of an outlaw in Louisiana because of it, but Daddy never had a man do work he wasn't willing to do himself.

6

New Town

The sun shining through the front room window into my face woke me up. It was already getting hot and the quilt I had wrapped around me wasn't helping any. Sometime in the night I had woke up feeling a wet spot. Harry had peed the bed again. I took a quilt with me and went and slept in the chair, I'd rather do that than lay in a wet bed. I didn't need the quilt for keeping warm though, it was to fight the mosquitoes. I couldn't figure which way was worse. Burn up under the quilt or throw it off and get ate up? I knew one thing though; I'd die before I'd ever pee in the bed.

It was time to get up anyway, so I headed to the breakfast table. Mama had made mush and biscuits. I had already made up my mind a time back that I didn't eat mush so I looked over the biscuits. Sometimes there would be white spots on the top from where Mama hadn't stirred them good. If there weren't too many spots I'd pick them out of the biscuit and eat, but sometimes they were all white and they didn't taste good.

Mama said I was about the only one of her kids that wouldn't eat whatever was put in front of me. I just couldn't eat something if it didn't look good even if it meant going without. Good thing about Mama, if you didn't like it you didn't have to eat it. I guess that left more for the rest.

Sometimes, if I didn't like the way the food looked, I just drank milk. A lot of the time, Mama had goat's milk. I could always get a lot of that since nobody else wanted to drink it. Mama told me she gave it to me as a baby and I still liked it. Elaine loved to tell about when I was just learning to walk. I had burned my feet by getting in an old ash pile. It has been left to burn out, but underneath it was still hot. I walked out in it and started hollering. Mama had to walk out into the ash to get me. I spent a few days not being able to walk.

7

Elaine's job had been to keep me on the bed. Mama gave me back my bottle as a comfort. I spent the next couple of years stealing bottles from the girls, first Sheron and then Esther. I was older now and didn't steal bottles anymore but nobody got tired of telling about when I did.

After everybody got to the table I took a biscuit and spooned preserves onto my bread. Sometimes we got ribbon cane syrup and butter and if there was no butter, ribbon cane and bacon grease. I figured out I could make anything taste good if I put enough sweet on it. Sometimes sugar, and if we didn't have any of that, honey.

Honey came from bees and trees. When Daddy or Grandpa would be out in the woods they would look up at the top of hollow trees for hives. They could be as tall as thirty feet high. If there was a hive, the bees would come in and out of the top. The men would cut a notch about half way up the tree and build a fire with a lot of smoke. The bees would fly away from all that smoke and when it looked like they were all gone, men would go ahead and cut the tree down and gather all the honey.

Rubin wasn't like me; he went after every meal like it was his last. When he saw me picking at my plate he'd tell me, "Well then, you must not be very hungry." He'd say it like he couldn't believe it. Rubin was getting big fast. Well, I guess he'd always been big. Mama said he weighed over thirteen pounds when he was born. Over at Grandpa Mac's Daddy liked to use Rubin to tease Grandpa.

"Hey Rube, what you want to be when you grow up?"

"I want to be like Bob Gay!"

Grandpa would get spitting mad. Daddy would slap his leg and Rubin didn't understand what the fuss was about. He wanted to be big like Bob Gay and didn't know why that was wrong. Grandpa said he couldn't believe any of his kin wanted to be like a colored man. I think Rubin just wanted the most to eat.

I swallowed down what I wanted of breakfast and when all the food was gone from the table, Mama and Elaine started cleaning up. They did up the dishes and got their house work started. Tonight after all the work was done, we were going over to New Town to visit Bob Gay and his family.

A black top road ran in front in our house and led to a store nearby. It went on to Coldwater where Daddy's folks, Grandpa and Grandma Miller lived. Beside the store was a gravel road that headed toward Oak Grove and the cemetery where a lot of Mama's people were buried. We had a baby sister, Lyndol Rae, buried there that had died before I was born.

Mama's people lived in Provencal. They were the McDonalds. A little ways down the gravel road, it forked and a dirt road with two white ruts headed toward New Town where the colored people lived. I guess they didn't get black top or gravel.

We bounced down the rutted road that wove its way through the thick woods and underbrush that covered the country. Bob Gay lived in the pines with all his family. Each brother had their own little shack, but they were all close together. The houses were built up on stilts about three feet off the ground. The ground was white clay, the yards were clean of pine needles and the ground was swept hard so there wasn't any grass around the houses.

The grownups shooed all of us away when we got there. Kids were to stay outside. I liked to play with Bob Gay's little girl, Chrissy, who was my age. Sometimes we played in the tire swing and sometimes under the house where the dogs lived. It was cool and dark under there and a good place to keep out of trouble.

The women were in the house visiting. They would send the girls around with tea or coffee to fill the cups of the men who sat on the porch talking. Sometimes I saw them add something from a little brown jug into their cups. They made sure none of the women saw. I liked to lay under the porch and listen to Daddy. He had the best stories. They were always 'before Mama.' Everybody listened to him.

"I had me a trunk of bootleg and so did Ted. We had met just down the road here and were talking to each other outside our car windows as we shared a few swigs. We heard it then, that ol' sheriff coming in that star car. I threw the bottle out the window but he saw me and got out of his car to get it from the weeds. I yelled at Ted, 'Let's head to Texas' and then we hit the air. We was out of the county before he could get back in his car."

Daddy whooped loud as he told the story and the colored men slapped their leg. Daddy told a lot of stories and laughter went on late into the evening. The kids ran around in the dark catching lightening bugs. As the evening wore on, the men got louder till Mama came out and told Daddy it was time to get us all back to the house. He didn't argue as Mama rounded us up.

Mama gave us cornbread and milk to eat when we got back. Daddy went out on the porch and listened to the radio that Mama turned on in the front room. I liked to hear the music too. There was singing and fiddle playing, guitars and dobroes. I like the dobro the best, it looked like a guitar but it was played face up and instead of a hole in the middle it had a big metal piece that looked like a hubcap. A train song came on as Daddy rocked his chair back and forth.

All around the water tank, waiting for a train
A thousand miles away from home, sleeping in the rain

Daddy said you were either a Hank Williams man or a Jimmie Rodgers man. Since Jimmie sang about trains, he was Daddy's man.

I walked up to the brakeman, just to give him a line of talk
He said, "If you got money, I'll see that you don't walk
I haven't got a nickel, not a penny can I show
Get off, get off you railroad bum, and slammed the boxcar door.

We loved it when Jimmie started making his train horn sounds on the radio. The train horn on the radio sounded just like the ones that left Provencal.

Nobody seems to want me, or lend me a helping hand
I'm on my way from Frisco, going back to Dixieland
My pocket book is empty and my heart is full of pain
I'm a thousand miles away from home, waiting on a train.

Daddy's train stories weren't sad like the song, though. He told them like he and Uncle Ted were having a great old time. It seemed to me like it would be a lot of fun making trips instead of working all the time like they did now. I looked over at Daddy to tell him, but he had dozed off in the chair. Mama came and got us all ready for bed. I lay in the front room on the bed I shared with Harry.

I heard Daddy tell Mama it might be time to move out, maybe to Oregon. That perked my ears up, Daddy always liked to move around. Even when he married Mama and had us kids it didn't slow him down. He didn't jump trains any more, but he could pack us all in a car and we would go. As they talked to each other in the night, the idea of leaving seemed to set in. It was fine with me if it was time to find a new town.

Good Bye

"Oh, Fonceal, y'all be careful," Grandma Mac told us as she brought out some bread and preserves for us to take with us in the car.

"Now, Mama, don't you worry none about us. We'll all be fine," Mama told her mother.

"I can't help but worry about y'all, Fonny, so far from home."

"It ain't like we haven't been gone before," Daddy said. He was ready to go.

Grandpa took some puffs out of his pipe and shook Daddy's hand. The kids didn't get let out of the car, because it would have taken too long to round us back up again. We didn't stay but a little bit and the car moved out of sight of the half yellow house.

Daddy nosed our red '41 Pontiac down the gravel road from Provencal towards Coldwater and Grandpa and Grandma Miller's. They came out of their white house when we drove up. They told us all goodbye. Grandma was worried about us making the trip, but she knew once Daddy made his mind up there was no changing it. We had left Louisiana before, the last time we had come back from Arizona where Esther had been born at a town called Show Low.

None of us were quite as sad to be getting away from Grandma Miller's eye. She loved us, but Grandpa and her didn't take any nonsense from a bunch of kids. We couldn't ride the mule. We couldn't chase the chickens. And they were quick to fly off the handle. Grandma had an old rooster that would come after us, trying to peck our legs. Once Daddy

12

told Louie and Rubin to go and knock the head off the rooster, so they did just that. Its body was floppin' all over Grandma's yard. Grandma came out hollering at Daddy,

"Wesley! Wesley! Your damn kids just killed my rooster!"

Louie and Rubin ran and hid.

Daddy hollered back, "Put him in a pot then!"

They didn't just get after us kids, but each other, too. If they got to fussing with each other we knew we had better lay low. Every once in a while Grandpa tried to tell Grandma what to do but she did just what she wanted. Grandpa did love to get Grandma worked up. They had bitterweed in their yard and if the milk cows got into it the milk would taste bad. So they were always trying to keep it dug up. Grandpa would make sure Grandma was in earshot and ask us kids, "You know how to get rid of this bitterweed?"

We didn't know.

"Pour a little whiskey on it and all them up yonder at the Baptist Church will be down here fast and take care of it. They'll have it all lapped up before you know it."

Grandma went to the Baptist Church so the fight was on.

Now it was time to leave them all. Traveling wasn't new to us so we settled in. I didn't look back as we headed down Highway 84 out of Louisiana. Just like Daddy told Uncle Ted in his story, it was

Georgia and Will Miller

13

time to 'head to Texas,' this time all the way through till we got to Oregon.

Driving

I turned my steering wheel to copy the way Daddy turned the wheel on the car. As he slowed down going up the hill he moved the column shift on the steering wheel. I felt the car shift down and the engine made a louder sound. I shifted mine as smooth as him, so did Harry. We grinned at each other.

Our steering wheels weren't exactly like Daddy's. His was bigger and had just three spokes coming out from the center. Ours were pie pans. There was a little lever attached in the center that came out past the edge of the pan. Mama could spin it around when there was pie in the pan to loosen the crust - or we could use it for shifting. Since there wasn't going to be much pie anytime soon, they made good steering wheels.

"We can really drive," I announced to the car. We were all packed in pretty tight, seven kids and Mama and Daddy in a '41 Pontiac.

Rubin wouldn't play along. "Ya'll ain't drivin', you're just bein' silly."

"Let 'em have their fun," Louie said from the front seat in between Mama and Daddy. Since he was oldest he got the best spot in the car.

Rubin wasn't going to be told nothing by Louie so he popped off right back at him, "You don't know much more about drivin' than they do. Remember when you were about seven and drove Daddy's brand new truck into the corncrib at Grandma's. Put a load of ties right through the back window. Your backside sure got warmed up that day."

14

"Ya'll don't fuss," Mama warned us. We looked at Daddy and he wasn't paying us no mind, so we knew we could keep talking.

"Shoot, that was nothin' like the trouble we got into when we were doing mechanic work on Daddy's log truck. We tried to use Elaine's leg to block the tires so the truck wouldn't roll. But her skinny old leg wasn't big enough to keep that truck from movin'. Every time somebody looked at her leg and saw the bruises from the truck rolling over it, me and you got a whippin'," Louie reminded Rubin.

"Well, I don't think it was funny," Elaine piped up.

"You probably don't even remember it, you just heard the folks talking about it, we hadn't even started going to school yet." Rubin looked at her. "We were just trying to do it like Daddy, when you work on a truck you gotta keep it from rolling back."

"What kind of boy uses a little girl's leg as a block to keep a truck from rolling?" Elaine just couldn't see it the boy's way. I don't know if it was from that story, but Elaine was always suspicious of the boys when they wanted her to play.

"I think we got nine whippin's for that, and sent to bed," Louie said.

"Well, I know we didn't get to eat supper." That probably hurt Rubin the worst.

Daddy stopped at a gas station off the side of the road. The man from inside came out and asked Daddy how much. He told him he'd take ten gallons of gasoline, the man pumped the gas into the glass tank on top of the pump. When it showed ten gallons he drained the gas into the tank from the hose. Daddy filled all of the water bags and Rubin put them around the radiator cap to hang in front of the car. We used the bags for drinking and in case the radiator needed a drink too. Daddy didn't let the flax bags dry out, that way

15

they stayed water tight. The girls went with Mama to the outhouse, and us boys peed in the woods behind the station. It was good to get out of the cramped car for a little while.

We stopped that day at a road side camp in east Texas where there was a little stream. That made water easy to get to and we stayed for the night. Harry and me carried buckets of water to Mama where she made a campfire from the wood gathered up by Louie and Rubin. Daddy rested on the ground with his back up against the car and strummed on an old guitar that he didn't know how to play. We all knew before long he would doze off.

While Mama made potato soup, we ran around the camp playing hide and seek and tag. Elaine played with us a little, but mostly tried to mother us. Elaine always thought we were going to get run over. We hardly ever saw a car so I didn't know how it would happen.

"Ya'll watch for snakes!" Mama hollered at us. Lickety split, Harry and me started trying to find some. We knew that wasn't what she meant, but if we got in trouble Harry said we would tell them that's what we thought Mama wanted. He was pretty smart. All we found were rabbits that took off as soon as we rustled through the bushes.

"Elaine, put the baby down on the blanket and help me with these bowls," Mama told her.

"Mama, what if something tries to get her, like a bear or a wild dog?"

"Ain't no bear or wild dog gonna get her, you scaredy cat." Rubin sounded put out with her.

" 'Bout the only thing that might getcha is a polecat," Daddy said. "Then we'll have to just leave ya behind, you'd stink to high heaven." He grinned as he walked up from the car to eat.

Mama handed him a bowl. "Wesley, we need to get these babies fed and put to bed."

16

"Listen to your mama," Daddy told us. He sat and started to eat, "this is mighty good, Fonny."

After we ate we brought our blankets out from the car and made pallets on the ground. Mama and Daddy had a mattress that they laid out and we all slept close to each other. Elaine took Sheron and slept in the back of the car. It wasn't long after everyone lay down that the night got quiet. The sky was black and the stars were bright. There was a little breeze that made the bushes move. I wanted to act big, but I kept checking to see if a bear or a wild dog might be nosing around.

It seemed like we were the only ones in the world until we heard the sound of a car coming down the road. Someone else was out there in the night. As I lay there listening, the sound slowly got louder and when it got close to our camp it broke up the quiet of the night. The headlights were bright as the car passed by the camp. I wondered if they even knew they were passing all of us in our beds right there beside the road. The two red taillights glowed and got further away as the sound of the engine slowly faded. I fell asleep before the sound was gone for good.

The trip was going to take a few days. When us kids weren't fighting or sleeping we watched as the country turned from piney green to fields of grass. The grass changed to rocks and gravel and flat topped hills. We went over mountains that had trees, and mountains with no trees. Water got harder to find and Daddy made sure our water bags stayed full whenever we stopped at stations or creeks. It could be miles and miles before we met anybody on the road and when we did many of them had the same bags on the front of their car.

When Daddy drove into the night I would take my spot under the front seat of the car on the floor. The hump in the middle made a pillow and I would put my legs under the bench seat where Mama sat. I was just the right size and it made a nice bed to lie down on. The motion of the car put me to sleep. I liked my spot, but I didn't dare tell anyone for fear they would try to get it from me.

The country outside turned again to timber. It was big timber and the trees went up the side of the mountains. The country wasn't flat like Louisiana. Out here if there wasn't a mountain, there was a hill and where there wasn't a hill there was the start of another mountain. As we crossed over the Siskiyou's it seemed we were so high we drove through the clouds. They seemed heavy as they rolled down the side of the mountain. Daddy had been this way before on a freight train. He told us how he used to ride the trains back before Mama.

RW Miller

"It was wintertime and cold and everything was covered in snow. The train would go slow up the mountain, so slow you could jump out of the boxcar and keep up with it running at a trot. Me and Ted would jump out as it moved up the mountain and run beside it to get warm. We made sure there wasn't a bridge coming up, or we could be in trouble. We would sing and shout and beat our chests to get the blood moving, stomping our feet in the snow. When it neared the top we'd jump back on and ride her down."

I looked out the window and in my mind tried to see Daddy running alongside a train. I could see him wrapped up

18

in a big coat with his hat low down over his head. I wanted to holler and beat my chest just like Daddy. Riding higher than the clouds I thought I was at the top of the world.

OREGON 1950

Down the Road

Daddy stomped his feet on the porch before he opened the door. Elaine ran to take his hat as he came in.

"Ya'll been good for yore mama today?" he asked as he washed his hands and face in the sink.

"I have, Daddy," Elaine hurried to pick up Esther and put her in her high chair. Daddy moved to the table and we all sat down to eat. I looked at what we were having and hoped it was something worth eating. I was glad to see it was beans and rice. There wasn't too much Mama could do to make that taste bad.

Daddy had moved us to Drew, a little sawmill town in the mountains down a dirt road way off the highway. Evergreen trees were everywhere. Every once in a while there was a clearing with grass and bushes. Daddy was working at one of the nearby sawmills. He walked to the mill every day and in the evening came back smelling like sawdust and sweat.

Daddy ate for a while and then looked at Mama. "Fonny, they told us men today not to come back on Monday. The ground is too muddy with all this spring rain. They're shuttin' down the mill till things clear up."

Mama looked at Daddy as she gave him another piece of cornbread. "What do you plan on doin'?" She didn't seem too worried, but she never did.

"I heard tell there's a road crew working down between here and Grants Pass. I'm gonna take off in the morning. With the little pay I got, I'll get y'all some groceries and get me enough gas to find work."

Daddy was leaving us. He didn't do that too much. Mama wasn't fond of the idea.

21

"I recall the last time you left us back in Louisiana and went to Vernon, Arizona to work," Mama frowned when she said it.

"What do you mean? I sent for you when I got settled. All of ya'll got to come out on the train. You were even payin' customers," Daddy said with a grin, teasing her.

"Mama doesn't love trains like you do, Daddy," Elaine added.

Mama remembered, "That train just drove on past our stop like we didn't need to get off. By the time I got the conductor to stop, we had to walk a mile beside the track back to Holbrook, me and six babies."

"Well, at least you didn't get bit in the back by Rubin," Louie laughed as he said it. Rubin didn't look up, he was eating.

"There were so many people in that train station I woulda bit somebody too if I coulda got away with it," Mama smiled as she said it. After that train trip Mama didn't want any part of railroads.

"I got to find some work. I don't see any way around headin' out and seein' what I can find." Daddy's mind was made up. After we were put to bed, Mama and Daddy talked into the night. I tried to hear what they were saying, but I fell asleep.

That next morning we all stood out in the road as Daddy steered the car down the dirt road to the highway. We ran after him till he was too far ahead and then we lost sight of him as he went around the curve and made his way down the road. It was a slow walk back.

We stayed there in the house, all of us kids and Mama. She kept the house up and had Elaine sing Barbara Allen and other songs with her. Harry sang too, and sometimes I did if I knew the words. We didn't know when Daddy would come back so we kept ourselves busy. When it was warm we played outside. It stayed pretty cool in the mountains, no matter what time of year it was.

Mama didn't let us get too far away from her eye. She was always afraid someone would try and get us. The older kids were always in charge of us younger ones. They got blamed for whatever we got in to. I liked the way that worked, since most of the time being younger wasn't too good. Sometimes Mama would come out and sit with us on the porch and she would look down the road for Daddy.

We ate beans and cornbread and drank powdered milk, which I hated. I thought dishwater might taste better and I decided to go without powdered milk from then on. After a while there wasn't any powdered milk for anybody but the baby so it didn't matter anyway. Mama couldn't make cornbread anymore since we didn't have the stuff that went in it, so we just ate our beans.

Louie found games for us to play. He took the top of tin cans and bent them in half. He nailed them to the side of a stick down at the end. We used them to roll other can lids down the road, as far as Mama would let us go. We would get the lid rolling on its side and run along trying to keep it up on the edge with the stick. When it finally fell over we stooped to pick it up and start again. We always looked down the road for Daddy.

I slurped my bean juice from my bowl. It had been more juice than beans. I looked at Mama but she didn't pay me any attention so I kept on slurping. Over the next few days we finished up the canned peaches we had and ate the oatmeal. Mama mixed more and more water into the milk for the baby. Before it got dark we sat outside and looked down the road for Daddy.

We played outside in the dirt making roads and ate up the last of the rice. We drank lots of water and sang songs. Sometimes we would fuss at each other and Mama would get onto us. She would walk outside and go to the road and I knew she was looking down the road for Daddy.

That next morning, I was sitting in the front room when Mama walked through taking off her apron. Elaine brought Mama her purse and she straightened her dress.

"You little n's behave," Mama said.

"Where are you headin' to?" Harry wanted to know.

"I don't want ya'll goin' outside while I'm gone. I'm goin' to the post office and check if there might be a letter. If I can I'm gonna see if I can't get a few groceries on credit."

Harry and me kept our nose to the window as we watched her walk down the road towards the store. She was looking for word Daddy might have sent at the post office, and the post office was in the store. I wasn't sure what credit was, but I sure hoped it got us something good to eat. We all guessed what Mama might bring. Some wanted canned peaches and some wanted canned cream to go in oatmeal. Everybody wanted candy. I thought we might get some light bread. Store bought bread was so different from cornbread and biscuits, it was like eating cake. We played that guessing game for a long time.

After a while the door opened and shut quietly and Mama walked in. She hadn't been gone long enough for us to get into any trouble so we were really glad to see her. She didn't have anything in her hands. No paper sack full of anything. Louie and Elaine met her at the door, and she shook her head at them. They didn't say anything, but gathered us kids up and started playing with us. Harry and me looked at each other wondering why there wasn't even any beans, but we knew better than to ask.

"What we have is good enough," Louie told Mama and she patted Louie and smiled. Mama made the gravy out of the left over bacon grease, flour and canned milk and stretched it with water. We poured it over bits of bread and

24

biscuits. Louie told Mama how good it was and Rubin took his plate last, after the rest of us had ours. That evening we all went on the porch and looked down the road for Daddy.

After a time Mama told Elaine she was going over to the neighbors to see if they would loan her some money until Daddy got back. One more time, Mama took off her apron, smoothed her dress and walked out of the house to find some help. When she came back we all looked at her and she shook her head, no help. The neighbors had said no to Mama, just like everyone else. They did offer to take her to Medford to see about something called 'assistance'. I thought assistance must be like money. She told them she would ride along with them when they went.

Mama had saved the last of the canned milk to feed the baby. If there was anything I didn't like it was grits, but like everybody else I ate my share and was almost glad to have it. We stayed in the house that day since it was chilly outside. Mama told Elaine she was tired of the cold and sure wished spring would settle in for good. The neighbors were going to take Mama and the baby to Medford later in the day.

The sun shone through the window warming a spot on the floor and showing the dust that floated in the air. I laid down in that spot of sun and it warmed me through the glass. The ray of light went dark as a shadow passed by the window. I looked up and saw that Daddy had walked by the window headed to the front door. I wasn't the only one that saw him because everybody started hollering. Daddy came in through the door and we ran to him, each one of us trying to climb higher on him. I didn't know why, but I started crying. I looked around to see who saw and didn't feel ashamed because everybody else was too. Even Daddy's eyes were watering.

25

He couldn't grab us because he had a paper sack in his hands. I hugged Daddy tight and breathed in his smell of sweat and the outdoors, but for once I didn't smell sawdust.

"Wesley." Mama sounded tired and happy at the same time as she said Daddy's name. We were glad to see him, but the paper sack held surprises for us and we left him to Mama as we all started going through the sack. He had cookies, big orange candy peanuts and candy orange slices. He'd also brought things for Mama to fix supper with. He sat down and started telling his story.

"Fonny, I got down by Grants Pass, about forty miles and I got a job with a road crew building tunnels. Lots of men were trying to get on. When the boss hired me on, I told him I needed to come back here and tell my wife where I was.

"He told me, 'You want work you'll stay right here. Work your four weeks and then you can go home for a couple days. If you don't, I'll hire one of these other boys that are ready to work now.'

"I had to work the four weeks and get the money to come back. I slept in the car at night and worried about y'all. When the last Friday night came, I got paid and headed back here. One of my best tires went flat and I had to fix it on the side of the road. Spent a while getting' it done. I slept on the side of the road a couple of hours and then came in here as fast as I could go."

"Well you're here now." Mama smiled as she said it. She told Daddy that she had gone down to the store to ask the man at the counter if he wouldn't help her even though she didn't have any money. He had told her no. I guess that's why she came back with nothing. We didn't have money or even credit. I wasn't sure if you ate credit or spent it, but we didn't have it either way. She told Daddy about the neighbors that didn't have any money to give but had offered to take her to Medford. She had planned to go with them that very day. I learned for the first time how worried and scared she had been.

Daddy thought it was a sorry state that a man's family couldn't even count on neighbors to help. Mama said they probably didn't have enough for themselves. There never was much extra in a sawmill town.

Foursquare

Harry and me sat outside watching the cars go by. They passed pretty regular, lots of trucks too. Our new place was off the highway and even though people went by all the time, nobody ever slowed down and stopped at our place.

We moved to a place by Talent, just off the road in front of a furniture store. Daddy had made us a house from pallets and two tents. He nailed boards in the pallets to make them solid. He laid them out on the ground and then we all helped him put up the big canvas tents. They were old army tents and he put two of them together to make us a little house. Inside it was bright with the light colored walls. There was a spot inside for the stove and a hole in the roof to let the pipe out. With the two of them together it made a house as big as some of the wooden ones we had lived in. Mama hung quilts on ropes from end to end to make bedrooms.

We were going to live there until Daddy got a little house for us built in Ashland. The town was in the middle of a green valley. A little river ran through the town and there was a bridge over it in the park.

Daddy worked for a sawmill. It was on the other side of the railroad tracks and not too far from the house he was building. He worked at the mill all day and then worked on the house 'til almost dark. He used scrap lumber, boards he brought up with him from the mill and used those to make the floor, sides and roof. He always got back to the tent before

27

the sun went down. He hadn't been back long when one of the cars that never stopped, turned into the house.

Harry and me were sitting outside, we stood up and watched as the car came to a stop. Rubin came up and watched as the man got out of his car. He was a tall, skinny man and wore a fancy black suit. He had dark curly hair and his eyes were sunk back in his head. He smiled at us but we didn't smile back. We just stood and stared.

"How you young'uns doing today?" he asked.

Nobody answered as Rubin ran inside, hollering, "Daddy!"

Daddy came out and shook his hand

"Howdy!" Daddy said to him. "You kids go on," Daddy told us and we scampered away as they went inside. We kept an eye on the tent and after the man had stayed a while Daddy and Mama walked him back to his car and he drove off.

At supper I was glad that Mama talked to Daddy about him so I could figure out who he was.

"Are you going to Brother Wine's revival?" Mama asked Daddy.

"I'm thinkin' on it. Every day I pass by his church on the way here. He talks to me and is pretty friendly. He asked about my family and where we lived. Said he had driven by and saw us here. I thought I might listen to his preachin' and find out what he has to say."

"Will you go tomorrow night like he talked about?" She looked at him.

"I believe I will."

The next evening Daddy came back early. He dusted the sawdust off his clothes with his hat, washed his hands and head and combed down his hair with some hair grease. He put on a clean shirt and went to see about Brother Wine's revival. I didn't know what a revival was, but I planned on staying awake so I could find out when Daddy got back.

He went again the next few nights and took Mama with him. He was excited about the meeting even after they got back and talked to Mama about it all. After that week Brother Wine came by to see us pretty regular. He always brought something with him, some food or candy. He was trying to warm up to us kids, while he did, Daddy warmed up to him.

The church was a little building in Ashland. It was on a corner a few blocks from the railroad tracks. All of us started to go to the Sunday meetings with Mama and Daddy. There was preaching and singing and learning about Jesus. We went to classes with kids our same size and were told stories from the Bible about how we ought to act so we could be saved. I didn't know what we were going to be saved from so I just sat there and hoped there might be some sweets handed out.

It was at Foursquare Church that Daddy got religion. Wherever Daddy went Mama always followed, so she got religion too. Things changed around the house and we spent hours at church. At first we went in the clothes we had but the church had a little place with all kinds of used clothes. Mama went through hand-me-downs and found things for all of us. I was hoping for some cowboy boots but I just got some brown shoes that somebody had given up. After we started going to church we had more than we ever had. Mama and Daddy weren't ones to just take and they helped who they could too.

Daddy sure did love preaching to us. After hearing the sermon at church, Daddy liked to come back to the house and preach to us all again. Sometimes when he got wild he would bang his fist on the table. It sure woke us up if we had dozed off. We listened and we didn't say a word, Mama just nodded and said, "Yes, Wesley."

Daddy started reading the Bible to us every night. It took a long time for him to get through the words. Mama would quietly look over his shoulder and tell him the ones he didn't know. The more Daddy learned, the more he had us start living the way the Bible told him we ought to. Daddy would read and read to us until Mama would tell him, "Wesley, these babies need to get to bed."

Hoyt Lynn

Daddy got the house done, with some help from men at church and we moved to Ashland. After being in the tent it sure was dark inside, even with the couple of windows Daddy put in. It was just a wooden square, made of scrap lumber. We still had to get water from a bucket and use the outhouse in back, but it made Mama feel better to have solid walls.

Of an evening, after he read the Bible to us, Daddy would sit and watch the trains go by and have us listen for the whistle as it got further away. He did that every night and at full dark we would all go into bed.

I came in from being outside and Elaine was lighting a lamp for us to eat supper. I looked around for Mama but she wasn't there and neither was Daddy.

"Where's Mama and Daddy?" I asked her.

"Don't worry," Elaine told us. "Just sit down and eat." With Mama and Daddy gone, there was no way we were going to mind Elaine. We ran in and out of the house even though it was cold outside, hollered in the house, and wrestled each other. I couldn't remember when we had been left alone and we made the most of it. It was all fun but as the night wore on, Mama and Daddy didn't come back.

30

"You kids get to bed," Elaine hollered at us, trying to get us to mind her. We wouldn't do anything she said and she finally got a broom after us and hit us with it. "You just wait till Daddy gets back! He's gonna light into you," Elaine was hollering now.

Daddy wasn't here now, so we didn't give it no thought. Louie and Rubin didn't help her, they just laughed at all of us. Louie thought it was all funny. Rubin tried to boss Elaine around and made her even more mad. It got so late we finally did lay down and even though I was going to stay up till Mama got back, I fell asleep.

I woke up to a baby crying. I got up from my pallet on the floor and went into the kitchen. Mama was holding it in her arms. Daddy was asleep on the bed in the front room. Elaine was bringing Mama a white cloth.

Louie walked through the front door and stomped the snow off of his feet. "There must be nine inches out there, and it's the fourth of May!"

Mama saw me. "Come over here and meet your brother, Hoyt Lynn." Elaine was so busy helping Mama that she didn't think to tattle on us. I sure was glad to see the baby. He was already good for something.

After that last snow it warmed up and summer came on. It was rainy a lot of the time but that kept us cool. We played in the trees and made forts out of strips, which was the bark end of the boards left over from sawing lumber. Daddy would make us power saws by taking a block of wood and hammering a board to it so we could pretend to cut down trees. We were busy sawing down the forest when Mama hollered at us from the house to come in.

"Ya'll walk down to that blackberry thicket and fill these buckets. Now that summers about over they should be ripe." She handed us each an old coffee can and we headed out. The berries grew down at the end of the road and I raced

Harry there and almost beat him too. The blackberries grew in a mess of vines with thorns. They caught on our clothes and tried to tear holes in our shirts. My arms were covered in red scratches but all of it was worth it. The blackberries were so big it didn't take any time to fill our cans and then eat as many of them as we could. It turned our fingers, our mouths and faces purple. Mama warned us if we ate too many they would make us sick. I never felt sick enough to stop eating them, but I did spend a lot of time in the outhouse.

School started for the older kids and they went to classes in Ashland. Harry went with them, so I was left with Sheron, Esther and the baby. Esther stayed inside with Mama but Sheron played outside with me. She was up for just about anything but Mama kept a close eye on us all the time.

After Bible reading one night we were all sent to bed. The days were starting to get shorter and it was already cool at night. Mama and Daddy were in their bed and I could hear them talking. It was about leaving. Daddy had enough money for the trip back to Louisiana. Mama wanted to go and Daddy said he was ready too. I wasn't sure if we were moving or just going on a trip. Either way, if Daddy was ready to go, I was ready too.

LOUISIANA 1951

Trouble with the Cousins

I had my head bowed and didn't even peek at supper while Daddy said grace. He thanked the Lord for all we had been given that day and said amen. Beans, greens and cornbread, supper looked good. We had canned goods from Grandma's garden and I guess they were all right. Mama liked to fix squash too, which I didn't mind as long as it was fried with sugar. Daddy always told Mama it was mighty good, even when I didn't think so.

We lived in the little red house on Grandma and Grandpa Miller's land. Mama and Daddy had their room with a bed. There were two beds in the bedroom and there was always a bed kept in the front room. The kitchen was in the back of the house and the L shape made a little porch out back. That was where we took baths.

The outhouse was way back from the house at the far fence line. When the hole would get full they would cover it up and move the outhouse forward. Mama had me take the old magazines out for when they were needed. They worked pretty good as long as the pages weren't the glossy slick kind.

Between Grandma's place and where we lived was an old, run down house with just a couple of rooms. It didn't look like anything but varmints had lived there for a while. The fence between the houses had steps that went up over it and down the other side. It was fun to climb them and jump off or see how fast we could run up and down it. I loved to race, sometimes I even beat Harry. We all took off as fast as we could when Daddy would race us down the sandy path that led to the bottom farm land. Daddy always got there first, no matter how hard we tried.

Since it was Christmastime, some of Daddy's brothers and sisters brought their families to Grandma and Grandpa Miller's. With Daddy having so many brothers and sisters the house was full. I didn't mind his four brothers too much, but with Daddy's six sisters there wasn't no way to not be in trouble with one of them. We were all over visiting, the grownups were anyhow, us kids were trying to find a way to fight with the cousins without anybody seeing.

When we got back to Louisiana the folks here had seemed like they were glad to see us again. The family fussed over us as if they had been worried about us but called us, 'Wesley's Bunch' like that wasn't any good. They all acted like they were better than us since they always had a roof over their head and plenty to eat. I didn't think much of them either. They'd never seen a thing but pine trees and swamp. When Daddy brought us back to Louisiana we didn't have much and they made sure to point out how little we had. That led to a couple of fist fights.

Since Daddy had gotten religion he had taken to preaching to the family. When he talked to them he got pretty loud, pointed his finger at them a lot, and sometimes banged his fist on the table. Grandma didn't pay him much mind. He told Grandpa all he had learned about living righteous from the Bible. Grandpa listened but didn't say much. Daddy finally had to tell them that if they didn't change they would all go to Hell. When he told them that I thought for sure there was going to be fist fights just like us kids out in the woods.

Daddy still got along with Uncle Ted, though. Back when Uncle Ted got married he settled down and he didn't ramble anymore like Daddy. I think sometimes he missed those days. If I had to stay in one place like him, I sure would miss the trips.

This visit everybody seemed to be getting along. The men were sitting on the porch, some in chairs, some on the porch letting their legs dangle off. I sat down behind Daddy, trying to stay out of sight so I could listen to Daddy's stories. The girls were sent out to see if anyone wanted a drink. There was a time when Daddy might already have a little something extra in his coffee he hid from Mama, but not

Grandma and Grandpa Miller's white house in Coldwater, Louisiana.

anymore.

Uncle Ted was telling us about the time he and Daddy were young men in Texas. I loved to hear about the time when Daddy lived fast.

"We got hired on together on a road job going from Ballinger to San Angelo. Now boys, that's when me and yore daddy went wherever we got the itch to. We had a job tying rebar together with hay wire. Now this was during the hard times and work was tough to find. We earned a dollar a day and was glad to have it.

"Was a feller workin' on the job couldn't get an old '27 Chevrolet truck up the hill with a load. Yore daddy talked to the old boy, got in the cab and drove it right out. After that he

35

got the drivin' job, which was a step up, 'cause it paid a dollar and a half. The boss man came up to me and said, 'It's a pleasure to watch that man drive.' I piped right up and told him that was my brother. Well, I went to drivin' and we both got that dollar and a half."

"That job didn't last too long though, good as it was," Daddy said.

"That was all right, we jumped the train for California. You remember, Wesley, we didn't get but to Lordsburg, New Mexico and the railroad bull throwed us off the train."

Daddy grinned. "That didn't stop us. Those railroad bulls walked around lookin' for fellas ridin' the trains. We's just trying to ride the freight, looking for work, but they'd take the club to you. They got a kick out of beatin' you with it. But we showed 'em. We got a bus ticket to the next town west, and when we got there we just jumped on again. That bull wasn't gonna stop us." I knew nothing could stop Daddy.

The men kept telling stories. I stayed out on the porch with the men. I always tried to stay outside when I was at Grandma's. I had to be careful not to get her white walls dirty and walk quiet so nothing would break. Grandma could get in a temper quick. She did favor Elaine, though, probably since her first name was Georgia like Grandma's. She didn't seem to think too much of Harry and me.

Grandma Miller wasn't much like Mama. She was tough and could do things like a man. She had a dresser in her bedroom she called a chifferobe that she had made herself with a hewing axe. Her daddy had been a saw miller and logger too and taught her about wood. He had come from Georgia and he had named Grandma, Atlanta Georgia, he was so proud of where he came from.

Grandma had taught Daddy how to use a hewing axe and he could make things too. It had a shorter handle than a long axe and the metal part was broad and wide. The sharp edge was about eight inches long and it took a lot of strength to use it. I knew from getting whipped that Grandma had plenty of hand strength.

Grandma had even taken on the army one time. Daddy had joined the service when there was a war going on called the Great War. Only thing was he wasn't old enough to join up. He ran off and got in, but Grandma wrote a letter to his outfit and told on him and they sent him home. Grandma said her sixteen year old boy wasn't going to no war if she had anything to do with it. Daddy had a picture of himself in his uniform and he sure did look  good. Too bad he was only in for a few weeks. About the time he got that picture took, Mama was about two years old. By the time he was old enough to join the army that war was over and Daddy had already found trains. Now he had plenty of train stories.

Daddy's sister, Aunt Hattavie came out of the house using a broom, trying to sweep us kids off the porch. She complained about how crowded the house was and ran us all out in the yard. It was cold so the older kids took off for the little, empty house and us younger ones followed. It wasn't much warmer inside, but there was a King heater. It was little and the metal it was made out of was tin. Louie got the fire started with some paper from the walls and a match. The fire from the paper didn't last long, so we all started peeling more

37

of the wallpaper off the walls to throw on the flame. The little stove got hot fast, but didn't stay hot. We shoved more and more paper in the egg shaped opening to keep the fire burning. It started to glow red. We were all busy playing and peeling paper when Elaine hollered, "The wall's on fire!"

All of us stopped playing and stared at the fire. We finally saw the smoke filling up the top of the room. Harry pushed me by the shoulders, "Run!"

It wasn't the fire that had us all moving. We were scared of the trouble we were going to be in. We all scattered, some headed to the woods, some of the cousins headed back toward Grandma's, but we headed to Mama's. None of the grownups saw what was happening until it was too late. It didn't take any time for the little house to burn all the way down to the ground.

The older kids were in charge so they got called to Grandma's to tell the folks what happened. I heard Mama tell Daddy, "Wesley, I just can't believe the kids would start that fire. I bet it was your sister's kids who started it." One of the best things about Mama and Daddy was the fact that they just couldn't believe their kids would do something wrong.

"Well, I asked what had happened but Louie and Rubin said they didn't know. They said they tried to put it out but they couldn't stomp fast enough." Daddy didn't seem too worried.

When the aunts started trying to lay blame for the fire, Louie, Elaine and Rubin kept their mouths shut. When Daddy brought them back from Grandma's they were grinning ear to ear. When we found out the cousins got whipped and they didn't, it really was a good Christmas.

Holdin' On

"Uncle Dave Moses is here!" Elaine hollered from the porch. In drove a '34 Ford truck with a big wooden shed on the back. He wasn't really our uncle, but a traveling salesman and we were all excited to see him, even Mama. She walked out to him and he greeted Mama,

"Afternoon, Mrs. Miller. Sure is warm for April. You and your children are looking fine this day."

"Why, thank you, but I don't know that I need a thing right now."

"Why don't you just look at what I brought? I have some fine ointments and salves for your aches and pains. This elixir here is to keep you from feeling poorly and tired."

"It'd be quite the thing if you had a remedy for tired!" Mama teased.

"Now, Mrs. Miller, it helps, not cures. I surely do have the remedy for feeling poorly for these children." We all gathered in closer. It was candy, shiny, colorful hard candy. Uncle Dave gave us all one, and that made eight pieces. I knew the baby couldn't eat it, so I kept an eye on that extra piece, but Mama put it in her apron pocket. Mama went ahead and bought a little thread, a needle and a package of something that went in cooking, but I didn't know what it was.

He thanked Mama and got back in his truck. The wooden box on back was full. Brooms, flat irons and a lot of things I hadn't ever seen before. Mattresses covered the top to make a roof. He slowly headed out the driveway to the next house down the lane and we all chased after his truck. I knew we wouldn't ever get a mattress from him. Mama made ours.

Mama had ticking she sewed into mattress covers and we went to the woods to gather up the inside. The inside of mattresses hung from the branches of big oak trees. It was called Spanish moss and it hung low from the limbs. Mama would take a stick with a forked end and put it up into the grey moss and twist it around and then pull it out of the tree. She piled it in the little wagons that Harry and me pulled. She went from tree to tree gathering all she could reach.

When we got back to the house Mama boiled it in her big wash pot that was used for washing clothes. She boiled it for a while and then grabbed it out with the same stick and had it dry up on the porch railings of the little red house. When it was ready she would take dried corn shucks to mix with it and stuff the mattress. After she stuffed them with all that would fit, she would sew up the side and we would have a brand new mattress.

I thought me and Harry knew enough about housework. Daddy must have figured that out too. I knew Harry and me were growing up when instead of having to play with the babies we got to go with Daddy and the older boys to the log woods.

We rode in the cab with Daddy. Little Jimmy and Ed, along with Louie and Rubin were riding on the log bunks in back, sitting across the beam with their legs swinging in the wind. We were headed over to Lysa Massey's to clear some timber for him. Daddy had made a trade. We would clear his land of some of the timber and get to keep it to saw at the mill. Daddy had already told Crit and Bob Gay to take the mules over; they had them in Massey's corral. Everybody always had sort of a makeshift corral so that the work animals could be nearby when they were needed.

Some of the folks around here didn't like Daddy too much. Louie said it was because Daddy was his own boss. There was a story in the family about a time before I could remember. Daddy's sawmill burned down and it was rumored that it had been burned down on account of Daddy mixing so much with the colored folks. That didn't change

Daddy's ways none though. You better take him the way he was.

Lysa Massey walked around his place with Daddy and handpicked which trees Daddy could cut down. One here and one there till there was enough to make a load. We had to stay out of the way, so Harry and me went to climbing trees and throwing pinecones at each other. When they were done the men shook hands and Daddy called us to work.

Rubin asked Daddy, "Why can't we use a tractor to skid these logs out, Daddy? Lots of folks do."

"Tractor'll tear up the ground, that's why Massey's hirin' us. With the mules we can clear the timber and leave the country in good shape. Mules are smart. He's sure footed and smart, can see all four of his feet at one time. Horse will eat till he's sick, but not a nice red mule, he eats just enough. Just can't beat a mule."

Daddy set the log truck up as close to the timber as we could get. The log truck was just a little '45 Ford cab with log bunks on the back. That's where the logs sat.

Me and Harry fell out and started making our way through the thick woods. Trees with leaves were hard wood, and trees with needles were pine and that was soft wood. The ground was covered in brush, sawvines and muskydine vines that were covered in little grapes. They climbed the trees and wrapped around anything that didn't move. I didn't mind the vines and neither did Harry as we began to glut ourselves on the little sweet muskydines.

"Wasn't none of this vine and underbrush here when I was a boy," Daddy complained as he had Louie and Rubin cut the vines to clear it from around the trees he wanted to cut. "Harry, you and Alton clear this out after we cut it." Grandpa Miller was a saw miller too. "When I was a boy, no bigger than y'all, Daddy would gather pine knots all through the woods. Those old dead pine stumps had nothing left but

41

the heart. It was rich light pine and the railroad would buy it to power their steam engines.

"My daddy had a wagon with wood wheels we loaded the pine knots in. The wheels had an iron ring around them that would get loose. We would soak the wheels in the creek all night long and make the wood swell. The iron rings would get tight and last all day as we made our way through the woods. We took the pine knots down to Peason and sold 'em to the railroad. Times weren't as easy as they are now."

Daddy sure knew the woods. I guess they were just like home to him. Now we were the boys and Daddy had us in the woods.

Daddy and the men started cutting the marked trees. The best ones were at least two feet around so they could get two cross ties out of it. Daddy put a notch in it with an axe to have it fall the direction they wanted. Little Jimmy and Ed got on either side of the tree, about a foot off the ground, and used the cross cut saw to saw it down.

The cross cut saw was longer than Daddy was tall and had handles on both ends. One man would pull the saw and then the other man would pull it back, back and forth until they cut it almost clean through. If the tree's weight started to pinch the saw they would put a wood wedge in the cut to hold it up. Once they cut through, down the tree would come. Little Jimmy and Ed cut the branches off with a hand saw and Daddy bucked it to nine feet. The truck could only hold a log that was about that long.

We had to be careful and stay by the truck when the trees were coming down. Little branches could come down anywhere and if they hit us, it could hurt us bad. If a tree didn't fall all the way to the ground, but leaned on a live tree it was called a widowmaker, so they couldn't be left leaning.

When the mules were hooked up to the logs with the harness called a single tree, they would drag it to the truck with this metal thing that had two sharp hooks that bit into the tree. The men had to stay way behind the mules, to stay out of the way of the vines catching and dragging limbs. Daddy said a good mule and someone who understood them didn't have to do anything but follow behind a distance and holler gee and haw and whoa to get the mule to do what he was supposed to do.

They put chains around each end of the log and a mule on the off side of the truck would pull the log up two other logs that were propped on the ground and the log bunk. The bigger end of the log would go up faster than the small end so they would move the chain up and down the log to keep the log going on straight. They did this over and over till they had a load on the truck.

When they cut a truck load of about thirty logs we were ready to haul it to the mill. Daddy chained them on tight and it was time to go. He jumped in the cab with Harry and me and we headed to the mill. Daddy was driving as fast as the loaded log truck would go. I was sure I could get out and run as fast as it was going. The men and boys rode the logs in back. They only stacked them up to two on top so there was a place for them to ride. I stuck my head out the window past Harry, who got to sit by the door since he was older. The wind blew on my head and cooled me off. I looked back at Louie and Rubin riding the logs and couldn't wait till I could ride the logs too.

That night Mama took our clothes off and looked us over good. Since we had been in the woods all day, Mama was checking us for red bugs and ticks. Mosquitoes were bad but once they bit you they were gone, ticks were worse 'cause they would latch on and itch till you got them off. Red bugs were the worst 'cause you couldn't hardly see them at all. They were red and as small as a speck of pepper. Sometimes you couldn't even tell if you had one till you scratched your leg bloody trying to get him out. The grownups would soak rags in coal oil and tie them around their ankles if they were in the woods for a while. Kids just got ate up.

Even though everybody worked hard during the day, on Wednesday evening we headed to New Town. Since Daddy had come back with religion, New Town was the place we went for preaching, Sunday and Wednesday. The church was a little building that all the colored folks went to. Daddy and Mama liked going there better than anywhere else.

Mama, Daddy and the little kids rode in the cab of the truck and the rest of us rode on the back. Daddy drove down that white trail like it was smooth as glass even though sometimes I thought the bumps would buck us off. We knew to hold on tight when Daddy went somewhere. He didn't look to see if anybody was left on 'til we got there. We had to sneak down the back road so Grandpa and Grandma Miller wouldn't see us. They sure didn't like Daddy going to New Town church.

The church was dark brown because of the weathered wood on the outside. It stood up on stilts a couple of feet off the ground. It wasn't very big inside. There were about ten sets of benches on the floor for people to sit and the pulpit was a foot above the main floor. There was a colored preacher who ran the church named Wilmer Lynch. He would have Daddy testify. When they would preach they would talk normal and then all of a sudden just shout a word like 'sin' or 'Jesus,' or 'repent'. I guess they were important words. Daddy and Mr. Lynch preaching made them sweat from their face. The colored folks would holler out, "Amen!" and hold their hands in the air and a lot of them would sway.

There was a lot of singing. The music made me feel something inside that sometimes made me want to move and sing along or make my eyes water. I don't think I was the only one who felt it. When those folks got to feeling something, they would raise their hands in the air and kind of moan. It was called getting the Holy Ghost. Sometimes there was a guest speaker and he could really get everybody worked up. People would pop up and say Amen and cry to the Lord. Benches would get knocked over and people would jump and shout. I don't know if I ever felt the Holy Ghost but it sure was wild to watch somebody else getting it. Sometimes it was a little scary, but I would never let on to Harry.

After a night in New Town, and the rough ride to the house, sometimes it was hard to get right to sleep. I liked trying to stay awake 'cause I would listen to Mama and Daddy talking in the night. It was about the only way I learned what was going on.

A man had been talking to Daddy at the mill. He was Wes Jackson from Winnfield. He had come over to hire sawyers and mill wrights to work his mills. Those mills were in a place called New Mexico, and he wanted Daddy to go there. I wasn't sure where New Mexico was but I knew Daddy and I knew it was time to go.

New Town Church

NEW MEXICO 1952-1953

Riding the Bus

I lay on my back looking up at the light green color of the roof. I felt the rough road under me and the rocking motion of the bus as it went down Hwy 84. My eyes started to close. I was stretched out on the blankets Mama had laid at the back of the school bus. Riding in a bus sure was the way to travel. There was plenty of room to lay out or play and nobody pestered me because I was touching them. I could look out any of the twenty windows, most all of them open to let the wind blow in as we drove through the dry West Texas heat.

In this part of Texas I could see for a long way. Even at night with the moon and stars we could see far. Back in Louisiana when the sun went down you could barely see your hand in front of your face what with the tall pines and the heavy air.

We were headed to New Mexico to work for Wes Jackson. He had come out to Louisiana to find a good sawyer. Daddy said that's 'cause the best sawyers came from there. When he had come to talk to Daddy, I couldn't keep my eyes off his car. It had to be about the ugliest thing I'd ever seen. Louie said it was a '51 Nash, dark brown on top and a buckskin color on bottom. The tires were all but hid behind the fender covers. I couldn't believe any man would buy such a car but I knew better than to say anything. I told Harry though, and he said he thought the same thing.

We had needed something to travel in so Daddy went into Many and found a '41 Ford school bus that was black and yellow and could seat twenty-six. The door opened on the passenger side with a lever and there was another door out the back. The seats ran length wise and backed up to the

47

windows. More seats went back to back down the middle between two poles.

Since it only had to seat ten, Daddy had taken the last few bench seats out of the back. Back there Mama had packed all that we might need for the trip and laid blankets down to make pallets to sleep on.

Another group was traveling with us that had been hired by Wes Jackson too. They were in an old Chevy pickup following behind. There was a couple I didn't know from Arkansas and Fatty Beard and his family. I figured they called him Fatty because of the way he looked, short and round with overalls unbuttoned on the side. You could see his skin in there and I always tried not to look. They had a mess of kids and I wasn't sure which kids belonged to who.

Mama spent most of the time on the bench behind Daddy. Me and the kids played around and took turns sleeping. I just rode and rocked. It was a long ways between towns and we all perked up and looked out whenever we went through any place with buildings.

"We made Sweetwater," Daddy said. Fatty Beard, who was following us, had got Daddy's attention by flashing his lights. Daddy slowed down and pulled over in the shade. I wondered where the shade was coming from, and looked out to see what was going on. We'd parked next to a drive in picture show and Daddy used the shadow cast by the big screen to keep us in the shade. I hadn't ever been in one to hear it; I had just seen the pictures. Mama and Daddy didn't allow us to go to the show because it was worldly, and worldly meant sinful.

Daddy got out of the bus, and walked back towards Fatty Beard's Chevy. The boys beat the girls out of the bus, and we ran around in the dust. Harry and me followed Daddy down to the men. Daddy was under the hood with

48

Fatty Beard, white smoke and heat came from the motor and the men decided the engine had blown up.

"Mr. Miller, I can't go on. But I sure do need to get to that job."

Daddy didn't think but for a second, "We can load you up with us. We've got plenty of room. What won't fit inside, we'll pack on top and keep going in the morning."

"Why, that would be just fine, Mr. Miller. Just fine." Fatty Beard was wiping the sweat from his face.

The women came over to help Mama fix us all something to eat. Harry and me eyed their kids, trying to figure out if we would get along with them or fight them. We still hadn't decided.

"There goes all the room in the bus," Harry said to me kind of down in the mouth.

The men stood around the car, Louie and Rubin stood close by. They were trying to act big and be with the men. The two men were smoking and taking a swig from a bottle. Not Daddy, he didn't smoke and he didn't drink. I figured it wouldn't be too long before he started telling them they were going to Hell. He didn't stay long with them, though. He came over to the bus, leaned up against a tire in the shade and dozed off. Without Daddy there, the older boys came back and started trying to boss us around.

There was a sign at the front of the big screen that had little letters that told what the movie was going to be. The wind had blown quite a few of them on the ground in the dusty lot that we were parked in. All of us kids started chasing around trying to gather them up and make words in the dirt with them. There wasn't a great many so there weren't too many words to make. Just taking them from the girls was fun for me. I didn't know too many words to spell anyhow.

I looked up when I heard a car coming close, it skidded to a stop close to us and a cloud of dirt rolled out from under a big green Cadillac. An old man with a chewed up cigar got out and started yelling and cussing us kids. We just stood and stared. He was saying we had been pulling the letters down from the sign. I thought he was going to whip us right there, so I was getting ready to run to Mama. The man from Arkansas was on top of the bus loading some of the stuff from the Chevy. When he heard that man hollering at us he came off that roof fast. He was tall and skinny and it seemed like he just stepped off the bus into the face of the Cadillac man.

Arkansas man then told the Cadillac man what for!

"That nasty Texas wind blew those letters off. Not these young'uns. They were just playin' in the shade, not hurtin' a thing." I sure was glad he was taking up for us. Most of the time if you got hollered at by a grownup, it didn't matter, you was in trouble.

Daddy heard the commotion and came over to see what was happening.

The man with the cigar kept on, "You all get these snot nosed kids out of here, and the rest of you too. This is my place and I don't want ya'll around here tearin' the place up!"

"Listen here, fella," Daddy started. "We aren't parked on your land. This is an open field where we're at. We'll leave after we're rested and that'll be after sun up. We'll go down the road then, and not before. We don't want no trouble, but we're stayin' the night."

I knew we weren't going anywhere and when Daddy decided we were staying, we weren't going anywhere until he was ready. The Cadillac man would just have to like it and I guess he did, because he left and we stayed.

That night when we turned in Mama had us give up the best spots on the bus to the grownups. She told us we had

50

to be happy about it. Ah, well, even with the new folks this was the best traveling we had ever done.

All the kids, except the babies, gathered some blankets and slept out on the ground. It had been hot in the day, but the night was cool. The moon shined bright and you could hear the trucks as they drove by. We slept close by the bus, and through the open window I could hear Daddy telling Mama we had about five hundred miles to go to get to the mill.

I didn't know if that was a long ways or not. It didn't take too long to get anywhere. Usually Daddy drove all the time day and night. We would always wake up in a different place than when we went to sleep. I was glad to camp tonight though, so tomorrow I would be able to watch out the window. We had already gone from wet, green Louisiana, where you couldn't see around the curve in the road to the wide open dry, brown of west Texas. I wondered about New Mexico. I hoped it didn't have any schools.

Fatty Beard sometimes spelled Daddy from driving. Daddy would doze off in the bus while Fatty drove but would have to get up and tell Fatty to quit lugging the engine. Daddy kept telling him when he ran too slow in a higher gear the engine would slow down and all the belts would move slower, that made the engine get hot. Sometimes Daddy would holler at him, "Rev it, rev it, and give it some gas." Fatty didn't drive very much. We had left the Chevy in Sweetwater; Daddy figured the man there was paid in full for letting us camp.

We crossed into New Mexico and the country was tan with hills with flat tops. There was scrub that grew out of the desert sand and gravel, but there wasn't much else. I wondered where the timber was that Daddy was going to cut. The country stayed pretty dry and spare for quite a while. We saw boney cows chewing, but I couldn't tell if they were getting much to eat.

We turned north and started going through hills and mountains. The country had little squat trees that looked more like bushes. Whenever we got on top of a hill we could see for miles. Mama said that flat topped hills were mesas. The narrow road wound around with nothing much to look at. There were a couple of rivers that went through a town Daddy said was Espanola. We could see mountains far away but we were in the low land. It was just dry and dusty.

Daddy told Mama that the Rio Grande River was in the valley between us and the mountains. It was in a deep cut in the ground so you couldn't see it. I still couldn't see where the trees were.

Mill after Mill

Folks called the town Tres Piedras. Mama said she knew 'tres' meant three, but she didn't know about 'piedras'. Rocks as big as houses stuck out of the ground, most of them too big and steep to climb but we all tried anyway.

All of the sawmill families lived in the shacks in the middle of town by the mill. There wasn't any grass, just dirt and rock and weeds. At night we could see lights across the valley. Daddy told Mama that was Taos.

"Why can't we get our groceries there, Wesley, it looks closer than Ojo Caliente."

"Well, it is, Fonny. Ojo is about fifty miles away and Taos thirty, as the crow flies. But there isn't a road over there that doesn't go down into the gorge. It would take longer and be a harder ride than just going to Ojo." I looked but I never could see the gorge Daddy talked about.

Just a month or so into working there, Wes Jackson talked to Daddy and told him he needed him at one of his mills south at Vallecitos. When we took off, we left the family from Arkansas there. The man had taken up for us kids in Texas, but that was about all I could say for them. They were planning to head back to Arkansas. They couldn't make it. Just Fatty and his family went with us. We didn't look back at them when we left.

We traveled high and dry in the school bus and it wasn't long that tall pines shaded the road. Driving around the curves slung us from one side of the bus to the other. We lay on the floor rolling, just like at a carnival.

I looked out the windows at the houses we went by. They were low to the ground and made out of large, rounded bricks that looked like mud. The doorways and windows were framed with boards and so low men had to duck to walk in them. I asked Daddy what the houses were made of and he said adobes, mud and straw. I hoped we got to stay in one, but when we got to the mill there were wood sawmill shacks to live in.

The house was a square room made out of rough lumber that had gotten dark over time. The windows didn't have glass, so Mama hung quilts over them to keep out the cool air. It made it dark inside but the cracks in between the boards let in light. Some shelves were built into the wall and a table was set up.

The smell of fresh cut lumber was still around, even though they weren't sawing right then. Harry and me filled buckets with water from the creek that ran close by. Louie and Rubin gathered wood for the fire that Mama wanted to make in the cook stove.

I was glad I wasn't getting the wood. Stove wood was a bother to gather. It had to be small enough to fit in the openings at the front of the stove. It could only be about twelve inches long and couple of inches around so it took a lot of splitting from the log. The fire would heat the black iron top to cook food and the whole thing would get hot enough to keep food warm in the top boxes.

The stove was black with four covered holes on the flat top. Mama used an old saw tooth file of Daddy's to pick up the burner covers. There were three sizes of flat iron so you could take off whichever one depending on how much heat you wanted. On the outside of the stove was a black cast iron tank that took up the whole side. It held the heated water and Mama called it the reservoir.

Daddy spent the summer sawing logs and keeping the mill running since he was the millwright too. He worked at night repairing parts of the mill and the day running the crew. We didn't have to go to church because Daddy said the one they had here wasn't our kind of religion. The weather turned cold and Mr. Jackson told Daddy they would shut down when the snow flew.

One night after Daddy read the Bible to us he told Mama that a man called Charlie Denton had come to the mill. He wanted to hire Daddy to set up the sawmill he owned in Elk which was further south. Daddy figured on going since the work here was about over.

He talked to Fatty, but he wasn't ready to move on. We'd be going on alone, which didn't bother any of us. We were glad to get shut of them. His wife was always

complaining and the kids were afraid of their own shadows. I didn't know what they were worried about; at least we had finally found the trees.

Look Up Ahead

Mama had us read road signs out loud to practice reading. It was kind of like going to school but we did it going down the road. Only Elaine got some of the longer

54

names, and sometimes even Mama couldn't read them either. Daddy had to tell us the names when we went south through Santa Fe, San Antonio, Carrizozo and Tularosa.

The inside of the bus was too big to be warmed by the heater that blew out of the dash. We had to wear our coats in the bus while we drove. Mama wrapped the girls and Hoyt Lynn in quilts.

The road south brought us out of the mountains and back into open country. The trees disappeared and there was more scrub brush the longer we traveled south. The country looked cold and lonely as I stared out the window. The road in front was just a gray line that went on and on, straight as a string, headed for another mountain. Snow started coming down and the ground got white.

We went through Tularosa and before we got into Alamogordo we made a turn onto Highway 82. Daddy told us about Alamogordo when he and Mama lived there before, one time when Louie was a baby, and another time when Mama was about to have me. She patted her stomach when she told us. She was going to have another baby soon now, too.

Daddy told us, "I drove a '41 Ford with a V8 Flathead motor. First thing in the morning we would leave the mill five minutes apart. And that helped you to know where the other fella was. There was a stretch of the log road that only had one lane so you knew you had to meet the other truck coming back with logs on the two lane part of the road. If you didn't you better start looking. He might be broke down or something else might be haywire."

Daddy tried to teach us and said, "Always look up ahead in the distance boys and you'll see the dust from cars or trucks coming. Trucks make more dust than cars. Look up ahead, and then you'll know when you might meet trouble. Always look up ahead."

Daddy whooped when telling us about going fast down the mountain. I knew how he felt about being able to sit and ride and go fast. Daddy must have liked the saw mill life better than the trucking life since he didn't drive trucks after that. It did sound fun to me. He told us how the mill had voted union so the owner had shut the doors. Daddy just moved on.

The bus started climbing the mountain in front of us. A rock wall on the right side of the bus showed where the road had been cut out of the mountain. The road was barely wide enough for cars to meet. The trees were little and bushy, Mama called them Juniper. The bus climbed slow. Daddy told us we would gain 4300 feet straight up in just sixteen miles.

As the snow came down harder the highway got more and more slick. Mama sat behind Daddy on the bench seat and they both paid close attention to the road. We went through a tunnel that was long and dark. On the other side bare trees were planted in rows, Mama called them fruit orchards. Tall pines were growing as we finally drove into town. Elaine read the sign and told us it was High Rolls. Cars were stopped. The snow was coming down heavier.

The highway patrol had the road blocked. Daddy got out to talk to them. Mama stayed in her seat and us kids stuck our noses to the window to try and see what was going on with Daddy and the men outside.

We saw Daddy point up the road. He talked a lot with his hands but we didn't know what he was saying. The men listened and then they did some waving as they talked. Daddy nodded and then he came back to the bus.

"They're gonna let us go, Fonny," Daddy told Mama.

"Do you think it will be all right?" Mama asked Daddy still worried.

"I got to get to the job. I told them I'd be there, so we'll keep on till we can't go no more." Daddy put the bus in gear.

Slowly, we moved up the road. Cars pulled off and stopped. I saw that Daddy had to drive with all his attention and it looked like Mama was praying in her seat. Sometimes the bus moved sideways but Daddy never let up on his grip. When we came to the town called Cloudcroft, Daddy said the worst was over. Mama sat back in her chair for the first time and let herself rest.

I thought about Daddy's story he had told us. I looked through the windshield and remembered - Always look up ahead.

Mary

We came into Elk and it wasn't much. A little school building, a post office and store in the same building and that was about it. We took a turn on a dirt road and went the two miles towards the sawmill camp where we would live at Elk Canyon. Several families lived in houses around the mill. We moved into one too.

Since we lived on the mill site, Daddy walked to work. He didn't come for dinner at noontime, so Mama packed him a lunch. She had a pot of beans going all the time and she would put a pint of beans and an egg sandwich in Daddy's lunch pail. At the end of the day whichever one of us saw him first would run to him. We knew he would usually have something saved for us. Most of the time one of the little kids would get the last few bites of the sandwich he made sure to leave.

Those of us kids that went to school would walk the three miles to the one room school house in Elk. Elaine got picked up at the cattle guard and she would ride the bus to the little town of Hope for high school. Louie was about ten months older than her but he had already lost a grade and was a year behind her. Louie didn't care a thing about school

57

and it was hard for the teachers to get him to do anything he didn't want to do.

"The first day I went to school I got in trouble for biting Elaine's finger and had to go to the corner. I never liked school again," he told us.

I kind of liked school but sometimes the other kids knew more about book things than I did. I had to pretend to know a lot more than I did. On the walk to school it was easy for me to get sidetracked by the sticks and squirrels. Sometimes wild turkeys would run across the road. Harry and me would get there late most of the time.

Mama had to drive the bus to Elk for food and mail, so Daddy went to Artesia, traded the bus and got her a red '41 Pontiac four door convertible. The bus had been the best traveling thing we had ever had but it was a little hard for Mama to get around in. That Pontiac was the slickest thing I'd ever seen.

The first time they drove it the gas tank fell off, they broke a spring and the water pump went out. Daddy took it back and got them to sell us a '46 Chevy pickup instead. It didn't look as good as that Pontiac but it ran.

One night before we even ate supper, Daddy and Mama left for Artesia. Elaine and Louie were left to take care of us. It was time for Mama to have her baby. Elaine tried to feed us like Mama and read the Bible to us like Daddy but we wouldn't mind or listen. She cried to Louie for help, but he thought it was all pretty funny. We wouldn't go to bed until she finally threatened to tell Daddy. That got us calmed down.

Early the next morning Elaine woke us up and said, "Come on, let's get up and go get our baby sister."

Daddy had come back to get us. When we got to town Daddy bought a dozen doughnuts from a store. He sat the box on the hood of the pickup and we stood around it, each trying to get an extra piece. They were the best things I ever ate. Before we went to pick up Mama, Daddy bought a small bed for the baby.

He left us outside and went into the hospital to get Mama. The boys played around the car and Elaine kept Hoyt Lynn and the girls inside it to stay warm. We waited a while and then watched Daddy come out alone. Mama couldn't come back to the house yet. She'd had a tough time having Mary and she wasn't healed up good enough yet. The doctor had to do some kind of operation to get the baby. We were a sad bunch as we rode back without them. Elaine set up the baby bed by Mama's and Esther put her doll in it so it'd look pretty.

Daddy went into town alone a few days later and this time came back with them. Mama was so happy to be back, but she had to go straight to bed. Mama kept trying to get up out of bed, but it was hard. Elaine tended her as best she could. Mama was upset she'd had so much trouble having Mary, "I would think after having nine babies before, I could have a baby without all this fuss."

Since Mama had an operation to have Mary, she wouldn't be having any more babies.

Elaine was holding the baby, "Well, Mama there's fourteen years between your oldest and your youngest, both born in February. I guess that's a good place to end."

"I guess it might as well be, sugar," Mama said to her.

Daddy would turn fifty this year and Mama was thirty-five. Ten babies in fourteen years was probably good enough.

He'll Make a Way

We had beans and rice for supper that night after Daddy gave thanks to the Lord for all we had. We were glad

Mama was back and the baby was so pretty. Daddy read the Bible to us and we sat still till Mama told him it was time for us to go to bed.

Elaine helped Mama make a bottle for Mary from canned milk and Karo's syrup. Elaine was careful when she mixed them. Elaine learned young how to do things around the house and at thirteen could do just about as much as Mama. Sheron and Esther were so much younger at five and six they sort of just played house.

That night I heard Daddy talking to Mama about the mill. There was trouble. The workers there were a rowdy bunch. Daddy was trying to preach to them about how they ought to live and they didn't like what he had to say. I heard hollering going on at the mill. Daddy had been telling them all they were going to Hell if they didn't find God. They didn't like it, but Daddy knew he was right so he just kept on telling them. Daddy would pound his fist on the wood ties and I knew he was telling them about Hell. Sometimes Daddy pounded his fist on the table when he told us about Hell, too.

Charlie Denton came to the mill and told Daddy he was going to fire him because of his preaching if he didn't stop. Daddy didn't stop. No man told Daddy what to do, especially when it came to the Lord. So we packed up the pickup for another trip. Daddy made a trailer for us to pull so we could take more of our stuff. The older kids rode in the bed and the younger ones in the cab. I sure felt good when I found my place in the back. The girls, Hoyt Lynn and the baby would ride up front. Daddy told Mama he was going to find Wes Jackson and see about working for him again. We bumped our way down the dirt road towards the highway.

Wes Jackson did hire Daddy back and we moved into a little house in Espanola close to the big mill. Living in town was a lot different than living in the woods. Louie and Rubin went to music lessons in town. Louie played the trumpet and

Rubin was on the trombone. Elaine learned the piano and practiced on the one at church.

Harry and me and the girls mostly played outside. We made all kinds of roads with our hands and used little blocks of wood for our cars. The dirt was like sand and it dried out our hands so much that sometimes it made them bleed. At the end of the day Mama would rub salve on them trying to get them to heal. She told us to find something else to do that didn't call for burrowing in the ground like a varmint.

Esther talked us into building a house with the two by fours that Daddy brought from the mill. Harry and me got started. Sheron and Esther worked on it for a while, but then they went in the house to help Mama. The sun was hot so Harry and me took off our shirts because that'd be cooler. We stacked the boards on top of each other to make walls and openings for windows. We didn't know how to make a roof so we just made the walls taller. My shoulders started to sting and were red, but we kept working. Harry's were red too. The sun shining on them made them hurt worse. I went to rub them and saw the skin had bubbled and I had water blisters. I crawled into the little house to find shade, before I could get good and cooled off; the walls came tumbling down on me. The boards hit those water blisters on my shoulders and hurt like fire.

I scrambled out from under the boards and ran to the house to tell on Harry as fast as I could go. I cried so Mama would know how much it hurt and get after Harry. I didn't care if he had done it on purpose or not. Mama met me at the back door and looked at my shoulders.

"Alton, why don't you have your shirt on?" In my hurry to tell on Harry, I forgot we weren't supposed to have our shirts off. So I just kept on crying.

Harry made fun of me for a while for being a bawl baby. So I went off to play on my own. I figured I'd ride a bicycle. The bike was a two wheeler with two little tires on either side of the back wheel that kept the bike from falling over. I took off in the dirt but the little wheels got stuck in the sand so I had to push as much as I rode. I dragged it to our yard and started looking for a screw driver; I was going to get rid of those little wheels.

Mama saw me coming and wanted to know where I'd gotten the bicycle. I looked up at her wondering what to say. I'd taken it from the boy next door, I hadn't ever seen him on it, so I figured I might as well use it. Mama told me all about borrowing and asking. I wanted to tell her when I had seen that bike I just knew I had to get on it. I knew better than to tell what I was thinking so I just looked at her sad-like so she'd know I was sorry. Mama made me take it back and tell the folks there I was sorry for stealing the bike. The only thing I was really sorry about was that the dumb bike hadn't been worth stealing, not with those baby wheels on it.

We were doing good, but that didn't matter much when Wes Jackson told Daddy he needed him back at Vallecitos. We loaded up and went. Daddy was always ready to move on, good times or bad. A few weeks there and then we went up to Pot Creek by Taos and worked at a mill there. Mama just about had a fit one morning when we woke up and in the frost on the window there was a bear paw. I don't know if the bear had anything to do with it but we didn't stay there very long. A man called Ted Groff came to the camp and hired Daddy for his mill at a little town south of Santa Fe called Madrid.

The road was little and wound its way up bigger and bigger hills. There were just a few trees here and there. We pulled a trailer behind our pickup with all the things Mama wanted to bring. We tried to make it up a steep hill but the Chevy kept giving out before the top and we would come to a stop. Daddy would let it roll back down the hill and try again.

He was getting mad as he tried to get us over that hump. He rolled back so many times; we got to doing it faster and faster. The last time the trailer jack knifed behind the pickup and turned over, dumping Mama's things to the ground.

"At least it didn't turn the truck over," Mama said. She was trying to soothe Daddy so he wouldn't get so mad.

"Maybe without that dad-blamed trailer we'll make it over this hill," Daddy told her.

He unhitched the trailer and we toted all we could fit into the truck. When we couldn't pack another thing, we climbed onto the truck and tried again. Those of us in back holding onto each other as Daddy mashed the gas. The engine roared and we started up the hill. This time we made it. Daddy left the trailer right where it was, turned over on the side of the road. When Daddy told the folks at the camp how we had come, they couldn't believe he had made it up the hill. A man told him nobody made it up that hill at all without being pulled and he couldn't believe that we had.

"He'll make a way when there seems no way," Daddy told us all, "Praise the Lord!"

Angel's View

Daddy walked into the house. Mama, holding the baby, followed him in. If we'd had a screen door, I think she would have let it slam. I don't know how it happened but the man Daddy bought the pickup from in Artesia had come to see us. When he left he took the pickup with him. I didn't dare ask, but Louie told us kids that Daddy hadn't been able to keep paying for it, so the man came to get it. I couldn't remember a time that we didn't have a vehicle. Daddy had been working hard here, but I guess there just wasn't enough money being made.

63

1951 Ford on road to
Marquez Canyon with
Wesley and boys.

Daddy caught a ride into town to talk to Groff and see if he could make a better deal. After waiting just about all day for Daddy to get back, we finally saw him coming up the road in a '49 Ford one ton. Ted Groff would loan Daddy the Ford if he would move out to his sawmill camp at Marquez Canyon. We could use the truck while we were there. Daddy didn't have much of a choice seeing that we had no car, so the use of the truck and someplace to go made deciding easy. Besides that, Daddy never chose staying over going, ever.

We left Madrid on Highway 14 headed south to Route 66. Everything we owned loaded on the flatbed, little ones in the cab and big kids on the back. We came out at Tijeras Canyon just east of Albuquerque and headed west through town. There were lots of cars and people as we went through downtown. Louie told us about places that had beds to sleep in if you paid for them called motels and the places that served meals already cooked. They were just something to look at as we went by in the truck. Mama always made our food and when we stopped, we slept on the side of the road and got to look up at the stars.

After Albuquerque we began to slowly climb a big hill Daddy called Nine Mile Hill. There were salvage yards and dumps on the right side that ran the length of the road. At the top was the Angel View Café and I thought it was funny that the view was nothing but piles of trash. Not much of a view.

When we got to the top of the hill we could see the long straight road as it went down and then it headed back up the next hill. The land was sandy with little bushes and there were hills and mesas up ahead. I knew by now not to worry about where the timber was. It would show up I was sure.

We turned right just after the iron bridge onto a dirt road. We crossed another little iron bridge with no top and struggled down the narrow dirt road. Nothing to see but juniper bushes, cactus and sand kicked up by the wind. I saw bluffs in the distance and little hills that came to peaks. There were different colors layered in the mesas and sometimes the rocks on the hill next to you seemed like they might fall down on you. The road wound around gullies that water had made during rain storms.

The road went on for over thirty miles and we drove west all day long, never getting up much speed so we could make it over the rocks and through the holes. The road was cut on the side of hills and it felt like the truck would lean so far to one side that it would tip over. We held on tight, to the truck and to each other. Sometimes we went straight up and straight down. The little kids got scared and Mama calmed them. We went up over a little hill and around a curve, and looked down below to see the little village of Marquez.

Mama sang to keep the peace in the cab as we slowly headed toward our new place. We were dusty, hungry and tired and I sat on the back of the truck trying to listen to Mama. I couldn't hear her but Elaine knew what she was singing. She sang along with her.

Down in the valley, the valley so low
Hang your head over, hear the wind blow

65

Hear the wind blow, dear, hear the wind blow
Hang your head over, hear the wind blow.

Roses love sunshine, violets love dew
Angels in heaven know I love you

Getting Started

"Fonny!" Daddy hollered at Mama, "Keep those kids back. There's rattlesnakes in this pile!"

"Rattlesnakes!" Mama repeated. She had Louie and Rubin come away from the mill while Daddy worked on the sawdust pile and the snakes with a D-2 Caterpillar. I headed toward him hoping Mama wouldn't see.

"Alton, you get over here." I stopped and headed back towards her. I had tried to see those snakes.

Daddy had started working on the mill the day after we got to Marquez Canyon. Before he could get much done he had to move the old sawdust pile from the mill. He revved the engine on the Cat to push the pile and he heard the sound of the rattlers over the engine noise. That's when he had hollered. Mama didn't want us outside while the snakes were awake so we had to go inside.

Daddy cleared out the sawdust pile, and the snakes lost their home. They slithered back into the woods where it was cool. Some that were slow to leave lost their heads to Daddy's shovel.

There was a house already built, the front high enough to crawl under but the back sat on the ground. A little creek flowed alongside the house. It had two rooms built out of rough slabs that were nailed up floor to roof. There was a bed in the house for Mama and Daddy, and a cot we called the couch in the front room. The two babies, Hoyt Lynn and Mary would stay in the house with them. Elaine, Sheron and

66

Esther would stay in a camp trailer that had a bed. The four of us boys would sleep in the shed which had two mattresses, one for Louie and Rubin and one for me and Harry. The shed and camp trailer were next to each other about a hundred yards from the house. I thought it was a pretty nice set up.

After we had gotten to the valley where the town was built we had driven through a little stream that crossed the dirt road. The village had about twenty houses. There was a church, but it was one of those that we didn't go to. A long building on the east side was the store and post office and just up from there was the school. I thought the buildings were made out of adobes like the ones in Vallecitos. When we got closer I could see they were made out of stacked rocks that were around the size of bricks, some bigger and some longer. They were stacked together and then mud was slapped on the side to make the wall solid. Most of the town seemed to sit on big, flat, orange-yellow rocks that poked out of the dirt.

We lived west of Marquez up a hill about a mile and a half where the tall timber started to grow. The road followed the creek that came out of the mountains that were to the west. The country was open to the east and we could see for miles. To the west it was like we were butted up against the bottom of the high country. The mountain was steep as it jutted up. The shade of the pines made it cooler than out in the open.

There was a corral with a tall pine tree in the middle. The whole place was built on a slope. The corral had a white horse and a black horse for Daddy and the boys to skid logs with. Daddy called them Jim and Joe. The mill was little and only took two men to run. Daddy was one and Louie and Rubin would make up the second man. The mill hadn't been used in a while and there was a lot of clean-up to do before Daddy got it up and running. A little Cat tractor owned by Groff was parked nearby and a '44 Army 6 x 6 GI trucks that

67

used to have a rag top. They were left for Daddy to use to bring logs out of the woods.

After Daddy made sure the mill area was safe enough we were all sent to sweep and clean the mill rig and help him get it ready for lumber. He, Louie and Rubin were going to cut the timber, skid the logs, saw the lumber, and hand load it on the Ford. When it was four or five feet high he would drive it in to Albuquerque to Groff's lumber yard. Daddy was working hard and fast so we could get a load out and get some money made.

An old gasoline Maytag washing machine had been left and Mama had the boys put it by the creek so she could wash clothes. Daddy got the engine running and smoke chugged out of the little motor. I stood over the tub and watched it, thinking how it would do all the work.

"Harry, you and Alton take these empty syrup cans and get water from the creek to fill this up," Mama said as she started putting Mary's diapers into it.

I hadn't thought about how the water was going to get in. We got our cans and started filling them from the creek and since Daddy had set it up close by, it wasn't much of a walk to dump our water in. It wasn't bad till Mama realized the tub leaked. That meant the water hauling job never ended. Keeping that tub in water before it leaked out was a race. The trip to the washing machine got longer every time.

I guess we didn't have it too bad. The older boys and Daddy were the ones really working. We could hear them running the power saw up the mountain. They would fell the trees and then use the horses to skid the logs out to the little road where the GI truck waited. They would cut a load and then skid all the logs at one time and load them on the truck like they did in Louisiana.

Mama could hear the GI truck coming from about a mile away and knew they were headed in from the woods.

"It's a good thing that truck is loaded downhill, and empty up, or I don't think Daddy and the boys would make it in," Mama said.

She would have supper on the table when they came in wore out. Even the horses were tired and Daddy would let them graze in the yard with just their leads. After saying Grace and thanking the Lord for all we had, he would slowly start to eat and talk about the day.

"This is about the roughest country I've ever worked. I can see the timber we want to cut, but I can't figure out how to get to it. If we do get it down, trying to skid it out is the next problem."

Just then Jim, the black horse, stuck his head in the window and nudged Daddy on the shoulder. He laughed and fed Jim a biscuit with sorghum on it. Mama shooed the horse away.

"Are the boys helpin' you all right?" she asked. "Do you want me to come out there and see if I can help?"

Louie was fourteen and Rubin twelve so they were doing the work of grown men. Even though Louie was older, Rubin was bigger. Harry was ten, and Rubin made two of him. Rubin stood out with his blond hair and size. All of us boys were dark headed and the girls mostly red and it seemed like Rubin was different in a lot of ways.

"We're doin' all we can, Fonny, no sense in you comin' out to the woods. We'll get it figured out." No log that came out of that canyon ever came easy.

When they had enough logs, they started sawing. They would feed the logs and grab the boards as they came out the other end of the saw. When Daddy sawed the boards he would watch to make sure the saw didn't get pinched. The board might not spread out far from the log and it would tighten up around the saw blade. If it did he would put an iron lumber wedge in front of the saw and spread the log from the board. The boards were ten to sixteen feet long depending on the length of the log. Daddy had an eye for knowing which way to saw the log to get the most footage.

None of the older kids went to school when it started. Elaine was already passed the grades the school had, and Louie and Rubin had to help Daddy. Sheron went with me

Wesley and Rubin bringing logs off the mountain at Marquez Canyon.

and Harry because she was six and it was time for her to start first grade.

Sheron would rather play outside with us boys than work in the house with Mama. Sheron played with trucks and cars and built forts. But she was still a girl and if we got to playing too rough with her, she would run to Daddy who always took up for her. Esther, who was about a year and a half younger, liked to play with paper dolls. Mama would cut out pictures in catalogues for Esther and then they would make paper clothes to put on them from the other pages. Sheron didn't have time to fool with dolls.

The three of us walked to school, almost two miles into town down the dirt road. Part of the road was sunk down below the dirt on both sides and a stick fence lined it on both sides. With those old crooked sticks holding up the fence it seemed like the road curved around forever and we were in a long trough.

The school was on a rise of rocks above the rest of the town. It had a bell on top and the front door was in the middle with windows on both sides. Outside big, flat rocks lay level to the ground where the dirt had been blown away by the wind. During recess we would carve our names onto the soft rock with sharper ones. There were lots of names where kids before us had done it, too. We didn't really make friends at school. Sheron was the only girl that went to school, and the boys seemed to all be kin to each other; we stuck to ourselves.

Sometimes Mama would walk to town with us and go to the little store and mail letters from the post office. Mama would visit with people who were there. They told Mama they had seen other sawmill families come and work for Groff and leave when things got too hard. Mama just nodded at them and went about her own way.

With the camp up against the mountain it got cool at night as soon as the sun went down. When it got really cold all four of us boys would get in one bed and use the second mattress to cover up. That helped with being warm, as long as no one peed the bed. Harry usually got blamed for it and we would throw him out of the bed. It didn't matter that I was younger, I didn't wet the bed and they knew it. Sometimes we laid awake and cut up and told stories. One night Louie had an idea.

"Rubin, you oughta climb that tree in the corral and jump on the camper to scare the girls. They're gonna think it's a bear and I bet they'll get to hollering and come out of that camper," Louie said.

"They'll get so scared they'll want to sleep with Daddy. Oh, we'll get a big laugh out of it. We'll see how fast they can run." Rubin was all for it.

"Harry and Alton you come watch, but you better be quiet as you can," Louie told us.

Rubin climbed the tree in the corral. We stood close by not making a sound. Rubin stood on the limb and then jumped to the roof of the camp trailer. He hit the roof, and then went out of sight going through the top all the way through the floor. The girls screamed all right, but with laughter. We ran to the door of the camper and saw Rubin just standing there with his feet through the floor, standing in the dirt. He was all scraped up and bloody especially on his belly from the boards he had gone through on the roof. He had got the scare, not the girls. Now we were all scared. What would Daddy do when he found out we had busted the girl's house? Harry and me ran back to our bed and got in quick.

"Louie and Rubin are gonna git it, we won't. They're supposed to be keeping an eye on us. Let's act like we don't know a thing," Harry told me. I followed along.

The girls had to run to the house because their bedroom was wide open to the sky. In the morning when we went in for breakfast, Harry and me were both relieved to find Daddy laughing over the whole prank. Rubin and Louie had to patch up the camper and we all laughed about Rubin having the joke on him. Rubin didn't think it was too funny.

Don't Get Hurt

We had been working out at Marquez canyon for some time and had a load ready to go to town. We took off for Albuquerque early in the morning because going and

72

coming took all day. Louie, Rubin and Elaine were left to do chores and to watch the babies. Esther, Sheron and me and Harry squeezed in the cab with Mama and Daddy. Groff didn't pay in money but in little pieces of paper that gave Daddy credit at a store in Albuquerque. We had to get diesel and gasoline so Daddy would show his piece of paper to the store where we also bought groceries.

Daddy just about always got us a treat which is why we were so excited to get to come to town. Daddy carried out big sacks of beans, sugar and potatoes. I carried the big bag of puffed rice. It didn't weigh a thing, but it made me feel big like Daddy to hoist it onto my shoulder and carry it to the truck. Smaller sacks of salt and coffee were picked out. Mama got canned meat in the square tin cans, Spam and some of those little Vienny sausages, canned fruit and vegetables. She always bought powdered milk which was awful. We didn't have any electricity so everything we bought had to be able to be kept without an ice box. We needed all of it to last at least till the

Road carved out by Wesley and the boys so they could haul logs.

next time we came to town when Groff would give Daddy his little piece of paper.

Leaving Albuquerque was the most fun because on the right side of the road were all the junk yards selling things collected at the dump. Little shacks with bicycle frames, car tires, steel and metal. At one of them they sold little wheels

73

that had been taken from toy wagons and tricycles. Daddy stopped there and bought us some little wheels to put on our toy wood trucks we played with. Sometimes we used jar lids as wheels, but these real little wheels would be so much better. They must not have cost more than a few pennies because I knew Daddy didn't have very much cash money.

The trip was long and we got to eat some of the crackers Mama had got. We had a bag of water and that kept our mouths from getting so dry. We dozed as we rode. The bumps were so big though, even if you drifted off you better have a good hand hold or get knocked to the floor.

We finally drove up the little hill to the house and Rubin rushed out to meet us.

"Daddy, somethin' bad's happened." Rubin was even more serious than normal, his face was red.

"Somebody hurt?" Daddy walked up to Rubin and started looking around.

"Louie's burned Daddy. Elaine's got him layin' down inside."

We all rushed inside. I knew one of Daddy's main rules had been broken: 'Don't get sick, and don't get hurt.' Louie was laid out on the couch and Elaine sat beside him. She had a wet rag on his forehead and a wet towel over his left leg.

"My lands, what's going on?" Mama asked Elaine and Louie both. Louie didn't look like he could talk, and Elaine started crying as she told Mama what had happened.

Louie and Rubin had changed the oil in the truck and filled it up with gas. Louie spilled gas on his pant leg but hadn't thought much about it. Later after the work was done Rubin and Elaine went in the house with the babies. Louie stayed outside and was making a smoke chimney. He put diesel in a can and had stuck a pipe over the top to watch the smoke come out the top. I knew that Louie did love to watch smoke come out of an exhaust pipe. He would watch the top of a stack on a truck in hopes of watching fire come out whenever we were on the highway. Elaine told us when the pipe was over the middle of the can it would put the fire out, so he had propped it on the side. The can turned over and the fire went up Louie's pant leg where that gas had soaked in when he spilled it.

Rubin and Elaine heard him hollering and saw him running. Rubin ran him down and got him on the ground to get the fire out. Elaine took his britches off. By then, though, the leg was burned bad. They carried him inside and waited for us to get back.

Elaine had been trying to keep him calm. He was hurting and he had sweat all over his head. Mama took the wet towel off of his leg. From knee to ankle it was red and the skin had already started peeling away. I didn't look too close because it looked so awful, but I thought I saw white bone. Daddy went grey and sat down on the floor beside the cot. Louie laid there with his eyes closed and didn't make a sound. Mama hugged Rubin and Elaine held Louie's hand. The fun we had in town was forgotten.

Daddy turned to religion and had us gather around Louie. We got on our knees, circled around the couch and Daddy began to talk to the Lord. He thanked Him for all we had and then asked his favor on Louie. He pleaded with the Lord to take away Louie's pain and for the leg to heal. He prayed for us all and left what happened to God's will.

We all were quiet that night for supper. Afterwards, Daddy read the Bible for hours. Mama finally told him, "Wesley, it's time to put these babies to bed."

When he closed the book, Rubin, Harry and me went to the shed, without Louie.

Work started the next day like usual, but this time only Daddy and Rubin headed to the woods. In the day Louie

75

lay on the floor on a pallet Mama made. At night he would sleep up on the couch if he wanted to. Mary was little enough that she would lay on the pallet with Louie and not get off. Mama kept Louie's leg covered in Vaseline and a towel. Esther waited on Louie for Mama and tried to care for him as good as a five year old could. She would sit down beside him and pat him and ask him,

"Does it hurt, Louie?"

He told her, "No, sugar, it doesn't hurt." I didn't know if it was true but I could tell Esther felt better. She told Daddy that night that his prayers were answered 'cause Louie didn't hurt no more. From then on, Louie never did act like it hurt again. I don't think he wanted to let Esther down. Mama dressed his leg every day, but Louie couldn't put any weight on it at all. Just laying there all day and night with nothing to make him hungry, Louie got thinner. Daddy or Rubin would have to carry him outside and to the outhouse. After a while Rubin and Louie got good at getting around together. Rubin would walk over and put his back to Louie, who would reach up and put his arms around Rubin's neck and hold on as Rubin leaned forward and stood up and walked for the both of them. It was a good thing he was stout.

With just two of them in the woods it was extra work for both. Daddy told Mama that at twelve Rubin could do the work of a grown man. Rubin felt like he was more of a grown up than us kids and didn't have much time or interest in playing. He got bossy and there wasn't a one of us that liked it. After a day in the woods, Rubin would eat everything he could and then go to bed. I guess it's hard to be a man when you're still a kid.

This went on for weeks but we got used to it. It started getting warm outside. Flies started coming out and Daddy made Louie a cage to go over his leg, Mama put a sheet over it and that helped to keep the flies off. Me and the younger

76

kids were splashing in the creek by the horses that were tethered on long ropes so they could get a drink. One of them butted Esther in the back and dumped her in the water. We wouldn't stop laughing at her and she ran in the house to Mama.

Wesley, Rubin and Harry

An old Mexican man came up to the house and asked to talk to Daddy. Mama pointed to the mill. Daddy shut it down to talk. Daddy dipped water out of the bucket and offered some to the man. We watched as they visited a while and he shook hands with Daddy. He left down the road back to town and Daddy hollered for us. We ran up and Daddy told us the people in town didn't want us playing in the creek. That was their drinking water and we were dirtying it up. We wouldn't dare argue with Daddy, but I didn't know why we couldn't be in the creek if the horses could.

That night at supper Daddy told Mama what else the man had said.

"He told me that there had been families working this mill before and if we didn't watch out we would be stuck here with no money and no food. They've seen it happen." Daddy said between bites of cornbread.

"Wesley, when I was in town, some of the folks told me that no one had ever been able to last here too long. That Groff don't pay enough to feed you, and it's too hard. I didn't think much of it at the time, but it sure is curious that they all say the same thing."

"We'll keep working and see how things go. Me and Rubin can't get as many bundles ready as fast as we could with Louie's help, but we'll keep at it. I don't like that we don't have a car of our own. I think I'll look around in Albuquerque the next time we go to see about a car."

"I don't know when Louie'll be back up." Mama looked worried over at Louie.

"I'm better, Daddy. I'm gettin' better every day." Louie was quick to tell him.

"I know you are son." Daddy patted Louie's shoulder as he headed to his chair. Although his leg wouldn't hold any weight, Louie had started scooting around on his hands and rear. He was good natured but I couldn't tell if he was better, or just better at it.

Daddy and Rubin kept working and the rest of us went to school and helped Mama with the baby and Louie. The sound of the saw echoed down through the canyons and we listened as Daddy and Rubin worked. When the sawing stopped, we kept an ear out for when the GI truck headed back. Daddy would load it down so heavy that sometimes it couldn't make it up the hills. Rubin would be driving and the motor would bog down so low that it would die, stop and start rolling backwards. It got to rolling so fast it was all Rubin could do to steer it as he flew down the hill. He turned around and looked behind his shoulder and acted like he wasn't scared.

Soon Mama ran out of baking soda, so the biscuits became hard and flat. The big gunny sacks stacked in the house were about empty. The little store in town didn't take the little pieces of paper as money even if Daddy had any. Daddy was thinking the man who came to talk to him might have been right. We ate potato soup. That night Mama told Daddy she didn't have anything left for breakfast. Daddy thought for a spell and then went out into the horse corral. He gathered up a big bucket of the oats that were for the horses and some of the molasses he mixed to feed them.

He took them to Mama and told her, "This'll do us for now, Fonny." She mixed them up for breakfast. It was sweet but eating horse feed was hard on your belly. We could all see that if we were down to eating the horse feed things weren't very good. Daddy started on what he said would be his last load of lumber to Albuquerque.

The Little House on the Truck

Daddy and Rubin left early the next morning for town. We knew it would take all day to go there and come back. That night just before dark we heard them driving up the road, we ran out to meet them and stopped in our tracks when we saw them driving up in a yellow '47 Ford F-6.

Daddy had left the Groff truck in town and used the money from the lumber to buy our own truck and a big sack of potatoes that Rubin carried into the house. It was just a little cab with nothing behind it, not even a flatbed, just two steel frame rails hooked up to the back wheels. I did know something though, Daddy said we were leaving and it was going to be in that Ford.

Daddy drove the truck to the lumber stacks and began making a floor on the back of the truck. He laid two boards down the length of it. He took fir boards and laid them across layer by layer. He nailed them to the boards that went down the length. He kept layering boards across until they were a foot thick and then he began making walls. There was a wall across the back of the cab and walls on the side. He made square windows on the sides and put on a roof. The back end was left open, but boards were layered at the end to make a little six inch lip so we couldn't just fall out when the truck

79

was moving. Inside he layered some boards from the cab halfway to the open end and that made the bed.

Cut out windows gave us light inside. Daddy then took broken pieces of glass from old car windows and put them up against the openings from the inside. He drove nails in around the glass and bent them to hold it in. From the outside they looked good. Inside, it looked a little rougher. We were ready to load up in our little house and head out.

Mama, Daddy and the babies rode in the little cab. It had a bench seat inside and they all squeezed in. The rest of us got in the back. Rubin, Elaine, Sheron and Harry sat or laid on the wood bed. I got on the floor by Louie. He sat with his back against the side and laid his legs across at the open end. Daddy had made him a little cover out of boards for his leg. The bottom was flat but it was a rounded frame on top and it covered both of his legs. Mama put an empty flour sack over all of it.

The sky was still dark when Rubin opened the corral and led the horses out to graze. With the creek and the grass they would be fine until Groff came. We took off and bounced our way over the thirty-five miles of dirt road to Highway 66. The big rocks and cuts in the dirt road knocked us around in the back and Louie made us stay up by the cab so we wouldn't fall out. By the time we made it to the black top and the metal bridge it was daylight.

Things smoothed out when we turned onto the blacktop at the iron bridge and made our way toward Albuquerque. We passed the junk yards, the car lots, the cafés and motels. We kept going east out of Albuquerque through the canyon. The road twisted and turned and the truck lugged down as it carried us through the mountain. The road straightened out as we rolled down the hill to the flat country as Mama and Daddy headed us back to Louisiana.

We couldn't look out the front of the truck so we were always looking back. We watched as cars came up behind us and then when the road was clear they passed. I inched my

The road out of Marquez Canyon

way to the back of the truck so I could sit by the open end and look at the cars and people while they looked at us.

Since Mama and Daddy were in the front, we acted up a little more than if they had

their eye on us. Elaine would have us sing songs and we would holler them out as loud as we could to hear over the road noise. Sometimes we played I Spy, sometimes we slept, mostly we fought and picked at each other but nobody cried. It seemed like we were all glad to have left that canyon.

We watched the sun get low in the west. Daddy pulled the truck over to the side of the road. He told us we could all get out so we jumped over Louie to the ground. Louie grabbed hold of Rubin's neck and he carried him over to where Mama wanted to make a fire. We were in a wide spot off to the side of the road. It was a dirt driveway that went off to the south but you couldn't see where it ended.

Now that we were stopped, without the wind blowing so hard, we could smell something hot coming from under the truck. Daddy laid down on the ground to take a look.

"Rubin come over here and help me look at this rearend." Rubin got down in the dirt with Daddy. Mama made camp while Daddy figured out what was wrong.

"All of ya'll go look on the ground and see if you can find some wood to burn to start a fire." I raced Harry to find the most to bring back to Mama. There wasn't much wood so she used what we found to start the fire and used some we had brought with us to keep it burning.

East towards Albuquerque on Route 66

She made potato soup in the big pot on the back of the truck and then Rubin carried it to the fire to cook.

"I'm going to need some parts to fix that rearend," Daddy told her.

"How are we going to get it, Wesley?"

"I'll flag somebody down in the mornin'. If I can get somebody to take me in to Santa Rosa they ought to have the part there."

Mama called us to come eat. Daddy sat down to say Grace. He thanked the Lord for all we had. We slept out that night on the dirt driveway by the road. Daddy was up early ready to head to town. I kept my eyes peeled to make sure that I would be the first one to spot somebody coming.

We heard it before we seen it top over the rise. A big Greyhound bus was coming. I thought how much fun it might be to ride on one. Daddy got close to the road and waved his arm. The bus driver saw him. We heard him gear his motor down and his brakes started to squeal as he slowly came to a stop near the camp. I hoped it would stop near to us so I could see it up close.

Daddy stepped a foot onto the bus and talked with the driver. He came and told Mama he had his ride to Santa Rosa

82

and told us all to mind Mama. He got up in that big old Greyhound and we watched as he headed east to town.

Fresh Milk

We played around the camp and looked for treasures in the dirt and weeds. There was always a little wind blowing and even though it was warm, it wasn't hot. We played hide and go seek and took turns being It. We didn't get near the highway. We were all road broke and knew not to get close. As the day wore on there were more cars and trucks on the road. It was fun to see if Harry or me could guess what kind of car the next one would be.

Mama was always telling us, "You kids don't go too far." She was always worried about snakes. We would walk as far as we dared from camp and then run all the way back, and sometimes I beat Harry. He acted like he let me win, but I knew I beat him

That night, those that wanted to could sleep in the little house on the back of the truck. I had my blanket outside with Harry. The stars were so bright we watched falling stars for a long time. The night was cool and we listened to the sound of the cars coming slowly toward us and then passing and moving on as we went to sleep. I made up stories in my head about where they were going and what they were doing. It was like having a bedtime story to go to sleep to.

In the morning the wind was already blowing and we had to keep the sand from blowing into our soup. The driveway to the ranch where we were camped was dirt and we saw the dust cloud as somebody drove from the south towards the highway. A tall man in a cowboy hat and cowboy boots, pulled up, got out of his pickup and went to talk to Mama. We all wanted to know what was going on, but didn't want to get too close to draw attention to ourselves, so we stayed close to the fire. Rubin went and stood by Mama. Elaine stayed by the babies.

"Hello," he said real loud to Mama as he walked up.

"How do you do, I'm Mrs. Miller, my husband's gone into Santa Rosa for parts for our truck. We don't plan to be here long, just enough time to get fixed. As soon as we're done we'll be gone."

"I own this ranch you're on," he told Mama. "I was told you folks were out here and came to check." He looked around. "Nine kids." He said it like we didn't already know how many of us there was. He looked at Louie laid out with his cage on his leg and saw the pot of potato soup we were eating for breakfast.

"Are you needing anything, Mrs. Miller?" he asked Mama.

"Thank you but no. We don't need a thing here. We're doin' just fine."

"Well, you all stay as long as you need to. I hope your man will be back to you soon."

"I'm sure he will be," Mama answered.

We all watched as he drove back down the dirt road. I sure did like those cowboy boots he had on, that sure would be something to have. I told Mama but she just laughed and told me "Maybe someday."

Just a little while later Mama put her hand to her eyes and watched the dust trail drift back up into the sky. We wondered why the rancher was coming back. He drove right up to us, got out and went to the bed of his pick up and brought out a big metal jug with a lid.

"Mrs. Miller, I've brought you some milk for all these young'uns."

"We don't want to take your milk. You didn't need to bring us anything."

"Yes, ma'am, I did." He said. He looked around again before he left and said again, "Nine kids."

"Maybe he hasn't seen nine kids before," I told Harry.

"He sure acts like he hasn't, some people don't know much. Race you to the milk!" Mama gave us all a dipper full of milk and then used some to thicken the potato soup. It was so good we had that jug emptied fast. What a treat to drink milk that wasn't made out of powder. I don't know how you could call them both milk they were so different. Supper was good that night.

With nothing much to do we laid around camp in the day and watched the cars come from both directions.

"Buick." Harry said fast.

Shoot. I knew that was a Buick. I got the next one, "Cadillac!" Harry grunted. We kept our eyes peeled to call the next one. We thought it was awful funny that the '49 Fords looked the same in the front as back. You couldn't tell the difference between them, coming or going. I didn't take my eyes off the road. I was trying to beat Harry on naming the cars. I watched as a pickup made its way from the east. I was waiting for it to get closer but it was slowing up. I jumped up to get a better look, so did Harry. Before he could shout, I beat him, "Daddy!"

It was a GMC and it slowed down and pulled off to the side of the road right by our camp. Daddy was back! He jumped out of the pickup and waved to the driver. We ran to meet him, all of us that could. He handed the part he'd brung off to Rubin as kids climbed all over him. He had us some penny candy and we all made sure we got our share. Mama fed him, and then he and Rubin got busy fixing the truck.

While they were working the dust cloud showed to the south and Mama told Daddy the rancher was coming. He drove up and out came the metal jug of milk. We all ran to him now and walked along side as he carried it to the camp.

85

Daddy told him hello and shook his hand, he and the rancher talked. Daddy told him we would be gone in the morning and took out his pocket watch and gave it to the cowboy. The man didn't want to take it but Daddy made him so we would be square with him.

We had stayed on the side of the road for three days and when Daddy and Rubin got the truck fixed we were all ready to move on. I jumped in the back and sat next to the boards that were on the back by Louie. It seemed like Daddy drove all night and all day. When we stopped to have our meals he would doze off and sleep. As soon as we were all fed and ready, back to the steering wheel he went.

Texas was a big state and it took forever to get across it. We left the desert and the mesas. The bushes and scrub became grass and there were more and more cattle grazing on it. The further we went it became greener and hotter. There were more trees and a lot more rivers and creeks. When we saw the standing water of the bayou we knew we were in Louisiana.

There was a little roadside park on Highway 84 just outside of Mansfield where Mama and Daddy had us get in the creek to clean up. We headed into Natchitoches, tired, hungry, and wet.

LOUISIANA 1953

The Lord's Hand

Word got out that Wesley's Bunch was back. We visited with some of the family and they told us about a house for rent in Natchitoches. It was two-story and sat on the east side of Cane River. It was the biggest house we had ever lived in. The boards were skinny and went across and over lapped each other. Mama said that was called ship lap. We walked up about ten steps to get to the porch which was on all four sides, shaded by big trees. Inside the front door there was a long hallway. There was a room on the left we used for a front room and a room on the right Mama made up for Louie. All the rest of us slept in the rooms upstairs.

Some of Daddy's sisters came by to see us and when they saw Louie they pitched a fit. The aunts went to hollering about Louie seeing a doctor. Daddy had three brothers alive too, but they didn't try to boss us like the aunts. One of his sisters even came from Longview, Texas to get after Daddy. Daddy told them all he didn't believe in doctors. He and Mama were going to count on the Lord to heal Louie and that was how it was going to be.

Those sisters weren't like Mama who always listened to Daddy. They were more like Grandma Miller. One or two of them came every day and got in a fight with Daddy. When we saw one of them drive up, us kids scattered to get out of sight.

Our house faced west and the town faced us and in between was the river. Mama's brother, Uncle Huey, had a place close by and his backyard was the riverbank. He would lend us cane poles for fishing. The pole was twice as long as I was tall. It was bigger on one end than the other. The big end fit in your hands easy. A line was tied on the end of the pole.

87

It took some practice to lob the hook, weight and float out into the river. We would go there and fish and take what we caught to Mama. I sure felt big when I was able to bring supper to Mama.

Daddy got Louie a metal cage to go over his leg. Instead of the flour sack, he put wire mesh around it from an old screen door. Louie's leg from knee to ankle looked like a big scab. Mama doctored it regular but he still couldn't walk. Daddy got a wagon that Louie could sit up in and he would use the handle to guide the wagon and push it with his good leg.

Harry and me were outside giving Louie a ride around the house. He was pulling and I was pushing from behind. The ground wasn't too flat and there were holes and tree roots hidden in the grass.

"Now come on Harry. You're tough, you can pull better'n that." Louie was egging Harry on.

"Push, Alton, push!" Harry hollered to me.

I put my palms flat across the wagon and dug my toes into the slick ground. Louie rocked back and forth in the wagon as Harry pushed and pulled him first one direction and then another trying to get the wagon to move. Louie got tickled and started laughing at us. He had been holding his foot on the ground keeping the wagon from going.

"Dad gum it Louie, I ain't gonna pull you no more." Harry had his hands on his hips.

"You better not let Mama hear you talk like that," Louie said with a big ole grin. He still thought the trick he had pulled was funny.

I gave him a big push right then and he almost tumbled from the wagon. Then Harry and me had the laugh on him as Louie barely caught himself from hitting the ground.

"You can just figure out how to get back in the house yourself." Harry wasn't going to cut him no slack. He took off into the house. I pushed Louie from the back and we made our way to the steps to get in the house.

"I'll go get Rubin," I told Louie and started to walk up the steps. A black and white car turned into the house with a light flashing. Behind that car was an ambulance. Daddy came out of the house, put his hat on and walked over to meet the sheriff at his car door. I stayed where I was and the rest of the family came outside to see what was going on. I couldn't hear what they were saying, but Daddy was starting to get loud. The sheriff kept on talking to Daddy. After a few minutes him and Daddy walked up to Mama who was standing by the screen door.

"What is it, Wesley?"

"They've come to take Louie to the hospital in Shreveport." Daddy was real upset and when he spoke to Mama, he kept taking his hat off and putting it back on. I had never seen Daddy act so fidgety and I was a little scared.

"Fonny, how do we let him go and the Lord think we don't have faith?" Daddy asked. Mama was quiet for a minute or two. She touched Daddy's arm.

"Maybe this is the Lord's hand, Wesley. This may be the way He is answering our prayers."

Daddy and Mama talked quietly for a few minutes. Louie sat in his wagon and didn't say a word. All of us kids just looked big eyed at all the people standing and waiting, the sheriff, the ambulance men, and the neighbors that had wandered close. And then Daddy went to Louie picked him up and carried Louie to the ambulance and sat him on the little moving bed the men had outside. Louie hugged Daddy for a minute, I'm not sure I had ever seen him do that. Mama came hurrying down the steps and put her hand on Louie's head.

"Don't you worry, Mama. These fellers will fix me good as new. Won't y'all?" I didn't know if Louie was acting brave or was relieved to have something done to his leg. Either way, he sure didn't act like he was worried about going with them.

The ambulance men picked up his bed and rolled him into the back of the ambulance. As one of them shut the door I heard Louie ask, "Think we could run with the sireens on." The whole town heard Louie leave.

Cotton Pickin'

Mama said the best way to deal with troubles was to work. It seems that's what we got to doing. Daddy took apart the little house on the back of the Ford truck. By the time we got done stacking the lumber we had quite a bundle. It was fir and that was hard to find in this country. Daddy traded the lumber for his share in a sawmill with Uncle Curtis, Mama's other brother. Daddy had been working on getting all that put together since we had got here, but we didn't have a paying job yet.

Mama talked to her brothers and they got Harry, me and Mama some work. I thought I was big catching fish for supper, but knowing I was going to go and work a paying job, I knew I was almost grown even if I was close to being nine.

Mama got us up early and we headed to the cotton fields. The fields were close to the house so the walk didn't take long. Mama wore a big hat in the hot July sun and she found a couple of floppy brimmed hats for Harry and me. Mine was too big on my head and was almost too much work to keep on, but Mama made me. When we got to the fields, the farmer gave us all big gray sacks. They were longer than Mama was tall.

90

The cotton was stuck to the brown boll and we had to pull it loose and put it in our sack. We would be paid by how much our sacks weighed when we were done. I couldn't pick but a tiny bit at a time. I looked down at that dab of cotton and then at that grey sack and it seemed like I would have to pick for a year to fill that thing up.

The hot sun beat down on us and there wasn't a cloud in the sky. I looked over at Mama in her row and she just kept picking. The rows of cotton looked as long as some of the highways we drove down. When we finally got to the end of a row we had to turn and then go up the other side that seemed even longer. Mama was always out ahead of me and Harry. He sat down in the little bit of shade the cotton plant made. Mama saw him and walked back to him,

"Ain't gonna be no lazy people in heaven, son."

"There's gonna be one, Mama," Harry told her as he looked up at her from under the brim of his hat, but he got up.

Sweat covered us causing the dirt and cotton to stick to our hands and skin. I got enough cotton in my sack to be able to throw a rock down in there every once in a while to make it seem fuller. We moved as slow as the day wore on, the heat making my clothes heavy.

When the day was over we took our sacks to the sheds where they weighed them. The scale had a line that came from a beam in the barn. At one end was a big hook that latched on to the top of the sack. The sack was picked off the ground even as long as it was. Our cotton was weighed and then the man paid Mama for our work. Mama looked at the money in her hand. I don't know how much we made, but Mama didn't have us go back to the cotton fields again.

The Sticker Patch

Elaine, Harry, me and Sheron started going to school in Natchitoches. Rubin went too, but only on Fridays. The rest of the week he had to work at the sawmill over by Marthaville. Daddy had gotten it running. He and Rubin cut timber on Monday, hauled it on Tuesday, sawed logs on Wednesday, and took and sold them to the big mill on Thursday. Louie was gone to Shreveport and everybody else was too young for school. I didn't like school. I didn't know as much as the other kids, and I didn't like them looking at me when I had to read out loud.

No matter what school we ended up going to, the other kids always thought we were different and it was the same here. We didn't talk the same way as them and a lot of the time we looked different, though nobody from here thought my name was funny. Just like a lot of the cousins, the kids here didn't think much of us. They ran their mouths, trying to act tough, but after me and Harry fought a couple of them; they learned they didn't want to tangle with us. I had to fight a few more times than Harry. He could joke and get buddies easier than me. Some of the teachers thought I was a bully after whipping a few well known kids. I thought that wasn't fair, if I didn't whip them right off, they might think they could whip me. I couldn't have stood anybody thinking that.

It was a big thing during recess to run foot races. I watched the kids race and saw that when they got close to the tree they all slowed down. I walked by there and saw there was a sticker patch. In Louisiana kids didn't wear shoes to school when it was warm so we were all barefoot. I decided right then that I was going to race those boys and I wasn't going to slow down at the sticker patch no matter what.

The next time the kids gathered around to start racing I came over.

"What're you doin' hangin' around here, you think you're fast enough to race with us?" asked the boy who always won. He was tall and looked stout, but I knew I could win.

"I know I can outrun you," I told him.

"I bet I could beat you easy. You don't look like much." He was sure talking big.

If I hadn't have wanted to race, that would have been a fistfight, but I let it go so I could whip him another way. I toed the line and kept my eyes on the tree we had to touch at the end to win the race. We took off running. I ran as fast as I could and when I got to the patch where I felt those stickers poking my feet, some of them making my spine tingle, I just ran faster. The tree got closer and I ran passed it as I reached my hand out to touch it. Everybody was behind me. I whooped like I always heard Daddy yell when he was excited.

"That didn't count, let's do it again." That same boy shouted. He knew it counted, but I was more than ready to show them all again. I brushed the stickers off my feet and lined up. I won, over and over again. I beat every one of them that came up against me. Every day I raced anybody that wanted to try. I became known as the fastest runner in school. I felt good, not just because I beat them racing, but I had outsmarted them too. Not a one of them noticed how they all slowed down when their feet hit the sticker patch. I knew if I acted like the stickers weren't there, they didn't hurt as much. It was kind of like that with a lot of things. If you pretended like things didn't hurt, pretty soon they didn't. At least not as much.

Britches

The more time we spent in school, I made buddies too, just like Harry. Those buddies came in handy when it came to the lunch room. The school sold lunches on metal trays and everybody that paid got a little carton of milk. Mama always packed our lunch. We would get an egg in a biscuit, peanut butter or cornbread and a little piece of meat. She did give us three cents to buy the little carton of milk.

Kids in Natchitoches didn't drink their milk. I couldn't get over the fact they didn't have to drink milk made out of powder and still didn't want it. Not too many of them ate their cornbread either. Since the school made you eat all the food off the tray, the kids would ask around if anybody wanted what they didn't eat. Well, I took their cornbread and I took their milk. The more friends I had the more food I got. I would have so many square little pieces of cornbread stacked around my lunch sack it was like a little fort. I could drink those little milks in just about one gulp. I got a pretty good reputation for that too.

I really walked tall the day I wore my new britches. I mostly wore Harry's old ones but Mama had got me and Harry both a new pair. I was so proud of those pants I wanted to wear them all the time. One morning I went to find them, but Mama had washed all the clothes and my new pants were wet. She had them out on the clothes line but said they were too damp to wear. I couldn't stand leaving them on the line so when we left the house; I went to the line, stripped off my old, raggedy britches and put the new ones on. Knowing I didn't have no holes or patches I felt as good as the other kids. If I only had a pair of cowboy boots people would know just how neat I was.

I sat at my desk in the back by the broom closet. I pretended to do my work like most days when the teacher came by. She leaned down to look at what I was doing then scrunched her nose and said, "What's that smell?"

"I don't smell anything," I told her.

"Do you smell that, Peggy?" She asked the girl sitting next to me. "It smells like something soured."

The teacher and a couple of the girls kept sniffing around and kept coming back in my direction. I started sniffing. I scrunched down in my desk and the smell was stronger. That's when I figured it out, the smell was my pants. They had soured. Mama had been right; they were too wet to wear. I didn't want them to know it was me stinking so I got up and went to the closet. Inside was a mop and it was still wet.

"Here it is teacher. It's this mop, it's wet and it smells." I held up that wet mop like a trophy. It was going to save me.

"Well, I'll have to tell the janitor not leave that wet thing in that dark closet until it dries out. That smell is awful."

"I'll just set it back in here for now," I told her. I couldn't wait for school to get over.

Mama got after me when I got back, and even though my pants stunk, she wouldn't wash them until it was wash day again. The next day I wore my old pants but I made sure I walked just as tall.

Grandma and Grandpa Mac

At school they would take time from the reading and arithmetic and let us do little crafts with copper. We beat thin pieces of it into shapes. I made a little bowl that could be used as an ashtray. I made a square bowl that could be used as an ashtray. I made a long skinny bowl that could be used as an ashtray. When I would show them to Mama she would ooh

95

and aah over how good they were. Her and Daddy didn't smoke but I kept them in ashtrays.

They didn't use tobacco at all. They didn't roll cigarettes or use snuff like Grandma and Grandpa Mac. The only time I ever saw either of them smoke was if one of us had an ear ache and Mama would light a cigarette and blow the smoke in our ear to try to make it quit hurting. A lot of the older men and women used tobacco, men might chew, but a woman dipped.

Snuff was a brown powder that was put inside the bottom lip. Grandma and Grandpa Mac were dippers. I tried a pinch once and it burned. The snuff made people need to spit all the time. So many old folks dipped, I thought for a while that old people just had brown spit. If they were inside they always spit in the fire place, fire or not. If they were outside they would just spit anywhere. I hated it because kids were always barefoot and if you weren't looking you would step in a big wet spot. That always happened at Grandma Mac's.

Emma and Henry McDonald

Grandma Mac's house was little with a bed in the front room and a couple more in the other rooms. The rough boards that were her walls were covered with newspaper and advertisements stuck with glue made from flour and water. A fire was going in the fireplace and they both took turns spitting in it. They moved their rocking chairs back and forth,

96

putting two fingers up to their lips to spit through. I saw right away one of my ashtrays wouldn't do them any good. Every time the spit hit the fire there was a hiss and a sizzle.

Grandma was a little skinny thing but all of her joints were big, her fingers and elbows and knees. When she worked out in her yard and squatted down her knees came up above her ears like a scrawny frog. She wore black high top tennis shoes that had faded to brown. Her yard had a garden and in the back there was a big corn crib made out of railroad ties where they threw old bottles. That's where we would get out brown snuff bottles if we wanted to play cars. The top of the bottle curved and had a cork lid; we pretended that was the front of the car. The dots on the bottom told us what kind they were. One dot was a Ford, two dots a Dodge and three dots a Chevy. Rubin told us which dot stood for what car. I don't know if he made it up, but that's how we played.

Grandma would leave biscuits and pear preserves on the counter in the kitchen at the back of the house. We would come in the back door from outside where we were to play, grab them and run. Harry would take the pan, but I had to get it put back. We would wolf them down and eat every drop of preserves. Every time we came over she had those biscuits set out. We sure were getting one over on her.

Grandpa had dogs that were for hunting, a German police dog, a little white dog that wore a bell because he couldn't bark and a bigger brown dog. He always liked to brag on them.

"Now if I want to hunt squirrel," Grandpa told us, "I just reach for my shotgun and walk out the door and those dogs will go out in the woods and get me one treed. If I want rabbit, I reach for my .22 and they'll nose me out a rabbit. I thought I'd fool them one day so I reached for my fishing pole. Well, wouldn't you know it; those dogs ran straight down to the pond and started digging for worms." I knew for sure they were smart dogs but Grandpa sure got tickled when he told me that story.

"Boy, come out back here with me," Grandpa said and I jumped up to follow him.

"I made this here shooter for ya." Grandpa pulled out a wooden sling shot with a piece of old rubber attached to it.

"Thanks, Grandpa!" I took it from him.

"Now, this shooter comes with a deal you gotta agree to."

"Okay."

"When you go over to your Grandpa Miller's I want you to use this to shoot his calves. Now every time you hit one, I'll give you a nickel. But you gotta be honest and make sure you don't tell me a story about a makin' more shots than you do."

A sling shot and make money? This was the best thing I had ever heard.

When we got to our house I practiced my shots outside on everything I could hit. I got Harry once but acted like I had been aiming at something else. He didn't know any better. Saturday we loaded up in the truck and Daddy took us over to Grandpa Miller's so he could help him with some work.

I had my slingshot and I was ready to get started on the deal I had made Grandpa Mac. We drove up to the house and while Mama went inside with the girls us boys stayed outside where we were supposed to. Rubin and Harry went with Daddy and Hoyt Lynn played by the house.

I had a job to do so I went straight to the field in back of the house and gathered up some rocks, little ones about the size of a big marble, and I got busy shooting calves. There were about ten of them. Each time I got one in the rear they jumped and took off running. They ran into each other and started mooing and making a bunch of racket. This was so fun I would have done it without the nickel. It was a sight as I kept shooting them. Hoyt Lynn came up where I was and he enjoyed the show too. I looked over at him to tell him I'd let him try, when behind him I saw Grandpa coming out of the gate.

He hollered and headed right towards me. I hadn't even thought about getting in trouble. I took off running and looked over my shoulder to see him coming after me. I ran as hard as I ever had to get across the field. I was about to hit the trees where I could hide when a hand grabbed my shirt and jerked me back to the ground. Grandpa stood me up, grabbed my arm and whipped me every time we took a step. I hollered and he just kept whippin', all the way to Mama who was out on the porch by this time. After I finished getting in trouble by all the grownups I wasn't sure Grandpa Mac's deal was too good. Harry laughed at me later when we were sitting outside.

"Why'd you let Grandpa Miller see you? You should've known he would get after you. Him and Grandpa Mac don't like each other one bit."

"I didn't know those calves mattered so much. I thought Grandpa Mac was just playing a prank. How was I supposed to know they didn't get along?"

"How could you not know? They never visit or talk to each other even though they're just about kin. I heard some of the folks talking that the two of them used to run whiskey. That's when their trouble started with each other. Grandpa Mac still ain't got over Mama marrying Daddy, him being fourteen years older than her and a rounder then too. Boy, he sure played one on you."

"Well, if he pays up, I don't care about a whippin' anyhow. I've had plenty of them."

Grandpa Mac couldn't stop laughing when I told him about my run in with Grandpa Miller. He gave me my fifty cents and told me that was about the best money he had ever spent.

Church Goin'

It was Wednesday night and we were headed to the church for the meeting in New Town. Bob Gay's wife was playing piano. This night Daddy and Elaine stood up in front and sang.

Precious father, loving mother
Fly across the lonely years
And old home scenes of my childhood
In fond memories appear

As I travel on life's pathway
Know not what the years may hold
As I ponder, hope grows fonder
Precious memories flood my soul

I was glad they sang 'Precious Memories.' It was about travelling and I knew all about that. They sounded so pretty together and sometimes I wondered if I was feeling the Holy Ghost inside. It didn't make me want to jump and shout, but sometimes tears would come to my eyes even though I didn't feel sad. Wilmer Lynch was the regular preacher, but had Daddy speak as a guest preacher that night. Daddy banged his fist on the pulpit and shouted as much fire and brimstone as any paid preacher. Folks shouted Amen and Hallelujah. Us kids stayed quiet.

Not much after dark we headed back to Natchitoches. Back in the house, we turned on the overhead light in the front room. This house had a single light bulb that hung from the middle of every room. It sure beat a kerosene lamp. Daddy was still filled with the spirit so when we got back he opened up the Bible and started reading to us. He hadn't got past just a few verses when car lights turned into the yard. We all scrambled up to see who it was. Harry and me beat everyone else to the window.

"You boys back away from there," Mama scolded us. But we weren't moving. It was the sheriff again! This was the second time he had showed up at our house. I couldn't believe it. There was no way we weren't going to try and find out what was going on. Daddy walked outside, he talked to the sheriff for quite a while. Daddy used a lot of arm movements to tell his story, while the sheriff nodded a few times. In the end they shook hands and the sheriff got back in his car.

Mama met Daddy at the door.

"What is it Wesley?"

"Ted Groff talked to the law in Albuquerque. They called out here looking for me. Groff's saying I stole from him. He wanted the sheriff to arrest me."

"Arrest you! My word, what are things coming to?" Mama sat down hard in her chair.

"I told him what I had done to leave New Mexico. What shape we were in. The way I figured it the lumber we took with us paid our wages for all that work. Sheriff said he would call them back in New Mexico. As far as he could see I hadn't done nothing but try to take care of my family."

"Well, I would hope so. Imagine thinkin' we would steal." Mama used her apron to wipe her face.

The next morning while we sat at the breakfast table, the family was still talking about the night before. Mama was stirring the pot of oatmeal she turned to Daddy, "I didn't sleep all night worrying about the sheriff."

"He's supposed to come back this morning after he talks to the law in New Mexico. I bet that's him." Daddy went outside when we heard the car drive up. All of us boys walked out with Daddy. We wanted to act like we were behind him, and I wanted to make sure I heard all that was going on. Mama came out too. The sheriff told the law in New Mexico Daddy's side of the story and as far as he was concerned 'wasn't nobody gonna arrest nobody.' We sure were glad to hear it, especially for Mama's sake. Maybe we were being helped after all that church goin'.

Learning to Win

Daddy had us move closer to the sawmill in Marthaville. He found us a little house by Shamrock. It had an artesian well and no electricity so we were back to hauling water and kerosene light.

Daddy got hired to log a big stand of trees, so besides hiring Wilmer Lynch and the Gay brothers, some days Harry and me would need to go and help at the mill. Daddy taught us things while we worked. One thing he told us was never to log trees in a fence row. There might be wire or nails from signs that were posted and they could get tangled in the saw. While we worked Daddy would tell us how to go about things smart. We didn't ask questions, we just listened and Daddy expected us to remember.

When we didn't go to work with him, I was working on my own things. I was building bicycles.

Down the road lived a tall, red headed boy named Albert. Every inch of him was covered in freckles and he looked to be nothing but skin and bones. His daddy worked for the light company and it must have been a good job because Albert had a brand new bicycle.

Watching him ride that thing up and down the road made me want a bicycle bad. I scavenged the country for frames, wheels, tires and chains. I gathered up old bicycle parts wherever I could, studied how they went together and built my own bicycle. I ended up with so many parts I was able to build more than one.

Harry didn't build bicycles with me but I let him ride. After the first time I beat him, he wouldn't race anymore, but he rode with me. I practiced riding and raced up and down the dirt road, getting faster all the time. If I bent a rim, I would change it out with my spare parts. Sometimes my back wheel was smaller than the front, sometimes the other way around, but I never settled for an 'every other link' chain.

I was feeling good when I got on my best bike and rode down toward Albert's house. I found him outside and asked if he wanted to ride bikes with me. We rode to Cooper's store and I had the six cents for a Coke. Albert had enough for a Coke and a candy bar.

We rode up and down the blacktop and the dirt roads. After a few days of that he told me that he thought we ought to race. It was what I had been waiting for. He got on his bicycle, and I got on mine. His was shiny and red. My bicycle was grey and rusty. He had big black peddles and I used big bolts for foot rests. My back wheel was smaller than my front wheel, but I had an every link chain, not a sissy every other link chain like Albert. I felt like I matched up with him pretty good.

We took off and I used what I had learned before at the foot races. Never back down. Never act scared, even if you are. And don't stop till the end. I had that red headed boy beat before we left the starting line and he didn't even know it. I pumped up the hill, and peddled down the other side. When I crossed the finish line, he was way behind me. He may have had a brand new bike, but I was the winner.

103

He peddled his brand new bike home and I rode mine head high and fast as I could go. I jumped off the bike as I rolled into the yard and let the bike slow to a stop and then fall over on its side. I hadn't learned how to make brakes yet.

Stubborn as Mules

Louie was gone for a long time, almost a year. He would talk to Mama and Daddy when they went to somebody's house that had a telephone. Once they had ridden up to see him. Rubin went with some friends in a red and white Pontiac to see him one time. The rest of us hadn't though. Finally Mama and Daddy brought Louie back.

He got out of the car and he didn't look in much better shape than when he had left. He was fatter though. He was on crutches, his leg was drawn up so that he couldn't walk on it. We all ran out to meet him and he laughed big as Mary jumped on him. He laughed and we laughed too. Good natured Louie was back.

He loved lemons and salt so Mama had got some for him for his first day back. He sat out on the porch with us and told us how he had got on up in Shreveport.

"I just sat up in that bed, day after day. I got so tired of being inside one time I just made my way down the elevator and walked outside. I just laid there in the grass. It felt so good to be out of bed and outside."

"I don't think I would complain about being in bed," Rubin snorted.

"Well, you spend enough time in one, you'd complain," Louie said real sharp to Rubin.

"After the nurses figured out I'd been gone for a while, they got to lookin' for me. The older nurse looked out the window and saw me layin' out there. She said just leave him alone. She told me about it and she helped me when I needed to go outside for a while."

"Did you do anything for fun?" Sheron asked.

"I got the idea one day to make a train. I gathered up four wheel chairs and tied them all together in a line. I pushed them down the hall and off they went. Well, I didn't figure on the turn. When they rounded that corner they didn't make it. The string broke I had them tied with. They ran smack into the telephone booth. All that wood and glass went everywhere. What a racket that made. The glass smashed into a million pieces. I thought I was going to get it then.

"The old doctor came to my room and bawled me out. He asked me what grade I had last been in. I told him seventh and he told me that they was going to make me go to school and do school work while I was in there. He thought he had me. Well, I didn't say nothin' to him, but when they brought those school lessons around I didn't do a one of them. He'd come in and get after me and I would just look at him and grin. I never did any of that school work. They couldn't make me."

"Well, I don't go to school but on Fridays here," Rubin told him. "Just in time to take tests on all the stuff everybody learned on the other days that I don't go. I got to do the work at the mill and try to do the school work too. That don't make for a good mix."

"Daddy don't care how you do in school," Louie told him.

"I just might care." Rubin left the porch.

Rubin sounded mad and worn out. A few days back he had gone logging with Daddy and Cowboy who was a dried up old man that always dressed like a cowboy. He was little and mean and Rubin didn't like him one bit. Daddy and Cowboy had partnered on some big red mules to skid logs with. They had bought them from a man down by Florien

105

who had brought them up to the woods near Clarence where they were logging.

They were stubborn old mules and Cowboy couldn't

get them to work. He beat them with a chain and only after that did they move. Rubin had been pretty upset about how Cowboy treated them, but being a kid there

Double Tree skidding logs

was no way he could say anything.

The day after Cowboy beat them, they wouldn't do anything for him and he finally left them alone. Daddy and Cowboy were ready to move down to the woods south of Bayou Natchez to log another stand of trees. Early in the morning Daddy told Rubin to walk the mules to where they would be logging. It was about twenty miles from Clarence to the job, so it was going to take all day long.

Rubin got the harnesses on the mules and started walking them down the road. They followed behind him with no trouble. After a few miles he got to the Grand Ecore Bridge. There was a rest stop before the bridge and some picnic tables. Rubin looked at those picnic tables figured he'd use them to get on one of the mules to ride bareback. He could get in trouble for riding. Daddy said mules worked all day just like a man, so they weren't to be ridden.

He rode through Bayou Natchez and didn't figure he needed to worry about somebody telling Daddy he was riding a work animal. It was a colored town and he didn't know anybody there. He jumped off before he got to the woods where Daddy was working. Daddy and Cowboy were

106

surprised to see him so soon. He hadn't accounted for how much faster he got there than if he just walked. They didn't ask anything and Rubin kept his mouth shut.

There was still daylight left so everybody was still working. Rubin led the harnessed mules over to a double tree and hooked them up. He had them go into the woods hook a log. When he told the mules to move and they skidded the log to the log pile. They obeyed every command Rubin gave them.

Cowboy didn't take his eyes off Rubin and the mules. He couldn't believe Rubin was having no trouble working the stubborn mules. He turned to Daddy and said, "If I didn't see what I was seeing, I'd call myself a liar."

Rubin kept quiet and showed Cowboy how it was done. When Rubin told us that story he was still upset over the beating the mules took from Cowboy.

I think sometimes Daddy forgot Rubin wasn't grown. Rubin was big enough to share clothes with Daddy. I thought it might be hard on Rubin at almost thirteen to be with men all day working while the rest of us were in school, and then send him to be a kid with us.

We all sat outside and watched the lightning bugs. I wondered if Louie and Rubin were going to keep fussing at each other, but Mama came to the door,

"Louie, let's doctor your leg."

"I'm comin', Mama"

I was glad Mama came, Louie was good natured, but he had a quick temper just like Daddy. Rubin was stubborn and wouldn't give an inch. Kind of reminded me of the red mules.

107

Strong Things

Mama took out a bottle of clear oil that had a perfume smell. She got down with Louie on the floor and worked the oil into the skin of his bad leg. The doctors had taken skin from his right leg up at the top and made it grow on his burn. The skin was puckered and tight below his knee. It needed to stretch and the doctor had told Mama she had to rub that oil in every day to help it.

Daddy took a nut from a saw mandrill and tied it to Louie's foot. It weighed a pound, was six or seven inches across and the hole in the middle was two inches wide. It acted as a weight to help pull on Louie's leg. Between Mama's oil and Daddy's mandrill nut, Louie's leg began to straighten out. We couldn't tell every day but over time we could see his toe get closer to the ground.

Louie went to work with Daddy and Rubin and became the scaler. The logs would be stacked in a pile and Louie would measure them across the cut end. A twelve by twelve log would yield a seven by nine tie. If it was smaller it would be sawed into lumber. Louie moved from pile of logs to pile of logs with crutches and pretty soon he could put his toe to the ground, then more and more of his foot. He put weight on it and his leg started to get muscle. Pretty soon it was hard to remember when Louie had been gone.

Mama's grandma, Grandma Reams, hadn't seen Louie since we'd all been back so she had Daddy drive us out to her place. Grandpa Reams had died in 1900 leaving Grandma Reams to raise eleven kids. She buried ten of them beside him in the Oak Grove cemetery. They had poor blood that ran in the family that had come from Grandpa Ream's side, which was why he had died so long ago. Grandma Reams had had to take care of her family herself and often told stories about hard times. She told us about the time she and her children had cleared a field for a farmer. She promised each one of them a nickel from the work. When they got done she went to the door to collect. He wouldn't let the kids stand on the porch since they were so dirty from work and for all their labor she got fifty cents. There wasn't enough to give the nickels out and she said it was one of her hardest times. When I heard that story I knew how good we had it. No wonder Daddy always thanked the Lord for all we had.

At Easter, which seemed a bigger holiday than Christmas, we went to the Coldwater church where just about the whole town turned out. We dressed up in our good clothes, shirts tucked in our pants, and new dresses for the girls. There was plenty to eat and the grownups did a lot of visiting. Most of the talk was about a revival coming in a few weeks called a Brush Arbor.

Grandma Lizzie Reams

The revival was outside and it could get hot in the sun. To make shade the older boys and men would put pine poles in the ground to make a square and use brush laid across them to make an arbor for shade. There were dozens of them in the open field and families would come and get under them to spend all day at the revival. Mama sent Louie and Rubin down to Provencal to make the Brush Arbor for us.

All of us went down to hear the preaching and watch the people get Saved. I wasn't sure about being saved, but I enjoyed watching the show. All the older boys gathered together just a little out of sight of their folks and hung out together. I sure wanted to hang around them, but whenever I tried they ran me off.

The sermons began, and slowly as the day went on and night fell, the preaching got louder and wilder. There was singing and moving and a lot of loud amens and folks hollering, 'Praise God.' Torches were lit as it got dark and a feeling came over the meeting that was kind of scary. People would scream and shout and dance around. If I thought church at New Town was wild, it wasn't nothing like a Brush Arbor.

After a while, even Louie and Rubin came over and stayed close to Daddy. People got up and fell on their knees at the feet of the preachers. Some wanted forgiveness and some wanted to be healed. Mary started crying. We were all glad when Mama told Daddy we needed to get to bed.

Sin City

It was the newest pickup I'd ever rode in. It wasn't ours, it belonged to the Freemans. It was a baby blue GMC, step side with a factory camper shell on the back. Old man Freeman and his boy were sitting in the cab with Daddy. I was in the back with Mama and all the kids. Ten of us made for a tight squeeze even though it was a long bed. Legs overlapped legs and quilts and blankets were laid on the bed of the pickup to soften the hard bottom.

It was tough not to fuss at each other, but Mama tried to keep us right. She had biscuits for us to eat, and we could chew on a piece of sugar cane if we wanted. I didn't know how long this trip was going to be, so I kept trying to squeeze out more space in the pickup. I figured we would be riding for a few days after I heard Daddy tell the Freemans it was over two thousand miles to Oregon.

110

The Freemans were folks Daddy knew from the log woods. They had been looking to find some better work. Daddy's log truck had broke down so there wasn't a way to make money. He had been looking for a way out of Louisiana. The Freemans agreed to take us if Daddy had the money for gas. We came from school one day to find Mama packed up and ready to go. Riding in the back of a pickup, there wasn't much room to take anything.

The camper had little windows in the side that had a crank so we could open the flap. It was hard to see the country out the little slits. The boys got the spots by the windows so we could have the wind blow in on us. Daddy and the Freemans took turns driving. Daddy usually took his turn at night. The Freemans never took a turn in the back.

There wasn't much to do but sleep and eat as we headed down the roads we had all been on before. When we stopped to stretch one time the Freemans wanted to go a different way to Oregon than Daddy usually did. Daddy agreed since they owned the pickup. We were going to be driving through Sin City! When we got close enough to see the lights I couldn't believe we were in such a place. We all found a way to look out the windows when we went through there.

"Ya'll are just being foolish, this place is called Las Vegas," Mama said and laughed at us.

"Look at all the lights!" Esther had sweet talked Louie in to letting her have a good spot to see out. There were so many lights and so many different colors. It lit up the streets even though the sun had gone down. I looked as hard as I could but I couldn't see anything that looked like sin. I wasn't sure what sin looked like, but I sure hoped I'd see it. I knew folks said things were 'ugly as sin' but I couldn't find anything that looked real ugly. I just saw folks wandering out of big buildings that were wide open to the street. I thought I might have seen sin if we stopped, but we just drove right on through.

Mama started singing, and I don't know if it was to ward off whatever sinfulness might have gotten through the windows but we settled down to sleep as she and the girls sang.

I've got a mansion just over the hill top
In that bright land where we'll never grow old
And someday yonder we will never more wander
But walk the streets that are purest gold

Don't think me poor or deserted or lonely
I'm not discouraged, I'm heaven bound
I'm just a pilgrim in search of a city
I want a mansion a harp and a crown

Mama always felt better after that song, and I guess we all did. I didn't know what was just over the hill top, but I was curious about what was on the other side.

It took a long while to find out. After the excitement of Las Vegas, the trip became long and hard. We fussed with each other and Mama had to get after us more and more. The small roll out windows made a lot of noise so it was hard to hear above the wind. Closing them made things quieter, but the pickup got stuffy. After getting out to stretch our legs when we bought gas, it was a misery to get back in and start again.

Finally, Mama had told us we were almost to Ashland. The pickup worked its way up the mountain when we went into Oregon. Knowing we were close, us kids were chomping at the bit to get out of the pickup. The engine was loud as the motor worked. After we made it over the hill the pickup went quiet. It had quit running. We coasted over to the side of the road. We jumped out of the back fast and scattered to pee and walk around. The grownups were talking about something with each other so I walked up to hear. We had run out of gas. The Freemans said they didn't have any money and Daddy had spent the last bit he had when we got some back up the road.

There was a house nearby so Mama and Daddy walked up there together and left us with the Freemans. Elaine kept watch on us and we played alongside the road. Harry found a frog and we were all trying to find another one. Mama and Daddy weren't gone long and when they came back they told the Freemans not to worry, help was coming.

Mama got out some sandwiches and we all ate a little. It wasn't long, just like Daddy had said that a green '54 Oldsmobile Rocket 98 drove up. A man got out and I thought I had seen him before. Mama and Daddy went up to him and shook his hand. He was tall and thin and his blue eyes were deep in his head. It was Brother Wine from the Foursquare Church.

"Brother Miller, Sister Miller, it's good to see you all again."

I was glad to see he had a gas can.

OREGON 1954

The Woody

Harry, Hoyt Lynn and me were laying in our bed when we saw Louie and Rubin sneaking out onto the porch roof. We jumped out of the covers and went to see what was going on. They were out there eating the cherries off the trees that surrounded the house. Long branches stretched to the windows. Our second story window was right over the roof of the porch and we could just walk out the window onto it.

I didn't ever shy away from eating something sweet and neither did Harry and Hoyt so we all crawled through the window. We must have made a bit of noise because Elaine came in our room to see what was going on, Sheron and Esther following behind. Out on the roof they followed us. All of us sat out in the cool night and ate cherries.

"Good thing Daddy's working at US Timber now. He would tan our hides if he caught us up at night," Elaine warned us all.

"Aw, he's too tired to pay too much attention to us. Since he's only here a little bit and then in the morning goes and saws at the Lithia Sawmill."

"How come Daddy don't have his own mill like before?" Hoyt asked whoever would answer.

Rubin loved telling us all how things were, "Why, these mills are big operations. These mills don't have little motors with flywheels; these are run by big diesel engines. Daddy's such a top notch sawyer; everybody wants him to work for them."

"Yeah, Daddy cuts more timber with the night crew than the day crew ever does," Louie said, then spit a pit as far as he could.

115

We all knew Daddy was the best circle saw man around. Here, in Ashland, they knew too. Daddy had plenty of work with the two jobs and we were doing pretty good. Not only were we living in a two story house, we had an inside bathroom. I wasn't sure if folks in Louisiana had ever even heard of such a thing. I didn't care too much about the peeing inside part, but I sure didn't miss squeezing into a washtub to take a bath. Using a real bathtub was almost like going swimming. It's a good thing that it was easy to get cleaned up. Harry and the other little kids all had red and scratchy skin. For the first time Harry didn't fight a bath.

We must have got to having too much fun and made too much noise. Mama caught us all outside on the roof. She blistered the ears of the older kids for having us out at night. We headed back to our bed, me and Harry on the outside and Hoyt Lynn stuck in the middle. I gave them a last warning before I went to sleep, "Nobody better pee the bed."

We had moved into the white house on Church Street in Ashland. It was built half way up a hill. It was so steep when Daddy parked in the driveway, the '49 Ford Woody that he had bought sat above the house. There was a wall made to hold the hill up so there was about eight feet of space between the house and the road. Everywhere it was green and pretty. Big trees made shade and the hills were covered in green vines and grasses.

In the morning when Mama fixed oatmeal we watched for Daddy walking up the road from town. The little kids ran to jump all over him, but us bigger kids just walked beside him. Daddy climbed the hill slow as he walked from his night shift. I walked close to him and smelled the sweat and sawdust that he wore.

Later in the day we played on the sloped street that ran by the house. Some of the neighbor kids played with us too. Down the hill from us was a house with a bunch of kids.

116

There must have been twenty of them, but no one looked alike. They all had different last names and some were in the same grade in school. They had to mind the grownups, but they weren't their folks. One of the boys there named Johnny had a burned arm that didn't work very good. He dropped things a lot and the people in the house would really get after him. I didn't like the grownups there at all.

Judy and her brother came from across the street. Judy was bowlegged and was the fastest thing I ever saw. I knew myself to be a fast runner, fastest in Natchitoches, but Judy was always right behind me when we got to the finish line. I liked to watch her more than anything and see her bowlegs just fly. I decided she was my girlfriend, but I didn't tell anybody, not even her. I just treated her nice and told her she'd done real good when I beat her in the footraces.

Just like when we were in Natchitoches we didn't talk the same as the kids here. They got a kick out of it, and we felt neat. We would spend our days outside and only come in the house when we were called or when it got dark. Further up from our house the hill was covered in vines. There were so many we could duck down and hide in it, make tunnels and play games trying to find each other. I was hunkered down in the vines when I heard Mama hollering for us from the door. It was time to come in for dinner.

We hurried into the kitchen to eat. Mama wouldn't let us get a biscuit until we were all inside and Sheron and Mary hadn't showed up. They'd been playing in the car when I raced passed them to come in.

"Elaine, I guess you better go see where those girls are..." Mama started to say when we heard a loud crash beside the house. The house shook and I thought it was going to fall down. We raced outside to see about it. In the empty spot beside the house we saw the Ford Woody on its right side. It had fallen from the driveway eight feet above the

117

house and was lodged on its side, some of the tires still going around. We could see Sheron and Mary through the windshield bawling their heads off. Mama ran to the car.

Louie and Rubin had to crawl up on it to get to the side window. By now, neighbors who had heard the crash were coming over. They helped to pull the girls through the window in the door.

Mama held on to Mary while Sheron stopped crying long enough to tell her what happened. They had been playing in the car, taking their own trip, playing with the steering wheel when one of them knocked it out of gear by hitting the column shift. It rolled down that driveway and fell down into the space between the house and the hill. After looking them over Mama told the girls they were fine, but the car sure didn't look too fine.

Mama had a neighbor call Daddy and he came from the mill. He looked the car over and then got to work. He and some men built ramps to use to guide the car. He used chains hooked to a neighbor's car and had him slowly pull the car back up to the road. The chains creaked and popped but they held and soon the car was back on all four tires. It was dented all along the right side, but just fine.

Mama just couldn't get over what could have happened to Sheron and Mary. Mama was always worried about us getting hurt. We were all told not to play in the car. I figured she just meant the girls, so I still got in there and pretended to drive it on my trips. I made sure I sat on the left side. If I couldn't see the scars on the car, I could pretend like they weren't there.

Worldly

Daddy was in his church suit and he looked sharp. He had us younger boys line up in front of him. First, Harry would get his black hair oiled up and combed. Daddy didn't spare the Brille Cream to keep our hair in place. Then it was my turn. Daddy would take my chin in his left hand and comb my brown hair to the side with his right. His hand was warm as it held my face. I looked at Daddy's face, clean shaven, with his ears and nose all trimmed. It was Sunday, so he smelled of Old Spice. I hoped I would get to use the Old Spice someday soon since Louie and Rubin got to rub some on. Daddy told me how fine I looked as he smoothed my hair. Then Hoyt Lynn nudged in between us and said it was his turn and Daddy started combing his black hair into place.

The church had built a new building they called the tabernacle. It was a little ways out of town and was bigger than the little building we had gone to before. It had a place inside with a microphone and it was heard out on the radio. They had gospel singing and sometimes Sheron and Esther would sing. They had preaching over the air and the congregation would get to talk on it too. Daddy didn't get to preach here; Brother Wine was in charge. Daddy did get to testify on the radio show some. He really got fired up and then Brother Wine would put his hand on Daddy's shoulder and tell him they were about out of time.

I didn't like going to the tabernacle much. It was too big and it felt a little empty inside. I heard some grownups saying that Brother Wine had a 'large vision'. I wasn't sure what that meant. I asked Mama but she just told me to behave. I guess it didn't matter. Mama still got to find clothes for us in their donations like before. So far nobody had given away cowboy boots but I always looked for them.

Mama and Daddy made friends with a family named the Thunderbirds who had five boys. Sometimes in the evening Mama and Daddy would take us over to the Thunderbirds to visit. The grownups went in the house and us kids were supposed to play outside. No matter how many

119

times we were told to stay outside we always tried to get back in. They had a television and we hadn't seen one before.

I knew the picture show was worldly and sinful, but I guess the television was okay since Daddy took us over there to watch it about twice a week. Sometimes they watched Red Skelton and I liked to watch the Cowboys and Indians. Most of the time, Daddy watched the fights. The men got loud and the kids could get loud, too. Mama didn't like to watch the fights so she would visit with Barbara Thunderbird in the kitchen.

It was fun to watch Daddy get excited with Billy Thunderbird as they cheered for their man. The evening would end and Daddy would talk about the fight on the way to the house. Daddy would talk about the punches that were thrown and Louie and Rubin would act them out as we walked.

"Wesley, don't go on so much about those fights. Why, it doesn't seem Christian," Mama said.

Daddy would calm the boys down, but he grinned all the way back.

Harry and me started acting out what we saw on TV too. We were outside the house and started to fist fight like we saw on one of our cowboy shows. Daddy came up on us and thought we were fighting for real. Nothing was worse to Mama and Daddy than us kids fighting so Daddy marched right over to us, grabbed up Harry and went to whippin' him hard.

"Daddy, we're just playing," Harry tried to tell him.

"Daddy, please..." I said as he started in on me.

He wouldn't listen to a word we tried to say and he tore us up for fighting. Mama was sure we had learned that sinful behavior from watching television. I guess TV was pretty worldly, but it sure was fun to watch, even for Daddy.

My Own Hill

Nothing was worse than the day school started. Only good thing about it was all the kids on the hill would be going. Mama walked us to the school and told the principal what grades we were all in. She had a bit of trouble with the fact that we didn't take shots. I guess it was a rule you had to have shots to go to school, but Mama and Daddy didn't believe in them so we were lucky enough not to have them. I heard about them sticking a needle in your arm, it just seemed awful.

Elaine was in the tenth grade. Louie had missed a lot of school due to his leg and his stubborn ways at the hospital. He was in the eighth grade and Rubin was in the seventh. The girls were all going too. Esther was starting first grade with Miss Prescott. Only Hoyt Lynn and Mary were still with Mama.

Harry scratched on the way to school, but I was getting used to him doing it by now so I hardly noticed it. I don't know if it was because of Ashland or the church but we all wore shoes even though it was warm. When we got there I saw all the kids wore shoes too. Like always I had to make a place for myself with the kids. Some of them made fun of how we talked and my funny name, but not for long. School wasn't just about learning to read and write, but about learning to fight, and I was good at that.

It seemed like every day there was another boy who wanted to try me out. It didn't take long before the boys didn't mess with any of us Millers. I just made sure that nobody thought they could get the best of me and soon enough they quit trying.

Since Daddy didn't work for himself like he did in Louisiana, the boys didn't have to do as much work so they could do their school work. Louie got to be in the band and found out he was still good at playing the trumpet. Before long he could play every horn they had. Elaine played the piano again and Rubin got to be on the junior high football team.

I struggled with reading and did a little better with arithmetic. What I was really good at was the arts and crafts. We got to make little paper mache dolls and used bbs to weigh down their legs so they could sit up. Since I was good at making things, I figured reading didn't matter much anyway.

Harry had some buddies that he ran with and I played with kids on the hill. Sheron and Esther played too, but Hoyt Lynn was still too much of a baby. If he got a little hurt, or didn't like how we played with him, he would run and tell Mama. Calling him a tattle tale didn't make any difference so we just left him behind.

Most of the kids had red skin and scratched all the time. Sometimes they didn't feel too good either. I knew Harry had been scratching for long time and it was just getting worse, sometimes I couldn't go to sleep for him moving around all the time. I didn't have any of it and I sure was glad.

Sheron, Esther, Hoyt Lynn and Mary

It was getting dark earlier and cooler so there was less time to be outside. Mama came out to get us one day off the viney hill when she got close to us she stopped and said, "I can't believe my eyes."

122

We ran to her and tried to see what she was looking at. The viney hill wasn't all green now; a large part of it had turned red with the cooling of the weather.

"Poison Ivy!" she said really loud. Mama just realized that part of the hill with all the vines was poison ivy. The poison ivy's leaves had turned red. That's what had all the kids sick. "I can't believe it," she told us. She herded us all in the house, while she got the kids bathed; Daddy went to town and brought back a bottle of calamine lotion. She had all of the kids but me start rubbing the pink lotion into their skin. I just watched, not a red spot or welt on me.

"Why isn't Alton broke out?" Mama asked Daddy.

"He just ain't one that's bothered by it, Fonny." Daddy answered.

"Well, I reckon that's a blessing for him."

From then on, all the kids had to stay out of the vines. They were glad to steer clear of them, after itching and scratching all summer. At first it wasn't too much fun with nobody playing there but me. It didn't take too long for me to figure out that the hill was all mine. I could do anything I wanted and when the older kids wanted to get after me I just ran to the vines. I made roads and tunnels and nobody could stomp it or change it. Sometimes I sat out there alone on the slope among the vines and looked out over all of Ashland, king of my own hill.

1955
Nob Hill

I had the smallest brush and the bristles were on the thin side, having been wore out by whoever used it before me, but I loved dipping it into the bucket of grey paint. Harry and me were on floor detail. Louie had the pink and Rubin the black paint for the walls. We had moved a street over from the house on Church to Nob Hill. Daddy bought a house of our own and we were fixing it up. It had burned up on the inside but the outside looked just fine. Daddy just had to replace a few of the Masonite shingles that had fallen off. Me and Hoyt Lynn helped Daddy with that 'til Hoyt dropped and broke too many of them and was sent to play.

Mama and Daddy weren't around, but had told us while they were gone we could paint our room. I had gone around asking neighbors and church people if they had any leftover paint. I got quite a bit of pink and some grey. I had little bits of a bunch of colors so I thought I would just mix them all up, that made about a gallon of black looking paint. Louie and Rubin had painted for a while but when it got to being work, they left. Harry and me were still painting. Things were looking really good.

Esther and Sheron passed by the doorway laughing and running. I wondered what was going on when Elaine followed them hollering bloody murder at them, "If you tattle, you'll be sorry!"

Harry looked at me. 'What's all that about?" he asked.

House on Nob Hill

We both stood up and looked at the floor. The doorway was on the other side of the room and between it and us was the wet grey floor.

"Nothin' to be done about it, I guess." Harry shrugged. "Let's just take big steps." Harry was eleven and I was nine, so our steps matched up close enough. I started off and put my right leg

124

out as far as I could go. I felt the slick wet paint on the bottom of my bare foot and stepped again with the other foot. Harry tried to put his feet in my footsteps. There were just three or four prints in the paint as we made it out and followed the commotion.

The girls had run out the front door and were standing in the yard.

"If you tattle on us, we'll tattle on you!" Sheron hollered at Elaine. The girls were acting snotty, both of them feeling brave 'cause they were together, and Mama and Daddy weren't around.

Elaine was on her way up to her room with a rag. I followed the gray foot prints Harry and me had left behind on the stairs. They were faded at the bottom of the stairs and got darker the higher we went up. I wondered if Mama might notice them so I used my bare foot to smear them. When I got to Elaine's room I saw what the ruckus was about. The girls had written on Elaine's mirror with lipstick.

"If Mama and Daddy find out you got makeup they're gonna tear your rear end up," I warned her.

"If anybody tells, then there ain't gonna be no more boogie woogie music on the piano. See how those little girls like that," Elaine said.

Daddy had gotten Elaine a used piano to play hymns. When we were left alone she played songs from the radio, sometimes we sat out in the car and listened to the rock and roll that came over the station. Elaine would play those songs and even on plain old songs everybody knew, she would add a little something extra that made you want to dance. All us kids loved it, but somebody always had to keep an eye out for the car in case the folks were coming back. If they knew we were playing and dancing to that worldly music, we might not have lived to tell about it.

I picked up a rag and helped Elaine scrub the lipstick. She was acting brave, but she was getting that lipstick off.

"Nobody's gonna tattle." I wasn't too sure Esther wouldn't, or Hoyt Lynn, but I wanted Elaine to feel better. And I wanted her to keep playing the piano for us.

I didn't come in the girl's room much, so I looked around. Esther had a dresser and on top of it sat all kinds of pretties she got from church. If you brought a friend to Sunday School they gave you a prize. Esther would have brought somebody kicking and screaming to get one of those little trinkets.

"They're back!" Hoyt Lynn hollered from the yard. Mama and Daddy drove by the front of the house, up the hill and parked above the house. Nob Hill was as steep as Church Street and the car sat above the house in the driveway. Mama got out of the car carrying a box. Daddy had the boys come and carry lumber he had sticking out the back of the car. He was still pulling burned lumber from the house and changing it with scrap from the lumber yard he worked at. He told us the house wouldn't smell so much like ash if he got enough of the lumber replaced.

Mama took her box in the kitchen and inside was a set of dishes. Esther helped her unpack them. They were made of plastic and had everything, plates, cups and glasses.

"Mama, have we ever had a set of matching dishes before?"

"I've never had a set of new dishes in my life, sugar. I can't get over it."

"Spose'd to be unbreakable. That's what the salesman said. Unbreakable." Daddy said as he came in. He sure was proud he had got something so fine for Mama.

"We'll have to invite company to supper, when the house doesn't stink of ash quite so bad," Mama told the girls.

I looked over at the dishes. Unbreakable.

126

Steep Hill

The next few weeks we worked hard on the inside of the house. Sundays we went to church and on one of them Mama invited Brother Wine and his wife over to the house for supper in a few weeks. Mama and Daddy were always trying to give back to the church. I just tried to get through it.

It had rained earlier in the morning but it was sunny when church got out. Daddy let us all walk to the house, some of our friends walked with us as we headed up the hill.

Harry and me drug behind, wanting to take all the time we could before getting back to the house. I watched as Esther walked with her friend Margaret. Every time they came to a puddle, Esther stepped harder and splashed Margaret's dress with mud. She did it on the sly, so Margaret wouldn't know, but she did it every time. When her friend turned off, I ran and caught up with Esther. I grinned at her, "I saw what you were doin'."

Esther looked at me with her big brown eyes and said, "Oh, Alton, her dresses are always so perfect. When Mama makes ours she doesn't even care if the pattern on the material matches. Margaret's are store bought and I just can't stand it. I just had to mess her up a little."

I laughed and said, 'Well, you got one up on her, she's sure a lot dirtier than you today." I kind of knew what she was talking about. I hated the corduroy pants Mama got from the second hand store. I always tried to act like they didn't fit, but that usually didn't work. Mama would have me come up to her and she'd pull and tug on them until they fit just fine. I tried to have them be too short or too tight. 'Too big' never worked since we could always grow into them. I figured I just ought to be grateful we got to wear shoes all year round. If we did go barefoot at least there wasn't any brown spit to step in.

Monday Mama started her new job at the nursing home. We were out of school for the summer and Elaine could watch us during the day. Elaine was fourteen and really only needed to take care of Mary who was almost two and Hoyt Lynn who was trouble at five. It was strange to not have Mama or Daddy around during the day. Since Daddy had done so good on the night crew, they promoted him to day, but he had to work with new men and he didn't like it as much.

I stayed outside most of the time in my work shed. It was a little shack at the back of the yard and I kept all of my  tools and parts there. I was back in the bicycle business. I found an old frame and I got started from there. I got a couple of handle bars from the old man down the hill. I had three bikes now, all different sizes. Harry would ride around with me some. I tried to teach Elaine to ride, but she ran into the berry thicket at the back of the house and then wouldn't get back on. I couldn't figure out what was so hard about riding a bike. Louie said he'd ride with me so we took off down the steep hill. Instead of stopping at the end though, he turned left and rode right into the screen door of the neighbor lady.

Louie

"I gave you the bike with brakes!" I was just disgusted with him.

"Well, I don't know how to use brakes! I never rode a bike that had 'em before!" Louie hollered as he lay there spraddle legged, half in her house and half out.

"You're gonna fix that door, young man!" The old lady came out from around the back of the house carrying a broom in her hand like she was going to sweep the floor with Louie.

It looked like a good time for me to git.

"You better bring my bike back!" I shouted as I took off. I had to head uphill so there wasn't that much taking off, just hard pumping and sometimes getting off and pushing. Louie came up pretty quick, threw my bike down by the shed and headed back down the hill with some nails and a hammer.

I went in the house to get a drink and saw one of Mama's new glasses setting on the counter. I couldn't stop thinking about them being unbreakable. I picked it up and tossed it in the air a few times. I walked out to the enclosed porch where Mama kept her wringer washing machine. I stood on one end, looked through the door to the kitchen and thought I could make it into the sink with the glass. I threw it as hard as I could. It missed the doorway and hit the nail that held up the lid to the washer. The nail stuck right through the bottom of the glass and there it stayed. I grabbed it off the wall and knew if Daddy found out he'd warm me up but good for breaking Mama's glass. I put the glass in the back of the cabinet and hid it among the other ones.

"Alton, fetch me a glass of water." I just about jumped out of my skin. Mama was walking in from the porch. She sat down at the table and pulled her dress above her knees. Both were bleeding and so was her hand.

I got her a glass of water and tried to keep my shaking hands from sloshing the water out of the glass as I gave it to her.

"I swear that hill is so steep. I just about fall up it all the way from work."

"Mama, you fell again?" I tried to keep my mind on poor Mama, but all I could think about was that broken unbreakable glass.

"I guess I should just be grateful I don't roll all the way down it and have to start again. I saw Louie working on

129

Miz Jones' screen. I asked him about it, but he didn't have much to say.

"Oh, you know Louie, Mama. He don't have much to say about anything."

I figured it was best to know nothing about nothing. I was starting to see that all kinds of things could happen when Mama wasn't looking.

Dinner

Having Daddy gone all day, and Mama gone half of it we all got to doing just what we wanted. We were busy having friends over, running up and down the hill, just about anything we could think of. It was a big time.

I was out working on my bike. Elaine was inside playing piano with Harry and some of his buddies. They were a little older than him so they sure didn't have time for me. Esther had come outside and was making doll clothes with Margaret in the car. I watched Margaret get out of the car and tell Esther she wasn't coming back till she could be nice.

Esther got out and headed towards the house.

"What'd you do to her now?" I asked.

"She said her mother won't let her use scissors. Well, I don't have to teach a girl seven years old to use scissors. I just can't fool with her."

Esther stomped her seven-year-old self into the house. She was always making doll clothes. Mama gave her scraps and if she wasn't doing that she was making paper dolls. She would like for Sheron to play with her, but Sheron didn't care nothing about dolls. Sheron was just a year older and they were like twins, but not when it came to dolls. Esther ended up being the mother to all of them, even thinking they loved her. Pretty silly I thought.

130

The front door slammed and out went Harry's buddies. The piano playing stopped and I went inside. We all looked at the clock to check on how close it was till Mama would be coming back. Elaine started making sure things were picked up.

"Harry's going to Hell! Harry's going to Hell!" Esther was screaming like a banshee.

"What're you carryin' on about?" Sheron asked coming from upstairs.

"I found a cigarette butt in the toilet." She started crying. "Harry's going to Hell."

"Now come on, Esther, that wasn't mine. That must have been one of my friends. I wouldn't smoke. Mama wouldn't allow it." Harry grinned at her and winked at me.

What was Harry's meaning behind that wink? Was he smoking? We were doing all kinds of things we shouldn't with the folks gone. Maybe we were all going to Hell. I was starting to be glad that tomorrow was Sunday and Brother Wine was coming. Well, that and knowing that the food ought to be pretty good.

***

Chicken, mashed potatoes, gravy and greens. Supper was going to be good.

Mama made a cake too. As she took it from the oven, she told the girls, "Cooking with gas is the modern way, but it just doesn't taste the same as food cooked over wood."

The table was set and all of us were acting just right since we had the preacher over. Mama and the girls set the table with her new dishes. The four younger kids sat at a table that folded down from the wall.

Elaine poured tea into the glasses from an old pickle jug. Brother Wine began to say Grace over the food. I squinted my eyes and peeked at the chicken. I looked from

131

the chicken down to where Brother Wine sat. How long was this prayer going to be? Seemed like he didn't just thank the Lord for all we had, but thought he ought to name things off, one by one. I sure did appreciate Daddy's praying right then.

He was just a couple of plates down and I could see his glass. Tea was slowly seeping out the bottom of the glass and pooling around it on the table. I couldn't take my eyes away from that seep. I was the only one that saw, because I was the only one with my eyes open. I knew what was going on with that leak.

I looked at Daddy and at Mama. I didn't know what to do. Did I warn them about the leak, or act like nothing was going on. I decided the best thing to do was act like I didn't know anything. That always seemed to work best.

Brother Wine finally said Amen, Daddy said it too, kind of loud. I figured he thought the prayer had gone on long enough, too. Brother Wine went to pick up his glass and then the tea really came out, all over his plate, down his tie, and in his lap. He jerked up from the table and dropped the glass. Mama sucked in some air and then jumped up to help him. She took the glass and looked at it.

"My word, this glass has a hole in it!" She looked at the bottom of the glass. Daddy looked at all of us kids. He looked us over pretty good. The other boys looked like they thought it was funny. I tried to look as surprised and shocked as the girls.

"Sister Miller, don't you mind. Nothing that can't be fixed," Brother Wine told Mama.

"I just can't imagine what happened to that glass. Esther you run and get Brother Wine another one."

Esther took off for the cupboard. Daddy kept looking at us and I was kind of sure he looked at me longer than he looked at the others. The meal went on and everything went better after that. Brother Wine left and Daddy questioned us kids pretty good. I think he may of thought it was kind of funny too. Just in case things got too rough, I was ready to blame it on Hoyt.

Wheels

I stood at the top of the street, nothing but hill above me and hill below me. I had ridden many a mile on my bicycle to the end of the road but today we were going to be on go-carts. Daddy had given us boys some scrap lumber and Rubin had taken the two by twelves that were about five feet long and bolted two by fours crosswise on them. The front could move a little but the back was solid. We gathered all the little wheels we could find from broken trucks and toys and nailed them to the corners, matching up the size in front and back. Rubin fixed a rope on the front end for us to steer by. He even went to the trouble of making us a back rest. We had three carts. Rubin, being the biggest, had double wheels on the back of his cart to hold him up.

"You go first," Harry told me. I didn't give it a thought. "Give me a push!" I shouted. Harry got behind me, put his hands on the board, and off I went. Rubin shoved off with his foot and he was right beside me. The wind blew our hair back and I whooped like Daddy. Rubin hollered too as we picked up speed. The bottom of the hill came up on us fast. The end of Nob Hill leveled out a little but was crossed by High Street, so we tried to keep a lookout for cars crossing in front of us. It was a rough ride, but the speed and cheering kept me going as we raced by the neighbor kids down the hill. The bar ditch on the other side of High Street broke our speed and we came to a stop in the weeds and grass. Rubin was right with me, and Harry drove in beside us.

We sat at the bottom of the hill going on and on about how fast we had went.

133

"I bet it was fifty miles an hour!" Harry was rolling off his cart to the grass.

"Ain't no way that you know how fast that was. But it was fast enough!" Rubin told Harry. "How're we going to do it again?" I wanted to know. I faced the hill, it was straight up.

"You runts just watch and see." Rubin told us. He gathered up the ropes from all three carts and began dragging them back up the hill, all three of them at one time. Harry was so glad he didn't have to haul his cart he cheered Rubin on and I did too. It was awful good that Rubin was as big as he was. At fourteen, Rubin was as big as some full grown men, and his work with Daddy had made him strong and tough. Even though Harry was just two years younger than him, he looked scrawny beside him.

I just couldn't get enough of riding on those carts. We got so good at using our feet to skid ourselves to a stop that for the most part we quit running into the cars parked on the street. We didn't have to fix our go-carts between rides near as much. A few runs down the hill and the little wheels started to wear out. We had to quit until we could find more.

We sat in the yard trying to figure something out when Mama drove in to the driveway. Esther got out of the car and ran to us.

"Mama got me a Coca-Cola and I didn't have to share with none of y'all!"

"Esther, I told you not to tell." Mama got after her. I don't know what Mama was thinking, there was nothing in Esther's head that could not come out her mouth.

"Now, you won't get to go yard sale-in' with me no more since you ran off at the mouth."

"I wanna go next Mama," I told her. "We need wheels for our carts."

The next time Mama went to the sales, I got to go with her in the Woody. Daddy was doing so good at the sawmill he bought a '49 GMC. We had two cars at the same time. Mama's money that she made at the nursing home gave her a little spending money and she went to yard sales looking for clothes for us kids. I kept an eye out for cowboy boots, but I was really on the lookout for wheels. Any of them I saw were on wagons and nobody wanted to sell the wheels off their wagons. I did get to have a Coca-Cola and I made sure that Esther knew about it when we got back.

I saw my girlfriend, Judy, outside skating on Scenic Street that went across the hill. When she got brave she turned and went down Nob Hill. As she got to going faster she squatted down, but it didn't help much, she swerved in front of her house and crashed into her yard. I think she was hurt, because she tore her roller skates off her shoes and ran into the house. I walked down to the roller skates and got to looking at them. I knew my go-cart problem was over.

I knocked on Judy's door and asked her if I could borrow her skates. She was red faced and teary and told me I could have them. It was a start. I went from street to street, house to house, asking to borrow the skates of the kids I knew. They all were a pretty nice bunch; their mother's being friendly with Mama and all.

I went to work on the skates. It didn't take much hammer work to flatten the metal and use the holes that were already there to drive the nails through and fix the skates to the cart. I had enough to put double wheels on Rubin's cart. Single wheels were on me and Harry's, with a few spare wheels just in case.

We were back in business. We figured we'd make one more cart, since we had the wheels and let some of the poor kids from the big family ride too. There were more kids than carts, but we took turns at riding down the hill, hollering all

135

the way. Rubin pulled every one of the carts back up the hill. He figured out a better way and nailed a hook on his cart and then ran the steering ropes through and toted all the carts up the hill at one time. After a few days, kids started coming around from the other streets to watch and ride. One smart aleck got to looking at the wheels real close.

"Hey, Alton, that's my skate you got nailed to the bottom of the cart. You smashed 'em flat."

I hadn't figured on this. The only thing I could think to do was fight him to keep him quiet.

Rubin spoke up, "All y'all get outta here. Ain't gonna be no more rides today."

I sure was glad for Rubin right then. The other kids started to leave. After we put the carts into the shed, we headed for the house. The best thing to do was act like nothing had happened and hope that kid didn't show back up.

That night while Daddy said Grace, he thanked the Lord for all we had. I thought about that. Two cars at the same time, go-carts, and I wasn't wearing corduroy britches. Supper didn't look too bad either. Mama had stirred the biscuits enough so there weren't white spots on top and there was plenty of milk in the gravy. I said Amen right alongside Daddy.

It was almost dark, so when we heard somebody knocking at the door us kids just looked at it. Daddy got up to go to the door, and even though Mama tried to stop us we all sidled over to see who it was. When I saw, I sidled right back to the table. It was Judy's daddy. He was really friendly to Daddy as he told him all about the roller skates and what I had used them for. Daddy barely shut the door after promising to pay for them, when somebody else came up on the porch wanting to talk to him about roller skates. Daddy paid for all the skates with money, and I paid with the whippin's he gave me.

Heavyweight Champs

G. Callahan, R. Johnson, M. Coke, S. Gray, H. Dickerson, B. Woodell, R. Miller, A. Mc Kinnis, R. Mickle

Rubin is Lucky 13

Acting Big

We were back to bicycles and walking but Mama let us go further away and we spent a lot of time at Lithia Park. There was always something going on down there. People put on shows in the park and acted out things. It wasn't very fun to watch so we just ran through the park, climbing trees and playing in the creek that ran through it. Some sort of Lithia water came out of the spigots in the middle of the park. It was supposed to be something special, but it just tasted like plain old water to me. Harry and me splashed it at each other for a while.

"Let's go see if we can see Daddy at work."

We took off. There was a shortcut to the sawmill, but we had to go through the mill pond. We talked about seeing the men walk the logs and I told Harry I thought we could do it.

The mill pond was crowded with big logs that had been cut down and stored in the water. They were forty to fifty feet long and at least a foot around. The logs were end to end and side to side. They bobbed up and down and sloshed around in the pond that was almost as wide as the football field at school. There was nothing but logs from bank to bank. I stepped out on the first log and Harry followed me. We didn't weigh enough to cause the log to sink down much, so we knew it was going to be fine. I stepped from one log to the next and the better I got at it the faster I went. Pretty soon Harry and me both were running the logs, sometimes they moved and tried to roll, but they were packed in so tight they didn't move much. We jumped from the last log to the bank.

We tried to see Daddy working, but we knew better than to go where grown men worked. Harry told me he saw him, but I never did and I wasn't sure he did either.

"Let's walk the logs back," I said. We were even faster and better at it than before.

"I bet we're as good as any lumberjack," Harry shouted to me. I agreed nobody could be as good as us. We weaved and jumped from log to log, sometimes I jumped on Harry's log with him and we tried to roll them like the lumberjacks we had seen. We made it to the bank, jumped onto it and headed back.

Fountains at
Lithia Park

"You figure Mama would have a fit if she knew we were walking the logs?" I looked over at Harry.

"Well, that's why we don't ask. If they don't know what we're doing, then they can't say no. The best way to do whatcha want is to not ask in the first place." I was learning a lot.

At the park we passed by a bench where Esther and Sheron were sitting. They sat with one leg crossed over the

138

other, a little purse dangling from their hands. Sheron was pretending to smoke an old cigarette butt, Esther had a twig.

"What're you all doin' down here?" Harry asked.

"We're playing 'big'," Esther told us. Being grown up meant smoking, but I wasn't surprised that Esther was too chicken to put a cigarette in her mouth. She sure didn't figure on going to Hell.

"You don't know what being big is. We're as good as lumberjacks." I said. I didn't have any time for their foolishness. After walking the logs not once but twice and knowing how good Harry and me were at it, I thought, boy, were girls dumb.

Summer

A case of soda pop didn't last near as long as we thought. Daddy had given it to us. His day crew had put out the most footage of any crew. The bosses had wanted to throw a party for Daddy since he was the crew boss. Daddy wouldn't have no part of it since a party meant being worldly and all. In the end, the mill gave him a case of pop and he gave it to us kids. He wasn't going to go back to the day crew either. He got them to put out a lot of footage, but he just couldn't get along with the men. He worked the night crew just as hard but he got along with them, so he was going back to working nights.

Being left alone in the house with twenty four bottles of Coke was just too much for us all. Sharing one bottle between nine of us kids, didn't amount to much so we opened up another. Even being room temperature didn't stop them from tasting sweet and good. Louie and Rubin tilted the bottles and downed them in about three gulps. Harry and me wouldn't be outdone and tried to copy the older boys. The girls wanted to be ladylike, but not for long, or they would

139

have fallen behind. The drinking contest became a burping contest, some of them so long and loud, I couldn't help but admire my older brothers.

"Do you think we should save these for Mama and Daddy?" Esther looked at the last two bottles left with their lids on.

As much as I wanted them, I didn't think my belly could hold another one.

We all looked at the last two bottles, then Louie and Rubin grabbed one each and had one last contest on who could down them the fastest. Neither one would own up to second so it just ended in another squabble between them. While the other kids lay on the porch trying to get over their belly aches, I had an idea.

"I'm gonna get these outta sight before they come back," I told them.

I took them to the shed and got them out of sight. Coke bottles were a nickel a bottle. As soon as I could walk to town, I was going to have a payday of my own.

Saturday I told Harry about it and he helped me load them in a wagon and down the hill to town we went. I had to split the money with him, but we both had a pocketful.

"We ought to go to the Roller Rink. I bet we could figure out how to skate." Harry headed to the building across the street.

We paid for our skates and went to trying to get them on. It might have worked better if we had socks on like the other kids, but it was summer so we didn't have any. Both of us worked up a sweat sitting on the floor trying to pull the skates on our feet.

"I think I need a bigger pair." I went over and traded mine for a pair a couple of sizes bigger. They were easier to get on, but a lot harder to keep on. Harry had got his tied up and out he stepped onto the hard floor. I held onto the wall and wobbled my way to the opening to the rink. We knew some of the kids already skating from school and they came over to help us. A couple of girls held Harry's hands and a couple tried to hold mine. I wasn't sure if I wanted them too, but after a couple of falls, I held on. Harry got better and better as he went around. It might have been my big skates but I couldn't keep my feet under me. I tried to watch what the other skaters were doing and tried to copy them. My girlfriends got tired of me, and took off, some of them skating backwards!

I gave it one last try, I pushed off, my feet started going in all kinds of directions and as I went down I hit my head on the wall and then the floor. I thought I was going to be knocked out. I laid there for a while, my head hurting in about three places. I was sure I could hear the girls starting to giggle. I couldn't stand for that. I crawled to the benches at the side of the rink, took off my skates, grabbed my shoes and left. I knew right then and there roller skates were better off as go-cart wheels and my skating days were over.

I started thinking about the parade for Fourth of July was coming. Rubin, Hoyt Lynn and me were wound up over it. The Ford place and the Kiwanis club had gotten Rubin to make a float for them and Hoyt Lynn and me were going to be on it. Rubin got together three wagons, one in front and two behind. He nailed plywood to the tops to make a boxing ring and that attached all the wagons to each other. Three foot up from the sides he had a rope going all around it, and it did look like a boxing ring. Hoyt Lynn was Ford and I was Chevy. We had signs on us so the people watching the parade would know. Since we were sponsored from the Ford place and Hoyt Lynn was Ford he knocked me out. So I lay on the floor beaten and Hoyt Lynn raised his hands and cheered with his foot on my chest.

It was fun for us but I don't know how much fun for Rubin since he had to pull us up and down the steep streets of Ashland. It was a good thing he got practice pulling those go-carts up the hills because three wagons, plywood and two boys was quite a load.

The parade ended at the Junior High. Rubin was winded, Hoyt was happy and I enjoyed the ride. Rubin was proud as a peacock when we won first place for our set up. The three of us walked back just knowing that everyone was looking at us. We were winners.

The Fall

I didn't have to fight at the beginning of school like usual since we weren't the new kids that year. After school I looked for Coke bottles along the ditches to sell and tried to keep a little pocket change on me all the time. I went to the Five and Dime by Lithia Park and bought Mama little things that she sure would fuss over when I gave them to her.

It got cold in Ashland, and snow fell before winter even came.

"Alton, run outside and fill this pan up with snow." Mama handed the dishpan to me.

"Yes, Mama!" I ran outside and filled the pan to overflowing.

One of the best things about snow was snow cream. She put vanilla, sugar and eggs and a little milk in a bowl and added the snow. She stirred it and kept adding more snow. The more snow she added the stiffer the ice cream would get until we could eat it with a spoon. You had to eat it fast, before it melted.

Louie came in from outside and took a big bite, "You sure you didn't put yellow snow in that bowl?" He laughed at the looks on our faces as we looked in the bowl.

"Aw, Louie, if you talk like that, you don't get any more." Elaine laughed at him.

Louie was in a pretty good mood all the time now. Daddy had let him quit school and he was working for Neil Stockerbrand hauling feed and hay for his store. Louie had gotten so far behind in school it didn't seem like there was any way he could get through all the grades. Daddy didn't think much about school anyway so it made everybody happy. After all, Louie was sixteen.

Snow fell all winter and we played outside whenever we could in the deep snow. There was a little extra money at Christmas and we got a sled. It was the first one we ever had and it just flew down those hills. Waiting your turn to go down was the toughest part. That and bringing it back up. But the ride sure made up for it.

Mama was always afraid we would get sick in the cold and I had to talk her into letting me go out as much as I wanted to. She wouldn't let me go out one Saturday afternoon. The snow had been melting and there were dry spots all over. It was then that I remembered Harry telling me about if you don't ask, nobody can tell you no. I wasn't going to forget it again. When Mama left to go to the store with Daddy to get groceries, I thought that would be a good time to go down the hill without anyone knowing. I climbed to the top of the hill and rode down the snowy hill to the bottom.

One more time led to one more time and I figured I had one last ride before it was too dark. I took off down the hill and tried to stay out of the dry spots as I made my final run. Boy, I was good at that sled, I thought. Just then the sled stopped but I kept going, right straight into a tree. I broke my fall with my face and half my front tooth. The other half was lost in the slushy snow.

I went into the house and acted like nothing had happened. Mama and Daddy got back and I worked hard not to have to open my mouth.

"Why is your lip twice its size?" Mama walked up to me and asked. I couldn't think of a good story and I didn't know how to pin it on Hoyt Lynn so I told the truth. Harry was probably pretty let down with me, not being able to think of something. I waited for Daddy to get ready to whip me, but when he saw my mouth he decided I had suffered enough. Washing up for supper I looked in the mirror in the bathroom and saw my front tooth broken in half. Oh well, Harry was the lady's man anyway.

Daddy said Grace and thanked the Lord for all we had. I stayed pretty quiet, not wanting too much attention to come my way. My tooth hurt a little, but not enough to keep me from eating. Daddy didn't say much as he ate. He finally started talking to Mama.

"They're bringing in a new-fangled machine to the mill soon."

"What does it do?" Mama asked as she helped Mary eat.

"It's called a band saw. Fella says it's the new and modern way to cut lumber. Say's the circle saw is old fashioned."

"Old fashioned? Why, what could be wrong with using what's been working for years?" Mama asked.

Daddy said the band saw worked different than the circle saw that Daddy was used to. The saw was a blade that was long and thin. It looped around a shaft on top and bottom and went around. Daddy had been a circle saw man for over thirty years, the best anybody had ever seen. I don't think he could see changing something that worked, when he was so good at what he already knew.

That night we all sat still and listened as Daddy read from the Bible. I listened to the stories and tried to understand. I knew Daddy's struggle as he tried to read the words out loud to us. Daddy hadn't had to do much reading in his life, so he was learning some of the same words I was learning in school. Mama let him read until she decided it

First Row: S. Deramo, J. Berry, S. Alner, F. Thomas, J. Byred, J. Lee, C. Bounds, R. Barnett, A. Joy, Row 2: P. Kearns, L. Hamilton, S. Rose, J. Nichols, J. Howard, R. Chambers, G. Stoffer, Row 3: D. Petitt, F. Robertson, M. Williams, A. Miller, S. Peterson, W. Covington, R. Wasner, H. Dickerson, Row 4: Miss Scripter, C. Shilling, R. Miller, J. Schuster, J. Skibby, C. Falls. Absent, F. Brown, B. Hardy, R. Hakes, L. Smith, S. Funk.

Miss Scripter ----- Homeroom 7-6

was time for us to go to bed. Then she quietly told him like always,

"Wesley, it's time to get these babies to bed."

As I lay in the dark, I was listening to Mama and Daddy talk. I had my part of the covers tucked under my leg so Harry couldn't pull them off me. The blanket was stretched tight so that very little of the quilt hit Hoyt Lynn who lay between us. I hadn't gone to sleep yet so I got to hear Daddy tell Mama about a gyppo mill that was running up in the Green Springs Mountains. He was going to talk to the boss, Ab Bush, and see about working on that little mill.

Gyppo mills were little mills owned by the saw miller. They could be taken apart and put back together and didn't have to stay on one spot. Since they were small and

145

could be moved they went into the woods so the logs didn't have to be hauled so far before they were milled. This kind of sawmill used a circle saw. He wouldn't make the change to the new ways so it looked like the rest of us would do the changing.

1956
Sling Shots

Daddy went to work in the Green Springs Mountains a few miles outside of Ashland. It was up a long, curvy road. Since school was going on, we stayed at Nob Hill and Daddy drove up the mountain every day. He was gone before the sun came up and got back after it had gone down. He had Sundays off and spent the day after church dozing in the chair. He did get back early one Saturday to get some work done on the GMC Panel truck so he could make it up the mountain on Monday.

Louie and Rubin helped Daddy. They had taken the tires off and screwed the nuts on the studs so they wouldn't get lost. They needed some more parts so the three of them went to town. Harry and me walked by the car.

"Lookee here. These fit right in the pouch," Harry said as he squatted down in front of the wheel well and started screwing off a nut.

We had just built sling shots and had been out looking for rocks. We had found some old inner tubes and used the rubber which was red and stretchy to pull back the pouch for speed. We made the pouch from the tongues of old tennis shoes. We screwed off a couple of lug nuts and they flew. Windows, birds, cans, just about anything we thought we could hit and most times, break.

When we heard Daddy driving up in the Woody, it was the first time I thought about what could happen. Harry

146

and me both ran to throw our sling shots in the shed and stayed clear of the car. Daddy saw the nuts missing and came to Harry and me right off. Harry thought fast and blamed it on Hoyt Lynn. I went right along with it and it didn't even bother me when Hoyt Lynn got whipped for it. I figured he'd got away with enough other things to take that whippin'. Hoyt Lynn was mad though, he may have been six but he had a temper.

He was almost five years younger than me, Sheron and Esther was between us so Hoyt Lynn was more of a baby than we wanted to play with. He wanted to run around with Harry and me but we didn't let him. He got even with us by tattling to Mama about things we did. When he wasn't being mean he was a crybaby so we left him behind and used him mostly to blame things on. Sometimes I felt sorry for him, but mostly he was too little to fool with.

When the slingshots came up missing, I figured Hoyt Lynn had got even. Harry and me hunted all over for them. When we looked at Hoyt Lynn's grinning face we knew he had something to do with them being gone.

"Where are they, Hoyt? If you don't tell, you're gonna be sorry."

He stuck his tongue out and took off running. We went after him and cornered him under the house. The dirt sloped under the house because of it being built on the hill. Hoyt Lynn climbed up the dirt until he was right up against the floor of the house. He was bawling mad at us. We couldn't get to him, so we grabbed up some rocks and started pelting him with them. He really started hollering then. It was just our luck that he was right under the kitchen floor and Mama heard him. Out of the house and down to us she came and Harry and me both ended up with the whippin' we thought we had got out of. When Daddy got back and Mama told him what we'd done, he tore into us too. No matter how hard we tried to find out, Hoyt Lynn never did tell us what he did with the slingshots.

Angels

We told Louie our sad story and he sure did understand. Louie had slapped Elaine when she was being a smart mouth. She ran and told Daddy and he gave Louie a whippin', even as old as he was. Louie told us that was the last one he planned on taking. He was almost seventeen years old and past being treated like a little kid.

Elaine was pretty upset with Daddy too since he wouldn't let her date. He wouldn't let her go to the football games and pep rallies at school unless Rubin went along. She thought having to take your brother along to everything wasn't very grown up. When Mama and Daddy were both gone she would wear shorts and prance around the house wearing lipstick and earrings. If Daddy found out, she would have gotten her hide tanned, but nobody told. We all had our secrets to keep.

Elaine had figured out that boys liked her. They were always hanging around her at school. She went to town and met with her friends and boys showed up there too. They gave her little presents that she gave to Sheron and Esther to keep them from telling Daddy on her.

In her room she had her jewelry hidden in a drawer. It was hidden from Daddy, but not from me. I took whatever I liked and gave it to my girlfriends. Elaine knew I was getting them but she couldn't say anything about it. She got really mad at me when I took a little ring with a turquoise stone to give to Judy. It was too small for Elaine, but she told me she was planning on giving it to Sheron. I figured I needed it worse than she did, after all Judy was my girlfriend, whether she knew it or not.

148

With money tight, I had to do what I could to find some. Harry came up with an idea.

"You know, Daddy's air compressor's just been sitting in the shed. He hasn't used it since I don't know when. We ought to see about selling it." Harry looked at me as we lay out in the front yard. None of the older kids were around, and Sheron had gone with Mama and the little kids to visit some friends.

"That's an idea. I bet we could do pretty good on it." I jumped up and headed to the compressor. It took the both of us to lift it and put it in the wheel barrow. We headed to town ready to wheel and deal like men. We walked the streets of Ashland trying to find somebody to buy it. The only men interested were the fellows that worked at the scrap metal yard. We had walked all the way across town by then and were tired of taking turns pushing the wheel barrow.

"What'll you all give us for the wheel barrow too?" I asked. I sure didn't want to think about walking that thing back up the hill to the house. They offered a few more dollars and Harry held out his hand to shake on the deal. We had more money than we had ever held and practically danced through town trying to decide where to spend it. Harry bought some rings at the dime store for the girls that hung around him. He thought he was pretty smooth when it came to girls. I didn't know how smooth you could be at thirteen, but I took his word for it that he was.

As we walked through Ashland, we decided to do something pretty daring. We walked past the park, past the candy store and the roller skating rink. We stopped right in front of the theater where they had picture shows. We were going to go inside. We knew that was sinful and worldly, but the movie posters and the building looked too good to pass by. I looked around to check for Mama, just to make sure she wasn't around. There was no sign of her, but Esther was over on the park bench with her friend Margaret. She had spotted us and was watching.

Harry didn't take his eyes off her. "The only way we're going to go in the show today, is if we make her go with us. That way she can't tell," he said.

"I'll get her," I told Harry and walked over to the bench.

"We're going to the show today, Esther. We got enough money for all of us. So come on, you're goin' in with us."

She looked around, looking scared, but I could tell she wanted to go. The three of us stood at the little cubbyhole and Harry gave the boy at the window our money. We all slipped in to the lobby. It was cool and dark inside. They sold candy and Cokes inside but we didn't buy any. Just the idea of being in the theater was almost too much. There were two doors that led to where they would show the movie. We went in the one on the right and found out that it took you upstairs to the balcony. We sat in the front row. Esther's eyes were big and I figured mine were too. For once I didn't mind that she held onto my hand. The lights were dim and we sat low in our seats and didn't say a word.

I couldn't believe we were inside this place. Soon the lights got dimmer and the movie started. I couldn't keep my mind on the movie. I looked all around the theater. The walls had curtains on them. They looked spooky because you couldn't tell what was behind them. The movie was a funny one and everybody laughed at the same places in the movie. I didn't laugh, my mouth was dry and I looked down at the people below. Esther wasn't laughing at the movie either. I thought she might start crying. Harry laughed with everybody else.

One of the scenes made the theater brighter and when I looked down I just about fell off the balcony. Louie, Elaine

150

and Rubin were in the seats below! I couldn't believe it. I sank down in my chair and nudged Harry to look down. I was scared to death they were gonna see us. The movie was a blur. When it ended, we waited until everybody was out of there and then Harry, me and Esther stopped at the doors to the outside. As soon as it looked clear, Harry, with me in the lead busted out of the theater and ran as fast as we could to get away there. Esther kept up with us out of pure fear. We didn't want to be anywhere near it if someone saw us that knew us. We didn't stop running till we got on the other side of Lithia Park. We sat down on the benches and crowed to each other about what we had done.

"So you think they saw us? Do you think they'll tell?" Esther looked at us.

"How could they? They'd have to tell on themselves. Let's just not talk about it to anybody." Not saying anything usually worked best for me.

"I sure ain't telling nobody," Harry said.

"I don't even know what you're talking about." I was feeling brave enough to grin at them. We both looked at Esther and knew she would go to the grave without telling. She wasn't just scared of going to Hell. Daddy and his belt were plenty enough reasons to keep quiet.

That night at supper Daddy said Grace and thanked the Lord for all we had. I bowed my head and kept my eyes shut tight. Not a one of us kids talked during supper and when it was over we jumped to help Mama clean up. Sheron looked at us like we were crazy. Daddy sat dozing in his chair, waiting to read the Bible. Mama couldn't move to do something that one of us was doing for her. She sat down with us all when everything was done it the kitchen. Daddy stopped reading and closed the book.

Mama looked at us all and said, "Why, I feel like I'm sitting in a room full of angels. You all have been so good today."

Nobody said a word.

Trying to Leave

Old time Fords and Chevys circled the dirt track. They skidded around the curves that made the circle track and dust blew up into the bleachers where we all sat. I didn't even care when it got in my mouth and nose. Daddy cheered the racers on, and we stood up and hollered with the rest of the crowd. Louie's boss had a car in the hard top races and let Louie bring Daddy and us younger kids in to watch. I just knew I could drive one of them if I had the chance.

The cars were older, mostly from the 30's and sometimes when they made the turn it looked like they were going to topple over with their tall cabs. There was a black and white clown car that made wrong turns and the driver would get out in the middle of the track and make us all laugh. It was driven by Leadfoot Lou Kerr and we cheered him on as he lost the race every time. Daddy hollered advice to the drivers who were trying to win and us kids echoed him as we shouted down to the racers. I sure was glad that racing wasn't worldly. I figured Daddy was glad too.

Daddy was gone a lot more now that the weather was warm. The Green Springs mill was busy but there wasn't as much money to be spread around as before. Daddy sold the Woody so we were down to the just driving the Panel. Louie's job played out with Neil Stockerbrand. Worse than the loss of money, the hard top races came to an end for us too.

Louie thought he needed to find a way to make more money and he talked Mama into letting him join the service.

Daddy said it was all right with him to see about it, but there was always work in the woods. So it was up to Mama to let him. He was still seventeen and he needed a letter for the Army.

They sat at the kitchen table while us kids stayed within good ear shot.

"What's wrong with working in the woods with your Daddy?" Mama wanted to know.

"Ah, Mama, the woods and the mill are always there. I can do that anytime. I'd like to see about the Army. I could make more money and be able to help more."

I figured that must have been why Daddy agreed to it.

"Son, how're you going to get up to Portland?" Mama asked him as she peeled some potatoes.

"Shoot, Mama. I can catch a ride with anybody heading north. There's trucks going every day. I don't need much money, just a little to eat on till I get enlisted."

It didn't seem to me to take much talking. Mama looked at Louie hard and said he could go. I was surprised she said yes. It wasn't but the next day that Louie headed down to the main drag in Ashland to hitch a ride to Portland.

With Louie being just about grown and leaving, it made Elaine want more too. Mama and Daddy were having a lot of trouble with her. She was almost seventeen, and thought she was old enough to run around with boys and go out on dates. Daddy still wouldn't have nothing to do with that. Elaine sure thought it was unfair. Sometimes she would run off and be gone late into the night. Daddy would look for her and when he brought her back she wouldn't be able to leave the house for days. Nobody told me where she'd gone, and I knew not to ask.

A couple of days after Louie left, Elaine was gone too. Daddy didn't find her till late that night. Daddy took the belt to her after that and had Mama keep a sharp eye on her all the time. She couldn't go anywhere that one of us kids didn't go along. I kind of felt sorry for her, so I didn't mess with any of her hidden stuff so she wouldn't have any more reason to cry. Supper got to be a pretty silent thing.

The girls were cleaning up the table. Elaine was in a pout so Esther and Sheron were trying to coax her into smiling. It was raining hard and loud but we heard steps on the porch. Mama went to the door to look and see who was out there. Louie walked in slow, soaked to the skin. Mama got him in the house and didn't care that he dripped water everywhere.

"They wouldn't take me, Mama," Louie told her.

"Girls, get Louie a plate." He was cold and hungry. He hadn't eaten much what with having no money and not figuring on needing to feed himself past a couple of days. He sat down at the table.

"I thought they might not. But I knew you had to find out for yourself, as hard headed as you are." She smoothed his wet hair back from his head.

"I barely even limp. I could do as much as any of them other boys. I've done more work that they ever thought about doing. This blasted leg."

Louie never talked about his leg, and never complained. To hear him talk about it that way now was something. I guess I hadn't given any thought to what it would be like to have a crippled leg like Louie.

Daddy walked over to him and patted his back, "You look for a job in town, if you can't get one, we'll go to the woods."

There was always the log woods.

The Model A

It wasn't only good for Louie when he found a job at a gas station in town. It was good for me and Harry too. Since Louie couldn't work with Daddy, he would take us to the mill with him to help. That meant missing school. I was always fine with that.

Ten miles of crooked road led to a turnoff to the log road. Daddy sawed logs all day and we helped Daddy with fetching water, carrying boards, and cleaning out sawdust. We knew to step lively when we were working with Daddy. We didn't stop till we had a load ready.

The cab in the log truck had one seat and the rest of it was full of tools and gear so Daddy couldn't bring us into town with him. He told Harry and me to wave down the woods boss when he came in and catch a ride with him. He'd be there in just a little bit.

With everybody gone Harry and me had the run of the place. There was an Old Model A car parked nearby and we got in it and played like we were driving it.

"I bet we could drive this thing to town, just us." Harry told me.

"Let's get it started. How hard can driving be? Daddy just about does it in his sleep."

It was too old to have a key; just a start button was on the floor board next to the door. Harry used his foot to push it. We had the car in gear, so when we pushed the starter button the motor turned over really slow and the car moved a little at a time. We had to get it turned around, facing the road.

We heard the tractor coming in from the woods.

"We better hide, so he won't see us and make us go with him." Harry and I got out of the car. Harry slammed the door to the Model A so hard, the back window behind the passenger side broke out. I thought the man would hear us, but he was whistling and busy getting in his pickup. He started it and drove off down the log road towards town. We watched the truck leave the mill and as soon as he was out of sight got back in the car. Harry pushed the starter button over and over and got the Model A turned around facing the direction of the road to town.

"You hear that?" I looked at Harry.

"He's comin' back!"

Back to the woods we went as fast as we could. We watched him drive through the mill and get outside the truck and get a thermos from the tractor. He got back in his pick up and left again.

"I thought he was coming back for us!" Harry said.

"Me too. He didn't even notice the Model A's facing the other direction!"

"Let's get her on the road," Harry said as he got in the driver's seat. I sat next to him with my hands on the emergency brake. It was a long lever that came up from the floor. He could barely reach the pedals with his feet. There were three of them. One was for reverse, one for slow and one for fast. There were levers at the steering wheel that were the throttle and fuel spark levers.

When we got the car going we learned we didn't quite know what we were doing. To get onto the main road we had to make a sharp turn to the right. We didn't know how to change gears so we could only go so fast. Harry kept mashing on one of the foot pedals to pick up speed, I kept pulling on the emergency brake.

We headed further down the road and got to going a little faster. The road hugged the side of the mountain and there wasn't room for a guardrail. It was just a cut out of the hill and only wide enough for about a car and a half. The few cars that were headed to Ashland started lining up behind us but we couldn't go any faster. We could barely see out the window. I never would have said it, but I didn't want to go much faster. Harry stuck his skinny thirteen year old arm out the driver window and waved the cars behind us to go around. The brakes started smoking on the car and no matter how hard I pulled we wouldn't slow down. The road went downhill and the curves went first to the left and then to the right as it switch backed down the mountain. Harry strained hard trying to turn the steering wheel.

"I can see the bottom of the hill!" Harry shouted. I didn't know how we were going to make the turn at the bottom. There was a car coming fast from the other direction. It made the turn on two wheels and head up the hill. It was the Panel and I knew by the way it was racing up the hill, it was Louie!

"We're not going to make it!" I hadn't seen Harry so stiff. On the left side of the road it sloped downhill into a valley. On the right side the road was up against the mountain except for a wide spot that had a big pile of gravel piled in the center of it.

Road down Green Springs Mountain

Harry swerved right and drove off the road at full speed straight into the gravel. We high centered on the gravel and came to a stop, both of us knocked to the floor.

Louie drove up to where we were perched. Harry and me didn't say a word to each other as we tumbled out of the car bawling at the top of our lungs. We both knew we better act hurt and scared if there was any chance of getting out of the whippin' Daddy was sure to give us. Louie was laughing.

"I never seen anything so funny as two little boys, nothing but eyes and heads a bobbin' looking out that windshield."

He laughed all the way to town and we told Daddy the mill boss had left us on purpose. Daddy got mad at him and I kind of felt bad about it, but not enough to take a whippin' for it.

I told Harry, "Next time, I'm drivin'."

1957
Salesmen

I sat outside the door of the shed in our yard. It was a warm day and with school over for the summer, we had time to look for ways to make a little money. Sheron and Esther were inside the shed, dusting and polishing the knick-knacks and trinkets we had for sale. They put them on our counter which was a door crosswise on a couple of stumps. There wasn't too much, some dime store rings and necklaces we had found in Elaine's hidden drawer, one doll Esther felt she could part with, even though she did cry a little. I had some rocks that were pretty and Sheron donated a little coin purse she had. She'd got it back when Daddy had enough money to hand out change.

Quarters had become hard to come by for us, just as dollars had become hard to come by for Daddy. We had started a daily rummage sale trying to drum up enough money to sneak into the picture show or buy Tootsie rolls.

It didn't seem like the neighbor kids had much money either. Harry was out in the street trying to get customers. We had a lot of lookers, but not too many spenders.

"I'm gonna get you kids if you don't stop!" Elaine hollered as the screen door slapped and she headed toward us. She must have checked her drawer.

I grinned up at her as she marched into the shed and grabbed up her stuff.

"Come on, Elaine, you don't care about any of this anyhow." Sheron tried to grab some of it, but Elaine took it from her and stomped back to the house.

Harry came back from the street and sat down beside me. The girls got tired of cleaning the shed and went back in the house, too.

"Old lady Foster has a bunch of plums hanging on her trees. We ought to go over and eat some," Harry said.

"All right, but let's ride the bikes." Being a bicycle man, I didn't walk when I could ride. We took off from our yard, rode around the corner, and two houses down from ours came to the Fosters. Johnny Foster, the woman's son, sat on the porch. We rode past it and then came down the hill and got to the back yard without being seen. We picked the plums that hung over the fence. We each ate a few.

"These are good enough to sell," I told Harry as I slurped on the juice that came from the big plum.

"We oughta do it, sell the plums I mean. People buy fruit all the time," Harry said. I told him that was one good idea. We rode back to the house and got some old coffee cans and walked back to the plum trees, the same way as before, no one seeing us. We filled the cans with the big fat plums.

"Where should we start?" I asked Harry as we walked to the street.

"Why not right here?" Harry pointed to the big two story house with Johnny Foster sitting on the porch.

"We're gonna sell her her own plums?" I looked at Harry with new respect.

"Why not?"

159

Harry walked tall as he headed up the walk towards Johnny Foster. He was grey headed and still lived with his mama. He was drinking a pint of milk when Harry and me walked up onto the porch. He raised the tall carton up to his mouth and didn't speak to us 'til he had squeezed every drop of milk out of it. He had a '46 Lincoln parked in the garage, all black, and never drove it on the road. He would just park it out front and wipe it down. He let me sit on the bumper sometimes. I figured we could do some business.

"What you boys want?" he asked us, looking us up and down. I waited for Harry to speak up. And waited some more. I looked over at him and he was froze. Like always, it was his idea, but I had to do the foot work.

"We wondered if you or Miz Foster might want to buy some plums." My voice came out louder than I meant, I figured I better settle down.

"Go on in, and check with her. Don't touch nothin."

"Yes, sir," I answered.

Harry and me went on inside and I had never seen anything like that place before. It was like they had never thrown anything away that they had ever owned. Newspapers were stacked higher than the chairs. Paper sacks were piled everywhere and full of stuff I couldn't begin to make out. We walked through the narrow path that went from the front room to the kitchen in the back. We found her in the kitchen and there were empty boxes and empty cartons and so much stuff on the table you couldn't eat on it, even if you wanted to, which I didn't want to at all.

"Well, hello there, boys. You the Millers from down the hill?"

"Yes ma'am."

"Aren't you handsome." I liked her right off. I grinned big at her, broken front tooth and all. I knew Harry was good looking with his black hair and hazel eyes. He always had a

160

girlfriend. My hair was brown, but I had blue eyes and Mama was always telling me they were pretty.

I almost hated to say to ask her, "We wondered if you might want to buy some plums?"

She took a look at the plums, held a couple of them up and then looked right at me.

"These look like fine plums. Why I don't think I could grow any better myself."

She looked at Harry. He looked ready to bolt. My face felt hot and my mouth went dry. I figured the best thing to do was keep smiling.

She turned and walked over to a pile of things in the corner and I looked sideways at Harry. He was smiling big too. She came back over to us and gave us each some change in our hands. I didn't even look at it. We thanked her, turned around and took off through the trail in her house and ran out the front door letting the screen slam.

When we got down the road a ways Harry turned to me and said,

"Nothin' to it!"

Football

One night Louie brought a buddy he had met at the gas station to supper. Don Smith was Louie's age. He was short, stocky and blonde. He worked as a lumberjack. He had supper with us and before long he was there almost every night. I guess he really liked Mama's cooking. Elaine sure was less of a sour puss.

Don would tell us big stories about all the things he had done and could do. I didn't know what to believe of them, but I did hear Daddy tell Mama he was a hard worker. He had come down from Alaska and had worked around

161

Ashland for a while. Elaine started laughing and smiling at supper.

Rubin wasn't too friendly to him. Don was a few years older than Rubin and I think Don thought he was tougher than Rubin. He didn't like that none. I knew nobody was stronger than Rubin. Why even the Kiwanis Club was interested in him.

During the summer they set up boxing matches to teach young men in Ashland how to box. They set up Rubin against a Navy middleweight boxer. Daddy whooped and hollered when Rubin took a turn boxing him and won. Daddy could have busted the buttons on his shirt he was so proud. We didn't talk about it around Mama.

Wasn't nobody more excited for the school year to start than Rubin. He practiced all summer and was going to be the football star the town wanted. Wasn't nobody less excited than me. I was headed back to the fifth grade for the second time. Sheron was going to be in my same class. I knew how Louie felt when Elaine passed him. I figured it ought to be easier the second time around, so I wouldn't have to work at it near as hard.

High school football started and Rubin didn't disappoint anybody. He played tough and the men in Ashland slapped him on the back when he was in town. I loved to go to town with him. Wherever we went, somebody bought him a Coke, mine too since I was with him. The only one who didn't seem happy about it all was Mama. Rubin would have cuts and bruises. Mama would shake her head and wonder why he wanted to play at something so rough.

After four games, Rubin was on crutches and the coaches had taped up his leg. That did it for Mama. Rubin was sitting at the kitchen table and we all sat down to eat. After Grace, Daddy looked over at Rubin.

162

"Yore Mama don't like you gettin' hurt at school. There's a lotta time bein' wasted playin' games. Tell those coaches at school that you won't be playin' no more."

Rubin didn't say anything, he kept looking down and his face and ears got red. I couldn't believe it, Rubin was a hero at school. I was going to lose out on a lot of Cokes if he had to quit. Rubin finally looked up at Mama.

"But Mama..." he started, and as respectful as he could he tried to talk Mama and then Daddy out of it. But when Daddy's mind was made up there was no changing it. Mama wouldn't be moved either. She didn't want him hurt. Afterward, Daddy let him leave the table, I don't know where he went but we didn't see him for a good while that night.

After Rubin didn't come to the game on Friday, the coach came to the house. We tried to stay out of sight, but in ear shot so we could hear everything. Rubin sat with them as the coach told Daddy how Rubin could probably go to college on a scholarship if they would let him keep playing. He kept talking about what a chance it would give Rubin to be able to go to school.

The coach didn't know that school didn't mean much to Daddy, and all this talk about college didn't make any difference. Mama and Daddy were nice to the coach, but he left with Daddy telling him they wouldn't change their mind. That kind of soured Rubin.

I don't think he cared as much about going to college as he did about being the star around town. I sure could see how that would be a letdown. Rubin didn't really try too much at school anymore and just got by like the rest of us boys. Pretty soon he just quit going to school altogether. He got a job being a driver for a Bible salesman. Daddy couldn't have been happier.

Rubin wiped down the Chrysler parked in front of the house for what seemed like hours. Just when he had every speck wiped off, he found another smudge and went at it again.

"You oughta take me and Alton for a ride in this big fancy car," Harry said as he looked at himself in the side mirror.

"Nobody gets in this here car but Mr. Simmons and me." Rubin shook his wiping cloth at us as he said it.

"What good is gettin' to bring the car to the house if you can't take her for a spin?" I asked.

"I take her around plenty, just ain't going to take you hoodlums around, probably mess up the upholstery and get the carpets dirty."

Ever since Rubin had started driving the Bible salesman car, he sure thought he was something. I guess he was. I might of thought I was pretty big for my britches too if I was driving around a big shiny Chrysler. He must have got paid pretty good because he bought Mama and Daddy a fancy Bible and was saving to buy himself a little '36 Ford with a rumble seat. He gave the man who owned it a little money on it every week.

"Why's he doin that?" Rubin asked no one in particular.

"What?" I looked to where Rubin was looking.

Johnny Foster was waving up the hill in front of his house. Rubin waved back, but Johnny went inside the house. He came back out and waved again, I tried waving too, but Johnny kept going back inside. Finally, Johnny hollered at us.

"Help us!" he finally yelled loud enough for us to make out what he was saying.

Rubin hollered back, "What'dya need?"

164

"Help!"

"What kinda help?" Rubin yelled louder.

Mama came out of the house, "What's going on out here?"

"Johnny Foster keeps wavin' and yellin' but won't say what he wants." Rubin told her.

We walked up the hill towards their house and that's when we saw the smoke rising up above the trees that surrounded the house. We could smell the smoke and fire, and the closer we got I could feel the heat on my face. We started to run.

Johnny had been bringing out things from the house and putting them in the yard. He would wave at us and yell then run back inside to bring out more things that looked to be no more than the trash they kept in the house. He couldn't get his mother to come out; she was busy trying to carry sacks loaded with what looked like more trash through the front room. The back of the house where the kitchen was at was covered in flames. Rubin and Mama ran in and came out with a blanket around Miz Foster. "How'd the fire start?" Mama asked them.

"I was making a fire in the stove in the kitchen and didn't realize that the sleeve of my housecoat caught fire. I walked into the front room to holler at Johnny to come in and have some coffee and must have trailed the fire through there. I stuck my arm in the dishwater, but by the time I turned around things was afire."

Knowing the state of her house first hand, I could see how the flames on that sleeve could catch that house full of newspapers and sacks on fire. Sirens sounded close and Rubin told Johnny he better not go back in. Johnny wanted to, but the neighbors who had come to look told him he better not. Rubin convinced Johnny to take his car from the street and park it down at our house to keep the cinders from burning it. The firemen took a hose to the house but Mama said it was dry as a tinder box. It burned to the ground.

The Fosters were upset and so were all the neighbors. Folks worried over them, but were thankful they hadn't burned too. Mary was so upset after seeing the fire; she had to sleep with Mama and Daddy for a while.

For days Johnny kept going up to the smoke pile trying to find something to save. Another of Miz Foster's sons came and helped them move. He made them leave all their trash behind and they were sick over it. They left Ashland. I was sad to see my best customer go.

Runnin' Off

Friday came and Daddy drove in from Weed with Louie. The work had played out on the Green Springs Mountain and Daddy had found a sawmill that needed a sawyer about seventy miles south in California. He took one of us boys with him each week and we helped at the mill and fixed the meals. It was my turn to go next.

After church on Sunday, Daddy and me loaded up and we went to Weed to batch together. The place was covered in Ponderosa pines and big fir trees that kept everything shaded. The mill was set up on a hill like sawmills always are. There was a space underneath it cut out of the hill that had been boarded in and made a little room for me and Daddy to stay in. There was a cast iron wood stove inside and two beds made out of scrap lumber fixed to the wall. There were no mattresses so we layered blankets to soften the bed.

I helped Daddy where I could and was in charge of fixing our meals. I didn't know how to do much. I had a pot of beans that Mama sent with us but when they ran out I had to cook on my own. We had flapjacks for breakfast, dinner and supper. Daddy didn't complain as long as we had plenty

166

of butter and syrup. My coffee was strong, but Daddy said that's how he liked it. It reminded him of the little cups of coffee they served in Louisiana, so thick you had to cut them with milk.

After a week at the sawmill we drove two hours back and to Ashland just past dark. Supper was waiting and I can say I was glad to see it wasn't flapjacks.

"Ain't much money to be made in Weed, Fonny." Daddy talked to Mama as he took a big bite of beans and cornbread.

"Thinkin' about asking around if somebody knows of some better work. May have to look pretty far out." Daddy said it out loud, but mostly to himself.

"Daddy," Rubin looked at him.

"Son?"

"There's a job over at Klamath Falls, I talked to a fella about it when I was over there with Mr. Simmons. Said they were lookin' for a custodian at the college. It pays pretty good, better than what I'm gettin' drivin' the Chrysler. I would have to live over there 'cause it's all week long."

"If it pays, son, no reason not to go. How're you goin' to get over there with no car?"

Rubin then told him about his '36 Ford. I could tell Rubin had it all figured out. There was no way Daddy would say no to a car if it got him to a job. A few days later Rubin drove up in his slick little dark blue Ford. Shiny, clean and so low to the ground if you put a pack of cigarettes on the ground it would knock them over. I know 'cause we tried it, and those cigarettes were almost the end of the Ford.

Mama walked out of the house to look at the car and saw the carton of cigarettes lying in the seat. She was madder than a wet hen. Cigarettes were just one step down from booze in sin.

"Mama, those ain't mine. My buddy Dean's daddy had me buy them for him and I just ain't taken them to him yet. He paid me to go get them. They ain't mine." This was almost as bad as when he couldn't play football anymore. Rubin got her convinced with some fast talking but he had to get rid of the cigarettes right then. It was a good thing she always thought the best of us all. Rubin convinced her, and he got to keep his Ford and his job in Klamath Falls.

Just when that all got settled down one morning we woke up to Elaine gone. None of us could believe this was starting up again. Mama drove around looking for her a couple of days and finally sent word to Rubin to come. We couldn't get ahold of Daddy and Harry in Weed so we had to wait for Friday when he'd be back. They spent all weekend looking for her and started to get mighty suspicious when nobody knew where Don Smith was either. Rubin had to go back to college to work and Daddy had to get to work too.

Harry and I waited a few weeks and then figured it was all right to go ahead and sell the things she had left behind. We went up to get it, and it was all gone. That's when we figured Elaine had run off for good. Mama cried a little all day long and we walked quiet around her, trying not to upset her. When Daddy came on Fridays they still looked for her, but nobody knew anything.

Saturday, Esther just about broke the door off the hinges running into the house.

"There's a letter! From Elaine! A letter!" She brought it to Mama at the table and she used a knife to open it. She read it to herself while all of us stood around her. Daddy sat at the end of the table waiting like the rest of us for the news.

"She and Don got married. They ran off to Reno. They're living up in Cottage Grove." She paused, "There's goin' to be a baby."

Mama sat back in the chair and closed her eyes, "My girl is married but she's all right. Praise Jesus."

Daddy called Don a no-account, and was getting pretty worked up; his fist hit the table more than once. Mama calmed him down.

Esther was still excited, "We didn't get to see her get married. What did she wear? Did she have a new dress?" She wouldn't stop asking a bunch of silly questions.

"Shush, sugar. I don't know all that," Mama told her. "I'm just glad to know she's settled."

"Well, I guess we can get ready and go," Daddy said.

Mama nodded her head. They had been waiting to find Elaine or we might have already left. Now that we all knew she was a married woman and gone for good, Daddy was ready to move on.

Elaine

Daddy said, "Heard tell about some work going on down in New Mexico. Louie and me'll head out tomorrow and see about it. Soon as we get things settled we'll come back up and get y'all. You all help your Mama pack up and get ready. When I get back we'll have a better place to go. Louie, go out in the shed and get my compressor, we'll take it with us just in case, might use it or might sell it."

Louie headed out to the shed. Harry and me looked at each other, but we kept quiet.

"Ain't a compressor out there Daddy," Louie said as he came back.

"Well, that settles it. If a man can't keep what's his in this town, he's got no business staying around a bunch of thieves." Disgusted, Daddy slapped his hat on his leg. I tried to feel bad about selling the air compressor, but it had bought

169

me my first ticket to the picture show. I knew I would go to the grave before I would tell what me and Harry had done.

NEW MEXICO 1957

Runnin' Hot

I never looked back as we pulled out of Ashland. Daddy had a pickup bed made into a trailer that we used to haul the extra stuff we had to take. We had been in Ashland so long Mama had been able to collect a few things to take with us. Daddy had come back from New Mexico and traded the Panel for a '41 Pontiac. He didn't think the old car could make the trip. Louie stayed down in a town called Chama to work and keep Daddy's spot where he'd been hired on as a sawyer.

The car was loaded pretty full with blankets and people. Having only eight in the car made for a pretty roomy trip. We drove to Klamath Falls to find Rubin, but he wasn't at his apartment or working. Daddy stayed around for a few hours hoping Rubin would show up, but Daddy was itching to go, so he had Mama write Rubin a note, telling him to come to Chama. Mama fussed around a bit, not wanting to leave Rubin, but Daddy's mind was made up. He said Rubin was plenty old enough to find his way to us and so we drove off without him.

Mama sat over in the passenger seat in front and pouted for a while, but it was her habit to keep the peace so she stayed quiet and looked out the windshield. Harry got to sit in front since he was oldest at home now. Elaine was left behind with her new husband.

We drove through the mountains of Oregon into the bright green hills that led to California. Trees grew right up the edge of the road making us feel like we were driving through a tunnel.

At the top of the hills Daddy would get out and add water to the radiator of the Pontiac. Then we would go downhill for a long time until the road leveled out again.

"The car keeps getting hot, Fonny," he told Mama.

"What're we gonna need to do?" she asked him.

"We may have to do something, but we'll keep on for now. We'll drive through the night and that might help it stay cool."

Daddy stopped a lot to keep adding water to the car, when daylight came we were close to a town.

"Well, we've made Reno, we'll see if we can't get the radiator flushed here." Daddy sounded tired but had gotten a second wind knowing we were close to a place where we could get the car fixed.

We parked at the edge of town in a wide spot beside the road. Mama had us get out and make camp. Daddy and Harry worked on the car and got the radiator out. The two of them carried it into town to a look for a shop. The rest of us kids ate our breakfast and played in the shade of the trees. Soon Daddy and Harry walked back with the fixed radiator and got it in the car in no time. We were back on the road.

We left the tall trees and headed over the bare hills on Highway 50. The road was as straight as a string and it seemed like it would never end. The heat blurred the road and made it seem wavy. A hay truck was up ahead of us.

"We got to get around this fella right away," Daddy said. "Never follow a load of hay, it blows off and can get in the radiator and make the car run hot. We just got that problem fixed, don't want another one." We all waved at the driver as we went by.

We drove across Nevada for two days. At a little place called Austin, the road started switch backing over a mountain. It got dark and it seemed like we never lost sight of the Austin lights out the back window. Daddy drove half the

172

night and Austin was still in the back window. We made it over the mountains and then we were in rolling hills. When it got dark again we saw lights up ahead, Daddy told us it was Ely. Just like we had watched the lights from Austin get further away, we watched Ely's get closer as we drove east.

During the day Mama would have us take turns sitting up front and we would have to read the road signs to her. I had good eyes and could see the letters from far away and it gave me time to figure out the words. I didn't want to read, but it got me a turn in the front.

When we went out of Ely we went down a long hill on a straight road that went on and on. The car went as fast as Daddy would let it, with all the windows down and the wind blowing in, we felt like we were flying so Mama had us sing,

Some bright morning when this life is over
I'll fly away
To that home on God's celestial shore
I'll fly away
I'll fly away oh glory
I'll fly away (in the morning)
When I die hallelujah by and by
I'll fly away
Just a few more weary days and then
I'll fly away
To a land where joys will never end
I'll fly away

I sure wanted to fly. The days didn't seem weary to me, but maybe they did to Mama. I guess sometimes the road did get tiring. Like when we made it to the bottom of the hill into Wendover and the ground went flat. We were in Utah and the country was dry and brown. There were places where white sand lay on top of the hard ground. There were treeless

173

hills of brown and the sun shone so bright I had to squint my eyes. The wind blew the road white. It looked like snow but it was sand. We had to roll the windows up to keep from getting pelted by it. Inside the car got hot.

After many miles we saw a thin strip of blue on the horizon to our left. The blue got closer to the road and turned into a big lake.

Mama told us, "There's the Salt Lake."

"Why is it called that?" Esther asked her.

"It is full of salt like the ocean. You can't drink it, and even if you couldn't swim, you could float in it."

I couldn't swim but I wondered about just laying in it like a bed. I would have liked to have tried. We drove by a building that had four strange looking corners with rounded tops that went up to a point. Mama had one of us read the sign. It was called Saltair. It looked kind of spooky to me. There were mountains to the east and a few to the south, but these had trees on them. We drove towards them and the country got a lot prettier as we drove through a big valley.

We headed into a canyon and the road went first one way and then another. In the back all of us rolled back and forth with the motion of the car as it went around the curves. Sheron kept telling Mama she was getting car sick and got to go up and sit between Mama and Daddy. I didn't believe her for a minute.

We made it to the top of Soldier's Summit and then headed down. The road had sharp curves and went downhill fast. Daddy was careful to keep the car from getting out of control. We had the trailer behind us and the curves made the car sway. Big rocks jutted out of the hills and we drove through Price Canyon. The valley opened up in front of us. There were hills and mesas beside us and the valley was full of farms. The road ran alongside big tan bluffs to the east. It looked like the wind had shaped them. All of it looked hot

174

and dry. We ran alongside those tall bluffs on the left, on the right there were hills but the tops were sharp and looked like broken teeth.

"We'll make camp at Green River," Daddy told us.

It was a small town and we drove through it to find a place to camp by the river that ran nearby. The river was wide with trees all along the banks. As we got closer we saw there were little covered picnic tables beside the road. Mama said folks came out and had picnics there. We went past them to the river bank. Nobody was around, so we had the place to ourselves for the night.

While we made camp, Daddy dozed off in the shade, looking up every once in a while to check on us. Mama started a pot of potato soup on the camp fire. It was cold at night, the girls slept in the car and the three of us boys slept close to the fire and each other, wrapped up in blankets. Usually, Daddy drove in the night, but after a few days of that he had to catch up on some sleep.

The next morning the sun woke us up. Mama was

The Mountain above Chama

making coffee by the fire and gave us cold flapjacks to eat with our hands.

"This is the last place for water, until Moab. Harry, you and Alton fill up the bags before we leave." Daddy told us as we picked up camp. To the east we could see tall mountains where trees didn't grow on the very top. They seemed far away.

The closer to Moab we got, the redder the big rocks got. They shaded the road as we went between them. Red bluffs shaded Moab on the west and those tall mountains we had watched for a long time butted up against the cliffs on the east as we kept driving. There weren't any towns or houses for a long time 'til we came to a house built into the rock wall called the Hole in the Rock. They let people look through it for money, but we just camped for dinner nearby.

Mama couldn't believe somebody lived in a hole in the rock. Mama thought they were crazy. She couldn't imagine anyone living like that.

We went around those big mountains we had seen for miles and made it to Colorado into Cortez. We went through Pagosa, Colorado and stayed on Highway 84 south into Chama. Big mountains were around us. Tall pines, fir and spruce covered the hills.

Chama was little and we turned off before we went through the main part of it and headed south towards the saw mill camp. There were hills to the back of the camp and it dipped down toward the highway. We turned on to a side road and then into the mill.

Tall mountains were to the northeast and big long rock cliffs stuck out of them. The whole country was made up of hills and meadows and groups of trees. The camp was located in a meadow. Daddy told us mills were built on hills so it was easier to tow away the slabs from the downhill side. The sawdust pile could be bigger too.

There were ten or twelve houses in the camp for the workers and their families. Daddy drove up to one of them. It was sixteen feet wide and twice as long. Boards were always cut at sixteen feet, so that's always how big a sawmill shack was.

Mama was so glad when she saw Louie walk out the door and holler at us, "Where you all been? There's work here to be done!"

Our Houses

After Louie grabbed up the girls and hugged them he put them down and showed Mama into the house. It was one big room made of rough lumber nailed up and down and taller in the front than in the back for the rain and snow to run off. It didn't have any electricity or running water. The outhouse was in the back and the windows didn't have any glass. Inside there were shutters attached with rubber over the windows. When you wanted to have light you lifted the shutter from the bottom and used a stick to prop it open.

Louie told me and Harry the best news of all. The house next to us was empty and the boys were going to get to sleep in there. Harry and I ran into the next house that looked just like Mama's. There were two bunk beds set up in the front of the house for me and Harry, Louie's bed was on the other wall. I could see his pallet laid out on the wooden bed bottom.

Over the next few days Harry and me got busy making our house ours. We decided since it was pretty chilly in there at night that we would build houses around our beds. We fanned out all over the camp and came up with all sorts of lumber. We could always find scrap lumber in a sawmill camp. We pulled long nails out of boards and houses to get enough to put our houses together. We stood back to look.

"They look like dog houses," I told Harry.

"Just about the best dog house you ever saw." Harry was proud of his work.

"What about a door for the front. That would help keep us warm," I told him.

We copied the idea of hinges from the windows. We took rubber from the red inner tubes of old cars and nailed them to the four boards we had hammered together. They shut but didn't latch, which was okay since we would be on the inside. We laid our quilts down in our dog houses and thought we were pretty neat.

We offered to make Louie's bed into a dog house but he wasn't interested. He was just about all grown up now. He worked with Daddy at the mill as a log truck driver. We could always tell when it was Louie coming up the hill, the truck engine just roared as he put the gas to it. The slope up to the mill was called 'Groundhog Hill,' because there were so many mounds. The truck would bounce and shake as it made its way to the saw mill. Sometimes me or Harry would ride along and enjoy the rough ride.

Daddy was hired on by Wes Jackson to be head sawyer. This was a pretty big operation so there wasn't work for Harry or me at the mill. We were too young. There wasn't much to do here like there was in Ashland. The store in town was a long ways away and we didn't have any money anyway. Mama got a job at the laundry a few miles back up towards Chama but outside of the main part of town. Sometimes we would go to work with her and see what we could find to do. I liked going to town so we could use a bathroom with running water. I guess we got spoiled having an inside bathroom for so long. Electric lights had been nice too.

The first time Mama went into town she went to the post office and mailed a letter off to the folks back in Louisiana. Mama always wrote the letters, Daddy never did write. He didn't ever use a telephone either. There was a pay phone at the laundry and Mama took change with her to call the folks in Louisiana.

178

She dialed the operator and asked for Natchitoches. She had to hang up and try again because they gave her Nacogdoches, Texas. It took two tries just about every time. They never could connect her on the first call. She wanted to let the folks there know where we were in case they heard from Rubin.

Daddy wasn't making much money at the sawmill so after a while he figured that hauling logs would pay better. He just needed to find a truck. Across the highway from the mill were two old trucks Daddy had seen from the highway. He went over and talked to the man about buying one of them. He found out one truck had the motor out and the other had the rearends out. Daddy made a deal to buy both.

He dragged them across the road to the house one at a time. When he got through with the mill for the day he would come and sharpen his hack saw. Right behind the cab he went to sawing the frame rails in two. They were steel beams that went down the length of the truck. There was about two feet between them. The engine was bolted to them in the front. The rear ends made the tires turn and were bolted to the frame in the back.

It took more than one night to saw through the thick steel. Daddy would saw for a while and then Louie would saw for a while. Harry and me took a turn too. We finally got the truck in two and moved the back end out of the way. Then they went to work on the other truck. When it was in two pieces they moved the broke down front part away. Daddy and Louie lined up the two halves and had a welder come from the mill. He welded the steel rails together. Daddy hooked up all the lines and wires and had him a running truck. He quit the mill and went to hauling logs for a fellow in the next town.

One morning when Harry and me got up and went outside we saw all the car doors were open. "Why is the car like that, Mama?" I asked her.

"You and Harry get your blankets and Louie's too. We're movin' to TA today."

"Where's that?' Harry asked.

"Just about fifteen miles down the road. Now eat you a flapjack and hurry and start loadin' the car," Mama handed him a bundle to load.

Since we lived in the other house and slept in our dog houses I wasn't able to hear Mama and Daddy talking in the bed like I could before. Since Daddy quit the mill he had to move from the camp. He had found a new place south of town. We sure did hate to leave our dog houses, but we knew better than to say anything as we got in the car with the girls and the babies and Mama. Daddy and Louie were already at work for the day, so we would see them that night at the new place.

We turned off the highway at the gas station onto a paved road. We drove by the two story school and just a few houses down turned into a house that had three front doors. It looked like some of the motels we had seen on the road. The house was just one room deep and inside the rooms all connected. It was built facing the road and on the other side of the road was a low area with a creek on the other side. The land was so much lower down in there that the top of a building would be lower than the bottom of our house. I was back to living in the same house as the family. It was fun to pretend we lived in a motel though, whatever that was like.

Freckles

Driving by that school was a sign, because before too long Mama marched us down to it and told them who we were and what grades we were in. We were different than the kids here but it was a good different. The girls loved our curly eyelashes and thought my blue eyes were something. Only Rubin and me had them, everyone else had brown or hazel and since Rubin wasn't around, it made me special. Harry strutted around the school yard making friends and it was kind of nice to not have to fight anybody on the first day of school.

I sat by a girl in class and she told me the town wasn't really TA, it was Tierra Amarilla but you didn't say the L's. I didn't even know that there were L's till she wrote it down. No wonder everybody just called it TA.

Old Man Garcia was the teacher. He was a tough little old man. He would whack your hands with a ruler for doing anything wrong and pull out the paddle if he thought he needed to really get your attention. It was a relief to get out of class at the end of the day.

Sheron and I had been down to the creek and we waded around in the knee deep water. The weather was starting to get colder and we didn't figure we would get to wade for much longer. We were laying in the field warming up in the sun when we heard horses coming. We watched a couple of cowboys riding their horses down to the creek. There was no wind and we could hear them talking to each other. They were far enough away that we could hear them talking, but not what they said. We heard some whining sounds but couldn't figure out why.

"It sounds like puppies," I told Sheron.

Sheron looked around, "Where are they, I don't see any?"

We watched the cowboys and saw that they each had gunny sacks in one hand. The tops squeezed shut in their fists.

"I think it's coming from them." I got up and started following the horses on foot. Sheron was right behind me. The cowboys made their way toward the creek. They weren't in any hurry as they walked the horses down the slope and across the field. We were like Indians as we tracked them and made sure they didn't see us. Ducking behind tall grass, and laying on our bellies in rocky spots. We kept close so we could keep an eye on them. They reached the edge of the water and threw the gunny sacks into the creek. Sheron and I kept hidden behind the big trees that grew along the creek bank.

They rode off just as slow and we waited for them to get out of sight. Sheron and me ran to where the sacks were resting on the creek bottom. There were little bitty puppies in each one. The sacks had only been held shut by their hands so when it hit the water the tops opened up. The puppies were coming out of the sacks and were so little they couldn't keep their heads above the water.

Sheron and me both jumped into the water and grabbed puppies with both hands. They had their eyes open but were really young. I got one and then another and put them up on the bank. Sheron did too and we were able to get all of them from the water. There were seven of them, all different shades of browns and blacks. We were worried the cowboys would come back, so we didn't talk loud, but when we had all of them in our arms, we grinned at each other and headed to the house.

I was pretty sure Mama wouldn't want seven puppies so Sheron and me went around the house and put them in the handmade trailer Daddy had brought from Oregon. There was a little black puppy with white feet and white spots on his nose. He just nuzzled me and kept licking me. I picked him up and decided that he was the best one.

"Mama ain't gonna let us keep these, Alton." Sheron was starting to worry.

"I'll figure something out. Let's find an old rag for them to lay on." I didn't want to think about trouble, I just wanted to take care of my puppies.

We kept them secret for the rest of the day. They slept a lot, probably worn out from their near drowning. Freckles stayed with me. That's what I called the one that loved me. At supper time I walked into the house holding him and told Mama I had saved the little dog and could I keep him?

Mama held him for a minute and put his little face up close to her and looked at him and then told me I could.

"One little puppy shouldn't be too much," Mama sighed as she said it.

I decided now wasn't a good time to tell her about the six others outside in the trailer. She let Freckles have scraps from the table and I got to sleep with him that night. He laid his neck on my neck and slept there. All night long I made sure I didn't move and wake him up. It was Louie that found the surprise the next morning in the trailer. He came in and got Mama. I was right behind them, Sheron too.

"Seven puppies, Alton? We can't keep seven puppies." Mama looked at them all laying on each other in the trailer.

"Just for now, Mama." I looked up at her, hoping to sway her.

"They were gonna just drown them," Sheron pleaded with Mama.

"You all find somewhere for these puppies and pretty soon. I can't be feeding a whole litter." Mama walked back to the house.

"They're so cute." Sheron said as she got in the trailer and they climbed on her. "How could anyone not want them?"

"Freckles is the best, though." If I could just keep Freckles, I knew we could find something to do with the rest.

"I'll help you kids," Louie told us. "After work I'll go to town and see who might want 'em. I'll ask around at the mill, too."

That night, after he got through hauling logs with Daddy, Louie gathered up a couple and left with them. In a few days Freckles was the only one left. I fed and watered him and he slept on me every night.

"Louie's probably just throwing them back in the creek," Harry said one night, laying next to me.

"You hush, Harry, you don't know nothin'." He made me mad.

"Who wants a bunch of scrawny dogs crying all the time?" Daddy didn't allow fighting, but Harry was getting close.

"I told you to hush, Harry. If you don't, I'll make you."

Harry laughed but he shut up. Harry had seen all that fighting I had done in school. Even play fighting Cowboys and Indians had taught him I wasn't any baby. He was two years older and fast, but I hit hard. Harry must of figured he didn't want any part of me. I was glad, I wasn't sure I could take him, but I'd have died trying. We had always been best friends and we hardly ever fussed at each other. Harry was getting older and that trip down from Oregon where he was oldest at home had got him thinking he was big. He was fourteen, but acting too big for his britches if you asked me. He didn't say no more about the puppies.

I had never had a dog for my own and I spent all my time teaching Freckles to be the smartest dog anybody had

184

ever seen. He grew fast and if I was worried there wasn't going to be any leftovers for him, I wouldn't eat all my food so I could feed him. I kept him in the trailer when I went to school, but soon he grew big enough to get out. Mama told me she would keep an eye on him for me. Since Chama was further away she didn't work at the laundry anymore.

TA was a small and slow town. When people went places they rode horses or walked. One night the town had a big bonfire and got together down in the bottom by the creek. We sat on the edge of the hill and watched. We knew we couldn't go down and be with them, but it was fun to watch the sparks rise up to the sky until Daddy called us in.

Mama checked the post office pretty often looking for a letter from Rubin that might come general delivery. She brought a letter one day from Grandma Mac in Louisiana. Mama cried when she heard Rubin was there living with Uncle Huey. Daddy had Mama write back to Grandma right away to have him come to New Mexico but we hadn't seen him yet.

The house at Tierra Amarilla

It was a good thing he hadn't come because Daddy decided we were moving to a place called Escabosa. It was about a hundred and fifty miles south. Daddy had talked with a fellow that had come from there. There was a saw mill and they were looking for a sawyer. Daddy thought he could do better there. It wasn't long before we were on the road.

Since we were leaving we didn't have to go to school and that was one of the best things about moving on. We had packed up the car and the trailer. The truck Daddy had built was just going to be left since it didn't have plates and we didn't have money to drive it. I guess it had served its purpose.

I was carrying Freckles with me and was getting in the car.

"Alton, we ain't takin' that dog. There's no room," Daddy told me.

I had a suspicion this might happen. I had hoped if I just didn't think about it no one else might either and I could slip him into the car. I had tried to think of a way to hide him, but I didn't see how I could without him smothering. I looked at Mama but I could tell she wasn't going to buck Daddy for Freckles. I looked at Freckles and I knew I couldn't just leave him in the empty yard. Mama said I could walk the few houses down to the school and see if someone wanted him. But I had to hurry. I walked over to the school and looked for one of my girlfriends. As I walked by Old Man Garcia's classroom window I thought I sure was glad to leave him behind.

Annette was in the school yard and I walked up to her with Freckles.

"We're movin' today, I thought you might want Freckles." I held him up to her as I talked.

"Why aren't you taking him with you?" She scooped him up and squeezed him.

"Daddy won't let me. There's not enough room in the car, but he said I could come over here and give him away."

"I'll take him. I think my mother will let me keep him."

As I walked away Freckles tried to wiggle out of her arms and go with me, but she held onto him. He whimpered

186

a little and I felt kind of good knowing that he was sad to see me go. I got in the back of the car and Daddy took off. We passed by the school and then got out onto the road. Before we went around the curve on the highway I turned around and watched out the window. It was the only time I had ever looked back.

Birthday

The table was quiet as we waited for Daddy to think on it. I had tried my best to convince him. I couldn't think of anything else to say to try and sway him. All of our faces were turned towards his. He was sopping up bean juice with some bread. I looked at Mama to see if she might be on our side. She was making sure Mary was eating and I could see she wasn't going to get in the middle of this. I looked back at Daddy.

"I reckon if y'all all stay together, the four of you can go. I'll come get you after a while, be watching for me outside the school." Esther clapped once and then stopped and put her hands over her face. I could tell she wanted to start talking, but if that happened who knew when she would stop.

"We will, Daddy," I said as serious as I could. I didn't want him to think this was a bunch of foolishness. We made sure not to fuss with each other and helped Mama clean up. When Daddy read from the Bible that night we made sure we were always paying close attention. Harry and me started out the door to get wood for the night. As soon as it closed we jumped we skipped. When we got off the porch, we whooped. We were going to get to go to the Halloween Carnival at the school.

We lived in Escabosa but the closest school was about four miles south in Chilili. The bus took us to the two room

187

school house on weekdays, but for the carnival we were going to have to walk the four miles. My birthday was the day before Halloween, so I figured that the carnival would be my own birthday party. I knew some kids talked about having parties for their birthday so I figured this one would be mine, even if I was the only one who thought so.

Waiting for the Carnival was a trial because none of us wanted to get in trouble and miss getting to go. Hoyt Lynn pouted around the house, with him just eight he was too little to go. Which we told him over and over.

Escabosa was a little town with just a general store and scattered houses on a winding road south of Route 66. The house Daddy moved us into was long and skinny like the house in TA but with just two front doors. Daddy said it was a trailer. It had a wood stove for heating and cooking. Wood was easy to get since we lived close to the sawmill. It was back behind the house in the woods, you couldn't see it, but you could hear the saw singing most of the time

Everybody but Mary went to school. Big kids went in one room, little kids in the other. Hoyt Lynn was the only one in the little kid class. There weren't a lot of kids and the teacher was nice. He learned our names and told me there was a place that sounded like Alton. From then on he always called me Altoona, Pennsylvania. I didn't mind because he didn't seem to mean anything by it.

At the end of the day the bus let us off right in front of a store and if I had a penny I always got me a Tootsie Roll. We walked by an old lady's house that was close to the road. We always waved to her and after a while she started coming out and giving us something to eat. First just a tortilla and butter then some with cheese, one time some with avocadoes and tomatoes. Sheron and Esther ate the green stuff like it was good. I couldn't get past eating something that looked so bad. I always took one though so I could give it to the girls to

188

eat. She let us into her house once. Her furniture was made out of cow hides on wood frames. I hadn't seen anything like it before and told Mama. She said she

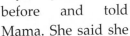
The house at Escabosa.

sure would like to see it. Mama's couch was a cot up against the wall with quilts on it.

The day of the carnival we got off the bus and didn't waste any time getting to the house. We wanted to get all our work done, so we could start the walk back to Chilili. The four miles didn't seem like anything since we just about ran the whole way there. We only stopped to walk so we could catch our breath. We walked up to the school and went in like all the other folks from town.

The two rooms were decorated with ghosts and pumpkins. There was a trough for apple bobbing and fishing poles lined up to fish for prizes. There was music on a record player and folks walked around in a circle hoping to win a cake. I couldn't figure out which thing to do first.

Sheron and Harry went over to a table where they were playing Bingo. I went over to the apples and the lady in charge told me I probably wouldn't get any with my broken tooth. I stuck my head in that water and came up with a big red one. I bit a half dozen before she shooed me away.

Sheron won gold clip on earrings in the Bingo game. She showed them to us and then hid them in her dress pocket so that Mama and Daddy wouldn't know about them. She was sure proud that she won. Harry hung outside a lot with

189

some older boys, cutting up and laughing. Esther won a cake and we all went outside with it. We sat on the ground in front of the school and ate all my apples but we saved the cake for Mama. We didn't know when Daddy was going to come so we were always keeping watch for him. When he drove up we ran to the car. Esther didn't stop talking the whole way back.

When Mama sliced the cake for us all, I sang myself Happy Birthday.

The Woods

Saturday afternoon the mill sang loud as it sawed the logs that had been cut during the week. They used horses to skid the logs out of the woods, but on Saturday they didn't work them. This was a little gyppo mill and it was set up in the woods. Trucks couldn't get into the woods to bring out the logs. Horses were used to tie onto the logs and skid them to the timber pile. One horse was black and one was white and they were both big. They were let off their ropes to forage in the woods behind our house. The only thing on them was a bridle.

Harry and me loved to play on those big horses. We rode them bare back but used the bridle to guide them. We walked them through the pine needles and leaves, the horses just clomping along. The trees were thick and we weaved in and out. Harry and me tense and waiting, keeping an eye on each other... then Harry leapt. The game was to knock the other one off the horse. As soon as Harry knocked me off he took off on my horse hollering. I got up from the ground and jumped on his horse and took off after him. He hid in the trees, but when I found him I jumped on him. We fell into the soft pine needles and underbrush, cutting up and wrestling. The horses just stood and watched, nosing for something to

190

eat and waiting for us to get back on. When we were tired, we left the horses where they stood and headed back.

One afternoon Harry was helping Daddy at the mill so I was by myself in the woods. I was scouting around and sat down at the foot of a tree. I was piling up the pine cones when I heard the whimper of a dog. It made me think of Freckles and I looked to find where the noise was coming from. He came to me as I sat there, a black and white herding dog, I think a border collie. He limped to me and was in a crouch. He had a gash in his foot that was red but didn't bleed. I put my arm around his neck and tried to look at the paw. He wanted to pull away but I held on to him. He whined, and I picked up his foot to see what it was. I talked to him but the dog was skittish and he slobbered all over me.

I heard the leaves rustling and looked in the woods, two men came out of the trees carrying rifles. I hadn't seen them before. They were a little out of breath and when they saw me they raised their guns.

"You better let go of that dog, son. He's got rabies," one of the men told me.

"Back away from him real careful in case he decides to go after you." They kept their guns on the dog. I saw that the wound on his paw was where they had shot him.

I rose up slow and couldn't figure out where to look, at the dog or the men with guns. I didn't know exactly what rabies was, but I knew if a mad dog bit you, you would go crazy and froth at the mouth.

"Get over here behind us," one of them moved his hand to point behind him. As soon as I was clear, the rifle fired. They blew the dog's head off. I just stood and stared at the dead dog I had just had my arm around.

The head was a mess of blood and bones. One of the men drug the limp body over to a burlap sack and dumped the dog in. The body flopped into the bottom. He draped the

191

sack over his shoulder and they headed back the way they came. They didn't say anything else to me. I stood there alone for a while looking at blood and hair on the ground.

Slowly, I started walking towards the house. I tried to wipe the drying spit off me as I walked. I was glad the dog hadn't bit me and made me go crazy, but I kept seeing the dog's open head on the ground. I don't know why, but I didn't tell anybody about the dog when I got back.

LOUISIANA 1958

Chores

I walked on one side of the wagon and Harry walked
on the other. It was big, made out of boards about sixteen feet
long. It had two wheels, one on each side and almost as tall as
us. Old Dick, the mule, pulled it along. Old Dick was
Grandpa Miller's mule and was thirty-one years old. He
would get to acting so worn out we would let him rest every
few feet. Grandpa didn't ever let us ride him, work animals
weren't for riding. Daddy had taught us that after they
worked all day long right beside a man, he ought to carry
himself back, just like the mule or horse did.

We were in the woods by the creek gathering drift
wood and dead limbs. The mule pulled the wood wagon
slowly down the rutted wagon road. The wagon barely fit
between the trees and bushes that grew right up to the road.
In places there wasn't room to walk beside the wagon. We
had to be quick with our feet as we walked in the narrow
spots. It hurt like the devil when the metal band that went
around the wood wheel ran over our feet. Sometimes Old
Dick would catch us off guard when he started up from a
stop. A mule always stepped back first before he started
forward. That roll back could get a toe before we knew it.

We were back in Louisiana, where Mama and Daddy
always went home to. Mama had wanted to come back,
Rubin was here and she was ready to see her folks. Daddy
was always ready to go somewhere, so in a day we had
packed up and left. He had driven us across Texas into
Louisiana. We had stopped at the creek near Many and
scrubbed up good to come in to town. It didn't take long for
folks to hear that Wesley's bunch was back.

We found Rubin living with Uncle Huey. Come to find out Grandma had never told Rubin that we were in New Mexico. She thought it was best that he stay with them. That's why he had never come. Daddy got mad about the family not telling Rubin where we were. Rubin was hurt that we had run off and left him. He was living with Uncle Huey and Aunt Hazel and going to high school in Flora. They lived in the front of a brick warehouse. There was a door at the back wall of the house that opened to the chicken coop. There were dozens of chickens roosting just on the other side of the door. Even I had a little trouble with that set up. I couldn't believe Rubin liked it. Talk about stink.

Rubin told Mama and Daddy he figured he had been cut loose, since he had been left in Oregon. Daddy didn't see it that way and was after him to come home. The way Daddy figured it Rubin's labor was Daddy's, not Uncle Huey's. The whole thing turned into a big blow up. It was a hard thing to buck Daddy so it wasn't too long until Rubin came back, mostly just to keep the peace.

We moved into the red house by Grandma and Grandpa Miller. Mama spent quite a bit of time over at Grandma Miller's helping her with work inside the house. Grandma always kept a tea kettle boiling in the back of the house in the kitchen. We didn't like to call attention to ourselves with Grandma around so if we wanted to talk to Mama, Harry and me would go to the back door and Harry would whistle like that tea kettle. Harry had to do the whistling since I couldn't. No matter how I puckered and blew, I couldn't get anything but air out. Mama would come in there thinking the water was boiling and find us at the door.

Grandma would call her, "Fonceal, where's that tea?"

Mama would have to tell her something because the water sure wasn't ready. I knew she understood why we kept

194

clear of Grandma. I heard her tell Daddy how hard Grandma was, but Mama always tried to do what Grandma wanted.

We had more to do living back in Louisiana and one of our chores was gathering wood. Harry and me brought the wagon full of wood back into Grandpa's yard to unload. As soon as we unhitched Old Dick and put him in the corral he got wound up. He would kick out his back legs and roll around on the ground. He sure lost the tiredness he showed while pulling the wagon. I was starting to wonder if acting worn out was something that old mule was trying to get over on us.

The hickory wood went in a pile by the smokehouse and the oak and pine in the wood pile to heat the house. The smoke house held all the pork. Hickory was burned slow to smoke the meat and give it flavor. Bacon was stored in a barrel. The bottom of the barrel had a burlap sack and then the bacon slab was on top of it. A layer of salt was put down and then another layer of bacon, all the way up till the barrel was full.

The hams hung from a hook. A piece of honeycomb robbed from a bee tree was put on top of the chunk of meat to have the sweet honey drip down on it. Whenever there was a hog killing several families would get together and help each other with the butchering. About six to eight hogs were killed at a time to fill everyone's smoke house. There was plenty to eat in Louisiana.

"Our names might just as well be 'get wood' and 'draw water' for all the folks want from us," Harry joked. I could tell it was mostly a complaint, though, as he dipped the bucket into the well behind the house.

"All right," I told him, "you be 'draw water' and I'll be 'feed the chickens.'" I went to the chicken coop, fed the chickens and gathered the eggs. Grandma Miller's chickens were in a pen at the back of her place. I hated to walk in there

195

and step on all the chicken manure in my bare feet. It was better than Grandma Mac's because Grandma let her chickens run around all over the yard. Between that and the tobacco juice folks spit, you could hardly walk in a clean spot.

Harry lowered the bucket down in the well. The well had two poles, one on each side with a timber across. The hole in the ground was about six inches wide. The bucket was lowered by a rope into the well. The bucket was shaped long and skinny, four inches around and three feet long. At the bottom of the bucket the end came loose and let the water fill from the bottom. When you pulled it out of the water the rope pulled on it and closed the end. It had a rubber gasket to seal it when we pulled it up out of the water to keep the water from coming out the bottom. The rubber gasket on ours was worn out and the seal didn't work. If we weren't quick all the water would run out before we got the bucket to the top.

Harry was pulling the well rope and I laughed when he got it to the top and poured a cup's worth of water into the kitchen bucket.

"You're liable to be there all night long if that's the best you can do."

"Go play with the chickens," Harry told me and then acted like I wasn't there.

He worked that well rope a lot faster the next time.

Farming

When the people around here had learned that RW was back, the locals had come over to hire Daddy to saw for them. He had to saw a few days for this man, and then saw a few days for another. They owned their own mills, but there was no better sawyer than Daddy. Daddy was always working, but he told us getting paid a wage didn't earn as much as owning your own mill.

Daddy got a black '49 Ford to use as a pulp wood truck. When he wasn't sawing, he cut timber to sell to the pulp wood mills for paper. Sometimes he hired help to work with him and the boys. Wilmer Lynch, the preacher at the colored church in New Town, came to work for Daddy sometimes too.

Daddy turned thanks over supper. He thanked the Lord for all we had. After a few big mouthfuls he told us his idea to make some more money. I hadn't known that we needed to make more we were eating so good.

Daddy said we were going to grow sweet potatoes. Daddy never had been much of a farmer. We didn't often have a garden. Daddy crumbled up a biscuit in coffee that had plenty of cream and sugar for dessert. I liked that too, a whole lot better than when we put mayonnaise on bread and poured sugar all over it. Daddy didn't read to us long that night. The next day we were going to farm.

At first light, Daddy walked to the bottom land where he was going to plant the crop. It was on the other side of the creek in a meadow on Grandpa Miller's land. He had a big team of red mules that he borrowed. Grandpa walked out to Daddy and told him something about the moon. Daddy listened, laughed and told Grandpa to go on back to the house. Grandpa shook his head and walked away.

Daddy took the mules and plowed long, straight rows into the ground. Row after row he made the furrows. I began to wonder just how big he was going to make this thing. He finished up and mopped his face with his handkerchief.

"Get to it, boys." He walked the red mules back to the corral. I stood at the end of the row with my sweet potato slip and looked across what looked to be miles of turned dirt.

"Better get to working. It ain't goin' nowhere," Harry told me.

He couldn't start till I did. I carried a bag of slips and about every foot I laid one down on the mound of dirt that was about a foot high and a foot wide. Harry came behind me with a notched stick. He took the slip and pressed it into the soft dirt. We started one by one, row by row. After all the slips were planted we got the sled that had a fifty-five gallon barrel on it. We filled the barrel with water from the creek and used old Dick to move it down the rows. We each had a coffee can and dipped the water from the barrel and watered every slip, added a little dirt in the hole and watered some more. After the planting, Hoyt and me were left to do the watering every day. I checked the sky every day and prayed for rain. It didn't take long for me to figure out why Daddy had never been a farmer.

The Bear

Rubin, Louie and Daddy were hauling pulp wood and they took Harry too. We were trying to make money every way we could. Pulp wood was fast money and if you had some timber to cut you could have cash just about every day

Pulp wood hauling might have been fast but it wasn't easy. Daddy would fell the tree with the power saw. Rubin and Harry would use the measuring stick and Daddy would trim to length, six feet and two inches. The boys would load it onto their shoulders and walk to the truck and load it by hand. Sometimes the logs were little and light, often times big and heavy. Trucks that worked in the woods generally didn't have fenders and seldom had doors. If we got to ride along the oldest always got to sit on the outside. When they had a truck full they would take it to the paper mill at Campti to sell. They got $14 a cord and tried to haul two and half cords on each load. Hard as it was, it sure seemed better than farming to me.

I was out walking the ditch along the roadside looking for old bottles to sell when I found a pair of faded blue canvas tennis shoes. The soles were good but the toes were worn through. I saw right away that these shoes had a lot more life left in them. When I tried them on they were a little too long for me, but not so big that they fell off when I walked.

I cut the canvas part off of the toe since they had holes anyway. That left a half moon shape with no canvas over it at the toe. I found some old inner tube and with bailing wire wired the inner tube to cover the hole on the shoes. I thought it looked awfully good. They weren't cowboy boots, but they were better than bare feet. I put them on and wore them around the place. I could walk in the woods easier, feed the chickens without stepping in manure and for sure stay out of the tobacco juice at Grandma and Grandpa Mac's. Most kids didn't have shoes in the summer in Louisiana, but I did.

Hoyt, me and the girls were sitting out on the porch watching it rain when Daddy and the boys drove up in the log truck. They came for dinner in a pouring rain which was unusual since Daddy liked to work in the rain because it was so much cooler. We ran out to where Daddy parked the truck. After the girls jumped all over him, he raced us all back to the house. I ran as fast as I could and so did the girls. Daddy was in the lead and I was right behind him. I tried to keep up with his stride, but I couldn't get my feet to go in his footsteps. I hoped someday I would. For now, second to Daddy was good enough for me.

He told us a traveling show that was setting up in town and we could all go on Saturday and look at it. The next morning all of us but Mama and Mary loaded up on the truck and went the few miles down the road to Bobby Cooper's store.

The little carnival had set up behind the store. What most of the men were paying attention to was a brown bear

199

inside a cage. It was walking from end to end of the cage and sometimes stood up and put its paws through the holes. The man in charge was talking to the crowd.

"Now, listen to me y'all. This bear stands six foot eight and weighs in at four hundred pounds. A bear is a natural wrestler. The bear knows holds by instinct. The choke hold, and as you all have heard of, the 'bear hug.' Who here in this community is man enough to go against Teddy the Bear? If you can throw him over, you win one dollar!"

The crowd talked among themselves and everybody was sizing up the bear and each other. A couple of men took turns and got in the ring with the bear and both of them gave up before they could throw the bear.

Louie looked over at Rubin and nudged him. "You can take that bear. Big fella like you oughta be good for something."

Rubin

"If I make my mind up to, I know I can tip that bear," Rubin announced to all if us.

"Do it, Rubin! Do it! You could earn a dollar!" I didn't know if he could do it, but I sure did want to see him try. Rubin went closer to the cage and looked over Teddy the Bear. He was muzzled and didn't have any claws, so it would be an even match as far as teeth and hands. Rubin looked at Daddy who nodded. Rubin walked up to the announcer and told him, "I'll wrestle him."

I couldn't believe it. The crowd cheered, we cheered and Daddy whooped loud. This was the best thing I had ever been about to see.

Rubin climbed into that cage. The bear and Rubin started circling. The bear had done this before so he stood right up on his hind legs and waited for the big blond man to make a move. Rubin lunged up under him and held onto him under the bear's front legs. Rubin's face turned red and he was sweating. His arms looked like they were straining. They danced around for a little while and then Rubin let go, he was breathing hard and didn't take his eye off the bear.

"Don't give up so soon, young fella," the announcer told Rubin.

"I ain't ever give up," Rubin told him. The announcer had made him mad, and the crowd cheered again. Rubin mad was something to see.

Rubin moved up on the bear and tried to get an arm over the top of the bear's head. He got a thumb right near the bear's muzzle at the back of his mouth.

"Watch that finger, son, that bear will bite it clean off. Don't get around that muzzle." The announcer was keeping a close eye on the fight.

Rubin didn't even look up. The bear ducked and grabbed Rubin around the middle in the bear hug. We could see the power that the bear had in his body. Rubin had his teeth gritted but he didn't let the bear knock him down. They split apart again and then Rubin went low with a lunge. The bear went down on all fours. Rubin got down low and they circled around with the bear on his feet and Rubin on his knees. The bear's head bobbed up and down. Rubin grabbed the bear tight and put his body into the side of the bear. He was a little higher than the bear and used his legs to push. Teddy the Bear all of a sudden went down on his side. Rubin moved fast and got the bear pinned on his back by lying across him.

Daddy whooped and me and the other kids screamed our heads off. Hoyt Lynn and the girls jumped up and down, clapping. Rubin had thrown the bear!

"Ladies and Gentlemen, this young man has thrown the bear and earned himself one dollar! They make 'em tough in the South! Don't they folks?"

The crowd cheered Rubin and he looked strong and proud. I knew he was feeling pretty cocky when he told the man,

"Let's go again."

"Ladies and Gentlemen, he wants to go again!"

Everybody went crazy. Hoyt Lynn moved closer to the cage and was all eyes. Rubin climbed back in and went after Teddy the Bear for the second time. It was almost as wild as the first round and he threw the bear again. The third time, we were all pretty sure he could whip the bear, and he did. The fourth time we started thinking about ways to spend Rubin's winnings. The fifth time, the crowd started drifting away. After the sixth, Rubin wasn't allowed in the cage any more.

Rubin was winded and sat down on a stump in the yard. He was breathing hard but grinning from ear to ear. I knew how he felt. I knew when I beat somebody at something I knew nobody was better than me. He told us how bad that bear stunk when he got his face in his fur. He said his thumb had got wet from the spit of that bear when he almost put it in the bears mouth. Men came around and beat him on the back, talking about how fine he had done.

Daddy collected Rubin's money and told us we could all get a soda pop at the store. Rubin didn't ask Daddy for his money, he knew Daddy figured what Rubin earned was Daddy's.

Daddy told him, "Mighty good, son."

"Thank you, Daddy."

Louie grinned and told him, "I knew you were good for something." Rubin was feeling so good he didn't even get mad.

Saplings

I stood behind the pines on the edge of the clearing a ways off from the house. I watched Grandpa Miller walk around the stand of trees between his place and ours. He looked the pines up and down, over half of them were dead and the needles turned brown. I didn't know how I was going to get out of this.

I had thought building a log house was good idea when Sheron and I had gone out to play in the pine needles. The pines were each about six inches around and twenty feet tall, straight as a string. The more I looked at those saplings the more I knew they would make a good log house. Sheron tried to talk me out of it when I went to the shed and got a hand saw, she took off after I cut the first one. It took some time but before long I had almost a dozen of them sawed down.

I was sweating from the work and took a break. I laid down on the soft ground and looked at all my handiwork. I looked up over at Grandpa's place and saw him come out of his yard and turn to close the gate. I was far enough away from him that to talk we would have to holler at each other, but he didn't look my way and I kept quiet. It was right then that I knew cutting down those trees was a bad idea. When he went around the house to the other side of the yard, I stood up and threw down the saw.

I looked at all the cut trees and finally came up with something. I picked up one of the felled trees and propped it up against a tree I hadn't cut. It looked like it had never been down. I did that with all the trees. The tops were just jumbled together, but the trunks look nearly straight. Nobody could tell they weren't standing up on their own, until they turned brown.

Now Grandpa was walking into them to find out why. I watched him squat down and find the saw marks. He headed towards our house and he walked over the ladder bridge like a young man. I stayed in the woods.

Him and Daddy walked over to the trees together and I watched as Daddy and him bent down and looked at the bottoms of the trees. They talked some, mostly Grandpa and then he stomped back home. Daddy hollered for us boys. I didn't want to go, but I did.

Harry, Hoyt Lynn and me stood among the dying trees.

"Which one of you boys cut down Grandpa's trees?"

Harry was first to pipe up and say it wasn't him.

"I didn't do it, Daddy." Hoyt Lynn wasn't taking somebody else's whippin' if he could help it.

I didn't say anything.

Daddy looked at me, "You cut down those saplings, son?"

I couldn't see any way out. I explained to him my plans of a log house.

"Yore Grandpa's madder than a hornet. He likes to keep his place neat and he's told me to get after whichever one of y'all done it. So Alton, you get to cutting them up for fire wood. And son, don't chop down Grandpa's trees." Daddy winked at me and headed to the house.

I knew right then, Daddy didn't care about those trees at all. He didn't care much about keeping the place looking nice or about a dumb stand of saplings. He only got after me because Grandpa was having a fit. To Daddy, a house was just a place to get out of the weather. Seemed to me Daddy had the right idea of things. Since I hadn't got a whippin' I was glad I hadn't blamed it on Hoyt Lynn.

The South

I was twice as glad the next day when Daddy told us we could drive with him to Natchitoches to deliver a load of pulp wood. Louie and Rubin stayed working, so Harry and me could go. Being younger, I was in the middle, but there was lots of wind that came inside the cab through the open doors that cooled us off. We drove through town past the statue of the old colored man stooped and tipping his hat on the main street in Natchitoches. Daddy said it was called the Uncle Jack, the good darky.

As we pulled into the train yard, colored men were singing and loading railroad ties onto a flat car for the train. They weren't little men like the statue, but big and muscled. I watched as two of them, one on each end, threw the tie up to the flat car. They were dressed in tan pants and plaid shirts and wore hats. There was a lead man on the train car making sure the ties fit together tight. The men never looked up as they threw the ties. They sang a song with no words. Just sounds they sang together made music, kind of like the slow songs that we heard in New Town church. The sound of the tie hitting made a beat. If it hit right it made a solid smack sound, but if it didn't fit right the noise was lighter and sounded kind of hollow. When the tone was wrong they would hold up for a minute and the lead man would straighten the tie up. They never looked up to see, just listened and knew. They didn't talk, they just sang the music.

We unloaded the wood by hand ourselves, when we were done we started up the truck. I listened to that music for as long as I could but the noise from the motor drowned it out. We drove along the road with the sun shining on us as it broke through the shadows of the pine trees. The wind whistling through the cab kept us from talking and I kept hearing the music in my head. I couldn't sing like Daddy or the girls, but the sound of the colored man's music made me feel something, but I didn't know what it was.

Mama and the girls were working in the house when we got back. They had the radio on and were listening to Mama's stories. It was fun to listen to the loud footsteps and doors slamming that came from the speaker. At night the radio signal could travel pretty far and Daddy listened to a preacher called JW Morgan out of Del Rio, Texas.

We still snuck off to New Town church to listen to the preaching. Many times Daddy would preach for a while too. I wasn't sure if I liked the music better or watching people get the Holy Ghost. Sometimes with all the swaying and jumping I was sure they were going to break the benches.

For Sunday dinner we brought Brother Lynch, the preacher, and his family over to eat. Grandma and Grandpa Miller wouldn't come over if the colored people were at our house. That suited me just fine. The old folks sure would be in a snit for a few days. Daddy didn't pay them no mind.

We'd had our sweet potatoes in the ground for a few weeks when Grandpa Miller figured it was the right time for him to plow his own garden spot. Harry and me were outside on our side of the fence when we watched him come out and hook Old Dick the mule up with a single tree harness. He walked behind the mule with a metal plow to dig up the dirt. He plowed a couple of straight rows and then took the strap off his shoulder and looked our way

"You two look big enough to plow," he hollered at us.

"Yes sir." I didn't ever say anything else to Grandpa but yes sir. Harry just nodded at him and we stood up straight. I thought this might be a good time to get back in Grandpa's good graces.

He showed us how to get behind the mule, hold the reins and to follow the row he had made so they would stay straight. Harry thought I ought to go first. He'd watch and make sure I did it right. I watched Grandpa and listened and I figured I could do it. I put the strap over my shoulder, and acting as big as I could, hollered loud to Old Dick, "Giddap!"

The mule took off and plodded through the dirt. I kept the plow straight and turned him at the end and made another row. I said 'gee' for right and 'haw' for left. Grandpa watched me for a while until he figured I could do it good enough. I kept my eye on the plow and heard the screen door slam as he went in the house. The mule heard it too.

As soon as Grandpa was gone, Old Dick became young again. He started pulling on the ropes and jumping. I tried to pull him straight, but he tossed his head, stomped his feet and made a turn and started walking. I pulled and said 'whoa' but he didn't care a thing about what I told him. He took off cross ways across the field. I couldn't keep up and fell face first in the dirt as I lost my handle on the reins. He tore up the neat rows me and Grandpa had made. I got up and tried to run the mule down, I got my hands on the trailing reins but all I could do was run behind hollering 'Whoa, Whoa!"

That red mule took me and the plow through the boards and wire that held up green beans and tore them all out of the ground. Harry ran alongside me hollering 'whoa' with me. The mule snorted and stomped. He came to a fast stop when the screen door slammed and Grandpa came out.

"You gall darn ignorant boy. What did you do? I can't leave you to do anything that you don't tear up. Let loose of those ropes and skedaddle back home. Both of ya."

He walked over to the mule patted his neck and started walking towards the field. The mule followed right behind him. When the mule walked by me he snorted and tossed his head.

It was a tough thing to be outsmarted by a mule.

Grown up Ideas

Mama killed two chickens, fried them up and with all the potatoes and gravy we had enough to feed everybody. The house was filled with all Mama's kids and she was happy with us together.

Elaine and Don and their new baby had come driving up in a black, four door '51 Pontiac about noon time when we were having dinner. Mama had held on to Elaine for a while. Sheron and Esther fussed over who got to hold the baby. Elaine had called to the store in town and left Mama a message they were coming, but we didn't know which day they would get here. So when they drove up we all ran to meet them. Harry shook hands with Don so I did too.

"The baby didn't have any trouble on the trip at all," Elaine told Mama.

"She's as pretty as a picture," Mama said as she held to her first grandbaby. With everyone together we were having a big time.

After we ate, it was still daylight outside so the men went out on the front porch. Don was outside looking the place over. He talked a lot, mostly about himself. He had a big job in Oregon working for a lumber company that sounded like "Warehouser." He seemed pretty full of himself. Louie listened to what he had to say and seemed interested in the work up in Oregon. With all the visiting, Daddy didn't read the Bible that night. Harry, Hoyt and me lay down with a blanket on the floor. With the company, we lost our bed.

In the morning the girls got our breakfast and I managed to get some of Mama's oatmeal down. She was feeding that to us a lot since she was getting new dishes out of oatmeal cans. Over time we had broken quite a few of Mama's unbreakable dishes and lost some too. *Mother's Oats* came with white dishes inside with the grain. Mama could tell what was inside by a drawing on the side, a cup, a bowl or saucer and she was working on putting together a new set of dishes.

The girls were busy in the house having a hen party. Don went to work with the men and I was left with Hoyt Lynn. I figured I would walk down to the road that went into town and look in the ditch for bottles to sell at Bobby Cooper's store. I let Hoyt go with me but since he was just eight, I made him get the bottles that were floating in the green water. We both walked back with a pocketful of candy.

Back at the house, we messed around making a phone out of green bean cans. We tied a string in the ends of the cans and stretched the string tight and when we talked into it our voice carried over the line. Mama came out of the house with all the girls and said they were heading over the ladder bridge to Grandma's to visit. I sure didn't want to go over with them. She wouldn't let us drink out of her fancy glasses. She figured we would break one of them. I didn't want to drink out of them anyway. It didn't bother me to dip water out of the kitchen bucket.

Hoyt Lynn stayed around the house and pretty soon Sheron came back. She could only be in the house with the girls so long before her tomboy ways got the best of her. I went to the outhouse and was shocked to see a roll of bright white toilet paper. There was catalog paper on the board too, but I hadn't seen toilet paper before Elaine showed up.

"Sheron!" I hollered.

She came out the back of the house and saw me holding that toilet paper.

"How much paper do you think is wound up in here? Hold onto the end and let's unwind it."

She walked to a tree and held the paper up against it. I circled the tree with the roll and then walked to another tree. I wrapped it around that tree and went to the next tree. Sheron quit holding the end when there was enough paper wrapped around the tree to hold it up. I was careful to not pull it too hard and break it. We walked from tree to tree until the roll ran out.

Sheron looked at the toilet paper wrapped around the trees in the yard. There was a lot of it. Some of it was starting to tear and fall down. About that time Mama walked up and just stared at the white toilet paper all over the trees. Sheron wasn't anywhere to be found. Elaine walked up beside Mama and then looked over at me and said, "Alton. What have you done?"

"Ah, it's not hurt." I started tearing the paper off the trees rolling it back up. The wad got bigger and bigger, it had dirt and little twigs in it, but I figured you could shake that out. I put the big wad back in the outhouse.

Elaine hollered at me, "Can't Mama have anything nice?"

Elaine sure had gotten fancy.

Losing Kids

It wasn't just the toilet paper. Elaine had different ideas about a lot of things. Just about every day, the older kids and Don spent time talking outside. Most of the time they were complaining about the old way Daddy did things and thinking they had a better plan. Louie talked about how hard Daddy could be. I tried to keep my surprise from

210

showing. I hadn't had any notion of how they felt about Daddy's ways.

"I know how you feel, Louie. The folks want to work you like a grown up, but you have to answer to them like you're a kid," Elaine was telling him.

"I'm thinking I could go into the service. Uncle Huey told me that it'd be the place to learn a different trade," Rubin said.

"It'd be good to do something on my own. Get away from Daddy and all this." Louie had his foot propped against the step of the log truck. We all knew Louie couldn't join the service because of his leg, so he had to look for something else.

"Come back to Cottage Grove with us, Louie. There is plenty of work there. You can stay with us." Don was ready to help Louie out of here. I knew to keep my mouth shut about what I had heard. That was a big part of getting to hang around the older kids. No tattling.

With the older kids backing him up, Rubin talked to Daddy about joining the service. Daddy was against it, but Rubin kept talking to him about it. Whenever Uncle Huey came over he talked to Daddy about it too, which I wasn't sure helped too much. Grandma and Grandpa Mac were on Rubin's side and after a while Daddy started listening to the talk a little more. Rubin told Daddy how the recruiter in Natchitoches was promising him all kinds of things.

One night I heard Daddy talking to Mama. He was going to tell Rubin that if he could cover the labor Daddy would be losing with him leaving, he would let him go. Mama said, 'Yes, Wesley." They never did fight with each other. Seemed like Mama always agreed with Daddy.

It had been a few nights since I had heard Daddy talking to Mama about letting Rubin leave. Rubin had quit bringing it up, he figured Daddy would talk about it in his own time. We all knew you didn't ask a grown up why or when, you barely asked how if you didn't know. They expected you to watch and learn and keep quiet.

Mama was the one that brought it up, "Rubin, you sure about the Air Force?"

"Mama, if I go in the Air Force I could fly. I would get a steady wage and learn something other than sawmills."

"Sawmillin's a good living," Daddy said defending his trade.

"I know that, Daddy, but I could learn something else too. I promise to send enough money home to make up for what you would make if I was still working for you."

"I figure that would be about $25 a month. Yore mama and me will sign those papers for you to go if you'll send that till you turn eighteen."

It wasn't no time and we were at the bus station in Natchitoches watching Rubin get on the bus with a bunch of other boys. He waved out the window to Mama. The old bus started down the road chugging along, all of us waving to it until we lost sight of it around the curve in the road.

"I just don't want him to get hurt," Mama said to us.

I guess she had forgot he could wrestle a bear. I hadn't ever seen him hurt yet.

While Elaine was still visiting, we went out to Mama's folks, Grandma and Grandpa Mac's, to visit. It was always a little more fun there than Grandma Miller's. We could chase the rooster, we were never too loud, and we could play in the pond. Since I had my canvas shoes now I didn't mind the poop and spit in the yard either.

They had a big water tank taller than Daddy that collected rainwater. It set out on the back porch of the house and held the rain water that came off the house. There was a spigot at the bottom that you turned to get the water in a bucket, and if we wanted running water we could put a hose to it. This way they didn't always have to draw from the well.

It was dark inside Grandma Mac's house since the walls were covered with burlap and cardboard. They just added layers to cover the cracks in the dark weathered boards. For pictures they used advertisements from the catalog that Grandma thought was pretty. They didn't have electricity, but I guess they didn't need it. They had lanterns and to listen to music she had a Victrola. Its cylinder had a song on it that she would wind up to play for us. She played a song for Elaine's baby and sat down in her rocker. Mama bounced the baby in her lap and talked to Grandma.

"When I hold this baby, I think of my own little baby I hope to hold again someday." Mama was talking of her baby Lyndol Rae who had died before I was born.

"You can hold your baby again, Fonny, and your own Mama can hold onto to you, too." Grandma spit brown juice into the fireplace. She still had her old brown high top tennis shoes that stuck out from under her skirt. Her gray hair was put into a bun, but long hanks of hair hung out of it, so she used pins to hold it back.

"I hope someday to see my Mama and know what she looks like. What a fine day that'll be," Mama agreed.

Fleaty McDonald

I looked from Mama to Grandma and couldn't believe what I was learning. Grandma wasn't Mama's own mother?

"Your mama is dead?" I asked Mama. She told me how her mother, Fleaty, had died at twenty-six when mama was two and half years old. Grandpa married Fleaty's best

213

friend, who I knew as Grandma Mac. She had raised Fleaty's two children, Mama and Uncle Curtis, as her own and had two more, Uncle Huey and Uncle Milton, her half-brothers.

"It's the Pernicious Anemia that got 'em. Puts a weakness in the blood. We're lucky Fleaty lived long enough to have you. Lucky that it don't weaken you more than it does, Fonny," Grandma took the baby.

"Oh, sometimes I get so tired, I just have to lay down a few minutes in the day, but if I get down too much, I go get a vitamin shot and that strengthens me for a long time," Mama told her.

I hadn't ever known Mama to ever let on like she was tired and wasn't sure I had ever seen her lay down in the day. If she did, it wasn't when I was around.

We weren't grandma's blood grandkids but she had never treated us any different from any of the cousins. I guess Grandma was Grandma and since it didn't matter to nobody if we weren't blood, it didn't matter to me. When we left she sent Mama with tomatoes from her garden and a big jug of ribbon cane syrup.

Mama made a big supper that night for us all. It was time for Elaine and Don to head back to Oregon with the baby and they were leaving after we ate. Daddy talked about the sweet potatoes getting ready to be dug. As soon as we got the crop in, Daddy would have enough money to buy his own sawmill.

I guess Louie couldn't hold back no longer and broke the news to Mama and Daddy. He was going to Oregon too. I knew the older kids had all talked about it, but I didn't know if Louie would really leave Daddy. Mama sure didn't want Louie to go, but she knew she couldn't make him stay. Louie was nineteen and ready to step out. Daddy didn't say anything at all. All Louie had was a change of clothes so it didn't take long for him to get ready.

214

We stood out in the yard and watched them leave.

Daddy finally spoke, "If I'd a known this was comin', I'd a never let Rubin leave."

I felt kind of funny inside. I had kept the older kids secret, and now Daddy was left with just me and Harry for labor. I wasn't sure if I had done the right thing, not letting on to Daddy about what I knew. I figured right then, no matter what, I'd work hard enough for Daddy to make up for it. I was thirteen years old and it was time I started earning my keep. Daddy walked back in the house and I stood outside, alone, and watched the red tail lights disappear around the curve in the road.

Sugar Cane

Sweat ran from my hair, down my back and soaked my clothes. I kept wiping the palms of my hands on my britches to dry them off before I lifted my end of the log. Harry had the other end and we lifted it together, put it on our shoulders and carried it to the truck. Harry and me loaded the first few layers of pulp wood, and then Daddy and Wilmer took over when the load got too high for us.

Harry and me were the oldest at home now, and working in the woods with Daddy fell to us. I didn't mind the work as much as I hated the heat. Folks in Louisiana didn't think much about how hot and sticky it was. I figured they hadn't been anywhere else and didn't know better, but I had been somewhere else and I did know better. Somehow that made it worse.

Close to dark, we packed up. Daddy and Wilmer got in the cab of the truck and me and Harry rode on the logs. Daddy stopped off at Wilmer's road and let him off. Harry and me stayed where we were, using the wind to dry the sweat off of us. Mama and the girls had supper fixed. Hoyt

215

Lynn tried to act big and loud when we got in. The girls all took turns trying to boss him around, when he'd had enough he'd pull somebody's hair or pinch them. The girls would run to Mama and before the night was over, Hoyt Lynn would get whipped.

There was a knock at the screen door and Ronnie McAlester stuck his head in. Ronnie was about sixteen or seventeen, a couple of years older than Harry, but they ran around together in town.

"Hidy, Miz Miller. Mr. Miller."

"Come on in, Ronnie, you want some cornbread and milk?" Mama offered him a big triangle left on the plate.

"Why, I believe I will," Ronnie took the cup full of cornbread and milk, salted it good and sat at the table.

"What're you doin' runnin' around, boy?" Daddy asked him.

"Me and some of the fellers are goin' coon huntin' tonight, wondered if Harry might want to come with us. You're invited too, Mr. Miller, if y'all all want to come."

"I guess it'd be all right if Harry went with y'all. But if you boys stay out all night, you still gotta work tomorrow, no lazin' about," Daddy warned Harry. We knew Daddy wasn't a hunter. We didn't figure he'd go.

"Alton, you go with 'em too. You help keep everybody out of trouble," Mama looked at us. I didn't know what Mama thought I could do, Harry was older than me and that meant I couldn't boss him. But if she thought I could, I was just as glad. I was getting to go with the boys and that made me seem awful big. Ronnie gulped down his cornbread.

Harry and me lost our tired and were fired up when we jumped in Ronnie's pickup, Harry in the cab and me in the bed. We were halfway down the road when I remembered we hadn't taken the gun.

216

We made a stop at Bobby Cooper's house, a big old time house with a breezeway that separated the two sides. Bobby jumped in the back with me and then we drove down a dirt road and stopped at a wide spot. The boys got out, lit up some cigarettes and started talking. That's when I learned we weren't going coon hunting.

"That damn AC Valentine ain't nothin' but a scavenger. We aim to play a trick on him tonight," Ronnie said as we stood in the beams of the head lights.

AC Valentine was a sugar cane farmer that lived down the road from us. When he had a crop ready he would use a big press in his yard to squeeze the juice out of the pulp. It was two big stones with long poles attached. He harnessed mules to the four poles. They walked around in a circle and the stones mashed the sugar cane pulp and the juice ran out. Sugar Cane was a big crop around here. It took about a year to grow so when a crop was ready it was a big deal.

When sugar cane grew it was green on the outside and got darker as it got ripe. Inside, the sugar cane had a whitish green pulp that was stringy, when we chewed on it the sugar came out and was so good. It was a treat to have someone cut off a couple of inches of it and let us chew on it. The juice would mash out in our mouth. When we had all of the sweet juice chewed out of the pulp we spit that out and started again with a new piece.

I guess it took so long for sugar cane to get ready AC had to come up with other things to make a living. He was always looking to get something for nothing. He was notorious for finding watermelons growing in a bottom and snatching them, no matter who was growing them. He had swiped some of Ronnie's daddy's watermelons and Ronnie was going to get back at AC.

Bobby had told AC he knew where they could get their hands on some sugar cane that was ready to cut. He told

217

us Ol' AC was chomping at the bit to steal some cane. We were going to go pick him up and play a trick on him.

AC was waiting outside when we drove up to get him. He had on overalls, the side buttons unfastened. He didn't wear a shirt and his gut hung low. He got in the front of the pickup and the other boys got in back with me. We took a dirt road up the hill towards the McAlester's. We drove down a couple of dirt roads, made a bunch of turns and got AC all turned around in the darkness. There wasn't anything darker than a thick, coal black night in Louisiana.

Ronnie brought the truck to a stop and we all jumped out and started chopping sugar cane. We used big knives and sickles. AC chopped like a crazy man, excited to be getting somebody else's sugar cane for himself. We chopped it and loaded it into the bed of the truck. When we had a load, Ronnie and AC got in the cab and the three of us sat on top of the cane in the back. Ronnie took off down the road and used the dirt road that AC used. When we drove up into the AC's own yard he finally figured out that he'd cut down his own cane.

AC jumped out of the truck and started cussing us with words I hadn't ever heard before. When he saw that we had got one over on him, he grabbed a big knife from the bed and held it up in the air as if he was going to bring it down on us. Harry laughed at him, so I did too. Bobby jumped in the front with Ronnie; he gassed that little pickup and just about slung me and Harry out the back. We left AC's yard on two wheels. The best part was AC's cane was still in the truck.

We all hooped and hollered down the road. I loved the feel of the night air as we bumped along the dirt road. We knew we couldn't get in trouble. How could AC tell anybody about him trying to steal somebody else's sugar cane? I sure was glad Mama sent me along to keep everybody out of trouble.

Time to Harvest

Getting older might mean more work, but it also meant more fun too. I didn't mind that trade off at all. I guess it was a good thing not to mind work since there was plenty of it. Most days I worked the woods with Daddy. I felt like an older kid then. Other times when we didn't have to work I would bum around, try to find bottles to sell for moon pies and Nehis. I loved the taste of that grape Coke. Sometimes I took Sheron on my handle bars to her friend's to play in her daddy's sawdust pile. We climbed the big mound, tall as a house and rolled down. Sometimes we sat on a shovel and held onto the handle, sawdust going down our pants to stick to our skin.

School started up and since we had been around so long, I didn't have to fight 'cause I was the new kid. These kids told us we talked funny too. No matter where we went it seemed like we didn't talk like the folks around us. If we were in the West we talked like southerners, when we were in the South, we talked like westerners. I figured I would be like Daddy and just go my own way, no matter what.

When the weather finally turned cool, Daddy started looking at the sweet potatoes. It was time to dig them up. Mama packed a lunch and all of us headed down to the bottom to start. Their green tops were shining in the sunlight and the whole field sure looked pretty. Daddy hitched up the borrowed red mules to the plow. Mama brought boxes and baskets for us to put the potatoes in. After we got a basket full, we were to dump them onto the wooden wagon that Old Dick would pull up to the house.

Daddy used the plow to go deep and turn the dirt over to bring the sweet potatoes to the top. He started on the first row. I thought we would see the potatoes come up, but since they were the color of dirt it was hard to see them.

Daddy made a couple of passes with the mules and plowed three or four rows. He had the mules stop on the outside of the patch and Esther ran over with the water bucket and he took a big drink from the ladle.

"You kids get in where I have turned them up and started pullin' them out of the ground," Daddy said as he mopped his forehead with his big hanky. We started digging in the dirt. At five years old Mary just ran around and fell in the mounds of dirt, which was funny. I moved my hands around in the dirt and came up with was a little potato about the size of a peach. Harry was digging close to me and he came up with the same thing. We showed them to Daddy. He walked straight over to us and got in the dirt too. He worked around a patch of dirt and came up with another scrawny potato.

"Let me try another row here in the middle," he told Mama.

He plowed a few more rows while we dug at the rows he had already done. Nobody was coming up with a big six inch sweet potato like we were all looking for. Daddy pulled the mules clear and walked into the dirt and dug around and came up with the same puny potato.

"Confound it!" Daddy stood up and threw the potato. That was about the worst cussing I had ever heard Daddy say. All of us kids stayed quiet as he kicked around in the dirt.

"Wesley, let's gather what there is. Try a few more rows and see what we come up with." Mama had us put what we were finding into the basket anyway, not a one of them bigger than a peach or an apricot. We worked the plowed part of the patch all day and where there should have been ten or fifteen big sweet potatoes to a mound, there were two or three little bitty ones. Every tiny sweet potato made Daddy madder.

Grandpa Miller walked down to us and looked at what we were digging up. Daddy told him he couldn't figure what had happened. Grandpa shook his finger at Daddy, "I told you when you was plantin' it was the wrong sign of the moon. You got to follow the signs."

That sure didn't make Daddy feel any better. I didn't know how the sign of the moon could keep sweet potatoes from growing and getting big, but I could see that it did. About all we had done was grow a pretty patch of sweet potato greens. It looked like Grandpa had been right.

Over the next few days we gathered up our little sweet potatoes and packed them on the wagon back to the house. The size of them meant we weren't going to be selling any. We ate a lot of them stewed up, fried and made into pie. Mama gave them away to anybody that would take some. That failed crop was a big loss for Daddy and all the plans we had for the money that wasn't going to come in.

Daddy figured on doing exactly what he usually did. It was time to go.

Wichita Falls

Daddy wound the engine up; we were headed out of town. We were in a slick green '49 Ford pickup with a black tarpaper house on the back. It had an engine that Daddy told us could really 'go'. We were headed to Oregon. With Louie and Don Smith having good jobs, Daddy figured he could find work there too.

I had heard Daddy tell Mama, "We got $56. That'll be enough to get us there."

It sounded like more than enough to me!

Daddy had built the house in the bed of the pickup. He took four wood posts and put them in the corners and layered boards across them on the sides. He left an open spot on each side and used old car windows for glass like he had done before. He even put a window where we could see into the cab of the pickup too. A curved post was put across the top of the standing posts on the front of the bed and on the back.

I watched him as he hewed the post with a hand axe and he hit the same spot every time. Boards were hammered from end to end to make a roof. Then he took tar paper and tacked it all over to make it water proof. He hammered little silver dollar sized circles of tin every foot or so to keep the tar paper from tearing in the wind. He ran boards across the back and made an opening for the door. He latched the door on with nails and rubber and used the tail gate to keep the door shut. When he'd got the pickup ready, Mama was ready.

Harry got to ride in front with Mama and Daddy, the rest of us climbed in back of our tarpaper house. Along with the usual bags of rice and beans, piles of sweet potatoes were stored under the benches Daddy had made along the sides. We could sit on them or lay down. Mama had a little kerosene stove she loaded in the back. It wasn't too awful cold here, but it could get that way as we went north.

Houses, shacks and farms went by as we looked from the side windows. I watched the piney woods give way to grassy hills the longer we drove and knew we were in Texas. Mama wanted to see Rubin who was in Wichita Falls. Since it was a different road, Daddy stopped at a service station and got some free maps to help us. Harry got in the back and gave me a turn sitting up front, Mama in the middle, of course.

The road through Dallas was further north than Highway 84, our regular trail. We had to turn off and we watched for the signs to tell us where. Mama started to look hard out the window. We went by farms and ranches and one looked just like another.

Suddenly, Mama started and said, "Wesley, we have gone by that same black horse three times." No wonder it all looked the same.

Mama looked over the map again and figured out we had been missing the turn to get off a big looping road that went around Dallas.

"Blast it, we've been drivin' around in circles!" Daddy was aggravated at himself.

"At least we got to see some new country," Mama tried to soothe him.

I had never been any place like the Air Force Base where we found Rubin. Everything was in a row. Men stood straight up and nobody had a smile on their face. Daddy spent some time talking to the man that stood outside the little shack to get in. After quite a while, and a lot of arm waving by Daddy, they opened the gate for us.

We got to go inside a visiting room and we all went crazy when Rubin walked in. His blonde hair was cut so short it was hard to see. He had on a tan colored uniform and under his buttoned-down shirt wore a white t-shirt. He hugged all the girls, and I could tell he was tickled to see us.

"Oh, they treated us like kings when we left Natchitoches on that bus," Rubin said. "We got to Shreveport and they put us up in a motel. There were a couple of beds to a room and all the bathrooms were inside. That's where we filled out the final paperwork and once we signed on the dotted line things changed. They knew they had us then. Down to San Antonio to boot camp and back to being nobody."

He laughed while he told us. Rubin had written and told Mama about his boot camp in San Antonio and then being sent to Wichita Falls. He had wanted to fly and he figured he would someday. Right now he was working on the airplane engines. We spent some time with him and then

223

Daddy was ready to go. We all got up to leave. Mama asked if he could use some sweet potatoes, but he told her no, they had enough to eat. I was beginning to think Mama was about sick of those things, but she never would let on if it was true. Daddy had Mama study the map as we left, he didn't plan on getting lost again.

A Dark Ride

In New Mexico Daddy got back to the roads we knew. When we would drive alongside a train, Daddy would see the hoboes riding in the open box car and always honk and lift his arm high out the window to wave. They lifted their arms back and I always waved too. I pictured Daddy as a young man riding along side of them. He looked a lot like me.

We camped at night and ate at the same roadside tables that we had on trips from before. Daddy knew where to find the creeks, the shade, and the best places to camp. At night it was cold so Mama and Daddy and the little kids slept in the camper and Harry and me rolled up in our blankets on the ground. We listened to the sound of cars moving in the night and I wondered if those folks were going to far off places, just like us. The stars were bright in the black sky and I liked being covered up by all that darkness.

When we went through Utah the wind blew and the little camper was chilly all the time. We stopped at Wendover, on the state line between Utah and Nevada. Mama said we could light the little kerosene heater in the back to stay warm. We had to take turns holding onto the stove handle so it wouldn't fall over. Nobody wanted to hold themselves and the stove up as the truck swayed and bounced over the road. Since I was oldest in the back I held onto it most of the time, but Sheron and Esther took turns with me.

224

We rode between mountain ranges and could see each of them out the side windows in the camper. There was nothing out in the big valley it seemed, but us and the skinny road. We made it to Ely. It had a park in town with tall trees that someone must have planted a long time ago and we ate some bread and butter. We finally went west and could see there were still mountains to cross up ahead.

The sunlight got dimmer as the day went on and it made it easier to go to sleep. The stove kept us a little warmer and we just sat around it and rode. Sheron laid down with Hoyt Lynn and Esther hugged up Mary and they all went to sleep. I dozed off a little and kept the stove standing up. I felt the pickup getting off the road and looked up at the window. The day sure had gone by fast. It was dark inside and out. We heard the tailgate open and Mama opened up the door. She looked inside and her eyes got really big as she looked at us.

"You kids get out of there right away!" She was almost hollering, but I knew she couldn't be, Mama never hollered.

I got up first and crawled out. I blinked at the brightness. The kids came out behind me and that's when we saw what had got Mama so upset. All of our faces, hands and clothes were covered in black soot. Everybody looked funny with their white eyes and teeth shining past their black faces. Esther tried to wipe her clothes off, but that black was stuck on. All the blankets; the bags of food, every square inch was covered in black smoke. The windows had gotten covered in it so sunlight couldn't shine in.

Mama fussed about how dirty we all were and how dirty everything we owned was. We tried to clean ourselves up with what water we had, but it just about wouldn't come off.

It wasn't often that Mama lost her temper, but she grabbed that kerosene heater and marched it out to the fence on the right of way and left it right there.

"That stove is not getting back in this truck!"

Mama cooked our supper with the girls and talked out loud, "When I think what could have happened with all that bad air in there." She seemed to be worried, upset, and mad all at the same time. She kept checking on us, looking in our eyes and wondering if we had a headache. Daddy told her everybody was all right. She just shook her head said 'Praise God' over and over. Nobody knew what to think. We hadn't seen Mama upset very much.

When we drove away from that roadside we left that kerosene heater right where Mama had left it, propped against the fence. Not even Daddy dared get it and we made sure not to complain about the cold. Nobody wanted Mama getting mad all over again.

We stopped at Fallon to get some more gas. There were mountain ranges in the distance and Daddy told us California was close by. We drove by a big dark hill that had a light colored spot in the middle of it just before we crossed the state line into California. Trees started getting thicker and the hills were more like mountains. The road wound through tall trees and all we could see were evergreens out the side windows.

Daddy drove just about all the time and it seemed like he never slept. When we stopped he would get out, stretch his legs and find a tree to lean up against to doze off. He used the truck to rest against when there wasn't anything else. Every time we stopped we tried to scrub more of the black off. The water sure was cold, but Mama told us to hush and we kept scrubbing. Daddy said we looked like a bunch of raccoons.

We climbed the mountains at the California line going into Oregon. The truck made a lot of noise as it pulled the mountains. Daddy said it was working hard and he would pull over after a long climb and give her a breather. He let the motor cool off and the transmission too. We crawled up the mountain and crawled back down the other side. The further north we went, the hills rounded out and there were a lot of meadows and stands of evergreens.

Crossing the Siskiyou's, the pickup gave out. The engine quit and silently the pickup began to roll to a stop. Daddy steered us off to the side of the road as we coasted and put us in the widest part of the shoulder. The car behind us pulled over and the man came and talked to Daddy. He would take Daddy to Ashland, the next town, to get help. Daddy was sure he could find Louie.

Daddy told us all to mind Mama and left. We ate our dinner and played around while we waited for help. Before dark, a big hay truck drove up. Louie jumped out of the cab and Daddy stepped out of the passenger side. It looked like we'd be rolling back into Ashland at the end of a tow rope. At least we weren't walking.

OREGON 1959

Setting Up House

A few days later Daddy took us to the new house he had found for us to live in. Mama got out of the pickup and just looked without saying a thing. We were in a clearing just off the road, back by the trees. I hadn't ever seen anything like it to live in.

"A train car, Wesley?" Mama asked as she shielded her eyes with her hand. Long and narrow, one end sunk down in the mud, the train car looked a mile long.

"Fonny, it's the dining car. So there is the makin's for a kitchen, and plenty of room to rope off bedrooms," he told her and starting walking towards it. Mama, seeing there wasn't nothing to do but follow Daddy, fell in behind him.

I ran on ahead, Sheron and Esther right behind. The step up to go in was high, so we jumped in the waist high doorway and hooked a leg inside. Daddy found a block to put down in front of the steps and Mama climbed inside. It was a long empty shell eight feet wide and about forty feet long. There were windows from one end to the other on both sides, most of them weren't busted. Mama walked about half way down and turned to Daddy,

"All these windows sure do let in the warm sunshine. I don't believe I've ever lived in a place so bright."

229

"You like this, Mama?" Esther asked. I didn't know how she couldn't like it. All Daddy's train stories and now we got to live in a train car. It was about as good as being one of the hobos me and Daddy always waved at.

"Y'all start bringing things in," Daddy told the kids.

"Not yet. We're going to move it first," Mama told him.

The train car wasn't on level ground and it stayed muddy back in the shade of the trees. Mama showed Daddy where she wanted it and he figured out a plan. Maybe this wasn't going to be so great.

Daddy brought in some logs with a two ton Dodge truck that he used at work. He sat the logs in front of the train car and jacked it up with a house jack. He used the Dodge truck and pulled the train car onto the first seven or eight logs, leaving some in the front. Then he moved the jack and raised up the train in the middle. We added more logs and the Dodge pulled the car up on them until the whole train car was up on the log road.

Slowly, Daddy dragged the car. When the first log came out from under the train car at the back Harry and me lifted and toted it to the front of the log road for the train to roll on. We had to be fast, Daddy didn't want the Dodge to stop moving because it was too hard on it to stop and start up again with all the weight. We never stopped running as we picked up the next log and moved it to the front while the truck creeped along. When Daddy finally let the Dodge come to stop, Harry and me both fell on the ground, winded and wore out. The girls brought us water from the bucket and laughed as they poured the dipper out on our faces. I didn't even move.

Daddy got out of the truck and walked over to where Harry and me laying.

"All we gotta do now boys, is jack her up and take all the logs out from under. Get to movin." I raised my head up and looked at Harry. He stayed where he was till he heard Daddy clear his throat. He sure got up then.

How to Live

After a few days Daddy had Mama set up with a stove to cook, a place to lay down, and table to eat on. It was time to get to work that paid. We were making pilings. Daddy hauled green logs, sixty feet long, with the Dodge and a trailer. Harry and me peeled the logs. We each had a log that we worked on. Each log was put up on skids and we took the flat side of an axe and hit the log on the side. That knocked off about a foot of bark at a time until we got to the end. When the log was green the bark fell right off, but only when it was fresh cut because there was juice between the log and the bark. It didn't work any other time. When we cleared all the bark off fifteen or twenty poles we had a load. Daddy would sell them as high line poles.

On the days Daddy was gone with the poles sometimes I got to ride with Louie in his hay truck. We went to the farm and we loaded hay with Bobby Thunderbird. We loaded fifteen hundred bales of hay, sold it from farms to stores, unloading some at each place, 'til we were empty. I worked hard to buck as much hay as they did. I didn't want Louie thinking I was a kid. I felt almost grown riding along side of him with the window down. I hooked my arm out the window like Louie and we cut up all day long. I kept his secret from Mama that he was cussing and smoking cigarettes. Sometimes he gave me one too. Feeling grown up sure was worth the work that went with it.

When school started I couldn't go with Louie too often. Down the highway from the house there was a man

231

with a second hand store and I got a job with him. He would take in people's old furniture, fix it up and then sell it. I was in charge of painting and the old man loved the color silver. Everything he gave me to paint-the old head boards and dressers, tables and even bicycles-was all to be painted silver from end to end, top to bottom. I liked silver too so I thought it all looked good. He didn't pay me money but gave me things from the store. I brought little kitchen gadgets for Mama mostly. I asked him for a harmonica and he told me I could have it.

I sure did want to play it. The older kids could sing and play and I loved the music they made. I never could sing as pretty as they did, and I couldn't figure out the keys on the piano or the valves on horns. I just knew I would be able to figure out how to play the harmonica and then I could play and sing with them. I carried my harmonica with me everywhere and every time I got a chance I worked on learning to play a song. I didn't let nobody hear me though. I didn't want them watching me try. I tried to play it during school at recess, but kids kept coming around so I quit. Harry wanted me to play football with the boys anyway so I did that instead.

I didn't have to fight much at school. Harry and me were both thin, and I wasn't very tall, but I think those boys could tell we were strong. I always looked like I was tough with my broken front tooth anyway, so nobody tried to push us around, even if we were new.

Harry was good at throwing and I was fast at running, so when we played football I caught all his balls. If it could be caught, I made sure I got it, no matter what. Harry hiked the ball and I took off down the field. I turned around and was running backwards waiting for the ball. I had to catch it over my head and when I fell to the ground I drove a stick through my wrist. It hurt so bad it took my breath away, but since there were girls watching I acted like I was fine. A teacher came over and took a look at it and had me go to the nurse.

I had never been in a place like the nurse's office. Everything was white, even her shoes. She took a ball of cotton and dabbed it in what looked like water, but when she put it to bloody hole in my wrist if burned like fire. I blinked fast to keep my eyes from watering. No wonder we didn't believe in going to the doctor. She asked me if I was all right and told her I was, even though I wasn't. She wrapped it up with some tape that was white too and wrote a note for me to take to my folks. She said I should get stiches from a doctor. I never was so glad to get out of a place.

When I showed up from school I went in to Mama and showed her my wrist. I gave Mama the note from the nurse. She looked it over good and when Daddy got back from work she told him about it. He didn't look at it but that night the family prayed for me.

I had broken that darn rule about not getting hurt and now Mama wouldn't let me play football. A few days later the nurse had me come to her office and asked if I had stitches. I told her no, that we didn't go to the doctor. She looked at me funny, but sent me back to class. A class I didn't like at all.

It was taught by a dried up, mean old man. If he caught somebody talking, not paying attention, or messing around, he would make them go out in the hall. He would follow after a little bit and then we would hear him hollering. My name got called one day when I was cutting up with a buddy and out to the hall he sent me. I stood out there for a while by myself and then he came out to yell at me. I stood there and just looked at him, hoping the spit that came out of his mouth wouldn't get on me. He got red faced and madder until he shoved me and pushed me while he yelled. I stepped back and he stepped closer. He was hollering at me close to my face when his hand came up and he hit me upside the head.

Before I knew what happened I hit him right back in the face with my fist. He stopped yelling and looked at me like he couldn't believe it. I couldn't believe it either. He grabbed a hold of his face with his hand and before he could say a word, I ran. I ran down the hall, through the doors, and across the school yard. I left that school at a dead run, hoofing it till I couldn't see the building when I looked behind me. This was one time when I knew I was in trouble right off.

I didn't go straight to the house because Mama would have known something was up. I loafed around in town until it was time for school to be out and then walked with the rest of the kids. Harry wanted to know all about it, and when I told him he couldn't stop laughing. He thought that was greatest thing I had ever done. The girls were worried sick over what was going to happen; even Hoyt Lynn didn't say anything to Mama. When a big, blue Mercury drove up to the house, I figured it was over for me.

Daddy walked out to meet the principal as he got out of the car. I stayed in the house, but I could hear them talk. A lady got out on the other side; I had seen her at the school before, some sort of a secretary.

"Mr. Miller, there was an incident today at school with one of your children. Alton struck a teacher in the face."

"Our boy hit a teacher?" Daddy couldn't believe it.

"Maybe they'll expel ya," Harry said to me. "Wouldn't be like a punishment at all." That made me think. Maybe this was all going come out okay after all.

"Alton!" Daddy hollered at me. It wasn't going to be okay. I jumped down the step of the train car and stood as far away as I could get away with.

"I am sure you know that that sort of thing cannot go unpunished." The principal kept telling Daddy how awful my behavior had been. The lady looked at the train car, at all us kids and wrote something down on a paper.

"If Alton will come tomorrow and apologize to Mr. Peters, we will allow him back in school, but only upon your assurance that this sort of thing will not happen again," the principal offered Daddy. How was I going to say sorry to that mean old cuss? I didn't know if I could.

"It won't happen again, will it, son? You'll say sorry tomorrow." Daddy gave me that look that meant this wasn't over.

"Yes, sir."

After the principal left I got my whippin'. Mama and Daddy just didn't allow kids to not respect their elders. Even when Daddy brought his belt down on my backside more times than I could count, I still wasn't sorry I had hit that old man.

I didn't like school before and I sure hated going now. Even after I told the teacher sorry, he had it out for me. I didn't do good in the classroom and the teacher made sure I felt dumb. It seemed like the best thing to do was to just not try and then I didn't look so bad.

The kids in school starting walking a wide path around me because of what I had done. If I was on the sidewalk, they gave way and stepped off. Nobody wanted to tangle with me. I might not shine in class and I might not make friends like Harry did, but I was known for being tough. In town, the boys from school would buy me a Coke and pat me on the back. I walked pretty tall.

After supper one night, when the girls were clearing the table, Mama pulled a letter from her apron pocket.

"A man came out here today, said he was from the county. He said he had been told we were livin' out here in this train car and he had come to see for himself. I told him he'd have to come back when you was home, so he dropped off this letter."

Mama sat down by Daddy and read him the letter to him. It said we couldn't live in the train car because it wasn't up to their code. I didn't know what kind of code there could be that told you where to live. It said some other things that I didn't understand. We all looked at Daddy.

He pounded his fist on the table, "Dad burn it! They ain't comin' out here and tellin' me how to live."

Mama looked back at the letter, "Says we got to move in two weeks, or they're going to come with the Sheriff. Says it's about the welfare of the children."

Daddy hit the table again. He read the Bible a long time that night.

Daddy didn't take somebody telling him what to do, so we didn't move in the two weeks. Another man came out and talked to us and Daddy ran him off. Daddy was fighting mad and waved his fist at the car when it left. But when the sheriff came, Daddy finally told him we would leave. Don Smith had told him about a job up by Cottage Grove. By the time we packed up the car to move, Daddy had decided leaving was his idea anyway.

Crit, Jesse, Jimmy and Ed

The scream of the saw drowned out any other noise so there was no talking as Daddy pushed the log through the saw. The first cut made a slab, a board with bark on the flat side. Harry was tail sawyer today and sent it down the roller bed and I threw it to the slab pile. The next cut would be a board. When it came off the saw Harry grabbed it and used the spike sticking up to pivot it and feed it to the edger. The edger sawed the boards into their widths, taking off any bark on the sides. The board rode down the roller bed and I

236

stacked it on the bundle. The bark strips were thrown into a pile and we would bring them to the house to use in the stove, once we got a house. As soon as we had enough boards we would work on that.

We hadn't stayed long at Cottage Grove, just enough to buy a grey '49 Ford panel truck with no side windows. It had two seats in the front and the back was empty. Howard Harpo hired Daddy out of there to work at Fossil. Harry drove us the three hundred miles in the Ford and Daddy followed in a flatbed truck with a gyppo mill on the back.

It took the better part of a day and a half to cross over the mountains to get to Fossil. When we got there we didn't really go into town. We headed to the mill site at Rosenbaum Canyon that was about thirty miles out. There wasn't anything there, just the dirt road we came in on and a creek to the right of us.

Daddy looked for the best slope to put the mill. It helped the logs roll down into place and the slabs, strips and sawdust were piled downhill. In the background we could hear the sound of the power saws in the woods. The cutters were already working.

Mama couldn't get her a house built until we had lumber so that meant the mill went up first. We lived out of the back of the panel truck and camped out. Daddy and us boys went about setting up the mill. Daddy set the saw cab first by bolting it to ties that were set on the ground. The saw cab held the main saw and the flywheels. To make it level he had me and Harry dig and bury the ties. He set the engine on the same kind of floor and made it level. He attached the belts from the flywheel to the engine and moved the motor until the belts got tight. He set the track next to the saw cab and then attached the carriage. The edger or small saw was set at the end of the track. The roller bed went out the end by the engine and stuck out about thirty feet.

237

When we got the boards sawed up it was time to build Mama a house. Mama's house was sixteen feet square. Daddy made the floor first with 2 x 10s and 2 x 12s. He would build the walls on top of the floor and add the roof, the front taller than the back to shed the rain. It had one big room with partitions made from quilts. There wasn't any electricity or running water so Mama had a cabinet with a place for her dish pan. Hoyt Lynn hauled the water to her from the creek.

Elaine's husband Don quit Weyerhauser and came to work too. He bought a light green Alice Chalmers crawler to skid the logs out of the woods. Elaine didn't make the move with us right away. She stayed in the house in Cottage Grove. She sure liked having that house. It had a big plate glass window in the front room. It was nice until Don's big boxer dog didn't like being left in the house and jumped through it. When they came back the dog was bloody and cut up, sitting nice as you please in the front yard. Mama couldn't believe they had a dog in the house in the first place. Elaine finally moved over into Fossil, closer to where we were working. She wouldn't live out in the woods where we were though. She wanted water and lights.

Every day but Sunday we worked. I would knock limbs off the trees with an axe and set the measuring pole. Harry used the power saw to buck the logs to sixteen feet. Don would go into the woods and bring the logs close to the clearing where we had set up the mill.

All the machinery in the woods had screens over their tail pipes and exhausts. It was the kind of screen that went on a screen door and it helped to catch sparks that might come out. Everybody was careful of fire because it was so hard to get water into the woods.

Daddy had an engine called a donkey set up on some skids. The donkey had a cable attached to a pulley. Harry would set the hand clutch on the motor and walk a cable out

238

to the end of the log and grab the end with tongs. Then he would walk back to the donkey and mash the hand clutch making the donkey pull the log toward the skidway.

The skidway was made of two poles spread apart so the log would roll onto them and head toward the carriage of the sawmill. The skidway was used to feed the logs into the carriage and that's another reason why we wanted the mill built on a slope, so they would roll into place.

Hoyt Lynn

Most days we worked from sun up until sun down. We couldn't keep up with the cutters. Don skidded more logs into us and we worked until dark trying to keep up with the logs. Sometimes Daddy had Sheron and Esther come out and help, too. We were tired at night and fell right to sleep after we ate what Mama fixed for supper. Sun up seemed to come just as my head got in the pillow good and then we were all up again and working. One night at supper Daddy told Mama he was going to need to get some help. The next morning they headed off to Fossil to get supplies and see about hiring more workers.

We all just hung around the house being lazy since we didn't have to work. I got to having a sweet tooth and wanted some cookies, and no matter how I asked them, I couldn't get the girls to make me any. So I figured I would make my own. I had seen Mama put oats and sugar, eggs and flour in a bowl and mix it up. I wasn't sure about how much sugar went in and since we didn't have much I added some syrup. I went ahead and put the rest of the sugar in there too. Mama was getting more anyway. I set a fire in the stove and baked them. When they come out they were flat and brown, and after I

239

tasted one I figured they weren't worth eating. I didn't have but the one, but ol' Hoyt Lynn cleaned up on them. He was like Rubin, he'd eat anything. The next time I had a sweet tooth, I figured I'd just drink the syrup.

I thought when Daddy got back from town he was going to have help for the work. He didn't find anybody, so while they were in town, he had Mama write to Louisiana and ask some of the boys from New Town to come up. He sent them money too. We kept on working hard and waited to find out if they would come. We finally got a letter telling us four of them were coming on the bus and when they would be getting to town.

A few weeks later Mama and me made the trip back to town to pick up the boys from Louisiana. I was close to fourteen so it was time for me to start driving. I drove the thirty miles to the black top and then Mama took over the rest of the way into Fossil. We went to the bus station and looked for the men. They stood off by the bus, no one around them. They were easy to spot being the only colored men in town. They had on their hats, overalls and boots and three of them had their clothes packed in old suitcases. One of them had his things in a box with a rope tied around it. They were big eyed and stood close to each other not talking to folks around them. When they saw us, I could tell they were thankful to see somebody they knew. When Mama walked up to them they took their hats off. I thought they were going to hug us but they didn't.

It was Crit, Jimmy, Jesse, and a man I didn't know named Ed. They got in the back of the panel and we all headed out to Rosenbaum Canyon. They didn't start talking till we were in the panel. Then Jimmy started talking.

"I ain't never seen nothing like what we been through. No trees, no creeks, just nothin' as far as my eyes could see. I didn't know how we were gonna work 'til we got back in the

240

timber. I've never seen no country such as I been through, Miz Miller, not never."

"Never been on the road so many days in my whole life. It was startin' to get me jittery wonderin' if we'd left the sight of God hisself," Crit added.

"Shore was glad to see you, Miz Fonceal. Felt good to see a face from home."

They never stopped talking as I drove the panel down the dirt road. Mama sat in the other seat and the four men rode in the back on the floor only being able to see out the front windows. They couldn't see out to know what the country was like. They didn't see all the rusted out cars and empty old houses all along the way. As they visited with Mama, I heard how worked up they had been on the trip. I didn't know why they were so scared.

Daddy hollered when we drove up. That made them feel welcome, and Daddy thanked them for coming.

"We'd work for y'all anywhere, Mr. Wesley, y'all know that."

Mama made a big supper for everybody and we all sat around the table and ate. They took their place at the table. The little kids took their plates and sat on the floor. Daddy thanked the Lord for all we had and for getting the men here safe. When Daddy got ready to say 'Amen', Crit just about yelled before Daddy could get it out.

Daddy hadn't had time to build them a room so that night they slept in the panel truck. They were spooked by the country and all four slept in the truck. Jesse went to the slab pile and before dark propped sixteen foot long slabs all around the Ford to keep out the mountain lions and bears.

The only animals we had seen were chipmunks, but they were safe from them.

241

Up a Tree

The four of them took over the work Harry and me had been doing. Harry still ran the donkey and I still knocked the limbs, but now I had some time to practice my harmonica. On one of the hottest days Harry and me were working with the men when we heard Don coming in from the woods. The crawler was moving pretty fast from the sound of it. When he came into the clearing he didn't have a log and Daddy looked over to him. Don made a motion of putting his thumb and finger to his nose. That meant that he smelled smoke. When Daddy saw that sign, everything got turned off and the men got ready to head to the woods to stop a fire before it could get going good.

Fire was a big fear in the woods. Working out in the middle of nowhere, the only water was from the creek. If there was a fire the best thing was to stop and beat it out with dirt and shovels right away. Harry went with them into the woods and they all started scouting for the fire.

I stayed around the house, hauling things for Mama. I even let Hoyt Lynn hang around with me. Sheron had got us some mayonnaise lids from Mama and we hammered them on a block of wood to make a truck for Hoyt Lynn. It had been a few hours since the men left and Mama was starting to look for them. The sun was close to going down when Sheron saw the men come out of the woods about a mile down the road. They walked slow and tired as they carried their hoes and shovels up on their shoulders. Sheron hollered to Mama they were coming and I asked her if I could take the panel and go down and pick them up. Sheron wanted to go too.

The panel had been parked on a hill to start it since it didn't have a battery. Daddy needed it to get the saw motor going so it was connected to the mill. By letting the car coast

242

downhill and then putting it in gear I could start it without a battery.

Sheron and I got in and I slowly started letting it roll. I let the panel pick up speed and before I knew it, it was going too fast to put it in gear. The steering wheel started going from side to side and I couldn't hold onto it. The car started veering from one side of the dirt road to the other and the tires on the driver's side felt like they were coming off the ground.

Sheron started hollering and I tried to hold onto the wheel and put it in gear at the same time, but I couldn't do either. In a flash the panel was on its side, plowing up the dirt. Sheron was bawling her head off. The panel skidded to a stop on its side in a big cloud of dust. I climbed out the window on my side and reached for Sheron to pull her out. The dust started to clear and I looked down the road and saw all the men running to the crash. I looked up the road and saw Mama and the kids running from the house. I started running towards the woods.

I got to the edge of the clearing and climbed the biggest tree I could find. I just knew this meant a whippin' from Daddy. I shimmied up the tree and watched as everybody saw to Sheron and looked over the panel on its side. Daddy and the men got on one side and heaved and groaned and turned the car back over on its tires. It rocked back and forth and then finally settled on all four tires. Then they looked around and Esther pointed towards me, high in the tree.

The kids came over to me and asked what I was doing. I told them I didn't want a whipping so I wasn't coming down. Hoyt Lynn laughed at me. He got plenty of whippin's from Daddy and thought the idea of me getting one was pretty funny. I wouldn't come down and they got tired of looking up at me and left. The grownups didn't have

243

time to fool with me and they went to the house. I got out my harmonica and figured this would be a good time to work on it. I played and sang up in the tree way past dark. I saw the kerosene light shining through the doorway in the house. I couldn't see much when Mama and Daddy finally came out to get me.

"Your supper is gonna get eat, Alton," Mama warned me from the ground.

"Come down from there, son, I ain't gonna whip you." Daddy kind of sounded like this was funny.

I climbed down and walked with them to the house. Daddy said the panel wasn't hurt and there hadn't been any fire so everything was just fine. He talked about the work for tomorrow and what we needed to get done. We walked inside and none of the kids said anything about the wreck. I guess as long as we got to keep working, wasn't anything I had done that was too bad. All that was left of supper was some bean juice to put on my cornbread. That was all right. After so many hours in the tree I was glad to have Mama's cooking, even if it was bad.

Kinzua

I sat on the car seat springs behind the steering wheel, my harmonica music the only thing that could be heard. The '29 Buick I sat in was mine. I couldn't drive on the highway anyway so the fact that it wouldn't run didn't matter at all. We had moved into Fossil to start school and the house we lived in had three cars that went with it. Harry got the '51 Ford. Since he could drive on the road, he got the running car.

Fossil was flat but all around it were hills that didn't have any trees on them. If I didn't already know better I would wonder how we were going to log. But a few miles out of town the road ran into the little valleys and that's where

244

the timber grew. A little lane off the highway dead ended at our house. It was a big two-story house with the bedrooms upstairs. At the back of the house one side went out a lot further, kind of like an add-on. There were little rooms down the length of it, each of them with its own door to the outside.

Daddy and the men stayed out at Rosenbaum Canyon and worked all week long and then come back on Friday night. The men stayed in the long addition on the house. Saturday, Daddy would get whatever supplies they would need for the week- groceries, parts, gas and diesel. They would head back on Sunday night.

Not having to work at the saw mill camp gave me time to build bicycles again. There were plenty of places around town to find parts so I got three of them built. I even had one with a knee action spring on the front wheel that let it go up and down with the bumps. Only one of them had brakes but I didn't find that too important. I could always stop it when I had shoes on by putting my foot on the front tire and pushing on it to slow down.

We started school in Fossil and I didn't like it any better than I liked school anywhere else. The walk up to the big building on the first day was long, not because of the distance, but because of the kids that thought they wanted to mess with us since we were new. I had made rules for myself that didn't allow any of them to look crosswise at me. If they did I took it up with them right away. There were a few fist fights right off, but it didn't take too many before the boys were walking a wide path around me. Peeling poles and working the mill put a few muscles on me that most of those boys didn't have.

Esther tattled on me about fighting. I always told Mama I didn't start it. She believed me. To my way of thinking, even if I did hit first, they started it by giving me lip, so I wasn't lying to Mama.

During recess, I walked around looking for things to do. Harry was at the junior high building on the other side of the road so I didn't have him to bum around with. Sheron was in my same class but I wasn't going to hang around with girls. I just stood in the shade and watched. The boys who had tried to push me around were in a circle around a little guy called Tommy. They were giving him a hard time. He was trying to hold his own, but I could tell when his face got red he was about to cry or run. I just couldn't stand to watch it anymore. Before I knew what I was doing, I was standing in front of Tommy just daring the other fellows to come at me. They left off bothering Tommy and I had a buddy from then on.

After fighting, the next best way to make a path for yourself in school was to be good at something. I wasn't good at anything in the classroom, except a little arithmetic, so I made my mark by running fast, jumping the furthest and winning in track. We never had balls and bats at home so I wasn't good at that stuff. Being fast and strong was a way to win and I made sure that I outran, out-jumped and outdid anybody that came up against me.

I was looking out the window watching the rain fall one day while the teacher was going over subjects and verbs. A man I hadn't seen before came around asking us if anybody would like to sign on to a paper route. When he told us we would need a bicycle to ride around to the houses and deliver the newspaper I knew I was his man. I signed up with him without asking Mama, telling him my folks would let me. Later, I told Mama about it and she let me go ahead and do it, but I would have done it no matter what. I was going to make money just by riding my bike and throwing papers at people's houses. It wasn't like any work I had ever done before. I got the papers after school and delivered them all in the afternoon. The town wasn't very big so it didn't take long.

The man who hired me collected the money and then he would pay me. I fixed up my best bike with a rack for the papers and started making money.

Having something to do was nice since Harry was always busy with his buddies. He was sixteen, driving regular now and the '51 Ford ran good enough to get him around. He slicked back his hair and ran around with older boys like Roger Easley and Billy Joe McMinn. They were always trying to find enough money to buy gas and cigarettes. Men smoked, and the quickest way for a boy to feel grown up was to smoke, too.

When Harry figured out I had a little money from my paper route, I started getting invited to drive with them over to Kinzua which was about ten miles away on the other side of the hill. Mama always let me go along to keep him out of trouble but I usually ended up being right in the middle of trouble with him. Harry knew how to have a good time, and he always had a crowd around him. I might have to pay for the gas, but I sure felt big being there.

Kinzua was on the property of a big logging company. A lot of people worked for the company and lived nearby so it had a bar on one side of the street and a store on the other. The property line of the corporation was right in the middle of Kinzua. The paved county road ended at Kinzua Corporation property and turned to dirt. So part of the store and bar was on county property and the other part on private property. The dividing line went right down the middle of the building.

The corporation part of the bar sold drinks by the glass and bottle. The county side had packaged liquor. Even though we were underage we could go into the bar and get a Coke because it belonged to the Kinzua Corporation. Sometimes Harry was brave and ordered a beer. He stood at the counter just like a grown man and drank it, wiped his

247

mouth and winked at me. I just took a drink of my Coca Cola.
I wasn't willing to risk Daddy finding out.

Saturday night was race night at Kinzua. All the
young fellas with cars would line up on the road and drag
race their cars down the dirt road. Harry and Roger went
there a lot. Sometimes Roger would bring a car out to race or
race with Harry and me. I liked running around with the
older boys. Even though Mama made Harry take me to keep
him out of trouble, Harry treated me good. I was the go-fer
and did all the fetching but I didn't mind. We would race all
those old cars until we saw Daddy's black work truck parked
by the gas station. If he showed up that meant we had been
out too late and he was there to get us. If we didn't spot him
right away he would get out of the truck and walk towards
us. When he was mad he pulled on the brim of his hat. We
knew to step high when that happened.

"I don't know what I'm going to do with you boys,"
was all he said. We still got to go just about every Saturday
night, when we had gas. We thought we had that problem
solved. Daddy's work truck carried big barrels that he used to
haul fuel out to the saw mill. One was for diesel and one was
for gas. Harry sure wanted to race and that took fuel. We

were sitting on the
porch waiting for
Roger when Harry
told me, "Come on."

We walked
over to the barrel
and found the
siphon hose. I went
and got his Ford and
we drove it up close.
We didn't want to ask
Daddy in case he said no. We kept real quiet as we filled the

Modern picture of house at Fossil

248

tank. He put the hose back and we didn't waste any time getting out of there. We'd find Roger out on the road.

We were talking about how we were going to whip out in Kinzua tonight. The car sputtered. The motor was making a lot of noise and it wouldn't keep running. Harry pumped the gas, jammed it in gear but the car quit. We coasted off the side of the road and got out and looked under the hood. No matter what we tried the car was dead. We started the walk back. Harry cussed since nobody but us was around. When we headed up the long driveway to our house, Daddy was on the porch with a cup of coffee.

"You boys having trouble?"

"The car quit running, Daddy, we can't figure out what's wrong with it," Harry told him.

"Well, next time, you might put the right kind of fuel in it." Daddy took a big drink.

"Y'all took the fuel from the diesel barrel, not the gas. I didn't figure you'd make it far. That's what you get. Go push your car back, no race night tonight." Daddy had let us hang ourselves by putting the wrong fuel in. I think he was laughing at us a little too.

All the way back to the car Harry blamed me and I blamed Harry for getting the wrong fuel. We didn't make that mistake again.

The Lake

After winter set in and the snow got too deep for racing, we went out to spin the car on the frozen mill pond. Harry would drive out on the frozen lake and then pull on the emergency brake. The car spun around and around, better than a ride at the carnival. Roger and Harry were in front and I was in back, mashed up against the door.

They got to inviting girls to go and showing off for them. Harry would spin faster and wilder so the girls would get scared and want to get in the front seat and hold onto him and Roger. Sometimes they would move up front and sometimes they stayed in the back and held onto me. I started to like it.

One Saturday, Roger's daddy let him take his big '47 Chrysler. It was tan on top and dark brown on the bottom. There was a lot of room in it and we really felt like we were something driving it. Roger drove us around and we picked up a couple of girls in Kinzua and took them out on the frozen lake. I was in the back with them like normal. Roger revved the engine and went out on the ice. The girls were already starting to scream and I think they were trying to act scared so they could have an excuse to climb up front with Harry and Roger.

The parking brake on the Chrysler worked a lot better than the Ford's, so when Roger pulled it to make us spin we really started going around. That big old car spun forever and finally came to a stop. By the time it slowly stopped all of us were laughing. It was quiet out on the ice and our breath had fogged up the windows. Roger leaned up to wipe the windshield from the inside when we heard, CRACK!

We all stopped talking and listened. There was another CRACK and the front of the car went down a couple of feet. The front tires had busted through the ice. The girls started screaming, this time because they really were scared. All four doors of the Chrysler flew open and we ran, slipping and sliding toward solid ground. Not a one of us looked back as the pops and cracks chased us to the bank. When we made it off the ice we turned around and watched as that big Chrysler's front end went under the water and then the backend went down too. It bubbled and sank, the only part showing was the tan roof of the car.

250

Everybody was silent. Roger looked sick. The girls said they had to get home and started walking. Roger stood there for a long time, looking at the spot where his Daddy's car lay in the lake. Harry told him it was a shame and then we starting walking too. I looked back and Roger was right where we'd left him, staring in the lake. I felt bad about him having to tell his Daddy.

"That Chrysler must weigh a lot more than my old Ford," Harry said. "That's why it sank. When the lake freezes back over, we'll go back with the Ford, it won't crack the ice."

I agreed with him. We'd play it safe next time and use the Ford.

Don't Get Sick

Word got around fast about Mr. Easley's Chrysler setting at the bottom of the mill pond. Half the town turned out to watch the car be pulled from the pond by pickups using log chains. It sure was a temptation to go and watch, but Harry and me didn't dare show up in case seeing us might draw attention to our part in the sinking.

Daddy had quite a cough when we walked in from working. Mama was busy fussing over him so they didn't pay much attention to Easley's troubles. The cold weather pretty much stopped the nighttime activities at Kinzua so we stayed close to the house.

Sometimes we drove into town and had a Coke at the café. Since I had money I played songs from the jukebox. When Harry was with me, folks always came over to listen to him tell stories. He got to where he would sing with the jukebox. He was as good as any we heard on the radio and it made me proud to sit beside him as he entertained the crowd. Seemed there was always a girl or two trying to hang on to him. It was hard to beat that black hair and big smile. I didn't smile with my broken front tooth, but I sure did like being with Harry and his buddies. I just kept the music playing on the jukebox with my dimes.

My paper route money kept me going. But money at the house was scarce. Work had slowed down at the mill and the boss told Daddy he'd have to wait for his pay. Daddy's cough let us know when he was walking in at night. He didn't say much when he came in; just sat in the big empty living room on the one chair we had and closed his eyes. It was just him, Crit and Jesse working now. The problems at the mill had caused Don to quit and Little Jimmy and Ed had gone home. They never had got used to being here anyway.

The Monday Daddy didn't go to work was when I knew he was in a bad way. Mama had to move his bed into the front room because he couldn't get warm. The bedrooms didn't have heat and the only room the fire made warm was the front one. One day I came from school and Daddy was in the bed. Mama sat beside him and fed him his meals in bed. Sometimes when I came in the house a man from church would be sitting with him while Mama got her housework done. Somebody gave us a white wicker chair and there would always be someone sitting in it tending Daddy. When they weren't rubbing him down with water or rubbing alcohol, their voices were low as they prayed over him.

Since Daddy didn't go to work, neither did Crit and Jesse. There wasn't any money coming in and we started eating mush for breakfast and soup for supper. Daddy could only get down a few mouthfuls anyway. He still couldn't get warm and Mama had all the blankets she could find covering him.

I gave my paper route money to Mama, but she couldn't feed ten people on it. Crit and Jesse were trying to find a way to help. I knew they had figured something out when I smelled the stew when I came in the house after

252

school. Even though Daddy was still in the bed, Mama, Jesse and Crit were happier.

Jesse was telling us how he got us some meat in our stew pot.

"I had spotted me that hole days ago. It's back where the ditch rides the fence line. Got to figurin' what kinda varmint might be inside that ol' hole. This country is full of odd creatures."

"I told Jesse, might as well stick our hands down in there and see what we come out with," Crit wanted in on the telling.

Crit went on, "I found us a good two by four and got up over the hole, then Jesse went to seein' what was in there."

Jesse had squatted down in front of the hole, put both arms in as far as he could and felt fur.

"I grabbed with both hands and pulled it out by its hind feet. It was a snarlin' and a hissin' and a fightin'. Crit swung that board hard and bashed in its head. Dead. And now we got some badger to put in the pot."

The badger stew was put on the table for all of us to dish up that night. It had a different smell to it, but Mama had boiled it so long there wasn't much taste. It took a while for the girls to put their spoons in it, but we all knew there wasn't no way around eating it. Mama did say she didn't want the neighbors to know we were eating badger and told us not to tell.

"Why, Miz Miller, this is as good as eatin' a 'possum." Jesse was proud to provide for us all, and didn't know why we wouldn't tell folks.

"That's right, Crit, but there ain't too many up here that's eaten a possum either." Mama was careful not to hurt his pride.

Daddy was fed a little broth at his bed. Mama tried to coax him to eat, but he ate less and less. Every day he seemed to get worse.

Sheron was helping straighten his bed when she heard Mama ask Daddy about seeing a doctor.

"Isn't the Lord gonna heal Daddy, Mama?" Sheron wanted to know.

Daddy heard it and told Mama he wasn't going to go to a doctor. He was going to show his faith, and he wanted to make sure Sheron at twelve didn't lose faith too. Daddy felt like he should count on the Lord to help him and that's what he was going to do.

Folks came in from church and must have seen how we didn't have much, since somebody sent Mama over a box of food. There was a bag of oranges and we decided we would wait and have them when Daddy got better as a treat. There were canned oysters and I didn't care how hungry I might get. That was something I wasn't going to eat. When Mama fried them the other kids, especially Esther, liked them. She kept telling me how good they were. I told her I'd just as soon eat a badger.

Oranges

Christmas was coming and Jesse and Crit went back to Louisiana. That just left the family in the house at Fossil. The room Daddy stayed in was warm and the rest of the house was cold so we stayed in there with him. Sometimes I wondered if Daddy was going to get back up again. He was so weak he couldn't walk to the bathroom and Mama had made a place for him to go on the other side of the bed. When we got back from school we spent the day in the warm kitchen and the night sleeping in Daddy's living room.

As it got close to Christmas, Mama was trying to find things to do to make the holiday special. The girls and her were in the kitchen making little cakes and coffee for us all to have. They sang carols together and Mama talked about times when she was a girl.

"My hands sure are cold today," Mama said. "Reminds me when I was back home and had to go out and pick poke salad. I picked it early in the spring, so it was still chilly and my hands would get so cold. After winter, we'll have to look and see if can find some to cook up."

"There's a car drivin' up, Mama." Hoyt Lynn hollered, running in to the kitchen.

"It's probably somebody from the church," Mama said, wiping her hands on her apron.

"But they already brought us a box of groceries," Sheron said.

I walked out onto the porch and saw a car drive up I didn't know. The door of the gray '51 Ford opened and out stepped Louie.

Esther

"It's Louie!" I hollered. Louie walked up to the house with barely a limp.

Everybody ran to hug him, especially the girls, and Mama had a big smile on her face. That's when I learned Mama had called Thunderbird's to talk to Louie and tell him we needed him.

He walked over to Daddy and told him, "All right old man, that's enough of this lazin' around. Time to get up and do some work."

Louie was twenty and grown and could tease Daddy if he thought he could get away with it. Daddy smiled up at him. Louie sat down next to him on the bed and talked quiet

255

to Daddy for little while. Mama and the girls finished up our Christmas cakes so we could have them with Louie. He told me and Harry to go outside and get his stuff out of the back of the car. We went out and saw that he had brought everybody presents-little suitcases with dolls, clothes for the girls, and trucks and candy for the little kids. There was also a .22 rifle that he gave to Daddy.

Having Louie back made us all feel a little better, especially when he got a job at a gas station over in Condon. It was twenty miles away and up a crooked road but it sure helped when he brought his pay to Mama. Daddy was weak and Mama talked to him every day about seeing a doctor. We had some money coming in from Louie, so they could afford to see one.

Daddy was struggling to know what was right. He said we were supposed to have faith in the Lord to heal us and going to the doctor didn't show faith. The doctors had helped Louie back when his leg was burned, but that hadn't been Daddy's decision. Folks had made him do it. Daddy had turned fifty-six on his birthday back in September. After he had been sick so long, his hair had just about lost all its color. Sometimes I had to look hard to see Daddy in the man who lay sick in the bed. Finally, he told Mama that if he wasn't feeling better in the morning he would see a doctor.

Mama went to put the food away she was able to get with Louie's money when she saw the bag of oranges.

"You boys might as well go ahead and eat these before they go bad." She handed them to me. Harry and me took the bag into the front room and started peeling them. They smelled sweet and so good that even Daddy could smell them. When she came in to check on him, his dry cracked voice told Mama, "Fonny, that smells so good, give me a taste of that orange."

Mama was excited that Daddy wanted to eat anything. I gave her a section from the orange. Daddy sucked on it and then slowly ate it, a little bite at a time. Mama was encouraged and had us peel another one for him. Mama held the orange to his lips and he ate more. Daddy ate every orange we fed him until the bag was empty.

The very next morning Daddy got up, got dressed and sat at the table for coffee. Daddy was well. I wasn't much of a believer. But as Daddy prayed in thanks for all we had that morning, I figured I had seen a miracle worked, because of Daddy's faith and a bag of oranges.

The Picnic

I finished up my paper deliveries and steered my bike towards the house. I got done pretty fast considering now I was the only boy Mr. West had on the route. As winter had come and settled in, the mornings got colder. Boys quit their routes one by one. Either they thought it was too cold, or their folks had made them stop. It didn't matter to me; I just took the route and counted my money. Now that it was starting to warm up they might want to get some of the routes back, but I had no plans to give up any of my work.

I bumped along as I got off the road to head down the dirt drive. There had been a late spring snow and to keep traction on my tires on the ice I had looped a rope around the tires and through the spokes to keep from skidding and wrecking. I had looked at the tire chains men put on their trucks and had figured out the rope would do the trick for my bicycle.

As I headed down the straight drive towards the house I saw Harry and Roger sitting on porch. They were waiting for me.

"Hey, Alton, when do you get paid for your route?" Harry asked me.

"Not for another week. Mr. West gives me my money every two weeks," I said as I jumped off the bike and leaned it up against the porch.

"Well, we had an idea, but we need some money to make it work. Roger and me and some friends want to go on a picnic and we wanted you to come along with us. But we don't have the money right now to buy the food. Think you could get the money?"

"I don't have any now. We'd have to wait till I got paid," I told him.

"Couldn't you go collect the money from the folks who get the paper? If you got that money now we could all go out and have fun. Roger and me'll give you the money back and you can give it to your boss," Harry explained.

There didn't seem to be anything wrong with the plan so I told them I would try. The next afternoon when I made my rounds, I delivered their papers to the door and told them I needed to collect from them now. Some of them wondered why and if they questioned me I backed off. I didn't want to draw too much attention to myself and what I was doing. Most of them were really nice and paid right up. I had a pocket full of money at the end of the day.

At the store I picked up light bread and weenies and a bag of marshmallows. I let Harry know I had got it done. It was time for a picnic. Harry patted me on the back as we got in the car and we headed out to have our party. It was starting to get dark, but Roger said we'd have a campfire.

The friends we picked up were two girls Harry and Roger had their eyes on. Like usual I was in the back seat with the girls, me in the middle. Harry told them we were having a picnic. They were worried about the cold but Harry said he and Roger would keep them warm. I didn't see how, but it wasn't too cold for me.

We headed a couple miles out of town and in a clearing we got out and made a camp. We got the fire going and sat around it while it got built up. I found sticks to put the weenies and marshmallows on and brought them back to the fire. I got the ends sharp and Harry and his girl said they was going to find some more wood. Roger said he and his girl would too. I sat on a log and waited for them to come back. And waited. And waited.

I finally put my weenie on the stick and started cooking it. I ate it, cooked another and ate it too. The longer I sat alone I got to seeing that this crummy picnic was nothing but a way for them to be alone with the girls. The longer I sat there the madder I got. I walked over to Harry's Ford, opened the hood and pulled all the wires out of the distributor cap. I walked back to the fire and threw them in. I sat back down and started eating everything I had brought to the picnic, eight weenies, a loaf of bread and I was working on the bag of marshmallows.

Harry and his girl came out of the woods first, then Roger. First thing Harry noticed was I had eaten all the food.

"What are you doin' eatin' everything?" He shook the empty bread bag.

I just kept eating. I didn't say a word.

Roger asked, "What's that smell, what you got burning in that fire?"

I just kept eating, didn't say a word.

Harry looked closer and said, "Damn it, that's the wires to the car!" He got a stick and reached into the fire and pulled out the wires, most of them were okay but a couple had burnt up.

I just kept eating. I was mad that Harry had me look like a fool in front of everybody. I hoped he felt like a fool, now that his car wouldn't run.

Harry and Roger went to the car and started working on it. The girls started complaining that they had to get home. I wouldn't keep the fire going for them, so they were getting cold. That's when it dawned on me I didn't have a ride back either. The girls went around and got in the car where it might be warmer. I thought it might be a good idea if I was already in the car if they got it running. Just in case, I climbed in too.

Harry was trying to figure out what to do and cussing me at the same time. I didn't care. I felt tricked by how I had financed a picnic that wasn't anything more than a way for the guys to get alone with the girls. Roger acted like he wanted to fight me. I told him to come on if he thought he could lick me. Harry told him to cool down. He didn't forget I was his brother.

Harry walked down to a fence and cut some wires out of it. He and Roger worked together and took one end of the wire and attached it to the spark plug and then other end of the wire to the coil. They had to be careful not to let the wire touch any other part of the car. It took them a while to get it done and the girls were getting upset. They were worried that they weren't going to make it home in time to not get in trouble. When they started sitting up close to me to get warm, I kind of saw why the boys had wanted to bring them along, but I never would have said so.

They got the car to start. It sounded rough, but it ran. Roger wanted to leave me there but Harry knew he had better have me with him when he showed up at the house. We slowly made it back to town. The car sputtered and they had to redo the wires a couple of times but we got the girls home. The car finally gave out as we headed up the lane to the

260

house. We pushed it the rest of the way. By the time we got to the porch, the whole thing seemed kind of funny. I guess it had all worked out all right. Harry's car never ran again, but I'd ate good.

The Paper Route

We still wanted to go to Kinzua on Saturday night so the next best way to get there was on my bikes. I had the best one. Harry picked his and gave Roger the one with the knee action spring on the front.

I warned him, "You watch that bike. If you don't ride it just right it'll throw you." "I think I'm old enough to know how to ride a bike, son." Roger said the last word as he took off on the bike, hit a hole and went over the top of the handle bars. Harry laughed. He had done the same thing and been thrown himself riding that bike. I just took off down the road in the lead, feeling pretty sure of myself as they hurried to catch up.

It was going to be hard to look cool riding up to the car races on a bike, so we rode in the back way, which was shorter anyhow. Harry had us park behind the service station and walk out to the racing so no one would know. We watched the cars and went inside and played pool.

There was a cop that liked to park on the side of the bar to see if he could catch anybody speeding on the pavement. Then he would give them a ticket. Once in a while somebody brave would get tired of racing on the dirt and turn and race on the blacktop. That cop would take off after them in his Ford, lights-a-flashing.

While we were inside warming up, we learned that some of the older boys had figured out a way to fix the cop. A guy and his buddy got a twenty foot log chain and on the sly wrapped it around the rearends of the cop car. They fastened

261

it around a big tree that was right beside the building. We all went outside to watch. Two cars raced down the dirt road. When they got to the pavement, instead of stopping, they gassed it. When they hit the pavement the cop threw on his lights and gunned it. That car jumped all the way to the end of the chain. The back axle came to a stop anyway. The body of the car lunged out a few feet further. The axle had been jerked clean out from under the car.

That cop came out of the car stomping, spitting, and cussing, wanting to know who had done it. Of course, nobody would talk. After the cop car got towed away and he left, the fellows who had done it soaked up their back slapping and approval from the racing group. Everybody went inside to play pool and talk about it over and over again.

When Daddy opened the door to the pool hall and hollered for us, Harry and me high tailed it out of there. He didn't pull on his hat brim like he did when he was mad though. He just loaded up the bicycles and drove us to the house.

"I don't know what I'm going to do with you boys," was all he said to us.

He had found some work but it wasn't every day. It had helped him to get stronger and he got better everyday. He thanked the Lord every day for getting well, more faithful than ever. I sure hoped some of that help from the Lord might rub off on me. I tried to forget but I knew my judgment day was coming.

I got a note in with my newspapers. Mr. West was coming to see me on Monday. I knew why he was coming. Roger and Harry had never come up with the money for the newspapers. He was coming to question me and collect. I didn't know what to do. Monday morning I woke up sick. Worried sick. It hadn't been too long since Daddy got out of

262

bed so I took to the bed myself. Mama didn't take any chances and didn't have me go to school. I was in the bed upstairs when I heard a car coming up the lane. I looked out the window. It was him. I felt a wave a fear so big, I thought maybe I *was* sick. What he wanted I didn't have. Oh, Lord.

I heard the man knock on the door and Mama open it and talked to him. He told her about the money and she told him she would get me. She came upstairs and found me in the bed. I must have looked bad, because she took one look at me and said for me to not worry right now. Maybe the pneumonia Daddy had had for so long was catching. I acted as puny as a healthy boy could act. Mama, knowing her kids wouldn't tell a story, went back downstairs and told the man I was sick and as soon as I got to feeling better she would figure it all out.

A week went by and then two. When I got to acting too well, Mama would ask if I was doing better. Right after that I usually had a bad spell. Harry stayed scarce by helping Daddy. He didn't want any part of the trouble he had got me into.

Things were busy around the house anyway since Daddy

1937 International

had a new plan. He bought a sawmill from Jerry Shriner at Condon. Daddy would mill lumber and part of the pay would go to owning the gyppo mill itself. Daddy had traded his work truck for an old '37 International flatbed and we

263

were going to move to Condon. I was beginning to think maybe the Lord did answer prayers. I didn't come out of my sickness until the day we were leaving and in all the commotion Mama forgot about the newspaperman.

I was never happier to leave a place as I was Fossil. I was feeling good again as we disappeared around the curve of the road.

Chirpy

I got up from my pallet on the floor and stepped around first Hoyt and then Sheron, past Mary and then Esther. We were all sleeping on the floor in the house we had moved into at Condon. The house was a just a square with fiberglass siding, and so little there was only room for Mama and Daddy in the bedroom. The rest of us made our beds on the floor in the front room. There was no reason to complain though since it had an inside bathroom and water and electricity.

Condon looked a lot different than Fossil. It was flat and treeless with wheat fields and other crops surrounding the town. We had to drive about ten miles out of town to the deep canyons to find the timber that daddy worked. Since the house was too small for all of us, Harry had moved into the house of a man that farmed wheat outside of town. Harry got a job driving the farmer's truck so that worked out pretty good. Since he had a good paying job and was kind of on his own he didn't go to school anymore. I saw him in town when he was off and he would give me a little spending money. He always had a pack of smokes and a buddy who palled around with him. I could tell he sure felt grown up.

Sometimes I went to work with Daddy, but I didn't have to do much since he had hired workers. Louie came out when he had a day off from the gas station and Harry came too when he could. I didn't mind the work at all. I was glad to not be in school on those days.

I would hear him at night talking to Mama about how hard it was for a man to make his way with all the rules and laws they laid on him. Kids had to be in school or the law got after you. Folks got to tell you if where you lived was good enough. Sometimes he got so worked up he would pound his fist on the table and Mama would tell him, "Yes, Wesley" and try to calm him down.

He read the Bible to us every night and covered a lot of pages. We could tell by the look on his face that what he was reading was important to him. He would stop and talk about what he had read to Mama. He read to us until we were worn out from sitting on the floor. When we would start to fidget, Mama would get on to us and tell us, "Listen to what your Daddy's sayin'."

There were things Daddy knew that were right and those that were wrong and nobody could change his mind about it. If it was knowing the Bible or running a sawmill, Daddy didn't need a fellow looking over his shoulder telling him anything. Daddy couldn't stand for somebody to tell him what to do. Out in the woods, he was left to work his own way. When somebody got to thinking they could boss RW Miller, he was gone.

I got to thinking maybe that's why we left so often. I don't know if Daddy ever got tired of working and moving. It seemed like sometimes Mama would. I wondered if she ever yearned to stay in one place long enough to make herself a house that looked like other women's. I don't think anybody ever thought to ask her. Daddy was just as happy on the road as in a house so I don't think he cared much one way or another what kind of place we lived. I guess I leaned toward Daddy's way of thinking. Making trips and working sure got us out of going to school so that was fine by me. I felt good when I was working like Daddy. Nobody cared if I couldn't read fast enough. They just cared if I could work hard enough.

After breakfast was over Daddy had me help him work on the '37 International. He used it to haul lumber out to the gyppo mill he had set up. He hauled the logs and then sawed them into lumber. He'd done good enough that he had bought Mama a car to drive. It was a lime green '51 Chevy with four doors and a bullet hole in the roof above the backseat. When I sat in back I always looked out that hole at the sky. I tried to figure out what might have happened in that car.

We were working on the '37 log truck to get it ready to make a trip. Daddy was having Louie go to Louisiana with the truck and get some sawmill parts. We had hauled in a bunch of timber over the last few weeks, enough to keep us sawing while he was gone with the truck. When we got though with the truck, Daddy cut me loose to do what I wanted.

Today I was going to meet my buddy, Chirpy Epply, at the picture show and see a cowboy movie. I had to keep quiet about it or Mama would have a fit if she knew I was doing something worldly. Chirpy's folks let him go, so I hoped he might have enough money to buy us some popcorn. I had met Chirpy at school. He was a tall, fat boy that the other kids made fun of. They called him lazy and clumsy. But when I looked those boys over who were mouthin' off, I didn't see nothing special about them. Heck, they were scrawny and some of them even wore glasses. I decided I would be Chirpy's buddy. I took up for him and when those boys came at us, trying to fight, I just knocked 'em down till they didn't get back up. Before long Chirpy wasn't being picked on anymore and I had a friend.

I got on my bike and headed into town. I rode down the main street then veered off down a side street and rode in behind the theater. I leaned the bike up against the back of the building where no one could see it. Mama came to town on Saturdays and I didn't want her coming across it on the front sidewalk. I walked around to the front window and bought my ticket. I waited for Chirpy on the inside, I didn't want to be seen milling around the front.

Chirpy came in and waved to me when he saw me.

"You want to get some popcorn or candy?" He reached in his pocket and felt around.

"Naw, I don't really want anything," I did, but I didn't want him to know I was out of money. He went to the counter and ordered two popcorns for us.

"Aw, thanks, Chirpy." I got my popcorn from him and we headed in. There were quite a few people in the dark theater. I always tried to look them over. They didn't seem like a bunch of sinners to me. Shoot, I'd seen a lot them out walking on the sidewalks, shopping and visiting with other folks. Mama told us that going to the show was sinful, but after sneaking in and watching a few of the shows, I couldn't figure out what made it so bad. There was no way I was going to ask about it. That might tip Mama off to what I was doing.

The movie lasted about an hour. It was a cowboy movie and Chirpy didn't think it was very good. I hadn't seen that many so it was plenty good to me. Chirpy headed out the front doors and I told him I was going to leave out the back. I didn't want him to know why, just told him it was closer to my bike. It was bright outside and I had to squint as I left the dark theater. The door closed behind me and I looked up with my eyes half shut right into the red face of Mama. It was too late to run.

"I figured that was your bike in this alley. What in the world are you doing, Alton? You know you're not supposed to be here." She had Mary by the hand, and her little six year old face was looking up at me. She looked scared to death. I knew how she felt.

"Mama..." I was trying to think up a good story, but I just couldn't come up with one.

"You get that bike and you get to the house now. I'll be right behind you."

Mama waited and watched as I got on the bike and rode off. I don't know if I had ever ridden a bike any slower. The front wheel veered first one way and then another as I barely kept the wheels rolling. I wasted as much time as I could. My chance for making up a story was gone and I could tell there wasn't any way around getting whipped.

Mama called to me and laid into me with the wire end of the fly swatter. When Daddy showed up she told him what I had done, he whipped me too. Daddy wasn't as mad as he could have been so the belt wasn't too bad. Sometimes Daddy's whippin' took my breath away it lasted so long, especially if he lost his temper. Those times he didn't know when to stop and Mama would have to call him off. I was glad this wasn't one of those times. There was a long lecture that night though. The kids were pretty put out with me when we had to listen to the Bible reading long into the night. I didn't hear much about what Daddy was preaching but I did figure on changing my ways. I wouldn't ride my bike to the show again. I would walk.

Alton- third from right, second row from bottom in front of Chirpy. Sheron- second row from top, second from right.

Breaking the Law

Sheron and Esther were cleaning the dishes, Esther talking a mile a minute. Hoyt Lynn was running around trying to pinch Mary. She was screaming and running around the table. Harry sat in Daddy's chair at the table trying to sing a song he'd heard on the radio. I was working on one of the chains to my bicycles.

It was just after supper, but still light outside. It was an unusual thing for us to be alone. Louie's boss, Buster, from down at the gas station had come up from town and got Mama and Daddy. He said there was call from Louie in Idaho and he was going to call back to talk to them in thirty minutes, so the folks had driven to town.

Louie had only been gone two days so it was quite curious for him to be calling. He'd left his red, white, and blue Ford that had 'Leapin' Lizzie' painted on the side for Harry to

269

drive and had gone to Louisiana in the International. We all hoped he hadn't had any trouble with the truck. When the Chevy drove up and parked, me and Esther walked to the door to see what Daddy had to say when they came in.

Mama walked right to the table and put her head in her hands. She just kept saying, "Lord have mercy," over and over again.

"What's the trouble with Louie?" Harry asked Daddy as he got up out of his chair.

"Said he's in jail. The police over there said the truck was a commercial truck and since Louie didn't have the right kind of paperwork He's gonna get fined. Only Louie don't have money to pay, and if he don't he'll have to spend thirty days in jail."

Mama started praying silently at her end of the table.

Esther was trying to soothe her, "Now Mama, Louie'll be fine."

Harry sat down beside Daddy and had an idea. "Daddy, why don't I take the Ford out there and drive over to where Louie is. I can take the money to pay the ticket. Then Louie can get goin' and I'll head back."

Daddy didn't say anything at first, but the more he, Mama and Harry talked about it, the more it seemed like a good idea. Daddy could keep working the sawmill while Harry took care of Louie.

"Could I go with him, Daddy?" I was hoping they would see I was just about as big as Harry was.

"No, son, you'll need to stay here with me and your mama and keep things goin'. Harry can go. By the time I was sixteen I'd already hopped my first freight car. It'll do him good to be on his own."

I sure was disappointed, but ol' Harry could hardly get ahold of himself, he was so glad to be going off and acting a man. He didn't waste any time going outside and getting

270

the Ford ready to go. The next morning, Daddy gave him the money to pay Louie's fine and enough to buy gas for the 450 miles he was going. They called the jail and told them that we were sending the money. Harry peeled the tires on the gravel as he left the house. Daddy shook his head as he watched. Mama started praying again.

It was even harder to go to school the next day knowing I was missing out. Normally, the only class I liked was gym, but that wasn't even good here in Condon. Since it was cold outside we had it inside and instead of being able to show my strength in rope climbing and long jumping, we were learning to dance. I did have a girlfriend named Joann. She was tall with brown hair and wore cat eye glasses. She sat next to me in one of my classes and I always tried to look my best in case she glanced over at me. Of course, she didn't know she was my girlfriend. I kept that to myself.

The teacher made the boys walk across the gym and ask the girls to dance. Then he would tell us how to put our arms out and how to count and move our feet. I didn't care how much trouble I got into. I wasn't asking no girl to dance, not even Joann. Sheron didn't seem to have a problem dancing, even as tomboy as she was. She said yes to the boy that asked and walked right out and started trying to move without looking at her feet. After a few days I think she got to liking that she was a girl and wore high heels to school. After she fell down the stairs in the hall she didn't do that again. Luckily there were more boys than girls and it got overlooked

Sheron

that I just stood on the sidelines. This was one time that I didn't mind being left out.

Most times I didn't like how it made me feel to sit and watch. Daddy never let us do too much in P.E. For a lot of sports you had to have the right clothes and tennis shoes. I didn't ever have any tennis shoes and neither did any of the other kids in the family. They wanted girls to wear gym shorts and Mama and Daddy thought that was worldly and said no, that left us to just sit and watch the other kids. I watched the boys play basketball and other games the gym teacher taught. I knew I could outdo them all if I was given a chance, but I just made out like I didn't care, sometimes to fool them and sometimes to fool me.

When we got let out of school we walked through town and I saw Mama's car at the grocery store. I headed her way and found her buying beans. While she picked out the rest of her groceries I looked at the candy. There were so many of the little brown chocolates in the bin I figured no one would care if I took one. I put it in my pocket and I helped Mama take her sacks to the car. After we got back the girls started putting the groceries up. Mama mixed up a big jug of grape Kool-aid, she stirred the sugar in with a big wooden spoon. I reached in my pocket and took out my candy and was about to unwrap it.

"Alton, what's that in your hands?" Mama had stopped stirring the Kool-aid and was staring right down on me.

What had I done? Right there in the kitchen I had got out my candy. Mama knew she hadn't bought candy. Mama's face was getting red and she was mad. I couldn't see any way out of this so I told her, "A Tootsie Roll." Mama about had a fit. She took the wooden spoon she had been stirring with and started walloping me from head to toe with it. I just ducked my head and hoped she'd run out of mad pretty soon.

272

"You get in that car and we are taking that back to the store and you are going to tell that store keeper you are sorry!"

"Mama, don't make me tell that man. Just keep whippin' me!" I couldn't think of nothing worse than telling that man what I had done. She laid the wooden spoon into me all the way to the car. I got in and begged her not to make me tell.

Mama scolded me all the way to the store. She went on and on about all the bad things that could and would happen to a thief. No matter how hard I begged, Mama wouldn't listen. It was a short ride back to the store. Mama marched me into the store and right up to the man at the register. She looked at me and I knew I had to do it.

I looked down at the floor and began, "Sir, I stole this candy from you and I wanted to give it back and tell you I am sorry and that I won't do it again and I hope you will not think bad about us because that's not the kind of people we are. We're God fearin' and I guess the devil must have got into me, and my mama and daddy won't stand for me actin' this way and if you want I won't come in the store again, but if I do come in, I won't ever do anything like this again."

I thought that was about all the things Mama had talked about in the car. I peeked up at him and he didn't seem mad at all.

"Son, that's mighty big of you to come in and tell what you did. I tell you what, since you ended up doing the right thing, you just keep that Tootsie Roll. You got a good mama here and you listen to her."

I wasn't sure Mama would let me eat it, but she did. The kids found out what I'd done and started calling me the Tootsie Roll Kid. If that's how bad guys got their names, I didn't want no part of it.

273

I thought the whole thing might bring on a whippin' from Daddy but it didn't. He had other things on his mind. Harry had been gone for two weeks and he should have been back by now. Mama went down to the gas station and called the number Louie had given her. They told her he had been moved to Burley, Idaho and she couldn't get ahold of him. We wondered if Harry was having trouble finding him. Maybe that was what was taking so long. Mama fussed around and Daddy kept working as we all waited for Harry and Louie.

It was almost a month when we came in from working at the sawmill to see the Ford and the International parked by the house.

Inside Louie and Harry were at the kitchen table telling Mama their story. They stood up when Daddy came in and both of them couldn't talk fast enough.

"Mama, this jail they had me in couldn't hold a cat. The bars were so weak I could've stretched them apart with my hands. I got to laughin' and cuttin' up so much about it, they took me on over to Burley so I could see what went on in a big town jail. It wasn't nothin' to talk about either.

"I waited for slowpoke here to show up and started to figure out this was a pretty nice place. They gave ya three meals a day and ya didn't have to work for 'em. It wasn't bad. I made friends with the guards and played cards with them and some of the other fellows in there. By the time Harry showed up, I was pretty rested up. Twenty one days it took him, by the time he walked in the door. I figured there wasn't any point in paying the fine. I had him get in jail with me and spend the rest of my time. I don't know what he'd done, but he did nothing but sleep the next two days."

"Anyway, I got him out, Mama, and here we are. All safe and sound," Harry added smiling real big at Mama. He sure wasn't wanting to explain anything he had done for all

274

those days. He told first one story and then another of flat tires, wrong roads, and helping folks along the way. I was pretty sure there were a lot of cigarettes and pool halls. I may have had my ideas, but I wasn't going to say anything. I wasn't a baby that would tattle.

"Why, Harry you look so handsome with your haircut." Esther said.

"This is called a 'Princeton.' The girls are crazy about it." Harry told us, seemed like he was crazy about it too. It was an inch long on top and a little longer on the side, combed straight back with plenty of Brill cream to keep his black hair in place. I had to admit, it did look good.

Pretty soon, what Harry had done for nearly a month between here and Idaho became less important than what we were going to do now. Daddy was glad Louie had come back, things weren't going good at the mill and he was thinking of moving on. Jerry Shriner had work at Rowe Creek and told Daddy he could put his sawmill up there. Daddy had Louie and Harry stick around while he read the Bible that night. He might not have said too much about their trip, but that night he sure preached fire and brimstone. When Daddy talked about the road to Hell, I looked at Harry. He turned his head towards me and winked.

Scared

It was the biggest load we had ever left with. Daddy was in the '37 International with the sawmill loaded on the back. Harry was driving "Leapin' Lizzie" and I was right alongside him. Mama brought up the rear in her green, bullet hole Chevy. It took from sun up to sun down to get to the new place. A mile or so off the blacktop down a long hill that curved to the left was a shotgun house. It was narrow but long and faced the road. The mill was back in the woods and

275

out of sight of the house. There was no electricity and running water but there was a little creek by the house. We used it to haul water to the house for drinking, washing and baths. The John Day River ran close by but it was too far to use for water every day.

The place was surrounded by hills, and even though we were close to the highway, we couldn't see or hear it. The trees grew thick but there were clearings every so often that grew wild flowers. The road hugged the side of the hills and was curvy as it wound its way back into the woods where the mill was set up. Further on down the hill were little houses that other mill workers lived in.

The mill wasn't owned by Daddy and was worked by hired men, just Daddy, Louie and Harry went to work there. They used an OC Oliver crawler instead of horses to skid the logs so not as much manpower was needed. The sawing hadn't started up yet, they were still working on bringing in logs. Since I was too young to work on the job, I worked on my bicycles. There had been enough room to bring all three so I hadn't had to leave them behind. Mostly Sheron rode with me, and Harry did on the days he didn't work. Hoyt Lynn wanted to ride bikes like me and Harry, but we didn't let him too much. He just hated being thought of as a baby. He was ten, but with Sheron and Esther being in between him and me, at almost fifteen I was too old for him. I was starting to feel bad about it so I'd started teaching him to ride every now and then. He was starting to get the hang of it.

There was plenty to do in the woods even without riding bicycles. Pines and fir shaded the ground and pine needles and underbrush covered it. The place was full of chipmunks. Sheron went in the woods with me and we watched the chipmunks jump from limb to limb and scurry across the ground.

276

"I got an idea." I told her one day while we were watching them.

"Uh oh," Sheron said, but she wanted to know what I was thinking.

"I bet we could catch one of them."

"What if they bite?"

"I saw a glove laying around the wood pile, I'll use that to grab 'em. They're so little, it probably wouldn't hurt anyway."

"All right, let's try it." She headed to the house for some food scraps and I went looking for a box. We met back in the woods and we propped the box up on one side with a stick holding it up. We tied a string to the stick and then went as far away as the string would let us, about twenty feet. We laid down on the ground and waited. After a while Sheron put her head down on her arms and kind of dozed off. I thought about closing my eyes too, but just as I was about to I saw movement around the box. I nudged Sheron and we watched as a chipmunk nosed around the box. He darted back and forth and then went in for the food. I jerked the string and dropped the box right over him.

We both let out a whoop like Daddy would and headed over to the trap. I eased up the edge of the box and stuck my hand with the glove inside. I had to feel around for the little thing and he tried to get away under the box when I lifted it. I got a hold of him and pulled him out. He looked at both of us with his little black eyes.

"He is so cute," Sheron said as she ran a finger down the fur of his tail.

"Now what do we do with him?" she asked.

We let him go and decided we would see if we could catch another one. We did it all over again and before long we caught another one, let him go, and then caught another one.

"Let's make a pen," I told Sheron.

277

I took a wash tub and put them in it and then laid boards across the top, with a little space in between but not so big that they could get out. We put little bowls of water and crackers in it and then went to the woods and set our trap some more. We got so good at catching them, that when it got dark we had about a dozen.

Mama and Daddy didn't mind what we were doing. Mama just said I had to keep them outside. I hadn't had a pet since Freckles in Chama, now I had too many to count. Sheron and I got so good at our chipmunk trapping that we had to make a bigger pen. We figured we would put it under two big trees that would shade it. The new pen was eight feet long and four feet wide. After I hammered the boards together I took some chicken wire and put it across the top. Before long, we had twenty-one chipmunks living in it. When we would lift the wire to feed and water them, they would all run to the other end. They didn't know it but that kept them from getting out. Some of them let me pick them up and hold them, and I got to where I didn't wear the glove anymore.

Every week or so, Mama and Daddy would take us all the two or three miles down to the John Day River. We would all play in the water. We didn't know how to swim so Mama was always after us to stay in the shallow part. The river had a rock bottom and had big boulders we could jump off of into the river. It was a great way to take a bath and Mama would wash her clothes out in the big river. She told us it sure made laundry less of a chore than hauling water from the creek to the house.

Daddy leaned up against a tree and talked to Mama about things at the mill.

"I sure don't like how these men work here. We been here all this time and we haven't put the saw to a log yet. They truck in the logs and set them in the pile, but nobody's in a hurry to get goin'. Fonny, I swear, seems like this job's

278

another dead end, just like Cottage Grove, Rosenbaum, Fossil and Condon." Daddy sounded put out by the way things were going. It seemed like over the last year he couldn't get anything going that would last or make any money.

He had talked to a fellow the other day that knew of a place over in Montana. Daddy thought maybe we ought to head there. There was a man looking for somebody to cut timber on his land, and then saw up the logs to sell.

"Well, there's nothin' here to stay for. Ain't like we can't find a place to live about as good or better than what we got." Mama was squeezing water out of the girls' dresses she had washed.

I wasn't happy about leaving like I usually was. There wasn't any trouble I needed to get away from and I had my pets to think of. I didn't figure there was any way Mama was going to let me bring them.

"No reason to stay, might as well move on. You write a letter and we'll go to town and mail it out to him, tell him we're comin'." Once an idea of leaving was put in Daddy's mind, I knew it wasn't going to be no time and we'd be gone.

After we got back to the house I figured I had better just do it so I walked out to the pen. I took the wire off of the boards and waited for them to all hurry away. Some of them left right off, but others of them seemed at home where they were. I walked away and figured they would be gone by morning.

I helped Daddy and the boys load up all the equipment we were going to take. Daddy loaded the sawmill onto the '37 International along with a 55 gallon barrel for water and the OC Oliver crawler. Louie gave Harry Leapin' Lizzie. He wouldn't be coming with us. He had a girlfriend in town with two little girls and he was going to stick around. Mama had a trailer behind her green Chevy for the rest of Daddy's things that didn't fit on the truck. I figured that's

279

where I would load my bicycles. I was in hopes that I could take all three, but I had picked out the best one to take in case Daddy didn't let me.

It took a few days to fix little things on the vehicles and every day I went out to my chipmunk pen to see if they were all gone. The fat one that I had had the longest acted like he didn't want to leave. I squatted down and told him it was time to go, just like I'd heard Daddy say so many times to us. He moved around the end of the pen but wouldn't leave. I finally got up and pushed him out of the pen until he ran into the woods.

There was still daylight left so I figured I'd let Hoyt Lynn ride my bike since it wasn't packed up. Harry said he'd ride too. I gave Hoyt Lynn the best one of the three. It was the only one with brakes. Harry and me just used our feet to slow the bikes. The three of us rode up to the highway, where the hill started and then headed downhill. I was in the lead, Harry right beside me, Hoyt Lynn brought up the rear. The hill was steep and it didn't take much to build up speed. The girls were out on the porch and waved as I went by. Swoosh, I passed the house. Swoosh, Harry went by, too. We were too far ahead to see Hoyt Lynn anymore. We flew past the other houses as we sped down the dirt road all the way to the end. Towards the bottom the road leveled out some and I used the sole of my shoe on the front tire to stop. Harry was right beside me and we talked about how fast we must have been going as we waited for Hoyt Lynn, but there was no sign of him.

"He was probably too chicken to go as fast we did. He must of stopped up by the house. I knew he was too much of a baby to come all the way down," Harry said.

"Let's go see where he is," I said as we started the slow ride back up the hill. The fast ride down was paid for by the hard pumping it took to make it back up. As we rode into the front yard a car pulled up and the man told Daddy there was a kid hurt and crying up the road toward the pavement. Daddy walked up the hill, and Harry and me drank some water from the bucket. It wasn't long before Daddy walked up carrying Hoyt Lynn hiccupping and crying. It seemed like he couldn't get a good gulp of air. He was bloody from head to toe and gravel was stuck all over him. Even his face was tore up and dirt and little sticks were stuck to his hair.

Hoyt Lynn was telling him, "It got to wobbling back and forth and it just kept getting faster." He sucked in some air. "The handle bars went back and forth and I couldn't get it to go straight." He started crying and he puckered up his face. "A rock caught under the front wheel and it stopped. I fell down the hill with the bike sliding with me. I couldn't stop fallin'."

Mama came out to take a hold of him. He looked pretty tore up but I didn't know how bad it was until I looked at Daddy's face. He was mad, about the maddest I had ever seen. Daddy turned towards me,

"You and your confounded bicycles!"

"Daddy, I didn't mean for him to wreck!"

"You are always acting the bully. And yore wastin' time on these fool things. Look what happens, somebody got hurt!"

I tried to tell Daddy that I had given Hoyt Lynn the one with brakes, I hadn't thought that he didn't know how to use them. But Daddy wouldn't hear me.

"I ought to whip your backside until you can't sit down!"

"Daddy, I didn't mean it, I didn't mean for him to get hurt."

He grabbed up one of the bikes and threw it as far as he could. He reached down again and came up with a board.

"Get over here."

281

"Daddy, no, please Daddy." I could barely get his name out as crying turned to a sob. I hadn't ever been this scared of Daddy.

All the kids in the yard, not just me and Hoyt Lynn were crying. Mama was on the porch tending Hoyt Lynn, she suddenly stood up and moved towards us, "Wesley!"

Daddy stepped closer to me with the board. He raised it over his head with one arm and I stood frozen staring up at the board waiting for it to come down. Louie stepped in front of him.

"No, Daddy, you ain't gonna hit him with that board."

Daddy kept coming at me and Louie grabbed him and manhandled him to stop. Daddy looked at me, a boy almost 15 years old crying. He looked at all the bawling kids and Mama. He was breathing hard and he didn't say anything. He walked over to the bicycle still close and swung the board down on it until it broke apart. Then he walked into the house.

All of us gathered around Mama crying. "Your Daddy's having a hard time, now. Things aren't going so good for him. We have to let him be for a while. Let's get supper on the table and get Hoyt Lynn doctored up."

I had forgotten Hoyt Lynn in my own problems. I stayed outside while Mama and the girls cleaned him up and put him to bed. Esther sat by his bedside and tended him. Supper got put on the table and Daddy walked from the chair at the front of the house and sat at his place at the table. I slipped onto the bench at the table and tried to not have him see me. Not a one of us spoke during supper. That night Daddy didn't read the Bible.

Socks

It seemed like trouble had still found me and I couldn't wait for us to be gone. We had stayed around for a few extra days waiting for Hoyt Lynn to heal up some. Whenever I looked at him laying up in the bed, I just wanted him to act fine so Daddy would forget all about what had happened. Esther tending him and babying him hadn't made things any better. I knew Hoyt Lynn was hurt. There wasn't a place on his body that the skin hadn't been tore off, but I just wanted him to get up.

When we finally were ready to leave, I couldn't help but go out and look at the mess that used to be my bicycles. I guess I didn't have to see if Mama would let me take one now. Daddy had said no more bicycles and so I guess my riding days were over. Harry walked up beside me and saw what I was looking at. He put his arm across my shoulders and said, "It's time you started drivin' anyway, you ain't a little kid no more! Come on let's get in Leapin' Lizzie and see what she'll do."

I followed Harry to the Ford, stuck my arm out the window and told myself I was too old for bicycles anyway. The warm wind blew in the cab as we made a big dust trail behind us. We headed out of the canyon slow and plodding like a train headed up hill. With all the vehicles working hard to pull their load, we were just as smoky as a train, too. Harry and me were in the lead when we got on the black top. Mama was next and Daddy followed behind.

It was over six hundred miles to White Sulphur Springs, Montana so Daddy told us it would take a few days or so to get there. The vehicles could only go about 35 or 40 miles an hour with our loads. Harry and me sat back in the truck seat, hot with the heat of the motor hitting us and the sun shine coming in the windows. The dry air blew in the window whipping our hair this way and that. Well, my hair anyway. Harry's Princeton was plastered down pretty good with Brill Cream.

Harry pulled out a couple of cigarettes and then I did feel grown up. He fished some matches out of his pocket and we went to light up. It was a struggle in the blowing wind so we rolled our windows up. After a few burned up matches we finally got an end of the Pall Mall's to light. I tried not to cough when I breathed in and made sure not to suck it in too deep. Harry didn't have any trouble at all. We flicked our ashes out the wing vent just in case Mama might see from the car behind us.

The road from Oregon to Washington

I was starting to sweat and so was Harry in the closed in cab. I puffed my cigarette a few times when I brought it to my mouth. It looked like I was really going to town on my cigarette, but most of the smoke wasn't going down my throat but back in the cab. I started having to cough even when I wasn't puffing on the cigarette and so did Harry. The inside of the cab started to smell like smoke and it was getting harder to see out the windshield for the cloud we were making.

"Harry we better get these windows down, I can't breathe," I told him.

We cranked our windows down as fast we could. The wind helped a little but even with the windows down, the smoke in the cab was getting worse. I looked down and saw smoke coming from under the seat.

"There's something on fire under here," I hollered at Harry to be heard above the noise of the wind coming in the windows.

"What is it?" Harry tried to look and keep the Ford on the road.

I reached my hand under the seat and pulled out an old sock of Louie's.

"Socks! Old socks are under here, and they're on fire!" Louie always made a mess and left a mess.

The smoke in the cab was getting thicker and was going out of the windows. Harry started to pull over as I tried to beat out the smoking socks. He came to a stop in a wide spot in the road.

"Don't worry about them socks. Get rid of these cigarettes before Mama and Daddy see!" Harry hollered at me.

Mama was coming up from behind and stopping behind us. Daddy saw the trouble and pulled in behind Mama.

Harry and me put out our cigarettes and put them in our pockets. Harry and me had to get out of the smoky cab to get a breath of air. Mama and Daddy had got to us and Daddy had a bucket of water in his hand.

"Some old socks under the seat caught on fire," Harry told them. He was pulling papers and wrappers, Coke bottles and more socks out from under the seat.

"How'd it start?" Daddy wondered. He poured some of the water on the floor board of the truck and Mama stomped on the things that were on fire on the ground.

"I don't know. Me and Alton smelled somethin' and then smoke was all over."

"How in the world?" Mama was looking the cab over.

"I guess a spark must have come from somewhere and it's been smoldering for a while. The wind finally helped

285

it catch." Daddy couldn't figure anything else out. "Well, it's all out, let's keep moving."

Harry and me drove back onto the road. We fished our cigarettes out of our pockets and as Harry handed me the match, he said, "That was close."

The Hitchhiker

This part of Oregon was filled with bare hills and fields. There were little canyons in the hills where most of the trees grew, but when we drove up out of them, the trees were gone and we could see for miles. Back behind us we could see mountains in the distance and up to the left of us was the faint peak of Mt. Hood. Harry and me didn't talk much. We sang for a while and since Mama wasn't around we sang, *Sixteen Tons*. Boy, if Mama ever heard that song on the radio we had to turn it off. I wasn't sure why we weren't allowed to sing it. I thought it might have something to do with the part about selling your soul. I was told a lot of things were sinful, but not why.

The first night we camped out at a roadside table. We stopped before dark to make camp. I looked out at all the dark brown, treeless country we were driving through. We were a long ways away but we could already see a dark blue river that ran through the bare country. Daddy said it was the Columbia River and Washington State was on the other side. We'd be there tomorrow. Mama was disappointed to not find a tree to camp under.

Supper was commodity beef, surplus army meat sealed in a can. Mama mixed rice up in it and it tasted pretty good. Daddy had brought along some wood for a camp fire in case there wasn't any around. It was a good thing because what was there was few and far between.

Mama and Daddy had a mattress to sleep on. It was always the first thing unloaded for the night and the last thing loaded when we took off the next day. The rest of us slept on pallets outside or on the seats in the car, wrapped in blankets. We were pretty far north, so the nights were cool.

Campsite breakfast was almost always oatmeal or mush. I thought mush was a good name because that is just what it looked like. Something I couldn't make out, mushed into something I didn't want to eat. When Mama fixed that, I would just wait for dinner time in the middle of the day to eat what Mama had then. All the days driving was just about like the first, the country desert like and lots of miles to make.

When we stopped at midday, Daddy told us he had felt something wrong with the truck while he was driving, now that we had stopped he wanted to look at it. The back tire needed to come off. Daddy, Harry and me worked to take it off the tire on the outside and get to the one on the inside. Mama and the girls set up camp for dinner. The green Chevy was parked beside the truck and Hoyt Lynn leaned up against it to watch us work. I think he wanted to help so he got close, but knew to stay out of the way.

The outside tire came off and I rolled it over out of the way. Harry and Daddy worked on the inside tire. Hoyt Lynn watched for a while and then Mama called him to come and carry something for her from the car. As he walked away Daddy took his little sledge hammer and banged on the lock ring. The lock ring was about as big around as a steering wheel and held the inside wheel in place. Daddy squatted down and hammered on it a couple of times and then BOOM! The lock ring blew off the tire. It got all our attention. It came off with so much pressure it hit Daddy's hand holding the hammer and then flew through the air and hit the Chevy broadside on the back and made a circle sized dent. After it hit the car it fell to the ground. Right where Hoyt Lynn had been standing.

"That could have hit Hoyt Lynn! He was standing right there," Harry said as he walked over to the dented car.

Daddy had hollered when the lock ring hit his hand. When we looked over to him he opened his fist and the hammer handle was broken right where he had gripped it. He stood up from where he had been squatting and groaned.

"Fonny, I think I've broken my fingers."

Mama hurried to him and looked at his hand. She felt it and they guessed that three of his fingers were broken. There was no way of knowing for sure. Mama took a rag and wrapped Daddy's hand as tight as he could stand.

The lock ring had to go back on even with Daddy's busted fingers. Harry helped him and they got it hammered back on the tire. It was only the middle of the day, but with all that had happened we made camp for the night. The little kids played and looked for treasure that might be found on the ground. Rocks that were shaped like an animal or something somebody might have left behind. Daddy laid down on his mattress and slept most of the rest of the day.

"Too bad we don't have any more cigarettes. We could have snuck off and smoked some," Harry said, looking around.

"Well, Harry, they don't last long when you have only four of them to begin with."

"Ah, we'll get more. We'll be in a town somewhere down the line."

"What are you gonna use for money?"

"Don't worry, little brother, I'll figure something out."

When Harry wanted something, he could always find a way to get it. He always made sure I got in on it too. Sometimes I wasn't too sure that I wanted in on all of his fun. Harry might get out of trouble with Mama since he seemed to be her pet, but it was always harder for me. One good thing was, Harry was older, and the older one was always in charge of the younger. I planned to use that if he ever got me into too much trouble.

Daddy seemed good as new the next morning. Mama retied his hand and we kept moving. Sometimes we saw fellows hitchhiking along the way, some with satchels and some with nothing. Every once in a while a man might have a dog with him.

When we pulled long grades, the Ford got hot and we would fill the radiator with water from the water bag hanging outside the truck. We used the barrel of water to refill the bag. Harry and me knew that before dark we were to look for a spot to stop. Sometimes all we could find was a wide spot beside the road. If there was a big tree or some shade we knew that was better than a place that didn't have any. The day had been long when me and Harry rolled into a spot we liked. Mama followed us in but Daddy took a little longer. When he finally came chugging in we saw he had somebody with him. Mama said she might have known he couldn't leave a fellow to walk. I was kind of disappointed when I saw he didn't have a dog.

Daddy got out and introduced the man to Mama. His name was Joe and his last name was hard to say. He told us it was Italian. He was out of work, but he was usually a camp cook for cowboys. Daddy sat down to visit with him, but since he was a cook he helped Mama fix supper. He was handy with the cooking and also helped the girls clean up. Daddy didn't doze off as quick with company so the grownups all visited.

"Where are you headed to?" Daddy wanted to know.

"Well, I'm not set on any place at all. I can go where ever I feel. I lost my job cooking for an outfit west of here, so I thought I would see what I could find this way."

"You're welcome to ride with us, one more won't hurt. Maybe when we get to the ranch, you can find work cooking there," Daddy offered.

Joe decided that's what he would do and the next morning after helping Mama with breakfast and cleanup he got in with Daddy and we all headed east. Harry was glad to have him come along because he had cigarettes. Well, not really cigarettes. He had Prince Albert tobacco and papers. He rolled his own smokes. He made it look easy and it didn't take him but a few seconds to roll one. He held the paper with his thumb and middle finger and used his pointing finger to make a cradle to hold the tobacco. He filled the paper with tobacco and licked one of the long sides of the paper and stuck it to the other, and then twisted it to seal the ends.

He gave some makings to Harry and me and we would slip around and try to roll our own. He didn't smoke around camp out of respect for Mama, but he didn't see anything wrong with it so he kept me and Harry's smoking a secret.

We crossed the line into Montana and the country got steeper and harder to drive. The hills became mountains. We blew out lots of black smoke as we tried to make it up and over the top of the passes. When we would head downhill we would meet big trucks trying to make their way up the mountain. The trucks went so slow anybody could get out and walk beside them. The cabs got so hot with the heat of the engine coming through the firewall and floor, the driver would stick his right foot on the throttle, stand outside the truck on the running board and steer the truck with one hand. I couldn't wait to try driving like that when I got the chance.

We camped outside of Helena. Mama and the girls drove on into town to get supplies. We were close to White Sulphur Springs, so Mama was going to get just enough to finish the trip. We stayed out at the camp and dozed off in the hot summer sun. Joe worked around camp and did whatever he saw needed to be done.

When Mama and the girls came back, they were excited to show what they had bought. Mama had gone to the second hand store and bought some clothes. The girls had a few new things and there were some shirts for Harry and me to share.

"Did you find me any cowboy boots, Mama?" I wanted some more than ever now that we were in ranch country.

"No Alton, no boots. Your shoes are just fine."

Mama just couldn't see how much I needed cowboy boots. I wore loafers in town, and when we worked in the woods we had old lace up boots that we wore. They were so big it was like one size fit everybody. I was going to get me some cowboy boots someday.

She did bring the Italian fellow some clothes. He got a denim shirt and pants to wear. He hadn't had a change of clothes before now. He was grateful to Mama and seemed to work even harder for her around camp. We slept there that night and Daddy told us we would make it to our place the next day.

We drove through the little town called White Sulphur Springs. Harry and I couldn't keep our eyes off the place. There were pickups parked everywhere and we counted at least nine bars. There was a big building that was built clear out into the street that the cars had to go around. There were only two grocery stores and one barber. People walked all over the place with beers and drinks in their hands. We could see into the bars because there were no walls, the buildings were open to the street. There were slot machines and gambling everywhere. It was loud and dusty and wild and one of the best places I had ever seen.

291

MONTANA 1960

Bucked

We drove straight through town without stopping. Like other times when we moved to a new town, we didn't really end up living there. We headed out about forty more miles to the sawmill camp. We were surrounded by mountains and trees and we drove through some hills to a big ranch. The place where we stopped had a couple of houses that were about a half a mile apart. There was a stream close by and a sheepherder's wagon set up. A man came riding up on a little pony that was buckskin and white. The cowboy was a skinny guy with his left arm missing below the elbow. He told us his name was Gabby and that he was the one that lived in the wagon. I wondered how he had lost his arm but wouldn't think of asking. Mama would have tore me up if I did something so rude.

He told us a family stayed in one house and worked up here in the summer. They chopped wood and hauled it to town to sell. Daddy was going to set up the mill further up the creek so we drove past the houses to a clearing. Gabby brought in two horses for skidding logs and Daddy had me and Harry make a corral for them. While Daddy talked to Gabby he pulled out a pouch of tobacco, held his cigarette paper on his stump of an arm and rolled a cigarette as pretty as any Joe had ever rolled. I sure thought he was something.

"You boys string this rope around these trees a couple of times and keep the creek in the middle of it." Daddy wasn't as impressed with Gabby as I was and wanted us to get to work.

Daddy didn't show us. He told us and we were to just do it. Harry and me just got to work tying up the rope to a tree. I held one end of the rope and walked to the outside of

293

the trees until I came back to the start. We tied it up again a little higher and circled the trees again. When we had the horses corralled we wouldn't have to worry about watering them, the creek would do it for us.

I sure liked the looks of Gabby's pony so I kept talking about horses. He told us the pony's name was Buck but that the work horses didn't have names. He stayed around for a while and I stayed close to him so I could look at his horse. He was just my size. Gabby went back to his wagon and we settled in for the first night.

We would be living out of the cars for a few days until Daddy got the mill running. Just like before when there wasn't any house, the mill had to get going to have the lumber for the house. Just before the sun went down deer walked out of the woods and ate grass close to us. Daddy told Mama there ought not to be any trouble with finding meat. Mama smiled a tired smile and had Esther and Sheron get the little kids to bed. Then she made the mattress for her and Daddy. It was so quiet in the darkness we could hear bugs and what I figured were deer walking through the woods. The snoring from Daddy and Harry finally drowned out the night noises.

The next day we started putting up the sawmill. Joe stayed and helped Mama. Daddy, Harry and me went to work. The three of us got the saw mill put up and then went about felling the trees. We used power saws and skid the logs out with the OC3 Oliver. Harry ran the crawler and I hooked the chokers. I would take a cable and loop in around the log and hook it with a ball and nubbin. When the cable was drawn up tight, it would choke around the log and get tight. Harry would pull the log out to the pile and we would do the same thing all over again. Sometimes the crawler wouldn't go as far back in the woods as we needed and we would hook up one of the horses to skid the log out.

When we got enough logs for the house it was time to saw. Daddy could measure the logs in his mind and know how many it took. With just the three of us working Daddy had to use the metal dogs that stuck up to turn the log himself to find the right spot to make the first cut. Harry worked as tail sawyer and I was to stack the boards fifty-two high, just a little above the cab on the truck. We didn't edge the boards, so they had bark left on the outside. When the load got tall I would hold one end of the board and prop the other on the load and push the board up into place. The first load was to go over to the site for the house. It was close enough to Rock Creek to make getting water easy, but upstream from the horse corral. Mama used the creek to keep fresh things cool, like milk or eggs, by putting them in a gunny sack and letting the cold water run over them.

Sawmill shacks that were just for the summer, like now, didn't need a pitched roof. The front of the house was taller than the back and that slope let the water run off. There was a spot for the door and a couple of windows to let in light. There was nothing to be done for the bugs that flew in and out. If we were there long enough and the green boards started to shrink, Daddy would take strips from the mill and nail them on top of the boards to cover up the gap. Inside, Mama had a portable cook stove and a stand for her dishpan. The beds were laid out in the corners.

After the house was done, we began working for money. We cut timber, skidded logs and sawed lumber. When we had a load on the truck, it was time to take it to town. Daddy and Harry took the first load to town and I stayed behind.

I visited with Gabby who was camped just a few miles from our place. It was a cool evening and we sat outside and smoked. He told me he had lost his arm in the war but we didn't really talk much. His pony was grazing nearby and I got up the nerve to ask him if I could ride him and he said I could if I took off the saddle and rubbed him down when I was done. I walked over to the horse and petted him, put my foot in the stirrup and swung on. I rode him all over the pasture and the pony obeyed all that I guided him to do. If only I was wearing cowboy boots, I'd looked just like a real cowboy. Gabby hollered at me to bring him in just before it got too dark to see. I trotted him in and took care of taking his saddle off and rubbed him down and fed him. I took a lot of care so that Gabby would let me ride him again.

I saw Daddy and Harry's headlights coming as they were driving back, so I walked back up to the house. I went by the corral where the workhorses were. We would be working them the next day since we would be back in the woods. I leaned up against the fence and thought that if these horses got out tonight, tomorrow I could use Gabby's horse to go and find them. I unhooked the gate and opened it. I left it and hoped they'd wander out so that I could use Buck to round them up. I couldn't wait for morning so I could be back on that pony.

When Hoyt Lynn brought in water the next morning he told Daddy that the horses were gone. Right off I spoke up, "Daddy, if you want me to I'll go down and borrow Gabby's horse and see if I can find them." It looked like my plan was going to work out.

"You had better, we're gonna need them today. Hurry up and see what you get done with the horses. I don't want to waste much daylight."

I ran down to Gabby's wagon. He was up and sitting outside his wagon sipping on a cup of coffee. I told him about the horses. The pony was already saddled and tied to the wagon.

"Think I could borrow the pony to go and find them up?"

"Go ahead, son, but he's fresh this morning." I didn't hear anything past 'go ahead' as I headed for Buck's rope. I got the reins, put my foot in the stirrup and swung my leg up. He reared up and came off all four feet. This couldn't be the same horse I had ridden last night. I bounced in the air, came down on the saddle with my belly, and bounced back up. He bucked again and I bounced up again and came down on the back of the saddle. One more time and I hit the ground hard. The wind was knocked out of me and I rolled around on the ground trying to get a breath. After I got a little air I tried to get on again. He wasn't going to let me. Every time I got close he jerked the reins out of my reach.

Gabby didn't say anything as he watched my battle with Buck. I was wore out, sweaty and beat up, as Buck grazed on the grass. I might have thought he was ignoring me if it wasn't for his ears twitching, telling me he was keeping an eye on me. Daddy hollered at me from the house to quit messing around and get to finding the work animals. I had to start off on foot to look for the horses, thinking this hadn't been one of my best ideas.

Gabby took a last sip of coffee and threw the rest on the ground. He walked over to the pony, got in the saddle, turned the horse so he could look at me and said, "I told you he was fresh."

Model T Races

Town was a long ways away so me and Daddy got an early start. It was my turn to go with Daddy to take the truckload of boards to the lumber yard. Most times Mama went with him to get groceries, but sometimes Harry or me would get to go. It took quite a while to drive the loaded truck down the dirt road. Daddy had me fill a water thermos to take with us and we chugged our way towards town.

The dirt road was wash boarded, full of holes and rough. The truck jerked us around in the cab and me and Daddy both had to hold on tight to keep from getting flung out. There was a steep downhill part to the road where Daddy had to be careful to keep the truck in the road and the load on the truck. He was mashing on the brake and holding onto the steering wheel with all his strength when the truck jerked hard. Daddy held on to the wheel, but it wasn't steering the truck. We looked and saw that the steering column had come loose and he was holding onto a steering wheel that wasn't attached to anything. The front left wheel was headed to the bar ditch beside the road. Daddy didn't let up on the brake and he got the truck stopped before we were wrecked.

The column under the steering wheel slipped down over a rod that went to the steering box. That's how the car was steered. The sleeve that went over the rod was broke in two. With it broke, there was no way to steer.

"We'll have to get this to town and find a welder to get it put back right," Daddy said, kind of to me. Mostly to himself.

"We just gonna walk, Daddy?" It was still a long ways to town.

"We'll start off, but somebody will pick us up."

Daddy took the steering wheel off the column and left it in the cab. He put the column on his shoulder and started down the road. I'd a whistled if I could, but I never did learn. I didn't mind 'cause Daddy couldn't either. He talked about the country and how pretty it was. We saw a bald eagle on the top of a fence post and even with us close by he didn't fly off.

Before we got to the black top we heard a truck, it was the family that cut firewood at the ranch so we caught a ride with them into town. Daddy had them drop us off at the yard

298

where we delivered our usual lumber. He said there were all kinds of tools there to get things fixed. That's where we went to get the column welded. Before long we hitched a ride back out to the truck and got busy fixing it.

When Daddy tried to put the welded column in the truck it wouldn't fit. The cab was too small for the long column to fit over the rod. I didn't know what Daddy was going to do, but he went to his tool box on the back of the truck and took out some tin snips. From inside the cab he looked up at the roof and eyed where the column needed more room. He went about cutting the top of the cab and making a hole about the size of a silver dollar. He cut a half moon and laid open the metal.

"Put that column up through that hole and see if it won't fit over the rod now, son." He told me.

I did what he told me. The column stuck out of the cab the six inches or so we needed to fit over the rod. He finished putting it back together and then folded the cut metal down back in place. We got back in and started for town the second time to deliver our lumber.

"A little ole thing like the steering wheel coming off ain't gonna keep us stopped."

I knew nothing stopped Daddy.

When we got to town, the mill workers unloaded the truck and Daddy and me walked around in town. Daddy let us look around a while. The town was full of people, ranchers, loggers and wild cowboys. Mama always called them that. She called the town rough and didn't want any of us coming into it very often. Getting groceries was a good excuse to get to come and look around. Daddy heard folks talking about a big Model T race on Saturday. They had it every year and it was a big time. I asked Daddy if we could come back and watch. I hoped Daddy would let us. I knew he sure did like a car race. I couldn't wait to tell the kids when we got back.

When Saturday came around we all loaded up in the car. The girls didn't really care about the car races, they were just glad to be in town. As we drove down the main street we were all wide eyed at the way the people drank and laughed and cut up right there on the street. There were all kinds of carts lined up on the street selling different things like peanuts and candy and Cokes. Daddy followed the main street and made the little jog around the hotel and café that stuck out in the middle of the road.

As soon as the car stopped all of us kids scattered. There was a big rock house high on a hill that looked like a castle. We were about to head towards it, when we heard Daddy was going to buy us ice cream, so we forgot the castle.

Daddy said he learned the Model T had to be older than 1916 and that was the year before Mama was born. Daddy teased her and told her she was too young to race. She just laughed at him. The crowd started cheering as the black cars lined up to the south and started revving their engines. Some had tops and some didn't. Some looked like they had just been drug out of the field and others looked like they had been slicked up a bit. They took off and strung out one after another as they tried to roar through town with their little motors. One car tried to edge out another one right there down the middle of Main Street. We cheered with the crowd as they passed us and headed north outside of town to the finish. I couldn't tell who won and didn't care. It was just fun watching cars go fast. Mama still didn't like the town so she was glad when we left.

Gabby met us at the gate when we got back and told us there was fire in the woods. Thunderstorms tried to kick up in the late afternoon, but not a lot of rain fell. There had been quite a bit of dry lightning and there was a fire a few miles into the woods. Since we were all hired by JW Rankin, and part of his ranch was on fire, we were all supposed to quit what we were doing and head to the camp where men were gathering. We were going to go and fight fire. This was shaping up to be one of the best summers I ever had.

They had a camp set up for everyone to report to, and Daddy, Harry and me and even Joe the cook headed up to work the fire. Gabby came along too, but he rode his horse there. Quite a few men were working and we overheard that some of them were hired out of the state prison. I tried to see which ones looked the meanest so I would know who the jailbirds were. Daddy and Harry were given shovels along with the other men to make fire breaks. Joe was made camp cook. I guess those in charge must have thought I was too young so I just ended up riding Gabby's horse around looking for hot spots. I tried to ride just like the cowboys, back straight and no bouncing. If only I had the boots.

After working all day we came in at dusk and ate beans and potatoes and drank coffee. The camp was out in the middle of the ranch property so just about every day we saw stray cows around the edge of camp. One night we rode up to see Joe facing down a big, Black Angus bull. It wasn't no more than ten feet away from Joe. The bull wasn't moving as Joe waved his apron with both hands and told him, "shoo, shoo.' It was like he thought that bull was a cat or something. Nobody helped Joe they were so busy laughing at the sight. The bull turned, and slowly walked off. Joe didn't think it was too funny, but it was.

We worked the fire for two weeks. We all slept on the ground, wrapped in blankets and the older men got up slower and slower every day. I might have got up a little slow myself, but I made sure nobody saw. I got used to the smell of smoke in the air but was sorry I hadn't seen much of the flames. Most of the work was digging up live grass and brush and burning fire lines so the fire wouldn't spread.

I was sorry to head back to the sawmill, my horse riding days over. The ranch owner paid Daddy $85 for all of our work so I guess it was a good job. Joe left us after the fire. He got a job cooking for an outfit a few miles away. It was just the family for a while, but with the money we made, Mama figured it was time to go back home. To her and Daddy, that meant Louisiana.

Batching

I waved at Mama and the kids as they headed out in the car, a trailer loaded up behind them. This was the first time I could remember that I stood and watched Mama's car leave and I wasn't in it. Daddy wanted to stay and work the rest of the summer and make some more money. Mama figured she'd head out now and get the kids ready for school. That was going to be in just a few weeks. I had been worried for a time that I was going to have to go with her but Daddy told her he needed me and Harry, who'd quit school after Fossil. I sure felt grown when Daddy told Mama he needed me and she said I could stay. The green bullet hole Chevy was lost in the dust cloud it made as Mama steered it through the curve in the road.

The three of us were going to batch together and work hard to make as much as we could. Every morning Harry and me argued over who was going to get water and who was going to make the fire. After Daddy cleared his throat, we just went about getting it done. There were still plenty of deer around and Daddy made use of the gun Louie had brought him in Fossil. We had venison just about every meal. The deer were just outside our door in the morning and came back around when the sun went down. Daddy said they were so

302

plentiful that you could just about walk outside and ask them to get in the cook pot. What he really did was shoot one and then hang it from two trees and cut the meat from it for us to eat. Every meal was pancakes and venison, usually with backstrap, the meat that ran down the spine of the deer. I started to miss Mama's cooking.

Before it got dark one night, Daddy told Harry to go in the house and get supper started. Daddy sent me in after we worked for a little longer. Harry was asleep on the bed with no fire made and no supper cooking. I kicked the bed and told him he better get to fixing supper.

"Alton, if you get the wood and water, I'll cook as many pancakes as you want." I knew we needed to get going on something before Daddy showed up so I agreed.

I hurried, I didn't want Daddy to come in find nothing done. When it came time to cook the pancakes, I sat at the table and had Harry wait on me. I wanted to make sure he worked, so as soon as he set down a stack, I ordered up some more until I had eaten twenty eight of them. I was making sure I hadn't got the short end of the stick. The next morning he made me the same deal and I ate eighteen more. By the time that meal was over I didn't want to eat pancakes for a while and Harry was glad to get the wood and the water.

Mama had us bathe pretty regular with the water that ran down through Rock Creek. With her gone though, Daddy didn't seem to think about us taking a bath. It was hard for me to keep track of what day it was, so lugging all that water from the creek happened less and less. Without the women around Daddy didn't bother to shave. Daddy's eyebrows grew longer than I had ever seen. He had so much hair coming out of his nose and ears and from his face I don't think Mama would have known who he was. He looked like a big grey bear. He was concerned about sawing the timber and finishing our job so we could follow Mama. We worked from daylight to dark and at night we were too tired to do much but eat and go to bed.

I wasn't too sad when a part on the mill broke and we had to quit sawing in the middle of the day. After a bit Daddy figured out what was wrong and he said he would send Harry to town for the part. Daddy and me would work on skidding while we waited for Harry to come back.

Harry couldn't get out of there fast enough. Daddy gave him a pocket full of money and the broke part.

"Be back before dark, son. Stay outta trouble."

Harry fired up the International and was gone before Daddy might have changed his mind. Daddy and me were left afoot in the woods, but we had plenty to do.

After working the rest of the day, we went to the house and made our pancakes with cold meat. Daddy dozed off in a chair while I kept a look out for Harry. Daddy woke up and said it was time to turn in. He turned out the lantern and we went to bed with no sign of him. The next morning there was still no Harry.

Daddy was slow to get up from the table when we heard the other family coming in to get a load of firewood. Daddy went outside and talked to them and then hollered over at me. He told me I was to ride into town with them, find Harry and bring him back. I was crowding in the car before Daddy finished talking.

I didn't know before we hit town that it was Saturday. So the place was jumping. Cowboys and ranchers had their pickups parked everywhere. People were coming and going from the bars, hollering and talking, dust was flying everywhere. We parked and I jumped out of the pickup and started scouting around for Harry. There were so many bars in town I was tempted to go inside and look in them, but I didn't dare.

There was a pool hall in the middle of town and I headed over that way. I walked in from the bright sunlight and had trouble seeing in the dark room for a minute.

"Hey, little brother!" Harry called to me.

There he was. Pool cue in his hand and a cigarette hanging from his mouth. His Princeton was in place and he had a big smile on his face. I grinned back when I saw him and headed over.

"Daddy sent me to find you," I told him right off.

"Well, you found me. Grab a stick and shoot some pool with me."

I hadn't ever been inside a pool hall before but I liked it. Harry told his new buddies I was his brother and showed me how to hit the ball on the pool table with the stick. He bet on shots with his buddies and was good enough that we had enough money for Cokes and cigarettes. Harry let me have a few silver dollars and they weighted down my pocket. They didn't use paper money for singles here, just the coins.

I didn't see the sun going down outside until they started turning on the lights. I just then remembered what Daddy had told me to do.

"We better get back to Daddy. He's waitin' on us." It was hard to say, since I didn't really want to leave.

"We can't make it before dark, anyway. We might as well stay here and go in the morning." Harry handed me a Coke, I took it and figured he knew what was right.

A lady that worked in the back told us there were beds upstairs that we could sleep in if they were empty. They were for the cowboys and sheepherders that drank too much and couldn't find their way home. Harry thanked her and told her we'd go up in a while. Just before the sun came up we went upstairs and shared a cot. We weren't too sure we'd have to pay for it or not, so just in case we only stayed in one.

305

The next morning we slept till the sun got hot. We figured it was too early to head back so we started playing pool. Harry said smoking kept you from getting hungry and gave me one to smoke while we played. I was getting hungry anyway so I thought I might walk around the town and see what there was to eat. Harry had a few dollars left from the parts he hadn't bought and he gave them to me to find us some food. I jingled the money in my pocket as I walked across the road. I squinted in the sun, my cigarette hanging out of my mouth and headed to the other side of the street to the café.

I didn't pay much attention to the man standing on the sidewalk across the street as I made my way towards him. He kept an eye on me as I got closer and when the sun got behind the building I looked him right in the face. Daddy! I almost didn't know him. He was wearing clean clothes and a new hat. His hair was cut and he was shaved, even his nose and ears. His eyebrows looked normal again.

I realized I had a cigarette in my hand and whipped it behind me and threw it on the ground as fast as I could. I managed to speak.

'Hey, Daddy."

"Go get Harry."

I ran back to the pool hall faster than I had ever run in any of my footraces.

"Daddy's here," I hollered like a little boy. All thought of being a grown up gone from my mind, replaced by the fear of Daddy showing up. I didn't know if Harry had thought about it, but I didn't have any idea what we were going to tell Daddy.

Harry threw down his cigarette and we both hustled out. Daddy was pulling on the brim of his hat, a sure sign he was mad. He marched us to the International and we got in. The part we had needed was bundled up and tied to the bed

306

of the truck. I guess he'd got that taken care of himself before getting cleaned up. Sitting so close to Daddy on the way back, knowing what we had been doing, was almost more than I could stand.

He didn't say a word as we headed out of town. Harry and me didn't dare make a sound as we bounced along the rough road. The forty miles seemed like four hundred and my mind couldn't stop thinking of the whippin' that was sure to come. When we pulled up to the house, Daddy got out and Harry and me got ready for what was coming. Daddy looked at us for a long time then said, "I don't know what I'm gonna do with you boys."

I almost cried.

A Cool Ride

The wind blew hard in my face as the old International worked its way up and down the hills on the two lane highway. It didn't have a windshield to block the wind any, but I didn't really mind all that much. Making sure I stayed in the seat took my mind off just about everything else. We were headed to Louisiana, back to Mama and the family.

Daddy got the mill running with the part we had all gone after in town and we finished up the job. We loaded the sawmill onto the back of the truck and everything else we could strap down to take with us. The little International had a narrow cab and it would be a tight squeeze for all of the two thousand miles we had to go. Just like always Daddy had the fix for that problem.

He built a little seat on the flatbed beside the cab on the passenger side. When one of us sat down in the seat we were just a little behind the window. We used a bracket that held the side mirror as a foot rest. There was just a few inches between all of us in height so it worked out good. It was a pretty secure seat and if you did doze off, the sides of the seat kept you held on. If it rained too hard, Daddy said we would just get in the cab till it let up.

It was my turn to be outside. Daddy was driving and Harry was riding with his arm out as we left Billings. Daddy had stopped at a store and bought us all brand new britches and Harry and me matching orange western shirts. We hadn't done any wash in the weeks since Mama had left so about the only way we could put on clean clothes was to buy them. The jeans were so stiff I could hardly bend my knees and I kept squatting to try and break them in. One thing about old clothes they were always plenty soft.

We headed into Wyoming, where the hills were bare and the wind never stopped. It didn't really matter if we were moving or not, the air seemed to always beat your hair and hit your face. After a few hours we switched and Harry or Daddy took turns in the extra seat. Harry drove when Daddy was out there and we would cut up with each other once we saw Daddy's head droop as he fell asleep out in the sun. He kept his hat tied on with a long rope around his head. The wind blew up his pant legs making them look fat like sausages.

We mostly camped at night and Daddy boiled coffee of a morning. We were out of pancakes we had brought along to eat so we had to find some food to stock up on. We drove into a little town in Wyoming and Daddy steered us to a café that was right in the middle of town. He stopped the truck and got out. When he saw me and Harry weren't right behind him he looked back at us.

"Come on boys, let's get us somethin' to eat." Daddy waved his hand at us as he walked towards the door. Harry jumped down from the seat and I got out of the door. We grinned at each other. For the first time in my fifteen years I ordered food from a menu in a café. Well, Daddy did anyway. He got us all an order of biscuits and gravy and coffee. As we ate our food, the waitress kept coming back over and filling up our coffee cups with more. I was kind of worried about it until Daddy told us refills were free. I scalded my tongue trying to get the cup drank down so she could fill it up again. When we went up to the counter to pay, all of us got toothpicks. I put mine in my mouth just like I'd seen other men do. I sure felt like a man of the world as I climbed back onto my perch and put my feet on the bracket. Daddy fired up the truck and we roared out of town.

At another little place, this time in Colorado, Daddy stopped at a little fruit stand. He picked us out some peaches, when the man told him he had some left over firecrackers from the Fourth of July, Daddy bought those for us too. It seemed like having just the three of us sure opened up what we could buy along the way.

The road was long and the country was big as the three of us made our way south. A lot of the time we drove all night, but sometimes Daddy would pull off the road and me and Harry would sleep rolled up in a blanket while Daddy laid down across the bench seat in the truck.Daddy would make a fire to boil his coffee and we would all have a few cups. When we were packing up to leave, Harry got those coffee grounds and set them on a tray on the flatbed to dry.

"What are you doin?'" I asked while I watched him.

"These grounds sure look a lot like the tobacco in a cigarette. I'm gonna dry 'em out, I got some cigarette papers. I figure in no time I'll have me a smoke."

"Just 'cause it looks like tobacco, don't mean it's gonna burn like it. Those things are soppin' wet," I told him.

"You just wait, little brother. When it's my turn to ride the outside seat I'm gonna be having me a nice smoke and you goin' to wish you had thought of it."

309

I laughed at him, "Ain't no way this is gonna work." But I was a little curious to see if it would.

After a few hours the grounds dried out and then Harry volunteered to sit outside. I watched him in the side mirror as he tried to roll those grounds into the papers. The wind blew them hard and Harry had to really work to get them rolled. It was a good thing he had so much practice watching Gabby do it with one arm. Finally, he got one together and now he had to figure out a way to light it with a match in the wind. After a bunch of tries he quit. When we stopped to pee on the side of the road I went up to him.

"How you doin' with your makings?" I asked. Harry didn't know I had been watching the whole time.

"I'm goin' to light the cigarette before we take off and then it will be lit and I won't have to worry about the wind gettin' it." Harry sure was working at this.

We hadn't gone more than a mile and Harry had his cigarette going. I watched him from the mirror as he put it to his mouth and took a big puff. He got a strange look on his face and he let out the smoke in a cough. That boy was wantin' to smoke. Daddy didn't pay no attention to us, he was just getting down the road as fast as he could. When it was time to switch I figured I'd try to smoke too. Harry gave me a lit cigarette as I climbed up into the seat. After we got going down the road and the mirror wasn't set where Daddy could see me I took a long draw. It was about the nastiest thing I'd ever tried to have in my mouth. I wanted to put on a good show for Harry so I pretended like I smoked it and enjoyed it. I figured Harry was doing a lot of his own pretending too.

Some days late afternoon thunder storms would build up ahead of us. Big white clouds would grow tall in the blue sky and it would start turning dark. We could see rain falling somewhere out there on the prairie and watched to see if it

310

moved our way. The sky would be full of sunshine on one side and shadows on the other.

The three of us in the little truck would face off against that blue-black wall of rain and drive right in the middle of it. All of us squeezed into the cab when the hard rain pelted the truck. Sometimes it turned to hail. The wind blew us around and it made me feel like we weren't much of nothing as we huddled together, no longer hot in the summer sun, but cold and damp in the storm. Either we drove through the storm or it moved fast, and just as quick as we were in it, we were out of it. The sun would shine on the wet road and the tires splashed through the puddles in the road. The air would smell sweet and I didn't think there was anything better than being right there, right then.

It was late in the day when Daddy told me, "We're in Texas, son." It was always good to get to Texas and know we were close to Louisiana. The only trouble was that Texas was so big it seemed to take forever to cross it. We had settled into a daily pattern of driving, eating, and sleeping. Daddy didn't have any trouble sleeping out on the extra seat and even when Harry slowed down to drive through town Daddy didn't raise his head up.

"Wake him up and have him put his legs down," Harry nudged me with his arm. Harry wanted to look cool when we drove through town in case he saw any girls he wanted to wave to or wink at.

It had been a while since Mama had taken care of us and we were looking like it. Daddy had on a pair of big brown pants, a pair of loafers and a blue sock and a white sock. They were different lengths so one was high up his leg and the other around his ankle. The wind blew his pants to his knees and with the rope tied around his hat he looked like an old railroad hobo riding there. Which I guess he kind of was.

Harry didn't think Daddy looked very good. Sometimes it did seem like folks stopped on the street and looked at us for a long time as we went by. It probably wasn't too often they saw an old man sitting outside a truck, a sawmill on the back and everything but the kitchen sink loaded on it.

"I ain't wakin' him up." I told him. If Daddy was asleep, me and Harry could cut up in the truck and Daddy wouldn't bang on the cab for us to settle down.

"If you want to try and look cool," I told him, "why don't you smoke some coffee?" Harry ignored me after that.

When the trees started getting thicker, I knew we were getting closer to Mama. The dry air turned humid and got heavy. The country turned green and damp and we sweated more and didn't cool off at night. We crossed the state line into Louisiana and Daddy seemed to lean into the truck. We stopped at the creek outside Many and Daddy had us clean up in the cool water.

"Boys, you wait here, I'm going to go in and get a haircut and shave. I shore want to look pretty for yore mama." Harry and me horsed around splashing each other in the creek and if we happened to get clean I guess we had a bath. We rinsed out our new orange shirts in the creek and they were just about as good as new. Harry and me were drying in the sun when we heard Daddy coming back. He almost looked like a young man with his grey hair trimmed up and his hat sitting cockeyed on his head.

After two thousand miles we were almost back to the family. We just had to get through the last few curves in the road.

LOUISIANA 1961

Whoa!

It was a happy greeting when we finally drove up to where Mama and the younger kids were living at Grandma Mac's. The girls hung on Harry and me and Hoyt Lynn tried to act big around us. We hadn't been together in weeks, I think that was the longest the family had ever been apart.

"Y'all look so fine," Mama told us while she smoothed our hair and patted us. "You sure do seem thinner though. We need to get you somethin' good to eat," Mama said and Daddy squeezed her tight and gave each of the kids a treat he had bought them on the trip.

"We weren't sure when y'all would get here, so the girls have been lookin' all day, every day," Mama said.

"I heard the truck comin' right off. I told Mama y'all was here!" Hoyt Lynn sure was trying to act big. He was ten and was always left with a bunch of sisters. Sometimes I was ashamed of myself, the way I never let him hang around Harry and me. I thought I might try and do better by him. Maybe I had missed him.

We told them all about our trip down and Mama told us about hers too. She had stopped in Lincoln, Nebraska and visited Rubin and his new wife Ruth Ann and then made her way on south. She told us a funny story about asking a man about the road while she was in the Ozark hills. He told her she maybe ought not to go on by herself since she was pulling a trailer. He asked where she had driven from, when she told him Montana, he waved his hand toward the road and told her just to go on. If she had made it with the car and trailer in the mountains, these little ol' hills would be no problem for her. And they hadn't been.

Daddy moved us to a little place over at Bellwood, a few miles south of Provencal. The house had electricity and running water so I sure was glad I wouldn't have to carry any water from the well. Not that I wouldn't have made Hoyt Lynn do it anyway.

An old friend of Daddy's, Lysa Massey, had us all over for supper one night. Daddy was anxious to talk to him because Mr. Massey had told Daddy he could put up his sawmill on the back of his property behind the house, and Daddy wanted to find out when we could start setting up. Massey had a pretty good sized house, a barn, and a big ol' chicken coop. There must have been a hundred chickens and the coop they were in was just about the worst place I had ever smelled.

Of course, the kids all stayed outside while the women fixed the food. The men sat on the porch and those that chewed tobacco spit in the dirt. With the six of us kids and the Massey bunch, it made for a loud time in the yard. Daddy and Mr. Massey walked over by the barn and Mr. Massey was showing daddy his new tractor. It was his first one. He had been slow to give up working with mules and his grandson, Milton Platt, who was around my age, told us it had taken his daddy quite a while to convince the old man to try the machine.

We heard a motor start and went on the other side of the house to see Mr. Massey firing up the engine on a little tractor. It was called a 'cub' because it was smaller than most tractors. Instead of the seat being in the middle it was on the side of the tractor. He sat down on it, and while talking to Daddy, put her in gear and took off straight for the chicken coop. As he got close to it, he pulled on the steering wheel and tried to plant his feet in the ground hollering 'whoa' over and over again. Even Daddy laughed as the tractor plowed its way through the side of the coop. Milton kept hollering for

314

his grandpa to mash the brake, but Mr. Massey couldn't hear him over the cuss words he never stopped yelling. Everybody came out of the house to watch. The tractor went in as far as it could and something stopped it, the tires kept spinning but it didn't go no further.

Massey got off, spit on the tractor and told Milton to get over and do something with it. He was going to stick to livestock. Chickens squawked and feathers flew. Massey said he probably lost a crate of eggs over that darn machine. Milton got on, put her in reverse and drove it out of the mess of boards and feathers. He made it do whatever he wanted. The old man went in the house and wouldn't have anything to do with the tractor after that.

When the older folks all went inside, Harry and me decided this would be a great time to bring out the firecrackers we had bought on the way down. Folks in Louisiana didn't have them for the Fourth of July. They usually just set them off for New Year's, so we were the only ones with firecrackers this late in the summer. Me and Harry were pretty popular with the kids, what with us being almost grown, but the firecrackers set us apart. We gave everybody a handful and some matches. Harry had a cigarette he snuck around with, and him and me used that to light ours. That made us quicker than the other kids at lighting and throwing. The girls sure screamed when the firecrackers went off close to their feet.

Milton kept getting braver and getting closer to me with his. We lit our fire crackers and slung them at each other right at the same time. Mine went off first right in front of him. I looked around to find the one he threw at me. I heard the little sound that the string made while it burned up, but I couldn't find it.

I looked down and saw that the fire cracker was in the left pocket of my brand new shirt. I swatted the firecracker

315

with the flat of my hand to try and make the fire go out. Just as I went to hit it again, the firecracker went off and tore the pocket clean off my shirt. The pocket was dangling from the bottom threads. About this time the noise from all that playing must have got the attention of the grownups because Mama came outside to see about us. Mr. Massey came out too. Mama saw my shirt and walked over to me and I told her what had happened. Mr. Massey started to get after Milton, but I told him Milton hadn't done it on purpose.

Mama told me she would sew my pocket back on, but my cowboy shirt wasn't brand new anymore. I guess that was why we didn't get new clothes much, they sure didn't stay new for long. Nobody got in trouble, but we couldn't throw firecrackers at each other anymore, at least not where anybody would hear.

Pulp Wood

Daddy was working fast to get the mill running but it still took about a week. The mill was a #8 Coilie and the number stood for the size of the sawblade. He wasn't worried about finding timber to saw. He had to do Mr. Massey's stand first since he was set up on his land. And just like  always, when folks heard R.W. Miller was back in the country, they lined up to hire him to saw their timber.

316

Daddy was known for being able to live saw. That meant he could look at the end of the log and tell where to make the first cut. By seeing the way the grain ran and the natural flow of the wood, Daddy's board didn't twist. If a sawyer just started slicing the log up, odds were the board would twist right away.

To make fast cash Daddy had us take a few days and haul pulp wood. If a man wanted his land cleared he would hire us out to cut it down and haul it away. We would take it to town and sell it to the paper mill. There were a lot of men working like us to make that fast cash but it was as hard a work as I had ever done, so not too many kept at it when they had another way to make a dollar.

Tree after tree fell to Daddy's power saw. The logs could be the size of an arm or leg up to as big as a foot through. After Daddy cut them down, I laid the measuring pole up against the log and Daddy made a second cut to get them to the right length. Harry lifted one end on his shoulder and I lifted the other and we walked it to the truck and loaded it. We had to save the really heavy ones until Daddy took a break from sawing so he could help us. He would stand in the middle of the length of the log and Harry and me would lift it up on his shoulder, he would balance it there and walk it to the truck and then we would lift it off him and load it.

Even in the early fall we soaked our shirts with sweat. With each load we went deeper into the woods to get a full load. We dipped water from the bucket when we were thirsty and ate the lunch Mama sent for dinner in the middle of the day. We ate in the shade, but when we had to 'go' and I don't mean pee, we went back and squatted down where we had already cut. That way we could use the stump to lean up against, in case it took a little while. I was coming back to where Harry and Daddy were resting after I got through when Harry looked up at me.

"You get sap on yer ass?"

"You wanna look?" I threatened.

Harry laughed, he knew I had it all over me, I always did. There didn't seem to be any way to not get sap on your butt, or to get it off without it just wearing off.

"Time to get back to work, boys," Daddy said as he woke up.

"Loud mouth," I told Harry. If Daddy dozed off when we ate dinner at noon we always tried to stay quiet so he would stay asleep as long as possible.

Daddy didn't want to use the International for hauling because he said it was a good road truck. So he started looking around till he found a truck that would do. Well, it wasn't really a truck but an old school bus. That's what they told us it was. All the bus part was gone, most of the cab was too. It had a hood, windshield and fenders, with two steel frame rails out the back that the rearends and tires were bolted to. Daddy built a wooden bench across so three of us could ride on it out to the woods. Even though school had started he would have us skip days and work with him.

When we got two and half cords loaded on the truck we drove to Campti. We rested as well as we could on the wooden bench. I had to sit in the middle because Harry was older and got to sit by where the door should have been. It took over an hour to get there. A big fork lift picked up half the load and in two lifts loaded it right onto the train. We got paid $28 on the spot and we headed back to Mama and supper.

After the mill got running good, Daddy didn't have us stay out of school as much. But he was waiting for us every day when the bus let us off. Hoyt Lynn and Mary went to the elementary school so they rode a different bus. Harry, me,

Sheron and Esther went to school together. Harry went even though he hadn't gone in Condon. He figured school was a good way to get out of work.

The bus stop was at a crossroads in front of Mr. Norsworthy's store. First the bus went north and then south to drop everybody off. When the bus stopped at the crossroads to go north, we got off and loafed at the store. If we had money I bought a Tootsie Roll or two, if we didn't have money I picked up a pack of cigarettes the store owner had outside on a table. He had two kinds out, one called Oasis and the other Wings. They were so bad I considered trying to smoke coffee again. At first I thought ol' Tater was pretty dumb to put his cigarettes outside on a table for anybody to pick up. After trying to smoke them I think he probably hoped somebody would take them off his hands. I told myself that anyway so I wouldn't feel bad about taking them.

RW Miller

When the bus came back from the north, we would get back on and ride south to where we were let off. There was Daddy in the truck waiting to take us to work. If he'd known about our time at the store we figured he would come and get us there so we never let on.

After a day of school and the rest of it spent in the woods, the trip to Campti got long. Daddy drove and Harry got the outside so I was tucked in between the two sweaty men. I felt a big yawn coming on and raised my hands above

319

my head to stretch and get it out. My feet pushed on the floorboard of the truck and the engine seemed to rev up. I pushed again and the engine revved and I know we got a little faster.

"Look at this Daddy." I mashed hard on the floor board and the truck picked up speed.

"Keep doin' that, son." Daddy pushed on the gas pedal all the way and I mashed with both my feet.

"I think we're going about forty!" Daddy was excited. He was just guessing. We didn't have a gauge to tell us, but we were gaining speed. None of us were sleepy anymore as the old truck sped down the road. We came up on a bunch of colored boys hauling pulp wood into town too. There were two fellas in the cab and two more riding the logs. Like us, they were trying to make it to the train to get unloaded and get their money.

Daddy didn't let up and we moved onto the wrong side of the road and inched our way up beside them. Harry hollered at them and grinned and Daddy whooped loud. The driver tipped his hat at us, but they kept looking straight ahead even as we passed them up. We might not have had a cab or doors, but we sure had a motor that could run. I didn't let up on the floorboard and Daddy kept the pedal mashed to the floor. We roared into Campti down the main street to the station. Daddy skid the tires to a stop. We beat the other load to the train. None of us quit grinning. The Miller boys had sure come to town that day.

The Carnival

Between the sawmill and 'pup' wood operation Daddy must of been doing pretty good. He bought Massey's tractor, the Minneapolis Moline, to skid with and that kept the logs stacked up ready to mill. Things were so busy that he had Mama talk to Louie on the telephone from Uncle Huey's and tell Louie to come down and get to working with us. It'd take him a little while to get here from Oregon, but he said he'd come. He told Mama he'd got married after we left and he was bringing his new wife, Janet, and her two little girls.

Mama told the girls, "I'd shore would've liked to have seen Louie married, but I didn't get to see Elaine married nor Rubin either so it's just as well."

"I'll make sure you see me married, Mama," Esther told her. Mama smiled in a tired kind of way at her.

With all that talk of marrying it was time for me to get out of the house. I was headed over to Milton Platt's. Sometimes he would come out and work the mill with us. He didn't show up every day but enough that Daddy let me go off and help him some too. I liked to work with Milton because it wasn't really work. He got to drive his grandpa's '59 two-door Chevy. It was solid red and shiny as a new penny. We loaded the hay bales on the trunk between the big tail fins and headed to the fields to feed the cows. I was up front. Harry had come and was sitting in the backseat. Milton spun around in a circle so the feed slung off on its own. Milton grinned at us, "That's how you feed cows."

Milton talked about the Halloween carnival that was going to go on at the school. He said the whole town just about showed up to it.

"I don't know about you fellers, but seems like we orta see about havin' some Halloween fun of our own, stead of just a bunch of young'uns runnin' around trying to get some candy," Milton said. He had the steering wheel turned to the left all she would do.

I had been looking forward to all that candy but I didn't want to seem like a kid so I didn't mention it. I braced my feet on the hump in the middle of the car. Harry jumped on Milton's idea.

"After it gets good and dark we'll see what we can come up with," Harry said between his clenched lips, trying to hold onto his lit cigarette. Since we were driving in a fast circle, Harry was mashed up against the door, trying to hold on. After we slung all the hay, Milton drove us back and said he'd see us at the carnival.

The days were busy so they went by fast. Harry and me went to school about every other day since Daddy needed us so much. We were clearing a patch of land and it was just about done. Daddy was felling trees and having to fight some scraggly branches that were called H-iron. They were hardwood with twisted branches that were tough on the saw. Daddy was sharpening saw blades while Harry and me were deep in the woods, cutting the marked trees. When Daddy was ready he was going to bring the tractor into the woods and have us hook up the logs to skid out.

Without any engines running it was quiet, just the sound of Harry's whistling and our feet crunching through the underbrush. We were shooting the breeze when we heard pine needles rustling to our right. When we heard the faint snort we both stopped and looked towards the sound. It was the thing we looked out for the most in the woods - a wild hog and maybe more than one. Harry and me looked wide eyed at each other, and then I pointed up.

Harry and me both scrambled up the same tree. We got about ten feet up when the hogs came out into the clearing. They made their way towards our tree, but they didn't seem much interested in us. They were long and fat, with thick snouts and short tusks coming out from their face. We didn't dare come down, at eye level we might look like supper to them. Folks let their hogs forage in woods all summer until the first freeze and then they'd round them up and butcher them. Those little pigs turned big and ugly.

They'd eat anything in sight and would attack a man in a second. We sure didn't mess around with wild hogs.

We hollered over to Daddy, but he never answered us. We thought he might start up the tractor and come to where we were. We waited up in the tree until the hogs moved on into the woods. When they were good and gone we climbed down. Daddy hadn't showed up yet so we went to see about him.

We walked up to the tractor and then the truck but Daddy couldn't be seen. We went around to the back side and found Daddy lying up against a tree. His shirt was red and his hand was bloody.

"Daddy?" When I spoke to him he didn't look up. His eyes were shut and he was slumped over. His head drooped down to his chest. Harry and me both didn't know what to do. We started shaking him and hollering. Finally, Daddy opened his eyes and looked at us. He cleared his throat, took off his hat, and wiped his forehead with his arm.

"Daddy, what happened?"

"I'm fine boys, I got to tanglin' with the H-iron and the saw kicked back and got my hand. I got sick when I saw my own blood. If there's too much it'll make me pass out." We helped him up off the ground. "Tie a rag around my hand, and I'll be alright."

"You got sick when you saw your blood?" I asked him.

"Yeah, sometimes it does me that way. Cover it up where I can't see it, and we'll get back to work."

While Harry tied a rag around his hand, it came to me that Daddy never had wanted to look at anybody's cuts and not even Louie's leg from when he was burned. Even if Daddy did pass out from seeing blood, it didn't seem to slow the work down much. After we dipped some water from the bucket and got a drink we got back to work.

We cleared all we were hired to cut and then got ready to move the equipment. Daddy was tired at the end of the day and while he drove to the house, he had Harry and me take the new tractor over to the next place to work so it would be already there when we started in the morning.

The ride on the tractor was long and boring. Just to keep ourselves awake, Harry and me went to riding on the hood, straddling the gas tank. We had a contest to see who could jump off and back on the quickest as it chugged down the road. I mashed hard on the gas throttle but it was still so slow. Harry got to looking at the fuel pump and rigged a chain on the side of the engine and got a little more speed out of it.

The faster it went, the more the front wheels wobbled back and forth. It was hard to handle with the steering wheel jerking back and forth. I sawed the wheel back and forth trying to get control. It didn't help much that I was sitting on it backwards, facing where we'd been instead of where we were going. That tractor seemed like it had a mind of its own as it weaved from one side of the road to the other, no matter how we tried to get it to go straight.

Harry jumped into the seat and tried to steady it, but the tractor took off down through the ditch that ran beside the road and up the bank. It was a wild ride and I yelled 'whoa', just like Mr. Massey. Only thing that stopped the tractor was a big old tree that grew up in the fence. It stopped the tractor but Harry and me set sail through the air and landed in the slimy water just a few feet away. While I was trying to get out of the muck as fast as I could, the tires on the tractor kept turning and digging up the ground.

"That was quite a ride!" Harry said as he ducked between the fence wire to get to the tractor.

"Man, I thought you could drive better'n that," I told Harry.

"What do ya mean? Isn't that what we wanted to do, take a wild ride?"

I grinned at him. Harry turned off the key to stop the motor. We took the chain off the throttle, restarted it and backed up out of the ditch, real slow. We got back on the road and headed out. We gassed it pretty hard and the whole back end of the tractor came off the ground. Only thing touching the road was the steering tires. Both of us got tossed off again, landing on the gravel road. The back end came back down on the ground, hard.

"What's goin' on with this darn thing," Harry revved her up again, and the back end came up like before. We saw the pivot pin was broke.

"That musta happened when it got stopped by the tree," I told Harry.

The only way we could keep all four tires on the ground was go even slower than we had before. It was after dark when we got to the stand of trees we were headed to. We watched the lightning bugs blink from the ditch next to the road as we walked on the yellow lines down the middle of the highway. We didn't have to say it, we both knew we would not be telling Daddy. There was no way we were going to risk not getting to go to the Halloween party at the school.

The night finally came. Mama kept shaking her head at the kids. They wouldn't stop talking about going to the carnival. Harry and me played it cool, not letting on that we were itching to be there too. We had big plans for the night, but it wouldn't be till after everything else was over at the school.

There weren't too many schools I liked to go to, and I sure didn't like it in Provencal. They had more rules in the classroom than I could keep track of. We all had to remember not to just say 'no' and 'yes' but 'no, ma'am' and 'yes, ma'am'. The ways in the South were different from the other places we went and sometimes it was hard to remember everything. Teachers didn't give you any slack either, they were always fast to bring out the paddle and have you bend over and take your licks.

Harry pulled the car into the parking lot. We weren't good and stopped before the kids were out of the car. The gym was decorated for Halloween and games were set up too. They ran us off from the fishing pond, said we were too big to fish for prizes. I walked around eating all the candy I could get my hands on and watching the little kids having fun. Milton showed up and we went outside in the chilly air. We spent a little while talking big, measuring ourselves up against each other with cars, work, and girls.

"You figure it's time to have our own Halloween fun?" Harry asked as he walked up with Billy Cook.

"What kind of fun?" Billy Cook looked at him.

"Well, all this in here is just kid's stuff. Halloween is about pranks and tricks. That's what we're going to do." Harry took his cigarette out of his mouth, threw it on the ground and then stepped on it. We waited till the carnival got over and folks started leaving. Sheron came out and wanted to go. Since we were staying, we told her to drive the kids herself. She was fourteen and could reach the pedals on the car so there wasn't any reason she couldn't do it. We herded Esther, Hoyt Lynn and Mary in with her and sent them on their way.

"What do we tell Daddy about why you're not with us? Sheron asked.

"Tell him we're helping clean up," I told her.

"Y'all better be good," she warned us. We just grinned.

When everybody had cleaned up and left, we looked the school over. It had a flat roof and was built with a main

326

building in the middle with two wings that came out from it on either side. All the class rooms were in the wings and had their doors to the outside. I looked over at it and had an idea.

"We could take all the door knobs off," I said. I was new at pranks so that was the best I could come up with.

"Let's get to it!"

We did get to it. After we had a good size pile of doorknobs, we threw them as hard as we could across the railroad tracks. I looked over at the gym and saw that the bell that rang for classes was on the outside of the building.

"Let's ring the bell!"

"How? It's rang from inside," Billy Cook asked.

"Don't ya know how to do anything?" I asked him.

We set about taking the bell apart, stripped the wires and touched them together to get them to sound the bell. We let it ring and ring. It wasn't long and we saw lights from a car coming down the road. It turned into the school. It was the principal. The wires were long enough that we hid around the corner of the building where we couldn't be seen. The Cook boys scattered, they didn't want to be anywhere near. When the principal stepped out of the car, we took the wires apart and the bell quit ringing. He stood there, looked around and kind of shrugged his shoulders. He got back in his car and drove off.

Harry touched the wires together and the bell rang out, long and loud. Here come the head lights again. When he stopped the car and opened the door, Harry quit ringing the bell. He must not have been wanting to see about it too much, 'cause he left again. We rang the bell one more time for good measure. He must have give up, because he didn't come back.

When the Cook boys showed up again, they told us they'd hid in the math teacher's livestock pen, and had an idea to put his calf on the top of the school building. It took some time to gather up all boards, pallets and blocks we

327

needed to get the calf up. I was beginning to think this was more work than fun. That is until I saw that bawlin' calf walking on that roof. What a sight.

We had put him on a pallet and then raised it up about two feet and put a block under the pallet and then did the same to the other side of the pallet, back and forth until we had him close to the top. Milton and Harry lay on their bellies on the roof and with all they had, they lifted the calf the rest of the way up. He started up that bawlin' when they wrestled him to the roof, but by then it didn't matter. All we had to do was throw the wood away we had used and get out of there. Harry and Milton jumped down, and without another word to each other, we ran off. We all knew we better git while the gittin' was good.

We ran for a ways and then slowed down and walked. The night was inky black and the closer we got to the house, the faster we walked.

"Think they'll tell?"

"Nah."

Getting Caught

The next morning was Sunday and there wasn't no way we weren't going to be at New Town at church sitting next to Mama. Harry and me had tried to figure out a way to get to town and see about the fruits of our labor, but Mama wouldn't listen to any of the excuses we had given her for not going to church. After the singing, preaching, praying and dancing, Daddy finally drove us back. We had all went in one car, so Harry and me couldn't even drive through town on our own to see if the calf had been rescued.

Two cars were parked in front of the house when we got there. One, a '52 Ford and the other, a brand new '61 Ford coupe. The screen door flew open and out came Louie, and right behind him, Rubin. The girls ran to them. Me and Harry walked over to the Ford. It was slick.

"What d'ya think of that little machine there?" Rubin asked. By the looks of the car, it looked like he was doing pretty good for himself. Two women came out of the house too. I'd seen Louie's wife before he married her and said "hey" to Janet. Rubin's wife was new to us all. Her name was Ruth Ann.

Mama made a big Sunday dinner for us all and we sat around all afternoon eating and talking. I heard Louie talking to Mama about Janet having a hard time getting used to living in sawmill camps and him working so much. Mama told him it just was taking a little while for her to get used to it. It would all work out. Louie said he sure hoped so.

Ruth Ann had come from Nebraska and hadn't ever been down south before. She was wide eyed and quiet. She called Rubin, Tiny, and for a while when she would talk about him or to him, we would forget who she meant. He said that the joke in the military was that it was run bass-ackwards. Since he was so big, they started calling him Tiny. It also helped separate him from the four other Millers in his unit. His wife called him Tiny because that was how he was introduced to her. I liked the name so I started calling him that too. Mama didn't.

Louie was the same old happy-go-lucky Louie. Rubin was different from before, though. He came down wearing white T-shirts under his clothes and had particular ways of doing things. He talked about the Air Force like it was something special. Louie didn't seem to like what Rubin was saying and would try to knock anything he said. Louie and Rubin squabbling? Now that hadn't changed.

Monday Louie went to work with Daddy skidding logs for the sawmill. Harry, me and Rubin went to get a load of pulp wood. Rubin was worried to death a trooper was going to pull us over in the log truck and check for a registration. Harry told him that everybody knew we didn't have papers and nobody cared. Rubin told us the military had taught him to do things right.

Harry didn't take too well to Rubin trying to boss us around. Harry had been the oldest at home long enough to like his place in charge. Harry smarted off to him a few times, but they stopped when we got to work.

Rubin cut the timber and trimmed the logs with the measuring pole that Harry set. When he made the last cut, Harry and me picked the log and took it to the truck like we did just about every day.

"You boys leave those big logs, I'll get 'em." Rubin told us. Harry and me eyed each other. Rubin, may have been working in the military, but that was not the same as hard labor in the woods. After we let him heft a few trees, and watched him sweat and huff and puff, Harry and me went to work. Rubin wiped his face with a hanky while Harry and me reminded him of how it was to work long and hard in the hot Louisiana woods.

Harry and me carried log after log to the truck until it was loaded. Sweat ran down our backs, but we didn't slack up. We worked harder than we ever had, just to make sure we showed Rubin. He sat on a stump trying to get his breath. It seemed to me the service had softened him a little. Harry and me didn't have his size, but we didn't need it to lift and carry with him. Rubin was in a sour temper but Harry and me grinned at each other all the way back.

That is until Daddy came out on the porch and said, "What'd you boys do?"

Harry and me stopped in our tracks. My mind went down the list of things Daddy might be asking about. The tractor? The school? Stealing cigarettes? Lying to Mama? Calling Hoyt Lynn "Alice" for being a sissy and getting carsick? What if I said one thing, and he was upset about another?

"Just worked in the woods today," I said. Harry didn't say a word, just left it to me like always.

"I'm talkin' about the trouble at the school," Daddy was a little impatient. I thought fast after having the exact trouble we were in nailed down.

"Something happen at the school, Daddy?" Harry was trying to be cool while he answered Daddy.

"Not just now, on Halloween, there was quite a bit of mischief went on over there. School principal was over here and told all about the bell and the calf. Said it took them half a day to get it off the roof. That Cook boy says y'all were the 'cause of it."

"What'd he say, Daddy?" I sure wasn't going to tell on myself for something that Billy Cook might not have said. After Daddy got through reciting what the principal had told him, it was clear that old Billy Cook hadn't left a thing out. Daddy didn't whip us, he hadn't ever come close to doing that since the day he almost beat me in Oregon. I wasn't sure he even cared too much about the pranks. He didn't like a man coming and telling him his boys had done something wrong. He didn't like that at all. He pounded the table with his fist that night,

"It's hard enough to make a livin' without two of my boys causin' trouble. And if that wasn't enough, the dad blamed tractor Massey sold me wasn't worth a plug nickel. The pivot pin's broke and she reared up every time I gassed her. I couldn't get no work done at all!" He pounded the table again. Harry drank his milk wrong, choked, and milk came out his nose. I broke out in a sweat. Mama tried to soothe Daddy with some vinegar pudding and as soon as we could Harry and me got out of sight.

The next day we had to report to the office and the worst thing that could have happened did. We got expelled from school. What that meant was we were going to do a lot more pulp wood hauling and saw milling and a lot less loafing. We were expelled for two weeks. Well, I was. School ended for good for Harry. Daddy said at seventeen he was too old for school anyway and he didn't get to go back. Rubin and his wife had gone back home in their Ford, so Harry was needed in the woods anyway.

I went off to school with Sheron and Esther on the bus. They sat up front, but I rode in the back and I kept my eye on Billy Cook. The more I looked at him the madder I got over his tattling about Halloween. I walked to his seat, and the kid sitting next to him slid out to make room for me. I lit into him about him telling on us.

"I didn't tell, Miller. I didn't. It wut'n me." He just kept a-lying.

"I heard different, Cook, and I'm going to tear you up if you don't tell me you did it."

There wasn't nothing for it, he was going to get whipped. Every day he said he didn't tell, and every day I whipped him. That boy was sure bull headed. After a week, I started to feel sorry for him. A boy his age getting beat up every day.

It was a relief the night Louie talked about going back west. I think his wife just wanted out of Louisiana. Daddy said that didn't sound like a bad idea, maybe he'd go too. I knew right then we were leaving. Mama sighed but didn't say anything. I was glad to find a way to quit whipping Billy. I was starting to feel ashamed of myself.

NEW MEXICO and COLORADO 1961

The Circus

Harry and me were back in the International. Mama and Daddy were following behind us in her green bullet-hole car, and Louie was bringing up the rear in his '52 Ford. We were headed west, all the cars full of kids and loaded with all we could fit. Daddy had convinced Mama there was some good money to be made in New Mexico, that it was time to leave. I don't know if she agreed or just went along with it, but it didn't matter, we were on our way.

Harry and me felt pretty grown since the two of us were in the truck by ourselves. It couldn't have been a better day of traveling, getting to smoke on the sly and cut up with each other. We figured Texas wasn't too far away, and when we crossed the line we felt like we had got somewhere. It took us a good little while to hear the engine making a noise that wasn't right. There was so much smoke coming out the exhaust pipe we couldn't see Louisiana or nothing else behind us. After a loud bang that came from under the hood, Harry had to pull off.

By the time Daddy pulled up behind us, the smoke had cleared 'cause the engine didn't run anymore. Harry folded open the hood on the driver's side of the truck and we could see a hole right there in the engine. It had thrown a rod right through the side of it. Daddy messed with his hat and scratched his head.

"Well, boys, the only thing I know to do, is to leave her right here. There's nothin' for it. We'll just have to load what we can onto the other cars," Daddy said.

We took about an hour to piece together places for the things the International was carrying. Some of it had to be left, mostly Mama's things. We pushed the truck further off

333

the road, down into the ditch. As we drove off, I looked back at the International, it was sad to leave that old truck. It had taken us from one end of the country to the other. Me and Harry were pretty sad too as we held the kids in our lap. Harry and me squeezed in the backseat of Louie's Ford with Janet's girls and Mary. This was not how the two of us planned this thing.

It took a couple of days to cross Texas and then it was into New Mexico. I don't think Janet ever quit complaining about all of us in the car, the dust or the food we cooked along the roadside. Louie tried to make her feel better, but told her Daddy was the boss and we had to just follow along. After a while she would sull up and then the ride was better until Janet's girl, Jeanne, peed on Harry and he tried to hand her up to her mama. I figured Harry should be used to it as much as he'd wet the bed. Janet got after her little girl but Louie told Janet it wasn't that big of a thing. The fight was on. Louie was in trouble for going against Janet with her girl, and whatever else she could think of. The long trip seemed to get longer with all the squabbling.

The country was without trees and the wind blew from Lubbock until we got in the mountains north of Santa Fe. We drove up highway 84 until we got to Espanola and then turned towards Taos. We moved into a motor lodge on the outside of town, it was just one room but it had a carport to park your car under and we had never had one of those before. Mama put up quilts to make the wall in front and we used it as a second room.

Mama told Louie that Janet might be happier living in town. We all hoped so, but it didn't seem to do much good. She didn't like living in one room with all of us, and she didn't like Louie working all the time, and she didn't like eating beans and rice every day. She sure seemed hard to get along with. I tried to stay out of the house as much as I could.

334

The mill didn't need me, so I spent a lot of time walking into town. Everything to do there needed money and I didn't have any so I just looked things over.

The middle of town had a place called a plaza. There was a park in the middle and the stores all faced it. The police station was underground in part of the park. The roof stuck out about four feet out of the ground. There were big trees that gave shade so the whole place stayed cool. A lot of folks spoke Spanish. Indians spread blankets on the sidewalk and sold jewelry to folks as they passed by. It didn't leave much room to walk. Women and men sat up against the wall and some of their kids played close by.

Since I didn't know much about the place, I was always walking down streets and having to figure out my way back. There were adobe houses with the bricks showing through, yards with dirt and yards with flowers. One night near dark I was walking down a little street when it crossed the main road I knew. I had walked down it alone, but when I came out there were five fellows following me. They talked Spanish to each other and about the only thing I could make out when they hollered at me was 'gringo'. I wasn't sure what that meant, but I was pretty sure it meant me.

I kept walking towards the plaza to keep myself ahead of them. I walked fast, but not so fast that they would see I was trying to get away. I knew no matter how tough I was, it would be a chore to take on five of them, especially all at once.

I walked faster and so did they. Pretty soon I was running and all of them were on my tail. I ran as fast as I could towards the plaza and figured if I could make it to the police station somebody would step in. At least there would be people around. I ran right in the middle of the park and towards the buried police station. Since it was late no one was walking in the plaza, so there was no one to help. Those boys

335

were right behind me and I hoofed it towards the police station and in one step jumped the four feet to get on the roof.

The local boys ran up to the building but they knew what it was. I was feeling pretty safe where I was so I figured it was my turn to have some fun.

"Come on, I'll take you all on," I shouted at them. They said some things in Spanish and I was sure they were cussing me.

"Don't y'all get chicken on me now!" I said. I laughed at them as they looked around. I must have not been worth the trouble they would get if they got in a fight right there, so they finally left, hollering things I couldn't make out.

I caught my breath and waited to see if somebody would come out to see what had been going on. Nobody did so I headed back to the motor lodge. I lit up a smoke on the walk back and figured I'd tell Harry I sure could use a knife. I figured he'd give me the money for one.

The next time I was in town I used the money Harry gave me and got me a little folding pocket knife. I didn't end up using it for fighting but I did get pretty good at whittling. I worked on a '58 Edsel I made from a scrap two by four. It was really looking good when I took a strip of chrome from Mama's car and cut it up and used a little hammer to tap into the wood so my Edsel had chrome too. Mama told me how good I was doing, until she saw where the chrome came from. She didn't get after me though.

Sometimes she let me take her car into town and I would go to Jack's Drive-in and buy a Coke if I had money. Sometimes I just parked and watched the people. The old man that owned the drive-in didn't mind if I parked and didn't buy anything. He always had old cars parked in the stalls. I think maybe he was trying to fool people into thinking more people were eating there than there actually were. The place was jumping the day I drove up and found out the travelling circus had come to town.

They set up in the parking lot. As I walked around I saw a little Ferris wheel and a roller coaster and other rides. Kids could ride ponies around in a circle or buy all kinds of popcorn and peanuts. At certain hours there were Indian dances, with chanting and drums. I loved to watch all the different kinds of people coming and going. I listened to the men calling out to people to get them to throw the ball and knock down the bottles or swing a big hammer to ring the bell. There were animals in cages, some you could pet and some you couldn't. A skinny lion slept in a cage and only seemed to wake up when the food bucket came around. The monkey never quit screeching.

I was around enough that the fellow that ran the place got to talking to me. He told me he could use somebody to help out and travel with them. It didn't look like it would be any work at all and I figured I was the man for the job. I told him all that I could do and he said if I could clear it with Mama he would take me on with them. I drove back thinking about how I was going to tell Mama I was leaving. I figured since it was work she would be all right with it. It wasn't any fun to walk around nearly grown without a dime in my pocket. This was the way to finally make some of my own.

I drove the car up to the motor lodge and parked out front. There was all kinds of racket coming from the backyard but I didn't pay it much attention. I had to tell Mama I was leaving and I was going to just tell her right off. I walked through the door, Mama was sitting at the table with her face in her hands.

"Mama, I'm gonna join the circus! I got it all worked out."

She looked up at me.

"I'm going to pack a bag and if somebody will take me back over to Jack's I can start today." I started looking for a paper sack to put my clothes in.

"What are you sayin' son?" Mama asked.

"I'm joining the circus. I told the man I would come clear it with you."

"Alton, quit with that foolishness. I've got enough on my mind. Janet's run off and left Louie, he's out back pitchin' a fit. Said she wasn't movin' one more time with our bunch."

It was then that I saw Louie was in the backyard tearing up anything he could kick, hit or sling.

"Louie's havin' a Miller fit," Sheron said. She was staying out of his way.

Mama said Daddy was moving us up to Colorado to work for Orville Jackson and wanted to be packed up tonight. Mr. Jackson owned mills all over and needed Daddy at that one. Janet had had enough and had driven the Ford to town to the bus station and left. I had been so busy thinking about my job I hadn't paid attention to the trouble going on. If I'd a known, I could have driven the car back instead of walking.

"Alton, you ain't goin' nowhere today," Mama just about raised her voice.

Looks like I picked the wrong day to join the circus. At least there'd be more room in the car.

Nothin' To Do

It was dark when we left Taos heading for Creede, Colorado. When I looked out to the west of town, the valley was big and looked flat but I knew it wasn't. The Rio Grande flowed through it, down at the bottom of a deep gorge. To look I couldn't even tell there was a cut in the ground, but we drove out on the rocky road to the edge of the gorge. There was no bridge across, so we had to use a switch back road

338

that went back and forth down the side of it. At the bottom we drove through the river, the car slowly going over big rocks and holes while the water swirled around. We used the switchback road to go back up the other side. We came out at Tres Piedras and then headed on north toward Alamosa. Mama and Daddy remarked on how little Tres Piedras had changed since we had lived there years ago.

As we drove north we came out of the mountains and went into a big, flat valley. There were mountains in the distance with snow on the top but we were quite a ways from them. Alamosa was in the flat valley but when we headed west from there the road started to curve around and we started back into the foothills to Del Norte.

At Southfork we headed up into the mountains but with the bright moonlight still saw the river alongside the road running fast. It was the same Rio Grande that cut out the deep cut in the ground in the valley by Taos. The sawmill camp was about twenty miles outside of Creede, off the highway, up a dirt road into the woods. We were moving slow through the curves when Louie pulled over as much as he could on the narrow road. His car had quit running. They stopped and him and Harry got out. Everybody else went into the woods to pee. Daddy and me walked up to Louie.

"What's the trouble?" Daddy asked.

"It just quit on us," Harry answered. Louie lifted the hood. It was dark so he lit a match to see what was going on. When he got the fire close to the dry battery, the acid in the air sparked and the battery blew up in Louie's face. Louie jumped back and hollered. Mama and Esther came running. Harry and me helped Louie to his feet. The girls tended Louie's face, but Louie told them he was fine and shooed them away. Daddy took an old rag and covered the battery and took it out of the car. Daddy said the battery had gone dead and wasn't charging the generator in the car. We'd have

339

to get a new one. He and Louie drove back to town. Louie did take a wet rag for his face, Mama made him. Harry drove the rest of us towards camp. We figured we would get there about daylight.

The camp was set up in the woods with big pines all around. It was always cool because of all the shade. Log trucks brought the logs in from the woods. The sawmill sawed them up rough and then trucks took them to Southfork to the big mill. During the week the camp was full of people. They went home on weekends and we were the only family to stay and live there all the time.

Cabins were already built so we just had to drive up to ours and unpack the cars. There were other families living in the camp so kids started coming outside as the morning wore on. We were at the north side of the mill and there were about six cabins at the south end for the men without families to live during the week.

Daddy had brought back a few groceries with him when he and Louie had come back from Creede. We used those for a couple of days while we set up housekeeping but Mama needed to go in herself to get what we would need for a longer time. Daddy and Louie were working, so Harry drove Mama to town and that left me and Hoyt Lynn to stay at camp.

We decided we would go in the cabins that the men lived in and look around. Hoyt Lynn opened a cabinet and found a carton of cigarettes. I told him to get a pack, they probably wouldn't miss one. Hoyt Lynn would do just about anything I said since he was getting to be with me. He was eleven and trying hard to be older like me and Harry.

We took the pack of Camels into the woods and smoked the pack in one day. We didn't suck in any of the smoke because it burned too much. Hoyt Lynn had a bad coughing fit, tears came out his eyes, but I pretended not to see since he was trying so hard. That worked out so good that for a couple of weekends we went back in the cabins and smoked the other fellow's cigarettes too. After a few weeks some of the men came up to Daddy telling him that his boys were stealing their smokes.

Daddy told them that his boys didn't smoke and they sure enough didn't steal. After they left Daddy hollered for me to come and talk to him.

"You boys messin' with their things?"

"No, Daddy."

"I told 'em so, but you make sure you steer clear of other folks' things."

"I'll make sure Hoyt stays out of trouble," I told him.

Daddy or Mama never would believe their kids would do something like steal or smoke. It was something we could count on and I was sure proud of it. I made Hoyt Lynn promise not to tattle. It would break their hearts if they found out what we were doing.

Since Saturday was when the family went to town for groceries, the cupboard was pretty bare. I remembered that Daddy had bragged on some cheap tuna fish he had bought. Mama had laughed at it, but I wasn't sure why. I didn't really know how to make tuna fish, so we just opened up a can and spread it on bread. It was real red, darker than I had ever seen tuna fish. I finished my sandwich in four bites, but it was strong tasting. We had a couple more cans but I wasn't sure about eating them.

"This is pretty dark meat, I think you ought to go over and ask the lady at the house across the road if something is wrong with this tuna fish."

Hoyt didn't want to go ask but he had to since I told him to. I watched as he talked to her, she shut the screen and he ran all the way back.

341

"She told me this is cat food. Look there's a cat on the label!" Hoyt Lynn pointed to a cat as big as you please right there on the outside of the can. No wonder it had been so cheap. I had already eaten my sandwich and was feeling a little sick at the thought of it.

"It tastes just fine to me." Hoyt Lynn had five sandwiches.

Salty Dog

Mama needed supplies from town and this time Daddy wasn't going. It was me and Harry. I sat over in the right side of Mama's car looking forward to seeing Creed for the first time. Harry told me it wasn't a big town, but big enough for what we wanted to do. We left a dust cloud behind us on the dirt road until we made the blacktop and then we ate up the twenty miles to Creed. The blacktop ended at town and we went down the main street. Creed had one road in; the other side of town was butted up against a rock bluff with a big crack in the middle. Most of the buildings were narrow and small

Modern picture of town ending at the mountain in Creede.

with a tall front facing the street. There was a brick building on the corner, bigger than anything else in town. Harry pulled up in front of it.

"I already scouted this place out when I came with Daddy. Let's go in." Harry said.

"What is it?"

"The pool hall."

Harry had been biding his time waiting for the chance to come to town without Daddy and check the place out. He had spotted another pool hall. We had so much fun in the one in Montana, we were itching to go in. We figured our errands could wait. I was right behind Harry as he walked through the doors. It was big and open with a wood floor. Pool tables were set up on the ground floor and a staircase went upstairs to the bar and dance floor. We said 'hey' to the man running the place as we walked over to the pool table.

Harry racked the balls and the two of us starting playing. We took turns winning, both of us good at finding the angle to drop the ball. Harry thought we could spend a little of the money Daddy has sent, so we bought cigarettes and Cokes as we played.

Empty bottles and a full ashtray sat on the table where we were. I picked up one of the empties, "Should I get us a couple more?" I asked Harry.

"Ya know, I don't see why we don't go upstairs and get somethin' to drink other than a Co-cola."

"You think they'll sell us liquor?"

"Our money's as good as anybody else. I don't see why not. Let's go." Harry was headed for the stairs, I fell in behind. We came up to the second floor, which looked a lot like the first floor, big room with a wood floor. Small round tables were set up by the long bar that ran the length of one of the walls which was covered by a big mirror. Little tables were set up close to it. There was a big area for dancing and a juke box was blinking in the corner.

Now that we had made it upstairs, Harry didn't move any more, just stood at the top of the stairs. He was always prone to chicken out of things. I wasn't going to stand there looking dumb, so I headed over to the bar. Harry came too. Two men sat at one end and the bartender was talking to them. Harry and me leaned into the bar and propped a foot up on the step that ran along the bottom, acting like we had done it a hundred times. We could see ourselves in the mirror, Harry's black hair was combed just right and he had a big grin. I looked like I was there for a fight, even though I wasn't. I just couldn't keep that look off my face. My blue eyes shown out on my tanned face, my broken tooth kept me from looking handsome, maybe it helped me look grownup.

The bartender looked at us, put down the glass he was holding and walked over. I tried to look like we had done this a million times as the bartender asked,

"What'll it be?"

It was then that I remembered we didn't know how to order drinks. What'll it be? What'll it be? What would it be? I looked at Harry and he didn't bat an eye,

"I'll have what he's having." He pointed with his thumb at the cowboy sitting down the bar.

"Salty Dog, comin' up."

I didn't know what that was, but we were about to have one. The bartender turned around dipped the top of the glass in salt, poured grapefruit juice from a can into the glass with what looked like water, but it came from a bottle that said Vodka.

Harry paid for the drink and took a swig, his face screwed up a bit, but not for long. The bartender grinned at him and Harry said, "That's real good." The bartender chuckled and walked away.

I had a swallow and tried not to cough. It was bitter and sour. Harry thought it was just fine. The second drink I took, I just sipped. We shared the one drink looking as cool as we could. Now we knew. It didn't matter how old you were, what mattered is if you had the money.

Oldest at Home

We sat around the supper table ready to eat. Daddy said grace and thanked the Lord for all we had. He sliced the cornbread and Mama poured the beans and juice on top for each of us. There wasn't any room at the table for the little kids, so Hoyt Lynn and Mary sat on the floor with their plates between their legs. Before too long Louie cleared his throat.

"Well, I think it's time I head to Oregon and find Janet. I aim to patch things up with her and see if we can't work it out."

"I think that's a good idea, son. You need to try and keep your family," Mama told him.

I looked over at Daddy, I thought he might try to keep Louie here.

"I'm not goin' to try and talk you out of it son, but you might as well know now, she ain't gonna live the kinda life ya need her to. Janet can't make do like Mama. Don't guess nobody could."

"I don't expect her to be like Mama, but I figure I got to see what I can do to fix things."

"I'm goin' with him Daddy," Harry said. This was the first I had heard of this. Harry too? I looked at Daddy, wondering if he would let him go.

"It's good for brothers to go together. Ted always went with me before I was a family man. Alton can take up the slack," Daddy said between bites.

I was torn between feeling proud that Daddy thought I was old enough to help make our living, and left out that Harry was going off with Louie. Harry was treated pretty much like a grown up. When we had come in late from

345

Creed, they hadn't said anything to us at all. We just had to be ready to work when the time came. I hadn't ever thought about what it would be like to not have Harry around, but I did like the idea of being oldest at home. I was fifth in line and it had taken a while to get to the top.

The mill hired me on to drive the old Dodge 4x4 army truck and I went to work. Slabs, which were the first cut of the log with bark on one side, were thrown in the back of the truck crosswise. When it was full I was to drive it to the gulley, raise the bed and dump the slabs. The sawdust and waste, like the strips the edger took off the side of the board, were thrown downhill. My money was added in with Daddy's, but at the end of the week, he always gave me a few dollars for my pocket. I'd been without money for so long I was sure fired up to work.

I had a lot of off time waiting for the truck to be loaded. Sometimes I helped the men throw the slabs, sometimes I just walked around in the woods. Even though it was a pretty good sized operation, it still used horses to skid logs for the small timber. The bigger timber was brought out with a dozer. I would go to the corral and make friends with the horses, feed them grass and pet them.

During the dinner break Daddy would walk with me. We didn't talk much but we would remark on the country, the weather or the work. There was a narrow, little creek not too far from the mill. When I went there with Daddy, he told me that was the beginning of the same river that had carved out the gorge by Taos. Daddy and me crossed the Rio Grande in one step.

Just when I was getting used to having a little money, it all came crashing to an end. Since school was starting we had to move closer to town. The school was in Center and that was about sixty miles, so it didn't make sense to drive all that way every day. Daddy found a place on the highway about halfway between Del Norte and Center. To get everything there we loaded up Mama's car and borrowed Mr. Jackson's Crummy, a turquoise and white '58 Chevy he used to haul people and supplies. We had to tow Harry's Ford 'cause it didn't run anymore.

It took a couple of hours to get down the road. Mama's car kept losing fuel pressure and dying. Daddy looked under the hood and found a leaking gasket. We didn't have another one, so Daddy took off his hat, beat out the felt till it was flat and cut a gasket out of the material. He put the makeshift gasket in place and told Mama she was ready to go. I got back in the Crummy and watched Daddy's grey hair blow all around his face in the wind. I looked at Daddy. He was probably close to sixty but just then I saw the young man he used to be, jumping trains and ramblin', the time he talked about before Mama. I must have looked at him a while, 'cause he turned to me, grinned and winked. So that's where Harry got it.

Red Faced

Center, Colorado was in a valley with mountains in the distance in every direction but south. The cold wind blew down the slope over the farms. It seemed like the temperature dropped a little more every day. We moved into a two-story house right off the highway. The bottom part of the house had two rooms and a kitchen and that's where we stayed. The five of us kids slept in one room and closed off the other so we wouldn't need to heat it. Mama and Daddy slept upstairs.

It was owned by a couple named Blackie and Goldie. They owned potato farms and this house sat right in the middle of them. Potato sheds were all over the country. The roofs were rounded and about ten feet tall, the sides came all the way down to the ground making a half circle. Potatoes

347

were stored in there after they were picked which was when the weather turned cold but before the freeze. That was the way a lot of folks around here made a living.

Kids were brought to the big stone school from all over the area. As I stepped off the bus I dreaded another school where I didn't know enough and didn't know anybody. I walked towards the school as cool as I could. Just like always, in the first few days I had to show the boys how tough I was. One guy a little bigger than me ran his mouth and before I knew it we were fighting behind the school after the last bell had rung. When I whipped him and one of his buddies, the others thought better of jumping in. After that, whenever I walked down the sidewalk and met somebody, if there wasn't enough room for us both to pass, they stepped off.

I did make some friends of my own, and me and my buddies would leave school and walk into Center to hang around. Storekeepers ran us out, saying we were trying to cause trouble, but we were just trying to have fun. Like one night when one of my buddies borrowed his daddy's pickup. We pulled an old outhouse into the middle of the street in Monte Vista which was about ten miles away. We set it down right under the only stoplight in town and set the toilet paper inside on fire. There was more smoke than flame so we didn't get into any trouble. This time nobody told who done it.

As it got colder and snowier in the mountains, logging got harder until they shut the operation down for the winter. It wouldn't reopen again until spring and that left Daddy without work.

Daddy talked to Blackie and he hired us all to pick up potatoes in the fields to pay the rent. Every one of us but Mama went out into the potato fields with our hundred pound sacks and picked. Eight-year-old Mary even helped. When we got the sack full, we just left them where they stood in the field for somebody else to come and load onto the truck.

My hands were cold, red and dry from pulling potatoes from the dirt. Rocks were scattered everywhere and as often as not, a rock was picked up and thrown down into the sack along with a potato. After a few days Mary started crying over the pain in her hands, so Mama didn't let her come and help anymore.

The wind blew across the fields. Sheron and Esther worked hard to keep their skirts down even though they had on long underwear. At thirteen and fourteen they didn't want anyone driving by and seeing anything they shouldn't. Hoyt tried to fill his sack as fast as me, I would slow up so that he always stayed close. Daddy held his hat on with a scarf that wound around his hat and his neck, trying to keep the wind from going down his shirt. Our faces got sore from the sting of the wind and seemed to stay red. Farming was hard work with little pay and I knew I wasn't cut out for it. The potato picking helped to make enough money to make the rent and keep us fed. Daddy spent Saturdays looking for something better.

Daddy hired on with a mill south of Ranchos de Taos. He had to drive a hundred and twenty five miles to the mill though. He went there for a week at a time with another fellow named Fred that lived over in Del Norte. He was the tail sawyer. He was a tall Mexican man with black hair that stood straight up except for a bald circle he covered up with a cap. After the first week, Daddy told Mama I could go with them and cook and help. I was glad to go, being the oldest at home was already starting to pay off by not having to go to school.

Mama's car was about done in, and with Harry's car not running, he took both of them to town to see about trading them for a newer one. He used Mama's to tow the

Ford and came back with a '50 model Mercury Daddy said would be able to handle all the miles he'd be going when he went into New Mexico.

The little mill was set up on a big sweeping curve close to the highway south of town. It was in the middle of treeless country so the logs had to be brought in by truck. Daddy and Fred worked there all day and I made the meals and worked in the mill doing whatever I was told. When we would head back on Friday, Daddy would take different roads back to Center trying to find a closer job. We went over Wolf Creek Pass in a big snowstorm one night, but Daddy drove us right on through it in that Mercury.

On the weekends I got a job that wasn't like any work I had done before. I babysat for a lady in Del Norte. She went to some kind of sewing school and needed me in the evenings when her kids were home. There were three of them, all of them old enough to be left alone if you asked me. The oldest

The house at Center in the potato fields.

350

boy was my age, but they didn't know it so I didn't let on.

As part of my pay she would embroider on my shirts with her sewing machine for practice. I had two shirts, a black one and a tan one. They were western shirts with a yoke pattern across the back. On the black one she used white thread and on the tan one she used black. She sewed my initials, AM, across the back about three inches high between my shoulder blades. She put fancy stitching all over the cuffs and wherever she thought it would look nice. I wouldn't wear my coat unless it was real cold so folks would see.

Her house was on the corner of an intersection that had a blinking light that warned traffic of the crossing. There was a store across the intersection where I bought myself donuts and milk before I started back to the house. It was a busy crossroad so finding a ride wasn't hard. The street lights lit up the area but it was full dark when I walked to the road and stuck my thumb out. I walked backwards when I heard a car coming and waited for one to stop for me. A yellow Chevy passed me, slowed up and stopped on the shoulder. I ran to the car and the back door opened on the passenger side. Two fellows rode in front, a lady and third guy were in the back seat where I got in. I told them where I lived right at the curve headed to Del Norte and the man in front said he knew where I meant.

It didn't take long to figure out they were a bunch of drunks. They took turns drinking booze out of a bottle in a paper sack. They made jokes that weren't funny and tried to get me to goof around with them. The girl kept showing me parts of herself with no clothes that I knew I wasn't supposed to look at. She was between me and her man and they kept kissing on each other and then looking at me. I didn't know what to do so I just stared straight ahead. They got to poking fun at me for being green. They laughed at me and told me how red my face was, which made them laugh even harder. They offered the bottle to me, but I didn't want anything to do with what they had going on.

I kept my eyes straight ahead and counted off the landmarks that got me closer to the house. They slowed down for the curve. As the driver steered the car into the pullout that led to my house, I put my hand on the door handle. As soon as they were going slow enough, I opened the door and just about jumped out. I didn't break my stride as I ran to the door. I heard the Chevy throw gravel as it got back on the highway. The bottle they threw out bounced in the ditch beside the road. Mama looked up from her paper she was writing on when I came in, and I tried to act like I hadn't run all the way in.

"You all right, sugar? Yore face sure is red," Mama said. I was beginning to wonder just how red it was, first the drunks and now Mama going on about it.

"It's just cold outside Mama." I didn't dare tell about what had gone on in that car for fear I wouldn't get to babysit anymore.

I could whip anybody, made my own money and could work up against any man, but whenever I thought about that ride, I couldn't help but feel like a dumb little kid.

A Good Time to Go

I was on one side of the mattress and Hoyt Lynn was on the other. I had the covers tucked around my leg so he couldn't pull them off me, and he had done the same thing. That made the quilt tight so some air got down between us chilling our backs. Sheron, Esther and Mary were laying the same way on their mattress, but they were snuggled up together so they could get warm. With the mattresses laying on the floor, the cold seemed to seep through from the bottom

352

"I'm cold," Hoyt said.

"Get up against my back, you'll warm up," I told him. I wasn't giving up my hold on the covers, but I figured that would warm my back up and him too.

"Do you think Daddy's really gonna go up to Elaine's?" Sheron asked.

"When he gets it in his mind to leave, it don't take long for us to be down the road," I said.

"But it's so far and so cold," Esther said. "Elaine told Mama we were welcome, but with the cold right now it would be too hard."

"How much colder could it be than where we are right now?" Hoyt Lynn asked.

The sun was starting to come up, so I knew soon Daddy would be hollering for me to make the fire. I dreaded getting up, so I put my pants and socks on under the covers. I heard Daddy clear his throat. He was in the kitchen, so I figured I'd go ahead and get up and start trying to warm up the house.

I walked out into the kitchen and went to the wood stove to add some kindling and start it up. Daddy was talking to Mama.

"Can't be much colder up there than it is here. Elaine and Don moved up there and they're doin' fine. He said there's some sawmills that will go to work after winter," Daddy told Mama.

"I guess winter will be over someday. It just don't seem like it right now," Mama said as she rubbed her arms with her hands. "She's got a new baby I sure would like to see."

After three girls, Elaine finally had her a little boy. He was just a few months old.

"Last word we had from Harry, he said he was heading up to see Elaine with a buddy. Said with Louie and

Janet gettin' back together, he felt like he oughta move on. I don't see why we don't go up too. I would like to look over the country and see what kind of timber they got."

I'd got the fire going and Mama just about had the oatmeal ready. She hollered for the kids to come and eat.

Daddy kept talking to her. "This'd be a good time to go, before we use up the money we got tryin' to live through the winter down here. We oughta be able to leave tomorrow. The car don't need much, maybe some better tires. We'll stop at Alamosa, put some on and head out."

With that, Daddy had made up his mind.

The next morning the car was loaded to the top. Kitchen pans, tools and heavy things were put in the trunk and on the floor of the car. Then clothes were layered on the floorboard till they reached the same height of the seat. Mama layered quilts and bedding on top of that till the back of the car was flat and as high as the top of the front seats. That's where the four kids would lay down and ride, facing forward or back, whichever way they wanted. They could look out the back or up ahead.

The trunk had canned meat, Spam, powdered milk and eggs, rice and, of course, potatoes. The last thing Mama added was a big blue speckled pot full of cooked rice and canned beef for us to eat along the way.

We rode with our coats on. The blankets and clothes made the car warmer, but not really warm. The kids were in the back laying down, but since I was oldest, I sat up front. Daddy drove and Mama was in the middle. I felt just about grown as I sat in the front. I had on my new straw hat that I paid six dollars for with my babysitting money. It had an eighteen inch brim and was almost too big for the car. If I turned my head I hit Mama with it so I tried to look straight ahead so we she wouldn't make me take it off.

It was the seventeenth day of December and we were headed to Alaska.

Cheyenne

The ribbon of road cut the acres of sagebrush in half. There were mountains in the distance, but we were still down in the valley. The kids had already started fussing. Mary had a fit because we had left her red and white book satchel. I know she wanted to ask Daddy to go back for it, but she knew better. Once we were gone there was no going back.

We stopped at Alamosa just long enough to change out the tires and then headed to Ft. Garland. After going through town we started climbing. The road hugged the mountains uphill toward La Veta Pass. Big trucks worked their engines hard as they slowly crawled their way up the mountain grade. Black smoke and fire came out of the stacks as they struggled. Those trucks gave it everything they had to get to the top. Black smoke came out the exhaust of the Mercury too as she gave it all she had to climb the mountain.

There were half a dozen buildings on top with a café and a truck stop. Daddy got more gas and I walked outside. Trucks were getting fueled, the drivers were eating, while folks in cars parked to use the bathroom. No matter which way you were coming, to leave you went downhill, so folks were relieved that the hard part of the mountain was over. The roadside was dirty with muddy snow and slush. Mama took the pan of food from the trunk and Daddy put it under the hood, propped on the manifold of the flathead engine so it would heat while we drove.

We headed down the narrow road. In some places the guard rails had cable on the edge to catch the car if it went off towards the side. In many places the side of the road just ended with nothing to keep a car from rolling down the

355

mountainside. When the road curved along the outer edge of the mountain, we could see for miles. Mountains and valleys went as far as I could see. At Walsenburg we hit Highway 85 and headed north.

It was so cold we kept our coats on all the time. I had a big leather jacket that Blackie had given me when Daddy told him we would be moving on to Alaska. With the bulky coat and my big hat I took up quite a bit of room in the front seat. When the kids got to fighting over room in the back Mama had Mary come up front and lay down in the floorboard under Daddy's feet using the hump as a pillow.

When we stopped again Daddy got Mama's pan from under the hood and we had a hot meal while we parked. Daddy drove down an alley in the little town we were in and used the buildings to keep the cold wind from blowing through the car. The rice and beef was a little more sticky than usual. I don't know if it was from cooking so long under the hood or just the way it came out. When we ate what we could, Daddy put the pot back in the trunk to keep cold.

We drove straight through the first night and into the morning. The country was rolling hills covered in snow. The wind blew the snow across the highway and some places were slick. Daddy didn't slow up none. We all slept where we were, but whenever I woke up from dozing, Daddy was always wide awake, Mama too.

Mama told us to look when she saw the sign telling us we were in Wyoming. It looked the same, more snow and more wind. We hadn't made Cheyenne when the Mercury's engine started to run rough. It was still firing, but not right. Daddy looked for a service station and we saw one just before town. We were almost there when the engine made a few rough sounds and then quit. We coasted the few hundred feet into the station. Daddy got out and talked to the mechanic that was working. Daddy told Mama to start it up so she slid over and turned the key. She cranked and cranked but the engine wouldn't turn over. They figured that the motor had seized up. It was done for.

Daddy and Mama talked about what to do.

"It's too cold to make a camp, Fonny. I don't know how long it'll take to find a way to keep goin,'" he said.

Mama pointed at sign down the street. 'There's a motel down there, all I know to do is to get a room and try to stay warm."

I was supposed to be near grown but I could hardly keep from getting excited. The other kids were talking all at once. I don't know how many places we had made camp, but we had never been in a motel. Mama and Daddy headed down the street, and the kids just about run all the way. We waited outside while Daddy went in and paid for the room.

The seven of us went into the room with two beds. Not only was there a wall furnace to get the place warm, but a television set too. I thought Mary's eyes would pop. We hadn't ever had a TV that wasn't at a neighbor's house. We couldn't figure out how to turn it on, but Hoyt Lynn looked it over and told us to play it, you had to put a quarter in the slot. Mama and Daddy must have had enough on their mind that they didn't worry about the TV being worldly. I gave the kids the few quarters I had. The quarter always ran out before the show was over and there was a scramble to get another one put in the slot.

Daddy had me go with him and we headed into town on foot to see what kind of vehicle we could find. Fixing the Mercury would take too much money and too much time. We found a car lot and walked in. The cars were covered in about six inches of snow so it was hard to tell what color or make they were. The salesman came out and we told him our story. He showed us a '54 Ford that cost $200. He told us we could take it for $100 and then send the rest when we got settled in

357

Alaska. I was walking around the lot and asked about a '51 Ford sedan, it was just about ten years old. The man told us $99 for that one.

Daddy was stewing on the deal when I thought about speaking up. I waited and then went ahead, "Daddy, if we buy the cheaper one, when we got to Alaska we wouldn't owe no money. There doesn't seem to be much difference in the two of them for the $100 extra we'd have to pay."

Daddy lifted up his hat and scratched his head and told me he thought I had a good point. He walked over to the '51 and looked her over and told the man that's what we would do. We'd take the cheaper one. Daddy paid the man and we got in the Ford and drove back to the motel. I sat a little taller on my side of the car, proud I had got to help Daddy decide. It was good to be the oldest at home and be treated like a grown up. It was especially good when Daddy told me that when they got another car this one would be mine.

Now we had a car but we were low on cash. Daddy had Mama go to the store and call Rubin, who was still living in Lincoln. Rubin told Mama he knew that they would need a certain amount of money before Canada would let them cross to Alaska. Daddy would have to prove he had enough money to make it through. Rubin said he would send the money to us Western Union. We just had to wait for it to come.

That gave us the time we needed to take what we could from the Mercury. We took the water pump and generator, anything that could be used later. We took the tires we had just put on and tied them to the roof of the car. The Ford was a little bit smaller than the Mercury and by the time we loaded it, there was barely enough room for the family to fit. The beef and rice was frozen so we couldn't eat it till we heated it again on the engine.

Rubin's money came in and we were ready to go. Daddy left the Mercury at the station. He told the mechanic he could get what they could out of it for parts. The wind hit and rocked the car as we left Cheyenne. Nobody looked back.

My Hat

"Mama, make Alton take his hat off. We can't see anything out the window," Sheron asked. The kids had been fussing in the back and now Sheron was trying to draw me into it. I know they thought I had it too good up front.

"Yeah, Mama we can't see." Esther joined in. I know she wanted up front, she always wanted to be next to Mama.

Mama looked up at my hat and I looked at her. There was a good chance the hat would have to come off since I was always hitting her head with it. She turned around to the girls and told them to quit fussing. She didn't say anything to me. Mama wouldn't ask Daddy to take his hat off, and she didn't ask me. After that, I didn't consider myself one of the kids any more.

The windows started to fog up as soon as we took off. Daddy used his hand and wiped at the windshield to make a spot to see out of. The heater and defroster worked but the amount of air they blew didn't amount to much, so there were just three-inch circles near the dash to look out.

The sun didn't shine while we were in Montana, the skies were gray and snow spitted at us all the time. When we wiped the windows, we could see we were in a big valley and the sharp mountains surrounding us, looking cold with their snow caps. The kids made up games to play and we spent our time sleeping, fighting and singing. Mama mentioned the grey skies and then had us sing,

O they tell me of home far beyond the skies,
O they tell me of a home far away
O they tell me of a home where no storm clouds rise,
O they tell me of an unclouded day.

Daddy drove through the night and just took cat naps in the car when we stopped to eat. After the hot food was gone, Mama gave us Spam sandwiches to eat. We ate in the car, nobody was in a hurry to get out and pee. The heater hadn't got any better so Daddy still tried to see out the window through the three-inch hole. We stayed cold all the time, the kids burrowed in the blankets in the back, and me hunkered down in my big leather coat.

We reached Babb at the Canadian border. Thanks to the Western Union from Rubin, Daddy had the $375 to show the fellow at the border crossing. We left Montana and went into Alberta. The flat country went on as far as we could see, the white of the ground blending with the grey of the sky when the sun was out. The road was packed with snow and we couldn't tell if it was pavement or dirt.

At Edmonton we turned west. We traveled in the dark most of the time. These were the shortest days of the year and being that far north we hardly ever saw sunlight. It was either snowing or dark. The snow was bladed high onto the edges of the dirt road making it seem like you were driving down a half tunnel. We hardly ever met another car or truck.

We fueled at a little gas station and added water to the radiator. Daddy said the car must have a bad water pump because we had to keep adding water every time we stopped. The kids got out to use the bathroom. Hoyt Lynn didn't know Esther still had her hand in the way and slammed her finger in the door. We heard the bang and then the scream. Daddy rushed to get the door opened. Mama grabbed Esther's hand and looked at it. It was bleeding, but just a little. Esther started crying and carrying on. Mama wrapped her hand with a rag Daddy had. Mama told her to hush but put her arm around her and walked her inside.

I was glad to stay outside with Daddy.

When they all got back, Esther's face was wet. Mama told Daddy that when they came from the cold into the warm bathroom, Esther had passed out. Mama had to splash water on her to get her to come to. They had her hand bundled up and Esther had calmed down. Seemed like it was always something with Esther.

When everyone was in we took off, the station was still in sight out the back window when we came up on a couple of people. They were bundled up big and bulky and when we got closer we could see one was a lady and one a man. They were hitchhiking. He had a mustache with icicles hanging off. Daddy stopped to talk to them. Daddy always stopped for folks. He reminded us we had been in need ourselves and probably would be again too.

Only the man talked and he told Daddy the station had thrown them out but wouldn't tell Daddy why. He looked like he had something under his coat. Daddy seemed leery of these two and didn't offer to let them ride with us. He told them they would be better off if they went back to the station, wished them luck and drove on.

Daddy told us he thought the man might have whiskey or worse under his coat. As far as Mama was concerned there wasn't anything much worse than whiskey. It was about the only time I could remember Daddy not giving someone a ride. It made this place seem that much more different. Mama worried over it for miles.

At Dawson Creek the road turned northwest and we were on the Alcan Highway. Daddy told us how the Alcan had been built during the war to haul supplies and men. For Daddy it was a way to get to Alaska and better work, but I think more than that, he wanted to see the country. Now the road was marked in miles and we could keep track of how far we had come. It made knowing how far we had to go tough. We had made two thousand miles, it was fifteen hundred more before we would reach Anchorage.

This was the only way to Alaska and even with it being the only road, most of the time it was just us out in the middle of nothing. Snow weighed down spruce trees that stood close to the road. It looked like growing was a chore for them.

We always worked on the frosted up windows. As fast as we wiped them, they fogged up again. We could only see out front, we didn't bother with the side windows. With all the kids and stuff in the back, we never saw out the back.

We heard a truck coming up on us from behind. The driver began to pass. He slowly gained on us and as his tires got even with the car it sprayed us with snow and ice. Daddy was slowing the car down, trying to get a spot where he could see. Mama wiped the window, but all that we saw was white. Daddy didn't want to slam on the brakes and 'cause us to spin, so he let the car coast.

Bam! The car came to a stop and all of us were thrown forward. The girls screamed and Mama sucked in her breath. Daddy told the girls to hush up. He didn't like to hear all that excitement when something happened. We rubbed at the windows to try and see where we were.

The snow was up against the windows on the passenger side. We had driven into a snow bank. The truck must not have seen what happened, we heard him going further down the road. With the truck gone, Daddy sat there for a minute trying to think what to do.

"Well, son, let's find a way out." Daddy opened the door.

My door was stuck so I had to climb over Mama to get out Daddy's. The car was buried in the snow from front to back. The only part we could make out was the left side doors and the trunk. There was snow on top, in front and underneath.

I pushed my hat down further on my head, trying to keep what warmth I could. Since it was straw it didn't really hold much heat. Daddy was looking everything over when we heard a car and saw a white Chevy Suburban pulling up. A man got out to talk to us and told us there wasn't much he could do for our car, he didn't have any chains and neither did we. He offered to take us to his house at White Horse to get out of the cold. He said the temperature was close to ten below.

Daddy talked to Mama and told her and the kids to go with the man. Him and me would stay with the car. No matter what, the car would have to come out of the snow bank. He was hopeful a truck would come along and pull us out. Daddy and me stood by the car as the Chevy left. We got in the car to watch and wait. Hours went by, the night got black and we couldn't see our hands in front of our faces. We waited for help or daylight, whichever would come first.

To save what gas we had we didn't keep the car running, just started it every once in a while to keep if from getting too cold to start. Daddy went to sleep in the front seat and I laid down on the blankets in the back. Daddy snored while I lay in the blankets and tried to pretend I wasn't freezing, I finally drifted off.

Bang! Bang! We were jerked awake by the sound of someone knocking on the back window. I opened my door and crawled out, Daddy did too. There was a little streak of daylight in the horizon.

"I wasn't sure anybody was in there but I thought I better check before I went on," said a man. He had driven up in a Kenworth with a flatbed trailer.

"We've had some trouble," Daddy told him. "I'm RW Miller. Me and my boy need some help getting the car pulled out of the snow."

"I've got some chains in my truck that I can pull you with." He headed to his truck to get them. Daddy turned to me, "Son, you get underneath the car as far as you can and start a trench so we can tie the chain around the rearends. I'm worried that if we just chain around the bumper it'll just pull off. Get as much snow as you can out of there, so it'll move."

I took off my hat and laid down on my belly and started digging under the car. The truck driver came back with the chain.

"Boy, do you have any gloves?"

"No, sir I don't."

"Just a minute, I think I've got some in the cab."

My hands already hurt just in the short time I had started moving the snow. I put one of the gloves on, only to have my thumb and fingers come out. My palm was the only thing covered. I held it up to look at, thinking there was something wrong.

"That's how they come, they're called driving gloves, but they're better than nothin'," the driver said. I figured he was right and got to digging.

I pulled at the snow, trying to clear a place for the chain to hook. The pain in my hands was starting to go away along with all of the feeling in them. I looked over at my cowboy hat. There wasn't anything else I could do. The eighteen inch brim along with the crown made a good sized scoop. I was able to pull a lot more snow out, but even with the hat, my hands started to feel like clubs. They didn't hurt anymore so that made it easier to dig, but I didn't have much control.

When the path was clear I was pretty far up under the car. They handed me the chain and I pulled on it to wrap it. I fumbled with it because I couldn't feel where it was in my hands. It took a couple of tries but I got it and then crawled out from under the car. I stuck my hands in the deep pockets of my coat and wondered if I would ever feel anything with them again.

The truck driver got in his truck and slowly backed the Kenworth up until the chain got tight. Daddy got inside to steer. After a few tries he got it started and revved the engine. The driver pulled a little harder and the car started moving. He slowly dragged the car. It popped over the mound of snow, the back wheels spinning. Daddy shouted 'whoa' when it came out and waved to the man in his mirror. He brought the truck to a stop and I unhooked the chain.

Daddy raised the hood and asked me for the can opener. I had it in the pocket of my coat and had a hard time getting a hold of it because I still couldn't feel my hands. I pulled all the stuff out of my pockets to the ground. Daddy picked up the can opener and opened a can of motor oil and poured it into the radiator because it was low on water. He said liquid was liquid.

I walked over to what was left of my hat. It was bent and broken and sure didn't look like a hat anymore. Daddy had ran over it when he came out of the snow bank. I picked it up, looked it over and then threw it as far as I could. I guess things like hats didn't matter anyway. It wasn't the first thing I'd had to leave. Daddy honked the horn, it was time to go.

When we got to the house where the family was, everybody was in bed. Mama fixed a pallet for me in the floor and took Daddy into where she was sleeping. Hoyt Lynn woke up and couldn't stop talking about the carpet on the floor. It was from one wall to another and he hadn't ever seen that before. I don't think any of us had.

In the morning they fed us breakfast. I heard Esther telling Sheron how good they were to feed us in the middle of the night. Sheron told her it wasn't night time, it was morning it was just still dark. I never really knew what time it was either. Staying in somebody's house was new to us, so we all tried to stay quiet and act right, so Daddy wouldn't get on to us later. The man and his wife couldn't get over us coming all this way in December. She was so worried, she made up a thermos of coffee to send with us. I didn't have too much to say, I just tried to keep my mind off my hands. They weren't numb anymore and I sure wished they were. They hurt like the devil.

Before we left the man warned us there was just one more fuel stop between White Horse and Alaska.

"Now, Mr. Miller it's a small place. It'll be on your right side. There should be a light shining. Make sure you go in there and fuel up. If it's late just knock on the door, they'll open up and make sure you get gas."

We still had a couple more days to go, but we were close. It was about three hundred miles to the border and then four hundred or so on in to Anchorage.

"We sure do thank y'all," Daddy told the man. He offered the man money but he wouldn't take it.

"Now don't forget to look for that light."

Lights

After having room to lay down and being able to walk around, it was sure hard to get back in the car. One thing about it, the cold and dark made sleeping in the seat a little easier. I tried to keep my hands tucked under my arms and that seemed to help with the ache.

366

We moved up the road towards the Alaska line. Daddy stared out the hole in the windshield. It was rare to meet somebody going the other way. Mama tried to keep an eye on the mile markers so we'd know how far we'd come. A few hours into the ride, Mama started looking hard for the station the man had told us about. It was even harder with the windows fogged up all the time. Sometimes I would wipe and for a few minutes we could see out. The moon wasn't much help, but the snow on the ground kept things from being so dark.

"Wesley, I think I see some kind of light over there," Mama told him.

"Do you think that might be the place?"

"It was just a little sliver of light, I'm not sure," Mama said. She wiped at the window herself trying to see. "I just don't know." She looked back from where we had come. Daddy went on.

"If we don't see something soon, we'll go back. I hate to turn around if it's just ahead of us." Daddy decided.

I had been trying to sleep. When I heard Mama and Daddy talking about missing the last stop, I started to pay attention. We drove on but no light ever showed. Daddy finally decided to turn back. He stopped the car in the middle of the road, put it in reverse and turned around. The kids in the back kind of roused up, but they didn't come up out of their covers.

Now, the three of us looked hard and wiped at the windows. After driving back for a while we thought we saw a flicker of light on Daddy's side of the car.

"I don't know if I should get off this road on to that turn out. It might not be the place." Daddy was almost talking to himself.

"I think that's the light I saw," said Mama.

It was the only thing we'd seen that was close to a light, so he turned into between two poles, hoping that was the road in. The snow wasn't as deep and when we got closer, we saw that there was a light. Our headlights shined on the building and we saw that it had pumps. This was it!

"Praise the Lord." Mama was relieved.

We drove up and then I got out and went to the door to knock. The light we were following was no brighter than a porch light, but Mama had seen it. I didn't know how.

After I knocked, the fellow inside hollered for us to hold on, he'd be right there. After a few minutes he walked out, so wrapped up in wool and fur that I couldn't tell what he looked like. He helped us gas up and Daddy paid. He told us how much further we had to go, that we'd need to be careful, there weren't too many more places to fuel before Anchorage.

We crawled back onto the road and then picked up speed. We made the border and drove into Alaska. All of us were tired, not just from riding but from holding ourselves so tight to try and keep warm. We couldn't go too fast with all the heaves in the road. Knowing we were close but having to drive slow and careful to keep from tearing up the car made it harder. We hoped we were getting somewhere. My hands were hurting worse than ever, but I didn't say anything.

It was morning but dark when we pulled into a station. Daddy and me got out to get the gas, fill the radiator and make sure the car was holding up. Mama went inside to call Elaine and tell her how close we were. She told Elaine we ought to be there sometime in the evening. The attendant came out and Daddy pulled the money from his pocket. The big clip we'd started with was down to a few dollars. Daddy gave the boy all the money we had.

"Well son, we better hope she makes it. That's the last of the money," Daddy told me.

368

Elaine's place couldn't be far if we were putting the last gas in.

"We burned a little more than we shoulda, what with missin' the station back there and havin' to turn around," Daddy said. "That doubled up a few miles."

We were worn out but knowing we were going to be there soon kept us up and talking. The girls couldn't wait to play with Elaine's babies, look at her house, or have her do their hair since she was going to school to be a beautician. When the sun shone we were all cleaning the windows to see out. There were mountains far away, completely white. We went through winding canyons, with a wall of rock on the right and nothing on the left. The girls sang in the back and Hoyt Lynn picked at them. Mama was turning around to get after him when the car sputtered... and choked... and died.

"We're out of gas," Daddy said. All of us sat up. We looked at him as he pumped the pedal. The kids got quiet, not wanting to make a fuss. The cold was already creeping in.

Daddy pumped the pedal again trying to start her up, just in case he was wrong. But the engine wouldn't turn over. The car was quiet and we were silent as we coasted down the road. Daddy steered her to a wide spot on the right and we came to a dead stop.

Out of gas, out of money, out of food.

Daddy banged his hand on the steering wheel, "Confound it!"

Of all the trips we had made, the dark and cold road to Alaska was the toughest. I sat there trying to think; I was sixteen and ought to be able to find a way to help. Mama got busy.

"All of you children wrap up tight, right away. It's gonna get colder fast. Esther, hand us a couple of blankets from those y'all are layin' on. You wrap up together to share

369

warmth. We'll all just rest and wait for someone to come."
Mama was calm as she told us what to do.

"I'm gonna leave these lights on, it'll help somebody
see us if they come up the road," Daddy said.

The car groaned and creaked as it lost what little heat
it held. The fogged windows froze until we couldn't see out.
Darkness surrounded us. Even though we strained to look
out the window, no car came around the curve to find us. We
were quiet as we huddled together for warmth. None of us
kids wanted to let on like we were scared so we didn't say
anything. The silence was broken only by Mama's whispers
as she prayed non-stop.

Nine-year-old Mary whispered to Sheron, "Surely the
Lord's heard Mama, she's said the same thing enough times."
Sheron shushed her. Being older, she knew better than to
complain.

Daddy patted Mama on the leg every once in a while
and told her somebody'd come for us. Lack of sleep made it
easy for him to doze off. He fell asleep with his head against
the door, using his felt hat as a cushion. We all tried to sleep.
Every time I opened my eyes, Mama was looking through a
spot in the window she had rubbed, hoping to see lights
coming.

As the night went on, the cold crept in. At first, it was
mostly my feet that were so cold, then my legs, until my
whole body seemed frozen. I couldn't stop the shivers that
snuck up on me every so often. I tried to ignore the cold, but
the ache in my hands wouldn't let me forget about them. The
headlights on our car got dimmer, the beams of headlights
got smaller and lower until they was gone. The colder it got,
the easier it was to sleep.

"Try to think of somethin' warm," Mama told us. I
closed my eyes and my thoughts slowed down as I imagined
hot coffee and wood fire. Something warm? There wasn't

370

anything much hotter than back in Louisiana in the summer. I saw myself running, red faced and sweaty in the humid heat, trying to find shade under the pines. The smell of cut timber drifted up from the sawmill as I listened to Daddy cut the logs. The song of the saw echoing through the woods...

Mama nudged me, "Alton."

I couldn't wake myself up from my dreams, or thoughts, whatever they were.

"What is it, Mama?" I didn't open my eyes when I answered her. The stories I had remembered still strong in my mind.

"Alton, come on son, wake up," Mama pleaded.

I shook myself awake. Our story wasn't over yet. We were still living it.

"Daddy's thinkin' we need to move around so we don't freeze. Girls, you get everybody woke up."

Nobody wanted to move.

"Come on now. We've got to get our blood moving. Beat our chest and holler, like we did when we rode freights," Daddy said.

We moved like frozen molasses. Trying to wrap blankets around our heads, nobody wanted to be the first one to start out. I wasn't going to get out until somebody made me. Mary started crying. Daddy had his hand on the door handle, not sure if getting out was a good idea.

Mama looked at the windshield, it was frozen over with our breath, and then there was a glow.

"Car's comin'," Mama said as she took a breath. Daddy started rubbing the window. Headlights!

"Are we saved?" Esther asked.

"We're saved." Mama told her. Then began, new whispered prayers of thanks.

All of a sudden I had no trouble being first out of the car. Daddy got out on his side and walked towards the front of our car, I was on the other side. The headlights got close, shined on us and came to a stop. A man got out in a big coat and hat and walked towards us, we couldn't make him out with the light shining on him from behind.

"We almost didn't see y'all! Don't ya know it's forty below out here!" He hollered at us.

Harry! It was Harry.

I walked to my brother and he hugged me around the neck. Harry had come for us. As we watched two more folks get out of the car, we saw it was Elaine and her husband Don too. His blonde hair was covered up in a wool cap, but I could tell it was him. After days of being proud to be oldest at home, suddenly I was more than happy to give that up for a while. I don't know if it was the cold or the pain, but I was tired. There were shouts and hugs as the kids got out and got in the Corvaire station wagon Don had brought. Elaine told us when we hadn't showed up, they had decided to come looking for us. They had been driving for about an hour. That's how close we had been to making it, an hour.

Daddy hooked up the battery cables they had brought to charge the battery. Don put gas in the Ford from a can. He told us people up here never left home without back up supplies. I stood outside with the men while the kids got settled in the car. They went on and on about the hot air coming out of the heater, there were even vents in the back.

Harry got in the Ford to drive it on in, and I stayed with him, the cold didn't matter as much anymore. I told Harry I was going to ride in the Ford so I could smoke with him, but that wasn't all the reason. I had been treated like I was nearly grown on this trip. Even though I was glad to see them, I didn't want that to change. I wanted Harry and Don to treat me that way too.

We made it to Elaine's house. Don saw my hands and had me stay in the kitchen so he could start treating them right away. He knew how to deal with frostbite. He soaked my hands in cold water and then heated some more and moved my hands to the warmer water. He did this a few times, each time the water was warmer than before. Some of my skin came off but it didn't hurt.

"Mama, is Alton gonna lose his hands?" Mary was scared and big eyed when she asked.

"Everything's going to be all right," Mama said. And I knew it was.

"I'll be fine Mary, they already don't hurt." That made her feel better.

Harry

It wasn't until I walked into the living room and saw the twinkling lights of the pine tree that I remembered. It was Christmas Eve.

ALASKA 1962

Getting Heat

The little house got crowded fast. Sometimes it seemed like it was wall to wall people. Mary, even though she was nine, took to playing under the kitchen table just to keep out from under foot. Not only was there Elaine, Don, and their four kids, Mama, Daddy, Harry and me, Sheron and Esther, Hoyt Lynn and Mary. Harry's buddy, Roger Easley, had come up from Oregon and he was staying there too. With fifteen crowding the rooms, I was always trying to get out of the house.

I ended up going with Don as he delivered heating oil to houses inside and outside of town. It took all day for him to make his rounds in the old Army truck he drove. Most of the roads were narrow and the trees grew right up to the edge. I couldn't tell if the road was gravel or paved with it covered in snow. We were driving along in the last bit of daylight when Don pointed out an animal standing in the road in front of us.

"Watch this moose now. He's probably going to ram the truck," he told me.

Don slowed down to a stop. The big, dark animal turned around and looked at us, put his head down, walked a few steps, took aim at the headlights on the truck and rammed us in the grill.

"They don't like the headlights. They ram the truck just about every time instead of trying to get out of the way. He's so big it doesn't ever hurt him."

"Why don't you turn out the lights?" I asked.

"Then you wouldn't have got to see it," Don said. He never did turn out the lights, that time or any other.

We got through early one day so we drove over to Don's brother's house. Billy lived just a few houses from us and was blonde just like his brother. Don said we'd hang out there before we went back. When we pulled up, I saw the Ford was parked there. I figured it was Harry and Roger. When we walked in the boys were all sitting at the kitchen table playing cards. They made room for us. I didn't know how to play, so they taught me. I hadn't ever held cards before, card playing was not allowed with Mama. We weren't just playing a little ol' game of Old Maid, this was Black Jack.

"Alton, we're not goin' to let you keep playin' if you keep bendin' the cards," Billy said. I must have been so uneasy I kept holding on too tight and bending the corners.

"All right, I'll hold 'em loose," I told them. "I still have a hard time feelin' with my hands." I didn't let on how nervous I was playing, worrying about somebody walking in and seeing us. I held them with just one hand and took a drag on my cigarette. I had snuck around doing that for so long, that didn't bother me at all.

Harry won a few hands and then we figured we'd better leave. Don said he'd stay a little while longer. We got in the cold Ford, and after getting her started up, headed towards Elaine's. The heater still didn't work so we wiped the windows to see out. We pulled up to the house I got out but Harry laid down across the seat, his head under the dash. The engine was still running.

"What're you doin?" I asked.

"I'm tryin' to see what's goin' on with this heater," Harry answered.

I left him. It hadn't worked since we got it, and I wasn't going to mess with it. I went on inside and walked into the warm kitchen.

"You been smokin' cigarettes son?" Mama asked. She was standing at the sink.

"No, Mama, just shootin' the breeze with Billy. They smoke over there," I answered.

"You sure?" She looked at me with her eyebrows raised.

I'd been worried about the cards, but it looked like I should have been thinking about the smoke. Just then Harry came through the door.

"Guess what I found?" He asked the room.

Daddy walked in from the front room.

"Shut that door, you'll let all the heat out," he said.

"This!" Harry tossed something wadded up onto the table.

I picked it up and smoothed it out, it was a piece of tissue.

"That was pluggin' up the intake hose for the heater! I pulled it out and the heater's blowing full blast now," Harry was excited.

Daddy took it from me and shook his head. We'd almost been done in by a lil ol' Kleenex.

Church

That night Daddy told us he was going to go out in the woods close by Anchorage and try to log. He couldn't stand being cooped up in the house for a day longer. Don had a buddy who would loan Daddy his '59 ton and a half Dodge to haul with. He wasn't working it now because folks up here didn't really work in the winter much. Don told Daddy it was too hard to work in the cold, but he had his mind set.

Not so bright and not so early, Daddy had me and Harry out in the snow trying to cut timber. The trees were frozen and we could hardly get a saw in them. When we did get some cut, dragging them through the deep snow was hard. We didn't have snow shoes so our feet busted through

377

the crust of the snow in places where it wasn't frozen solid. It took up so much time we couldn't get enough work done to make it pay. At the end of the week we were so worn out, Daddy finally gave up on it and said we'd wait till spring. He told us he was beginning to wonder why anybody lived up in this cold.

That left only a couple of things we could do to get out of the house, neither one fun-- church and school.

They sent a bus around to take Hoyt Lynn and the girls to school. Elaine packed them a lunch in the morning and when Mary came from school the first day she was about to bust. She told Elaine that was the biggest lunch she'd ever had, a Coke, and sandwich and a little Milky Way candy bar all at one time. Elaine hugged her and got a little teary eyed after finding out what a feast that little meal had been to Mary.

I walked to school just in case I found something better to do on the way. Another boy lived nearby named Tommy. We walked together. After I got the hang of it, the school was one of the best ones I'd been to. They had four classes a day and a study hall after each one. That's when I did my school work and I wasn't too far behind. Daddy said schoolwork was for school, not in his house, so having the time to do it kept what I'd been taught fresh in my mind.

They had recess in the gym. They taught a lot of track, running and jumping, rope climbing and flipping. I got to where I could run up a wall and flip in the air and land on my feet. Nobody could jump as high or as far as I could. I told Mama about it.

Daddy heard us talking, "Sounds like a bunch of foolishness, jumping around for no reason. What are they teachin' in that school? If this weather would warm up, we could be out, tryin' to make some money."

Sitting around was about to drive Daddy crazy. Mama walked up to us.

"Go in the bedroom and look at what I got you today from the Salvation Army," Mama told me.

I came back out with a suit on a hanger. "This?"

"I think it's just your size. Go in the bedroom and try it on."

"Mama it's worse than corduroy pants."

Mama held out the green plaid suit. It had a jacket and pants with four inch squares in three different shades of green. It was the most awful thing I'd ever seen. I put the pants on and pulled them up as high as I could to show how short they were. The jacket fit me like a glove, so I tried to scrunch up the sleeves so they didn't come all the way down to my wrists.

"It don't fit," I announced.

"There ain't nothin' wrong with that suit. You'll look fine goin' to church in it." She straightened the pants and pulled down the sleeves. Her mind was made up.

I took the suit back in the bedroom, dreading the day I'd have to leave the house in it. How would folks know who I was, wearing that thing?

"If you were gonna buy me a clown suit, you should have let me go ahead and join the circus," I told Mama, but not loud enough so she'd hear.

Sunday came around and we all went to the new church. Daddy wasn't sure if the preacher believed just like he did, but he'd see what the preaching was like. Elaine came with her little kids and I was pretty sure this was the first time she'd come too. We walked into the main part of the building and that's where the preaching went on. Classes and other activities went on in the basement below where they had the heater. Little vents came out of the floor in front of the pulpit to help heat the whole building.

Harry was old enough not to have to go to church so I was left there with the family, green checkered suit and all. My friend Tommy came and a couple of other boys that were my age. The service dragged on and it was hard to stay sitting on the narrow benches. I told Elaine I would sit with her babies and help them be quiet. I gave the preacher five or ten minutes and then the littlest ones, Debbie and Speedy, would get a pinch. They let out a squall and there was nothing for me and Tommy to do but pick them up take them downstairs so their crying didn't bother folks. That was the polite thing to do. They never got good and calmed down until church was about over.

When Elaine didn't come to church one Sunday, we had to figure something else out. I told Mama I was feeling sick and needed to get some water. Tommy followed me out and we went downstairs to the basement. Tommy had got his hands on a couple of cigarettes. We felt just like outlaws as we smoked in church. It wasn't but a few minutes we heard footsteps coming down the basement stairs. I tried to get my cigarette out and threw it across the room. Somehow, Tommy got rid of his too. One of the deacons came into sight.

"What are you boys doing down here?"

We just stared at him.

"You were smoking down here," he said it like he was sure.

"We were just tryin' to get warm," I said, I thought that sounded pretty good.

"Boys, smoke was coming up through the vent under the preacher's feet. He might preach fire and brimstone, but he doesn't usually smoke while he's doing it. Now you get out of here and don't let me catch you again."

Tommy and me both hightailed it out of there. I was scared to death that the deacon was going to tell Daddy. I figured the best thing for me was to stay gone for a while. So I asked Mama and she let me go to Tommy's. I stayed there until his mama ran me off. I walked back to Elaine's and didn't get there 'til pretty late. I wasn't sure I'd got my cigarette out and worried that the church had burned down. I slowly walked into the house and waited for Daddy to start in on me.

Mama looked up, "Are you feelin' any better?"

I didn't understand what she meant at first, I'd forgotten my lie about not feeling good.

Daddy was asleep in the chair. That's when I knew the man hadn't told on us and the church hadn't burned down.

I was getting as good as Harry.

Break Up

After folks at church found out how many of us were living at Elaine's, a friend there offered Daddy a place to live. Harry didn't move out there with us. He floated around between Billy's and Elaine's.

The new place was outside of town but it had a lot of room and was the biggest place we'd ever lived. It was at the small local airport and the building was called an airplane hangar. It was a Quonset hut so the walls curved up to make a half circle. Jack, the owner, kept his plane on one end of the building. He came out pretty regular and worked on it. Me and the kids went over on his side and visited with him when he was there.

On our side of the building Mama took quilts and hung them from rope to partition off bedrooms. There was a stove for Mama to cook on and heat the place, but since the rounded ceilings were so high it was pretty cool most of the time. We didn't wander too far from the fire.

We were back to using an outhouse, but it wasn't too far away. I went out there to smoke and every time I came in, Mama asked,

"Alton, are you smokin'?

"No, Mama, I'm not."

She shook her head at me, I figured I had her fooled. She'd got a job cleaning houses in town and was tired at the end of the day. That must have kept her from studying me too close.   When Tommy came out, he brought his Husky pup. We tried to turn him into a sled dog by putting a harness on him and tying ropes to a sled. By the time we loaded the sled with our supplies, it was too heavy and we had to drag it ourselves. The puppy just ran alongside. We'd found an old miner's shack and used it as our clubhouse. Tommy and me were the only ones in the club.

The shack didn't have any windows and the roof had fallen so far down that we had to stoop to be inside of it. We built a fire in the middle of the shed and used it to heat up. There didn't seem to be a place for the smoke to get out so it hung heavy in the air. After a while it was so thick Tommy and me had to lay down on the ground to keep breathing. The Husky wouldn't come in.

When spring came, the locals called it break up. The snow turned the ground to thick mud. It thawed one day and the next it froze again, over and over, until the weather stayed warm. Our miner's shack was hard to get to for the mud. We sunk so low in the muck, we didn't go under it anymore.

Daddy was ready to try logging again so we borrowed the same Dodge truck and went out into the woods. Leaves and brush were wet from the melting snow. Mud was deeper than our boots and it took all the toe clenching we could do to keep from walking out of them. The truck was stuck more than it ran. As the ground dried up we walked further into the woods. That's when mosquitoes as big as hummingbirds flew up and ate us all alive.

Harry was batting them left and right. "One thing about these skeeters, you can hear 'em comin'. They don't sneak up on ya, like in Louisiana."

They were big and slow, but there were too many to fight off. Logging didn't last any longer than when we had tried it in the winter.

One night I heard Daddy tell Mama from their bed behind the blanket he was going to take a job carpentering until we had enough money to come out of Alaska. There were apartments being built near the church and that would be enough work to make what we needed to leave. He was going to have me help him after school. There was daylight since the days were getting longer.

Nobody was happier than the girls to find out we were leaving. It had been a cold dark time for them. Mary had stayed sick most of the time and Hoyt Lynn was in trouble all the time, having to stay inside so much.

I wasn't so happy to leave. I had done good in school, hadn't had to fight anybody and had a couple of buddies. I knew one thing though, that green suit was not going to make the trip out of Alaska.

Heading South

It was a sad story being squeezed into the backseat with the little kids. I thought I was done with the back seat, but it hadn't worked out that way. The same Ford that took us to Alaska in the winter was bringing us out in the summer. This time Daddy had made a trailer to haul all the supplies, tools and blankets. That made more room in the car, but that was taken up by Harry and Roger, who took turns riding up

383

front with Mama and Daddy. No matter how you sat, nine in one car got tight.

The car jerked and bounced along as we drove the eighteen hundred miles of gravel road towards Washington State. We crossed over into British Columbia and the narrow road got better as we headed south. Mountains with snow and glaciers to the right and hills to our left made a canyon that we travelled through. Even though it was summer, this far north the air stayed cool and sleeping at night next to the road got chilly. Mama made camp in the evening when there was a wide spot and we cooked soup and ate biscuits she had packed for the trip.

Daddy tried to make good time as we headed out of Canada but the gravel road kept slowing us down. The sharp little rocks went through the tires and put holes in the inner tube. Daddy would feel the tire going flat, look out the side mirror and tell us, "We got another one boys." He pulled to the side and the boys got out.

We had to take the wheel off the car and bust the tire off the rim to get to the inner tube. Harry cleaned the rubber and sand papered it so it would be rough. He took the Campbell's Tire Patch glue and put it on the inner tube and then put the patch on. Once it stuck we had to air it up. Harry took the hand pump and stuck the end of the hose into the valve stem. He took the pump and sat it on the ground. He held it with his feet and with his hands pumped air into the tire. I took the valve out of the stem so that the air would go in faster. Harry pumped till he was give out and if we were where Mama couldn't hear, he would cuss. When the tube was full, as fast as I could, I put the valve in the stem. The trick was to get it put back in before the tires lost too much air, because then we'd have to start again. Then Harry cussed no matter who was around. We put the inner tube back in the tire, put the tire back on the wheel, and put the wheel back on

384

the car. By the time we did it eleven times, I could have done it in my sleep.

The trip was long with so many people in the car and trouble almost every mile it seemed. The road was as hard as any we had been on. When we were off alone, Harry and Roger talked about things never working out for Daddy. They were starting to think maybe it was Daddy's own fault on why he didn't make a go of it. I thought it was just hard times. It seemed like most folks had them too. Daddy found a gospel station and we sang along to the hymn.

Farther along we'll know more about it,
Farther along we'll understand why;
Cheer up my brother, live in the sunshine,
We'll understand it all by and by.

That song told me that folks all over had trouble, just like us. I figured Harry and Roger thought they knew more than they did. I got tired of hearing them complain. Daddy sure never did much of it, so I didn't either.

Roger's folks had a line on a job for him, so we went through Washington so we could drop him off at his folks' place. When we got there, Harry decided to stay too. Daddy was looking for sawmilling work so we headed down to Oregon to his old stomping grounds to see what he might find. We saw Louie there and surprised him with a visit. We didn't stay long. The whole time Janet was afraid Louie was going to take off and go with us, but he didn't. With no luck finding work, Daddy kept on south.

We went back down through Nevada and Utah, Colorado and then into New Mexico. Daddy stopped all along the way at places he knew. Mills weren't hiring or had been moved. There was no work. We kept on south until late in the afternoon we stopped in a little town called Bernalillo and camped alongside the Rio Grande. There was a big mountain to the east of us and the west stretched out to desert.

I unloaded Mama's pots as we made camp. Hoyt Lynn took the buckets to the river to fill up. After the work was done, the kids played in the river and cooled down. Big cottonwoods shaded us and even though it was July, the clouds built up in the sky and the gusty winds cooled everything down. Mama made potato soup and we all sat around the camp fire.

"We're not goin' any further," Daddy said.

"You think you'll find some work around here?" Mama asked.

"I'm going to unhitch from the trailer and leave it here with y'all. I think I'll go on into Albuquerque, it's about ten miles. It's a bigger town so there's more of a chance to find work." He tipped up his bowl and drank the last of his soup.

"How much money do we have left?" Mama washed the bowls in the buckets of river water.

"Not a dime. I got enough in the gas tank to go into town and come back, that's about it."

"Then I'm sure you'll find us something," Mama said.

Daddy left before we all woke up. The sunshine quickly warmed up the cool ground we slept on. The New Mexico sun was strong and made it hard to remember the winter of bitter cold we had spent in Alaska. Mama heated the soup from supper and we ate it for breakfast. All of us played in the river, Mama sat on the bank and watched and laughed at us. She said it was the easiest way to wash clothes that she ever saw.

We didn't eat any dinner so we could wait and eat supper when Daddy came back. We watched every car cross the bridge from the east, waiting for one of them to turn

386

down to where we were at the river bank. A familiar one finally did.

Daddy stopped the car and stepped out. Mary ran to him and he handed her a loaf of bread. He opened the door to the back seat and pulled out a big box full of groceries.

Mama smiled. "Looks like things are gonna be fine."

NEW MEXICO 1962

Good Kids

The next day Daddy took us into Albuquerque and we drove down 4th Street. On the west side of the street were two big houses. Daddy drove the car up alongside one of them and drove in back. In between the big houses were little apartments. Three of them were connected to make a u shape, we moved into the middle one.

In one of them a lady lived with her daughter who was about grown. The daughter was crippled up with something wrong with her muscles. Another family lived in the other apartment and had three little boys.

The street was lined with big trees, cottonwoods and elms. White fuzz floated from the cottonwoods through the air like dust in a sunbeam. Hoyt Lynn found the ditch that ran out behind the house, and him and Mary got in it with their feet. Red Sanders lived in one of the big houses. His kids were just bigger than babies and played on the porch. Daddy talked to him and told him that some folks at the church had loaned us this place to live until we got on our feet. He told Daddy that was fine as long we didn't chase the turkeys and chickens that were pecking around. Daddy told him we were all good kids.

We pulled the trailer up against the house and used a tarp to make a lean-to and that made a room for me and Hoyt Lynn. The girls stayed in the house. I didn't mind being out there at all. Sometimes at night me and Hoyt would go to the ditch and catch crawdads. It got to where we didn't even notice their pinch. We put our catch in a bucket of water and took them to the house. Mama rinsed them good and then boiled them so we could eat the tails.

Daddy found work as a carpenter, but it was fifty miles away in Santa Fe. Since we were getting help with our house, he didn't want to try and move. Before he could go though, he knew he had to get a better car. The $99 Ford had taken us to Alaska and back but was about done for. Daddy figured he better get a new car before it quit altogether. When we started it in the morning, the engine was cold and air would build up in the engine and blow the oil filler cap off. Once the air got warmed up, it quit trying to blow off the cap, but we had to add oil all the time.

He drove the Ford around until it got warmed up and then drove it to a used car lot. With it warm they couldn't tell that the motor was about gone. He traded it straight across for a '47 Chevy panel truck with two bucket seats in the front and nothing in the back. Daddy had given the Ford to me, but I didn't say anything when he traded it. I figured he had to do what the family needed.

With Daddy gone so much in the day, there wasn't much to do around the house. I sure was too old to hang around with Hoyt Lynn much. Sheron and Esther, at fifteen and fourteen, took turns babysitting for the neighbors. When they had a little money, they would walk downtown with me and look at the dress stores. They didn't have enough to buy a dress, but Esther would look at how they were made and buy thread and rick rack and hand sew hers to look just like the store bought ones. After Esther had her a little sack of do dads and we headed back.

As we walked past the big house to get to our apartment we noticed something all over the ground. As we got closer we saw it was feathers. We walked into the house to find Mama plucking what was left from one of the turkeys that roamed the yard.

"Did you kill a turkey, Mama?" Esther asked.

"No, I did!" Hoyt piped up.

Mama was acting like everything was just fine.

"You killed one of the turkeys?" Esther was already starting to worry about what Red Sanders would say.

"One of those ol' turkeys got out of the pen while the little kids were out in the yard. It started chasin' after the youngest one. It caught up to him big wings flappin' and started peckin' him all over his head. I heard him screamin' to high heaven. So I ran to the wood pile and found me a two by four. I ran up on the turkey and swung at it, just like I's playin' baseball. His head went flyin'." Hoyt Lynn was not bothered a bit by lobbing its head off.

I couldn't think of anyone that was more suited to killing a turkey than Hoyt, ornery as he was.

"Red Sanders went on and on about Hoyt Lynn saving their son, said they'd never forget it and gave us the turkey to eat," Mama told us while she worked on dressing it out.

Hoyt Lynn sat at the table like he was big as Daddy. He was already hard to get along with. I could tell it was going to get worse. And it did, not for me too much, but for the girls. Day after day he pestered and picked at them. Mary was tough as she could be for little girl, having Hoyt Lynn boss her around. But he didn't just boss her, he was after his older sisters too. Mama got after him with a switch, but that didn't seem to make any difference to him.

I got to where I left all that kid's stuff with them to tend. I went off to town in the morning and stayed gone all day, loafing at pool halls and sitting on street corners. Daddy wished he could take me to work with him, but the boss wouldn't let somebody not of age on the job. So the summer was long.

I watched the thunderstorms start up in the afternoon and that's when I usually headed back. The clouds would build up in the sky to the north, big and fluffy. Before too long they'd get taller, forming what looked like an anvil. The clouds darkened up, and then it looked like they were sitting on the air, flat on the bottom. Rain would fall and I could see dark streaks reaching towards the ground. The temperature cooled and the wind got gusty, blowing the rain in.

One storm came up fast, and I had to sit under a canopy on the sidewalk and let it pass. Water ran down the streets, moving rocks and tree branches in the current. Fields were flooded and roads were washed out.

I walked up to the house to see the girls sitting outside. Daddy had got back early and him and Mama had left to go visit some friends. The girls' hair was pulled out of their pony tails, their faces were red and they were out of breath. Hoyt Lynn wasn't anywhere around.

"Don't go inside with those muddy feet, Alton. We just finished giving the floor the scrubbin' of its life," Esther warned me. They didn't usually look this tired when they cleaned the house.

"What did you do in there that wore you out so bad?" I sat down beside them.

"When Daddy left, he told Hoyt Lynn, 'Now, Hoyt Lynn you behave while me and your mama are gone and don't pick on your sisters.' Well, Daddy didn't get out of sight and Hoyt Lynn wouldn't stop pestering us. We kept tellin' him to stop and he wouldn't. We warned him, said if you don't quit, we're gonna mop the floor with you. Well, he didn't stop and we mopped the floor with him."

It had taken all three girls to wrestle twelve year old Hoyt Lynn, but they had got him pinned and tied the clothes line around him. Each of them held on, got him picked up and turned upside down. They dunked his head in the water bucket and mopped the kitchen floor with his black hair. He had screamed like he was dying, but they didn't stop till they mopped every inch of the floor. When they were done, they carried him outside and threw him down. He ran off when he got loose, probably because he was crying.

They had just finished telling me about it, when Hoyt Lynn came around the corner of the house, his hair all matted it up, sticking every which way with soap and kitchen floor crud. I laughed at him. He got mad all over again and threw a rock at me and ran off. It didn't come close to hitting me and that made it even funnier. He didn't come back around till Daddy and Mama drove up to see all of us sitting outside like the angels Mama knew we were.

Castle Rock

Daddy and me were back to work on the sawmill, I guess back to what we knew best. He had talked to Bates Lumber and they hired him to repair a sawmill that had burned. They wanted it hauled north of here, and then they would hire Daddy to run it.

The mill was on a little lane off 2nd Street, just a mile or so away from us. We took off the burnt timber and replaced it with wood supplied by Bates. We used three by six timbers to make a new saw cab and carriage, built a stand for the roller bed so that it was about waist high and fixed the track. When it was ready, Bates brought a fork lift from the South Valley to load the sawmill and had their lumber truck driver, Melvin Lane, haul it up to the mill site in Castle Rock. Daddy and I watched it go. In a few days we would be right behind it.

Daddy figured he'd take Esther with us to keep house so the three of us headed north. Sheron stayed behind to help Mama and the little kids pack up. Before we left town, Daddy drove us over to Lotaburger and got us three cheeseburgers. We ate them in the car and shared a Coke. Esther talked about how good it tasted for the next five hours.

393

Castle Rock was a little over two hundred miles north up highway 85. We went west at Springer and then north at Cimarron. There was paved road for about eight miles until we got to the white ranch house that marked the turn off, then thirty miles of dirt road until we got to the camp.

When we drove up we were surprised to see two other mills owned by other companies in the same area. Daddy found where our mill had been unloaded. Close by was the house we would live in. We weren't the only family there. We met the Taylors, the family of Truman Waldo, and a Mexican man named Sipi Montoya.

Esther went to work cleaning the house, and by the time she got through scrubbing, I was surprised it was still standing. Esther was thirteen and loved to play house, but it wasn't quite as much fun with no inside plumbing and just a wood stove for cooking and heating.

It took a few days to put up the mill. We set the wood ties and attached the saw cab, the carriage, the feeders and the circle saw. Esther would walk out to the mill and check on us, tell us when supper was ready, and try to tend us like a mother hen. Daddy and me went along with it for the most part since she took care of us so good and kept the house.

With just the two of us working it took a few days to set up. We were close to being done when Esther ran out of the house screaming. When she got to Daddy, she was trying to tell him how she'd got hurt, but she kept passing out while she tried to talk. Daddy looked at the wound and Esther was finally able to get out she had burned her hand by spilling hot grease on it.

Sipi Montoya heard us and came over. He told Daddy that he would take her to Raton to the doctor. Both me and Esther knew that going to the doctor wasn't what Daddy believed in, but he nodded yes to Sipi and let him take her. Daddy had softened a little as he'd gotten older. I figured a

394

man could only keep so much fire burning in him, even if he was a Believer.

Esther came back with a white bandage that afternoon and boy did she act pitiful. Our housekeeper wasn't worth much after that. When Saturday came I stayed, and Daddy and Esther went to Albuquerque but he brought back Sheron. She was pretty put out with Esther because she just knew she had burnt her hand on purpose to get to go back to town. Sheron spent a lot more time outside at the mill helping us work so I was glad she came.

The next time Daddy went to Albuquerque he brought the family. Since I stayed behind, the Taylor's invited me over to their house to eat. As hungry as I got, I sure didn't want anything she fixed. Mrs. Taylor was as nice as she could be but their house was a wreck. The place was so piled up with things I couldn't even find a place to sit down, which I didn't want to do anyway. The kitchen was piled with dirty dishes. It looked like whenever somebody was through with a dish, they just tossed it in and left it where it lay. Mama kept a clean house, I thought maybe it was easier to do that when you didn't have very much to get spread around.

Their whole family played music and those Taylor boys could play just about anything. I'd never been any good at my harmonica and had ended up losing it somewhere between there and here. Duane Taylor used an old board to make a steel guitar. He used wire and nails, old handles he found lying around and nuts and bolts. His steel guitar wasn't electric, but it made a good sound. I sat over with the family and listened, some of the songs sounded so good it made my hair stand up.

They played late into the night and invited me to stay over. I tried to get out of it, but they just insisted. I lay there in the bed with sheets so dirty I could see the dark spot where somebody laid before me. I don't know if those sheets had ever seen any soap. I didn't move from where I lay, stiff as a board and not anywhere near sleep. It smelled like nasty bodies and sweat. I just couldn't stand it so I got up and snuck back to our house in the night. After that I made sure I wasn't visiting with them anywhere near bedtime.

The kids living in camp played baseball in a field, so the girls and Hoyt Lynn started playing too. Mary was as much a tomboy as Sheron ever was and her red braids were always coming loose as she out played and outran all the boys close to her age.

I went over to the Taylor's to listen to them play music. Before it got too dark I walked towards the house. The kids were out in the open field standing around a body laying on the ground. As I got closer I saw it was Hoyt Lynn. He looked like he was sleeping. Esther was squatted down beside him and Mary had a stick in her hand. Sheron had run to get help. When Mary saw Mama and Daddy coming she went to crying and carrying on.

"What happened here?" Daddy asked.

Mary started explaining, "Hoyt Lynn kept takin' my turn to hit. I told him to quit and so did Sheron but he wouldn't listen at all. He wouldn't ever give me a turn. He kept shovin' me back and takin' the stick from me."

Mama went to Hoyt Lynn and got him to wake up. He had a lump on the side of his head, big as an egg. Mary cried a little louder with each word. I think she was hoping that would help to get her out of trouble. Daddy took the stick away from Mary and whipped her with it.

"Y'all know you're not to fuss with each other." Daddy hollered at them all.

Sheron spoke up, "Hoyt wouldn't ever let Mary have a turn. So after he hit the ball and threw down the bat to run. Mary picked it up and when he came runnin' into home base, she hit him upside the head with the stick. He fell like a sack of taters."

I sure wished I'd seen it. I guess Mary had had enough of Hoyt Lynn. It took three days before Hoyt started picking on Mary again.

No School

It was time for school to start and Mama learned the closest one was at Cimarron. For the first time, that didn't bother me at all. I had finished up the ninth grade in Alaska and was going on seventeen. Daddy figured that was good enough so I didn't have to go anymore. That was just about as far as the other boys had gotten. Since it was close to forty miles to Cimarron and the school, I would drive the kids in and wait there for them to get out. This wasn't going to last long though. I had a job starting and Daddy planned to move us to Cimarron as soon as he found a place.

The first day the kids loaded up in the panel truck. Hoyt Lynn sat in the one other seat in front and wouldn't move. Esther and Sheron wore new dresses Daddy had bought them in Albuquerque. They were the same except Esther's was pink and Sheron's was yellow. They were put out with Hoyt Lynn for taking the seat, but they crawled in the back by Mary and tried to sit ladylike.

It took about an hour to make it to town. When we drove into the school, the girls got out the back doors. Sheron looked around, "It's so dusty and dirty. It's ugly here."

It didn't look bad to me. The town was little but there was a park in the middle and some stores. The highway ran through the middle of it and to the west, mountains pushed out of the ground.

The kids waited by the truck for Mary but she wouldn't get out.

397

"Come on Mary, time for school," I told her.

"I just hate school, Alton! I'd druther do anything else but go inside and sit." Just like Sheron, Mary was a real tomboy.

"Come on now, you're gonna be late," I told her.

She scooted out of the back of the truck and stood there, skinny and freckled, her long red hair already coming out of its braids. Sheron and Esther waited, they didn't want her to have to walk in alone. I tried to fix Mary's hair a little and put it back in her braids. I knew she wouldn't bother with it herself.

"Let me do it," Esther said and she worked on Mary's hair.

I worked on convincing Mary, "You got to go to school. Mama says. Didn't you get a brand new pair of shoes to wear, just for startin' the third grade? You're gonna look just fine up against the other kids. I don't think I ever had a new pair of shoes for the start of school."

Mary looked at her shoes, "Thank you for tellin' Daddy I needed them." She sat back down in the car, trying to stall again.

"Get to school, Mary," I told her in my best grown up voice.

"Oh, all right."

"I'll be here when you get out."

Mary drug her feet as she followed Sheron and Esther in. The older girls had gone to plenty of new schools and new classes, but being the new kid wasn't ever very easy. Esther was still so shy Sheron had to take her to her class and come for her afterward until she got to know some friends.

I could have whooped out loud, just like Daddy when those school doors shut behind them. In just a few days I was going to work.

High Altitude Al

Trucks dragging trailers came in and out of Castle Rock, mostly to haul the milled lumber to the big sawmills in town. I got to know a few of the drivers. Kid White had skin dark as charcoal. Melvin Lane came up with his truck from Bates Lumber, and when Daddy needed some parts for the mill, I rode with Melvin back to Albuquerque. After we got the parts back to Daddy, Melvin told me I could come along anytime. Pretty soon, I was driving the thirty miles of dirt road to the black top.

I learned to shift the 5 and 4 transmission fast and smooth. Melvin let me drive more and more. When Melvin's buddy, Jack Berry, would show up in his pink and white '56 Ford station wagon, I would drive alone while Melvin and Jack followed in the car drinking something out of a brown paper bag.

I never dropped a gear and I revved the engine steady as I shifted from one gear to another. Just when I was feeling pretty proud of myself, it got a lot harder to do when my nose started bleeding. I scrounged around the truck for paper and rags to help stop it and still drove the best I could, knowing they were watching me from the station wagon. At least they were quite a ways back since Jack was trying to stay out of the dust I was making.

When the rags got full I just threw them out the window and kept on going. I made it to the black top and waited for Melvin and Jack to come in the car. After just a little while, the station wagon pulled up beside me, screeching to a stop. Both men jumped out and Melvin climbed up the side of the truck to talk to me.

"Son, are you hurt?" Melvin asked me pretty concerned. "We seen all those bloody rags!"

"No sir, just a bloody nose." I was worried they'd think I was just a kid, if I let a bloody nose slow me down.

"Ohhh. Some folks get them up here because of the elevation. We're at about eight thousand feet. We thought maybe you'd cut your head off." He joked and then hollered to Jack, "Just a bloody nose."

They gave me some water to wash up with and decided they'd start calling me High Altitude Al. Jack drove off in his car and Melvin got in the truck with me and we headed off to Albuquerque. Before I knew it I was driving the truck while Melvin slept in the passenger seat. Driving on the black top in a lot of ways was easier than the rough and ragged dirt road to the mill. I learned to handle the big truck and trailer through town and traffic. It was my first paying job, not money, but all I wanted in eats and smokes.

1963
Cimarron

Barney

Daddy had just finished saying grace, thanking the Lord for all we had. Mama passed around the oatmeal saying it would help warm us up. It was cool outside, the door latched to keep the cold air from coming in. Doyle Holbird had bought the sawmill in Castle Rock and wanted it moved to Cimarron, so as quick as we put it up, we took it down. Holbird had hired us and given us a place to live in the shacks at the sawmill. The mill wasn't running yet and Daddy was waiting to get word on when to start. Since there wasn't any work we were still at the table after sun up.

There was banging at the door and Mama went to open it. Harry stood there with a big grin on his face.

"Hello, Mama!"

"Well, my lands! Look, Wesley, look who's here," Mama was swallowed up in a big hug from Harry.

"Get in this house!" Daddy welcomed him. We hadn't heard from him since we had let him off in Washington.

"How did you find us?" Mama asked. Esther jumped up to get Harry some coffee.

"I called Elaine a few days ago when I was leaving Louie's place in Oregon. She told me you had been in Albuquerque, but she thought you were coming up north here to work. So I headed this way. I made pretty good time. I was driving a pretty slick Chrysler Saratoga but when I was coming up that big hill out of Albuquerque just before Santa Fe, she quit on me. I hitchhiked on in here and got here last night late. The sheriff let me sleep in the jail."

"This morning I told him who I was looking for. He told me he knew right where you were and drove me over." Harry grinned at Mama.

"Oh, Harry, why didn't you just come and try to find us. I don't want you sleepin' in a jail," Mama fussed over him.

"Now Mama, it wasn't like I was arrested. It was a pretty warm place." Harry winked at me. I figured by now he'd probably seen the inside of a jail more than a few times.

Everybody talked at once, and we caught him up on what was going on. We told him how we were waiting to find out when we were going to go to work. We were supposed to saw logs for Holbird but that hadn't started yet. The mill was just planing rough lumber to make it smooth. He'd let us move into the house, but right now we didn't have a paying job until Melvin Lane starting hauling in logs. Harry told us he'd start looking around to see what he could find.

The weather turned colder and it froze a few nights later. Melvin Lane hadn't put antifreeze in his engine so it busted and he wasn't going to be able to haul the logs. That ended the job we had been waiting for.

401

Daddy scouted around for other work, but with winter coming on it was hard to find. Harry got a job for Don Koble setting tongs, but that was a young man's job. A big machine called a loader would swing out a cable through the air and Harry would catch it. Attached to the cable were tongs that Harry would take and set on each end of the log so it could be picked up.

The loader would then pick up the log and set it on the log truck. I tried to hire on too, but they didn't need anybody else. He worked long days and at the end of the week he brought his money to Mama.

Holbird came and told us since we wouldn't be working for him, we would have to move out of the mill shack. With Harry working, we were able to move across the highway to a little white house. It was better than a sawmill cabin, besides the kitchen and living room, it had three bedrooms which was more than enough for us. There wasn't any inside plumbing, just an outhouse by the fence. With a tall wood burning heater in the kitchen that part of the house stayed warm. A door off the kitchen led to Mama and Daddy's room, the living room and the girl's room. Harry and me shared a bed in the back room where there was a door to the backyard.

It was a lot of fun having Harry around. We didn't have a car of our own but we used the panel truck when we needed to. In Cimarron you could walk to anywhere you wanted to go anyway. We took Sheron, Esther and the little kids over to the Halloween Carnival at school. After getting handfuls of candy, Harry and me sat at the top of the bleachers looking sharp. None of us dressed in costumes, we just came to get sweets. Sheron hung out with her friend Sharon Padmore, and Esther found her friend, Cleta Pigman. They came and sat by us for a few minutes then went off to talk to other girls.

When they started shutting things down we left. On the way out to the car Hoyt Lynn tried to steal some of Mary's candy. She put up a fuss and I made him give it back. We were waiting on Harry to come get in the car. When he didn't show for a while, we went on without him. I thought he might get after us when he showed up, but when he came in he was whistling. I figured then he must have been trying to warm up to a girl. I wasn't sure who it might be, but I didn't care enough to find out either.

Harry worked six days a week and on Saturday nights came in late...and drunk. We could tell by the loud singing and laughter when he walked into the house. Mama would holler out to him from her bed, "That you, Harry?" He would holler back, "Yes, Mama!" and that was the end of it. She never questioned him about drinking. I thought maybe because he was breadwinner for the family. I was sure she had to know that was what was going on. The whole rest of the house did. With Harry supporting us all, maybe she figured she would look the other way. I had begun to see that both her and Daddy knew more about what us boys did than they let on. I was sure by now Mama knew Harry and I were smoking but she didn't say anything. Maybe it was easier sometimes just to not notice things.

After talking to just about everybody in town, I got a job with the Bradley brothers. They were working the mountain north of town. It was the same stand of trees Harry was working but he worked for the logging company hauling the logs out. Bradleys were hired to cut the timber, and skid it to the road. Fifteen loads a day were hauled out to Taos mills. That's why Daddy couldn't find a job in Cimarron, the logs weren't being hauled there.

Don Koble came and picked Harry and me up about four in the morning. Harry had found me some gloves to work in, and that helped with the cold. We got to the woods

403

right at daylight. The mountain was steep so they had to use mules and horses instead of machines. I was young but I had experience using livestock, and they took a chance on me. I think it helped that it was cheaper to hire a kid. I was to get three cents a log and I was happy to have the work.

The horses and mules were kept in a corral out in the woods close to the job. I broke the ice on their water and fed them oats and hay out of a coffee can. If it had just been mules, the food could have been kept out, but not with horses around. Daddy said a mule eats until he's full and then quits, but a horse will eat until he makes himself sick, so you had to measure out what he got. Daddy always did like a mule.

I worked with another skidder called Burmeister, who worked the mules and told me to use the horse. That suited me just fine. I didn't care if the mules were smarter, I liked the horse. His name was Barney and he was all black except for his white face. They said he weighed around 2200 pounds and his hooves were about eight inches across. At about 800 pounds apiece, the mules were puny beside him.

I got Barney out of the corral and rode him bareback with a bridle out to where they were cutting. I talked to him and patted him while I got to know him. He stood tall and silent while I hooked him up to the single tree harness. He was so tall it was easy to just scrunch down and walk under his belly. When I had him all set, I gave him the command to move, but he just stood there. 'Giddap' I told him again, pushed at him and slapped him on the rear. I did everything I'd ever heard of to get an animal to move, short of beating him, and he wouldn't move a muscle.

I walked over to Burmeister and some older men who were standing by a fire. They had been watching me, but not a one of them said anything as I walked up. I know they wanted me to feel like a dumb kid, but I had to eat my pride and ask them what to do.

"What do I gotta do to get this horse to move?" I asked them. They snickered.

"Well now boy, what you gotta do is light a fire under him. That'll show him whose boss and get him movin." Burmeister finally spoke up. He handed me a stick.

I didn't know what else to do, so as much as I didn't want to, I figured I better try what they said. I walked over to the horse, gathered up some smaller sticks and brush and with a match lit a fire under the belly of the big black horse. It was mostly smoke with little flame, but the heat reached under Barney's belly and he got the message. This time when I told him 'giddap' he moved right to the logs.

I looked over to the old men around the fire and they were fit to be tied.

"Son, that's not quite what we meant," one of them said. That's when I figured that 'lighting a fire' had been a figure of speech. They had meant for me to beat him with the stick, not set it on fire. I guess I had done all right though, Barney was working. I didn't have a bit of trouble after that. If he got stubborn I just had to rattle some brush and Barney would get to work.

I walked him to the first sixteen foot log and he stood while I dug the log out of the snow and hooked the tongs around the end. Even with gloves the iron was cold on my hands. We skid the logs downhill to the log road and piled them up in one spot. Daddy had taught to always pull the logs downhill, never sideways. The log could start to roll and if it did it could pull the horse over and kill him and possibly you too.

When I unhooked the tongs at the log pile, Barney would walk back up the hill and stop at the next log without me leading him. I followed him back up the mountain about thirty or so feet and we did it all again. Hook the tongs on the log, pull it down the hill, unhook the tongs and walk back up to the next one. When we got a full load set there, we would skid to the next spot.

At the end of the day I walked the horse back to the corral. The logs had all been hauled from this area, so tomorrow I would go to where the cutters had worked with a fresh bunch of trees. Burmeister had me tie the animals together and take them over to the new area in the woods. I had to cross a cattle guard, Barney walked right over it, but the mules balked. I tugged on their lead, but they wouldn't budge. I got tired of it so I nudged Barney on and they didn't have any choice but to follow since they were tethered together.

After a few days one of the men told me the feet of the mules were so little they could step in between the slats of the cattle guard and break a leg if their hoof went through. I hadn't paid any attention and felt bad about dragging them over it every day. I figured if they were gonna fall through they'd a done it by now so I kept pulling them over.

We'd been working for a couple of weeks when one of the Bradley brothers came over to talk to me.

"We're wantin' to finish this job at the end of the week. If you can keep up with the cutters and by Friday have all the logs skidded down to the log trucks, we'll pay you five cents a log instead of three. Think you can get that done?"

"I can do it."

"All right, then, let's get to work and we'll get this job over with."

I figured if I could skid more than one log at a time I would have a better chance of keeping up with the cutters. Instead of tongs I would use Tennessee dogs that would let me skid two logs at a time. Tennessee dogs were like a big railroad spike with a hole on one end. I drove the metal into the end of the log with a hammer. I could have Barney pull two, sometimes three down the hill at a time and make the

406

log pile faster. Thirty to forty logs made a load, depending on their size.

By the time Thursday came I had a rhythm and on that day I walked up and down the mountain enough times I skidded one hundred and twenty three logs, six dollars and fifteen cents worth. The older men didn't treat me like a kid anymore. They called me Al and offered me coffee when I showed up. I knew I had made a spot for myself.

Friday morning we drove out to the woods to finish the day and collect. When we got there, everything was gone--the horses, the equipment and the Bradley Brothers. We learned that when we had finished up Thursday, they skipped out. I cussed them like everybody else.

Word spread fast over what the Bradleys had done to everybody. Rumors flew about where they might be working, some said over by Raton, other folks said they were up in Colorado. Some of the men went to hunt them and collect. About a month later I got word of where they had been. The Bradleys had gone to work over by Taos with a different crew. The log skidder had Barney skid the log sideways down the mountain. It rolled and Barney went with it. A stick had went through the horse's stomach and they'd had to kill him. I'd been mad for what they'd done to me, but I was sick for what they'd done to Barney.

The Edsel

I was in the kitchen eating a bowl of stew Mama had left on the stove. I was all alone at the table. The rest of the family had already eaten and were in the other room. Harry had taken off in his Plymouth after he got his dirty shirt changed. We had rode in together from the woods where both of us were working now.

407

When one of the men who worked the loaders quit, Harry talked to his boss and got hired on to work the machine. That left his job hooking tongs open and Harry got me hired to do it. We had spent our whole lives working together so when it came to this job it was smooth. He sat on the loader and pulled the cable up the heel boom, which was a long arm that stretched out from the body. He would give it a little slack and sling the arm out causing the cable to fly through the air. I just had to raise my hand above my head and the cable would land in it, Harry's aim was that good. I set the tongs six foot from the end, then he would pick up the log and butt one end of it up against the heel boom and then swing it over to load onto the truck. We got to the job at daybreak and worked till sundown five or six days a week, depending on the amount of logs.

I didn't see much of Harry when we weren't working. He changed clothes and left and always got back late. I learned he was slipping around seeing Sharon Padmore pretty regular. She had just come over to see Sheron at first. Knocking on the door asking if Rebel was home, Mama told her there wasn't nobody here by that name. But there was; that's what they'd taken to calling Sheron at school. Mama asked her about it and Sheron told her there were four girls with the same name and since she was from the south, they had pinned that nickname on her.

It wasn't like Harry to just run around with one girl. Mama had remarked on how he seemed to give this one all his attention. Harry usually had a crowd he kicked around with. I thought Harry could do just about anything, run any piece of equipment, sing songs like the fellows on the radio and just get along with people. What took work for me always came easy to him.

Harry and me for the most part always got along. I don't think either one of us wanted to try the other. He hit

408

fast, but I hit hard. I wasn't sure I could match his speed, and he said he wanted to keep his pretty face. It was all said in fun, but I don't think I wanted to tangle with him anymore than he wanted to tangle with me.

At nineteen, Harry had a few inches on me, and was a little bigger but he didn't have much growing left. I was seventeen and thought I might get a little taller, but at 5'8 what I lacked in height I made up for in strength. Mama said the way I packed away groceries you'd think I'd be fat, but I didn't have much extra on me.

Esther and Mary

I scraped the bottom of the soup bowl with a piece of bread and was chewing on it when the door opened. One of Esther's friends walked in. She was about fifteen, tall and thin with a lot of curly brown hair. I couldn't tell what color her eyes were, because she wore cat eyed glasses and they had fogged up when she came into the warm kitchen from the cold outside. She stood there a minute waiting to be able to see. I said, "Hi."

"Hi! Oh...," she looked surprised, "I thought you were Harry sitting there," she told me when her glasses had cleared. Girls always knew Harry.

"Nope, I'm Alton."

"Oh, is Esther here?"

"Cleta, I'm back here," Esther called.

She didn't say anything else as she walked through the kitchen to find Esther.

I left my bowl on the table for the girls to clean up and headed outside. The car was blocked in by a '58 Edsel, white on top and pink on bottom with a big chrome front end. I went back inside and found Esther and her.

"Hey, I need you to move your car so I can get out." I smiled at Cleta when I talked to her.

"It's not my car, its Mama's," she said.

"I still need you to let me out."

"Go ahead and move it. The keys are in it."

"Okay, I'll do that."

I sat down in it and reached for the gear shift. It wasn't on the column and it wasn't on the floor. I looked all over the dash, on the right side of the wheel and then on the left. I was going to have to go inside and look dumb and tell the girl I couldn't find the gear shift, or walk to town. I headed inside.

I walked to the girl's room again. Esther and Cleta looked up at me.

I cleared my throat, "Does that thing have a gear shift?" I couldn't help but feel like a kid.

She looked at me for a minute and then said, "Oh, it is in the middle of the steering wheel. It has buttons to push to change gears. Do you need me to go out there and show you?"

She smiled and I saw she had a gap between her front teeth.

"Naw, I can find it now."

"I'll show you," she said and got up and walked towards me.

I followed behind while this girl went outside to show me how to drive a car. I wasn't feeling too smart right now. How was a fellow supposed to know to look for the gearshift in the steering wheel. No wonder they'd quit making Edsels.

She went ahead and got in the car and said to me, "See, they're right here."

410

I leaned into the window to look and then looked at her. Her eyes were blue.

Learning to Drive

Harry and me made such a good showing working with Don Koble, he told us he would hire on Daddy to haul logs if he had a log truck. When we told Daddy that night about Koble's offer, Daddy got busy putting a truck together.

He got his hands on a red International but it didn't have a front axle. He talked to another fellow with a Ford that didn't run at all and made a deal for it. He put the Ford's axle under the International and he was ready to go. Daddy wanted me to haul logs with him and had me quit hooking tongs to drive with him. I liked working in the woods with Harry, but driving was a lot easier work.

We headed to the log woods. Koble used eight trucks to haul with. Once an area was logged out, the equipment would be moved to the next spot. We hauled out of Vermejo Park, then Castle Rock, Cimarron Canyon and the McDaniel's Ranch.

Daddy was finally making money hauling logs. Daddy and me spent a lot of time together driving the mountain roads. I watched everything Daddy did and tried to do just like him when he had me drive the truck. When it was time to move fast and make a decision and when it was time to slow up and be careful. He showed me the way up the mountain and the way back down.

He gave me a few dollars at the end of each week. I saved up my money and at the end of the summer was able to buy a green '53 Buick with a white top for $125. With Harry either working or off with Sharon Padmore. I hung out with my buddy was Wayne Holloman. Now that I had a car we did a lot of driving around Cimarron. Neither one of us had much money, but we looked cool. We went into Dee's café to get a cup of coffee. It cost a dime so I ordered the coffee and drank the first cup and Wayne drank the refill.

I was in pretty bad need of some tires so we drove over to old man Whitton's garage and asked him if he had some tires that would fit the car. He had some that were on the narrow side, but he was willing to sell them to me on credit. I could pay the $40 when I had it. I wasn't sure they were the right size but he told me they would be fine so we put the tires on.

I wasn't too happy when I saw them on the car. They were too narrow and spun out real easy. When I told Whitton they didn't look right, he told me a deal was a deal. He wouldn't take them back.

Wayne and me didn't let the tires stop us from cruising, that's just about all we could afford to do. We learned there was going to be a dance over in Eagle Nest on Saturday night. It was about twenty miles over there and Wayne and me figured we would go. We drove the car down to the Cimarron River to wash it. The river ran so shallow we drove right in the middle of it and started cleaning her up.

"You know, Wayne, this car would look sharp if the dark green were more like a black."

Wayne looked at the car, "I do favor the way black and white look against each other."

"Well, hell, let's go to town and buy some spray paint and paint this thing. How much money do you got? I got a few dollars."

Wayne dug in his pocket and we headed to the store. We bought the paint and went to work on the car. It took ten spray cans to cover up the green, but when it was done it did look sharp...if you looked at it from a few yards away.

That night we slicked back our hair, put on our best shirts and headed to the dance at Eagle Nest. Harry drove out

412

there too, with Sharon. When we got to Eagle Nest, we parked my car and rode around town with Harry in his white Plymouth. His car had a radio and a song came on called 'The Long Tall Texan.' The beginning started with the guy singing:

I'm a long tall Texan, I ride a big white horse
I'm a long tall Texan, I ride a big white horse
When people see me walking down the street
They say haw haw, is that your horse?

From then on, Harry's car was the Big White Horse.

The town and the dance hall were jumping with folks from all over the area. I didn't know how to dance, but I wasn't too shy anymore to ask the girls out onto the floor. I let them show me how and we had a big time. When they shut down the dance at midnight, we all stayed outside smoking and cutting up. It was almost morning when Wayne and me drove back to Cimarron. Harry wasn't there when we got there so Wayne just stayed at my house.

The next morning we headed to Dee's to share a cup of coffee. We were turning left from the highway when 'wham' we were hit in the back by another car. Wayne and me got out to look it over. We'd been hit in our left rear fender. When the fellow got out, he told us it was his fault and he would take care of it. It wasn't really the big dent that bothered us, but the fact that when the two cars hit, it caused all the black paint we had just put on to fall off the back of the car.

Johnny Arnello the town cop showed up and looked things over. Johnny saw that the wreck wasn't my fault and there wasn't going to be any argument. The guy in the other car told me he had insurance and that would handle it. I hadn't had any dealings with insurance but a week or so later when the insurance man handed me over a check for $150.00

413

to fix my car, I was grinning from ear to ear. Of course, it was made out to Daddy since I wasn't grown yet. The family used it to live on and I felt like I had helped out.

I decided to wheel and deal on my car anyway. I was having trouble with the tires I had bought from Old Man Whitton and he wouldn't do a thing about it. I didn't get too upset with him, seeing as I hadn't paid for them yet anyway. A new car might be the best thing.

Carl Dunkerson had a sharp off-white '49 Lincoln he was looking to trade. He was leaving to go to Mexico and he couldn't take the Lincoln because it didn't have a title. That

didn't seem like much of a problem for me so I traded him straight across, my Buick for his Lincoln. That worked out all right for a few days until I learned that a title was a lot more important than I thought when I

Harry and Sharon Padmore

couldn't get a license plate for it. I got pulled over a few times for not having a tag. I didn't know what to do about it so I just kept driving. I guess Johnny Arnello finally had enough.

"Miller, the next time I catch you driving this car without a tag, I'm going to impound it," he told me.

"You're gonna arrest the car?" I teased him.

"This ain't funny, boys. I don't want to see you driving around in this thing no more," he told us.

"And one more thing, Miller, next time I pull you over, you better have a driver's license." I figured I'd better

414

not push my luck, so I parked the Lincoln at the house and either walked or rode with somebody else.

Daddy and me weren't hauling logs that week so I decided to hitchhike to Albuquerque to have something to do. While I was there, I found a '53 Chevy. It was green with a brown hood, had an oil leak, and there wasn't any exhaust under the car. The right window was gone and it wouldn't go in reverse, but it had a title and the salesman told me he would take $10 for it. I knew I couldn't leave it there. I drove back to Cimarron and in just a few days I used a long gas line that usually was used on a house to make an exhaust pipe for the car.

Wayne and me were driving around a few days later when we saw the Driver's Ed teacher out with his students. He would have the students drive south out of town towards Philmont. Somewhere along the road he would reach his hand out the window and fire a starting pistol. That was the signal for them to stop as fast as possible. Then they would get out and measure the skid marks to see how far it took to stop. He was wound up as he shouted 'twenty feet! Or thirty feet!' It was about the dumbest way I'd ever seen anybody learn to drive. I'd known how to drive for so long, I couldn't remember a time when I didn't know how.

I looked over at Wayne and joked. "You know, Johnny told me I needed to get a driver's license. Maybe we oughta follow along so I can learn."

We pulled in behind them, looking for a way to poke fun at how foolish they all looked. We followed them around and when the teacher fired the gun off, I slammed my foot on the brakes. One of my brake pots were out, so when I hit the brake it squalled so loud they could have heard it in Taos. Wayne and I jumped out, ran behind our car, and shouted as loud as we could, 'thirty feet!' After a few times the teacher ran us off, but he was back at it the next day so we were too.

The gun went off, we hit the brake and when we jumped out, Johnny Arnello pulled up behind us, lights a flashin'.

Wayne stood by the driver's door. Johnny walked over to us, shaking his head.

I grinned at him. "Hey there, Johnny, we're just out learnin' how to drive!"

Wedding Dress

Daddy and Mama were gone to buy another truck. He'd made a deal on a '56 Ford but it was in Breckenridge, Texas. A man had come out to the mill and sold Daddy the truck, sight unseen. The mill had shut down for a few weeks and this was a good time to leave. Daddy said we were doing so good hauling logs there wasn't any reason that I shouldn't be driving too. We could make double the money. Daddy said if we hauled into Taos, we could make $100 a load. I was up for that, driver's license or not.

With no work, Wayne and I drove around town and then sat in the city park watching people go by. I saw Mary running down the road with a boy called Roger hot on her heels. Her red hair was strung out behind her and they were all laughing and carrying on.

"Mary! What're y'all getting into?" I called as I waved her over to where me and Wayne were. She ran to me with her buddy right behind her. They were covered in dirt.

"We were just foolin' with the people at the show."

I remembered how I was always tempted by the picture show. "Were you trying to sneak in?"

"Na, I don't want to get whipped. But we found a place under the building where we could crawl under it."

"What are you doin' crawlin' under that building?"

"We use boards and hit the floor with them as hard as we can, right under the peoples feet. The folks in there can't

416

figure out what is going on. Some of them left 'cause they couldn't hear the show because we made so much racket. We figured we oughta run before somebody came lookin' under there."

"Well, don't let Mama find out your crawlin' under buildings. She's liable to get after you for even messin' around at a movie theater."

"We're through with that right now anyway."

The two of them were running down the street before I could say anything else. Even at ten years old, Mary was in charge.

A few days later Mary and Roger were at it again. Harry had left early, the girls were gone, so I was working on my car. Mary's red braids were a-flyin' as she rode off towards town after I fixed the chain on the bicycle I had built her. Before long, she and Roger were back and then gone again. The next time I looked up, Roger was wearing what looked to be like a wedding dress.

I had to find out what was happening. I hollered at Mary to come over to me. The two of them came over on their bikes.

"What're you doin'?"

"Well, we rode over to the Catholic Church where Roger's cousin was gettin' married. Don't tell Mama we went over there, Alton. Mama will whip me if she knew we crossed the river. We couldn't go in, but we got to watch them come out of the big doors."

"But why is *he* in a dress?"

"Oh, that's one of Esther and Sheron's petticoats. I thought we ought to dress up like the bride and groom, so I had Roger wear the wedding dress. Don't tell the girls' I got their petticoat, they'll never quit squallin' over it."

"But why is he in the dress" I asked.

"Well, I sure don't want to wear it!"

417

She took off and Roger followed her, like he always did. He didn't have much to say, but I guess I wouldn't either if I was wearing what he was.

Harry was gone all night and no one seemed to know where he went. The next day when we heard the Big White Horse drive up, me and the girls walked outside to see what he'd been up to. His girlfriend, Sharon, was with him and she couldn't keep the smile off her face.

"Where you been?" I asked.

"Trinidad, gettin' married!" Harry told us.

"Wait'll Mama finds out," Sheron said under her breath.

At least he wasn't the one wearing the dress.

Fast

When Mama and Daddy got back, the three girls raced to them trying to be the first one to tell them Harry had got married. Mama said she'd not seen any of the other ones get married, so she reckoned it was just as well. Harry had loaded up the trunk of the Big White Horse with all of his things. There was plenty of room in the trunk left over. He and Sharon were moving over to a little house on Main Street.

418

Her daddy tinkered on radios and television sets, so I figured Harry would have a set now to watch, which might be worth going over to visit him, even if he did have a wife now.

Daddy had brought back a '56 Ford F-9000, yellow and blue, and that was my truck to drive. I followed him down the road to the log woods and back to the mill every day. Daddy always had the loader put on a big load because we were paid by the footage and the more we hauled, the more we got paid. Daddy told the loader to keep putting them on until the last log, the brow log, went on.

We hauled out of Pot Creek, through Black Lake to Ranchos De Taos where the mill was located on the road headed toward Espanola. When we got to the mill, we unloaded ourselves using the forklift they had there. The driving wasn't hard, but the days were long. By the end of the work day it was too far and took too much time to drive back so we stayed at the sawmill. As usual, it was built on a hill. Under the mill they had a saw room where they stored saws and files and parts for the mill. The room was about ten feet by ten feet so it had enough room for Daddy and me to sleep. We made a couple of beds out of boards and threw a blanket on them. We slept there during the week and went back on the weekends.

At the end of the week Daddy gave me a few dollars to run around on. I picked up Wayne in the Chevy and we headed into town to drag main with the rest of our buddies. That always led to racing.

We didn't race them side by side because there wasn't room on the road, but we timed them from start to finish. I was in the Chevy but it wasn't doing that good. George Dobyne was there spinning the wheels on his '56 Ford Coupe. He was called the millionaire because his family had money. He was getting quite a bit of attention and there was just no way I could let him win.

419

Wayne and me figured we could do a lot better if we were running the '49 Lincoln, so we went to get it. We took a few turns driving the car around, getting her warmed up. Then we got at the line to race her down the street. She really moved, and Wayne and me had to clinch our cigarettes in our teeth we were grinning so big. We beat George's time, and figured for good measure, we'd do it again. We started down the street one more time, that's when we saw Johnny Arnello start up his patrol car and turn on his lights. We figured he was headed straight for us.

When we got to the finish line, we just kept on going west. We rode out of town as fast as that Lincoln would run. Johnny was behind us, but with the head start we had and our big motor he couldn't gain any ground. We drove into Cimarron canyon, and we lost sight of him around the curves. When we couldn't see his headlights anymore we turned off into the woods and hid behind some brush and trees with our lights out.

We heard Johnny before we saw him, his patrol car was gunning it through the canyon and he drove right past us.

"He'll probably go all the way to Eagle Nest," I said as we laughed.

"Looks like we got plenty of time to get her back," Wayne said.

We laughed our asses off as we headed back to Cimarron, but we drove straight to Daddy's and parked the car.

The next morning started early and Daddy and me went outside to start the trucks and get them warmed up. I looked up when I heard a car coming. Johnny Arnello had come to visit. He drove up behind the Lincoln and got out to talk to us. Daddy walked over to him. They talked and then Daddy hollered at me to come over.

420

"Son, were you out driving that Lincoln last night?" Daddy asked.

I might have been grown and making money, but when Daddy asked me about the Lincoln, I felt just like the kid I used to be. I answered the same way I had all my life when I was in trouble.

"No, Daddy." I denied it and I looked both of them in the eye.

"Mr. Miller, I saw that car racing up and down the street last night. I know it was this Lincoln."

"He said it wasn't him, must have been another car. That car don't even have tags."

"Mr. Miller, it was that car."

And then Daddy did what Daddy had done all my life when somebody accused his kids of something. He took up for me.

"If he says it wasn't him, it wasn't him."

"But..." Johnny tried to keep talking.

"Let's go." Daddy looked at me and motioned with his thumb for me to get in the truck.

Johnny eyed me pretty good, but he got in his car and left. When Daddy walked by me to get in his truck, he winked. Maybe he wasn't too old to remember when he lived fast.

Don't Let Go

When Daddy and me came back at the end of the week, a little red, white and blue '47 Chevy flatbed pickup was parked outside the house. Louie had come from Oregon. Inside the house, all the kids were around him, listening to him talk and taking the little presents he'd brought for them. Nobody brought up the fact that he had come down without his wife and family.

421

Daddy had told Mama to write to him about how much we had going on and that he ought to come down and haul with us. Mama told Daddy that Louie and his wife were having trouble. As far as I knew, they always had. Louie and her had had a baby boy named David back on my birthday in October so he was about nine or ten months old. Looked like that hadn't helped much.

Fonceal and Wesley

When we were outside looking over the trucks Daddy asked him, "Where's your wife, son? She didn't come with ya?"

"No, Daddy, I left her back in Oregon. I'm not sure I'm even gonna stay married to her. She's from town, and she don't like living the way we do. She can't do like Mama always could."

"Your mama tried to show her."

"I know, Daddy, seems like there ain't too many like Mama. Maybe I oughta let her go."

A few days later Louie went to work for Herman Lane hauling logs. He loaded tree length logs which were a lot longer than the sixteen footers that we hauled. He came out of the same mountains and went to the same mills but we didn't run together. Sometimes we met each other on the road but we really didn't see him until the end of the week.

Since Louie was apart from his wife, he thought it gave him a right to see other girls. He found a girlfriend in town who didn't seem to mind going to the show in the log truck he picked her up in. One Friday night he came back early.

422

He pulled into the yard and shut the motor off, I walked over to him.

"How come you're back so soon? I thought you was going on a date."

"I was, but she's mad at me now."

"Why's she mad at you?"

"Well, I was picking her up with the truck and when she ran around behind she didn't see the trailer pole." The trailer pole was a big piece of pipe that stuck out a few feet past the end of the bunks at the end of the trailer.

"She walked into the pole, right square in the face and knocked herself out."

"She wasn't too interested in going to the show after that, huh?"

"She wasn't too interested in riding in a log truck anymore." When we told Mama the story she didn't think it was funny.

"You shouldn't be foolin' around anyway," Mama told him.

As the summer wore on, the trucks worked hard up and down the canyons. Mine began to smoke quite a bit. Daddy decided when we got back at the end of the week we would work on my motor and fix it.

When we raised the cab and tore into the engine, there was a lot that needing fixing so Daddy figured we would rebuild it, which meant we would take it out of the truck. Since we would have to work after dark to get it done for Monday, we needed a place where we could have some light. Daddy decided the best place to fix the motor was in the boys' bedroom at the back of the house. It had a door to the outside so we could bring the motor and parts straight in.

We took the alternator, the exhaust and other pieces off to lift it out of the truck. We used a rope and a pulley to lift it and set it on the ground. The four of us, Daddy, Louie, Harry and me carried it into the back room.

Daddy and Louie knew a lot about rebuilding engines so they taught what they knew to Harry and me. Daddy would tell us what to get done, and then go to Raton to get parts. We took it apart, cleaned and added the new parts Daddy brought back. When we put all the parts back it was beginning to look like it might not fit out the door. There was no way Daddy was going to take some of that motor apart without trying to make it out first. So we each got on a corner and found a handhold. With all parts added back onto it, the engine was quite a bit heavier than when we brought it in.

"When I say, boys, we'll pick her up. Whatever you do, don't let go," Daddy told us.

We were all straining and trying to keep a good grip. At just about the same time, our feet busted through the wood floor and we landed a foot down on the dirt foundation. The engine hadn't budged.

We may have fell through the floor, but we hadn't let go.

First Date

Esther met me at the truck when Daddy and me got back late Friday night. We'd gotten the engine back in the truck after taking some of it apart and putting it back together outside. It ran good and we'd been hauling for a few weeks.

"Alton, Sheron is sick and Mama won't let her go out tonight. I got a date with Robert and I can't go if you don't go with me."

The only way Mama and Daddy would let them go out with boys was if they would double date with each other. I sure was glad the rules were different for boys and girls.

424

"I don't have a girlfriend right now, Esther, who would I go with?"

I didn't seem to keep a girlfriend for long. There had been Barbara Davis and then Linda King, but they said I was gone working too much and didn't have enough money. I couldn't really argue with them about that.

"What if you went with my friend, Cleta? She's cute and fun. You've seen her. She's real nice."

I knew who she was talking about. She had the Edsel... and the blue eyes.

"I'll go with you. But you gotta set it up."

"I knew you would. I'll go over and ask her."

Esther took off walking towards Cleta's and it didn't take her long to get out of sight, that girl could cover some ground. Mama had bought me a new pair of $5 Levi's so I was glad to have a new pair of britches for my date. I rolled up the sleeves on my shirt, slicked back my hair and cuffed my pants over my loafers, I couldn't help but wish I had some cowboy boots but I'd never found any I had enough money to buy.

Robert came and picked up Esther and me and then we went to Cleta's to pick her up. Esther told me not to go to the door, Cleta's folks thought she was out with some friends from school. She had on a white shirt and pink skirt with her hair done up. I smiled and said hi when she got in the car. We all watched the picture show together and then went for ice cream. Cleta didn't talk much. She did smile and laugh at what I had to say. We drove her back home first and I walked her to the door.

"Do you want to go out sometime, maybe next Saturday when I get back from work?"

"If Mama says I can."

"I'll come pick you up and your mama can see I'm all right."

"Okay, I'll tell her you're coming over next Saturday."

I got back in the car and Robert took off. Esther talked her head off and I didn't hear a word of it.

When Saturday came around I was over at Cleta's as soon as I could get away. Her Daddy met me at the door and had me come in. Their house was very neat and clean and up against one wall they had a TV. Her Daddy was a tall cowboy, a few inches over six feet, with dark skin on his face and arms. I could tell he wore a hat most of the time, because his head was much lighter from his bald head to halfway down his forehead where his skin turned to leather. He was easy going and told me his name was Leon.

Cleta's mother, Polly, was a smaller woman, shorter than Cleta and always busy. Both her mama and her daddy smoked but they seemed like nice people. I figured I wouldn't have to hide my smoking from them, like I did my own mama. Cleta acted nervous until we got out of the house.

"I'm not sure Mama is happy with me going out with you," Cleta said.

"Just me, or anybody?"

"Well, I think anybody. I told them you were Esther's brother and they like her. I just haven't gone out a lot and it's kinda new for them. "

"Do they know my family?"

"Daddy said he remembered when you all moved to town. It was about a year ago, wasn't it?" I nodded my head. "He told me that he knew you were loggers, and loggers are drifters. So he was surprised you were still here."

I thought about what her daddy had said; that we were drifters. I knew Daddy was called a rambler by his family. That didn't seem like anything bad. To me drifters seemed like people that didn't know where they were going and didn't work. I knew Daddy always had a place in mind for us and I darn sure knew we always worked.

"We're not drifters. Sometimes you just have to go where things might be better," I told her. I was feeling a little prickly about the name her daddy had put on us.

"Oh, he didn't mean anything by it. We just haven't moved around like you."

"Well, I don't know of too many that have." I figured I'd let it go.

Her mama and daddy had come out to New Mexico from Oklahoma when she was about five. Her daddy had gone to work at the McDaniel's ranch as a cowboy. Her mama cooked for the cowboys and Cleta grew up herding cows and living out at Sweetwater on the ranch. After her mama went to beauty school, they moved to town closer to where her mama worked.

She was sweet and told fun stories and I liked to watch her while she talked. She was always putting her tongue up against the gap in her teeth. She didn't mention my broken tooth. She just had a sister three years younger and a baby brother, not yet a year old.

I didn't have much money so we didn't go to the show, but had ice cream at the Creamee and drove around town. I knew that the school was going to have a dance in the next few weeks so I asked her if I could take her and we made a date for it.

The night of the dance I pulled up to her house and she met me at the door. We drove up to the school for the dance and started walking in. The principal stopped us at the door. Unless I attended school I couldn't come in.

I looked at Cleta, "What do ya wanna do?" I asked her

"I'm not going in without you," she said.

I grinned at her. We turned around and walked into town. We went to the city park and talked. I told her I liked her hair.

"Since mama is a beauty operator, she always does my hair. It's so curly she has me keep it up, or she wants it cut awful short. She says she loves the curls but it always seems like she is trying to cut them off!"

Cleta hadn't had much to say the first date but she warmed up to me on this one. I couldn't believe I hadn't noticed her all the times she had been at the house with Esther. She was about the cutest thing I had ever seen. I took her home and gave her a kiss at the door. Just as we got started the porch light came on so I figured that meant the date was over. Cleta hurried inside and I grinned as I walked to the car.

The Brow Log

Every Monday, Daddy and me started the week again. Now working out of town all week hauling logs seemed to drag on. I couldn't wait to head back on Friday. I was at the house just long enough to clean up and head to Cleta's. I would take her out and then spend some time at her house, until her mama started slamming pots and pans and then I knew it was time to go.

I was in a hurry after we unloaded in Taos to head back to Cimarron on Friday. When we pulled in just before dark, there was a lot going on at the house. Louie had got back from his haul and was getting ready to leave. He hadn't even cleaned up and was jumping in his little pick up.

"Where you goin?" I hollered at him.

"Janet called from Espanola. She was headed this way but got lost, so I'm goin' to git her," he said as he drove away. I knew Louie had been going over to a buddy's house talking to Janet on the phone, but I didn't know they had patched things up. Looked like they had if she had driven down here from Oregon."

428

Harry was at the house too. He'd bought a new car because he and his wife had decided to move to Paradise, California. They were leaving in a few days and he'd driven over his white Plymouth.

"Hey, Alton, thought you might want to buy the Big White Horse?" Harry asked.

I always had liked that car.

"Hell yeah, I'll buy it," I told him. We were outside so I went ahead with the cuss word.

I gave him what I could for a down payment and he told me I could pay it out as I got the money, just Western Union it to him when he got to California. I took Harry back to his house and then went to pick up Cleta. We drove around town showing off in my new wheels. I gunned the engine, we raced up and down the main drag and spent some time in the front seat...having fun.

A lot of the time we double dated with my buddy, Wayne, and whatever girl he had. I still didn't have much money so it was an ice cream or the show. Sometimes Cleta had to pay for me, but she didn't let Wayne know about it.

Me, Esther and Sheron would see each other at the show, but we all kept it secret from Mama and Daddy. The show was still worldly and wrong to them, so we just didn't put it in their face. Kind of like my smoking, I think they both knew what was going on, but as long as I didn't do it front of them, they didn't say anything. I wouldn't disrespect them that way anyhow.

On Monday, like always, Daddy and me had a load of logs to haul to Taos. We drove into the log yard and parked. We unloaded my truck first, then I drove out of the way and parked. I got back on the forklift and we started on Daddy's. I drove the forklift to the side of the logs and raised the mast so I could hold them. When Daddy loosened the load I saw the brow log shift and then waited for Daddy to drop the lever on the load. I sat on the fork lift and waited with my foot on the brake. It was taking Daddy so long to untie the load, I finally put on the parking brake. Still, Daddy didn't come around from the other side of the load. I hollered at him a couple of times, he didn't holler back.

I figured I better go on the other side and see what was going on. I got off the fork lift and walked around the front of the truck to the other side. When I looked by the trailer, I saw Daddy laying face up on the ground, a log was laying on him and he wasn't moving.

"Daddy!" I ran to him. The cable had caught the sixteen foot brow log and pulled it off on Daddy. The weight of the log was across his chest and belly and had him pinned to the ground. I grabbed the log; it was so big around I couldn't get my arms around it, but I got a good hold on it, and heaved it off him. Daddy still wasn't moving and I hollered his name and shook him. His face was white and his mouth was slack. He didn't answer me back.

Some of the mill workers heard me, and came to see what was going on. When they saw Daddy they got real serious. A lady across the street who heard all the hollering called for an ambulance. Daddy didn't wake up even when we heard the sound of the sirens. He just laid there.

The ambulance came into the log yard, but they couldn't get close, because the log I threw off Daddy was in their way. A couple of workers went over to pick it up and move it, they couldn't do it by themselves so they had a couple of more fellows to come and help.

The ambulance workers brought a rolling cot to pick up Daddy. The mill boss was there now trying to help. The men were telling him what had happened.

Front end loader unloading the logs at Taos.

"How'd you get that log off your father?" he asked.

"I threw it off." I didn't know why he was so concerned with the log.

I heard them talk about me throwing off the log by myself, but I didn't pay them too much attention. They were hauling Daddy away to the hospital, I wasn't sure Daddy would have agreed to go, but he wasn't in any shape to tell them no.

A fellow from the mill took me over to the hospital and I waited outside in the waiting room for news. They came out and told me Daddy was going to be there a while so I should go and get my mother. I rode back to the mill, got in my truck and for the first time drove alone through the canyons towards Cimarron and Mama.

I parked in front of the house and Mama met me outside.

"Alton, what's the matter? I just heard one truck comin' and this is the wrong time of the week for you to be comin' back." She was wiping her hands on her apron.

"A log fell on Daddy, Mama, and he's hurt bad. He's at the hospital in Taos and the doctor said you should come right away."

Mama didn't act excited, but she prayed under her breath as she quickly got ready to leave. Esther ran to Louie's and told him and he came to drive Mama and the girls. I followed in my car and brought Hoyt Lynn. We drove to the hospital at Taos and went in, all except Mary who couldn't

431

because she hadn't remembered to put shoes on before we left. The girls had her sit on a bench that was just outside the hospital. When we looked out the window we could see her with her dirty face and loose hair looking sad and scared.

Soon the nurse told us Daddy would be there for a while. He had a broken collar bone, but the real trouble was with his insides. Somehow they were hurt and shook up and that was the worst thing. Daddy had only woken up a couple of times and not for very long. They had him on some kind of medicine that made him sleep. Mama stood beside him, her hand resting on his arm.

"Y'all might as well go on back. Yore Daddy is gonna be here a while and I'll stay with him. Get the little kids to bed, we'll see what tomorrow brings. I'm prayin' with all my strength your Daddy will be all right," Mama said.

"Mama, you call the neighbors if you need us sooner. We'll tell them you'll be callin'," Louie told her.

"I'll be fine, and with the Lord's help I'm sure your Daddy will, too."

Mama walked outside with us and sat on the bench by Mary and hugged her for a minute. Mary's face was streaked with tears. She must have felt lonesome sitting outside alone, I thought then I should have come out and sat by her. We left Mama by herself there at the hospital and got in the car. Mary and Hoyt Lynn rode with me.

"Is Daddy gonna die, Alton?" Mary asked me as she leaned up from the back seat.

"No, sugar, Daddy ain't gonna die." I just knew in my mind that there wasn't anything that could get the best of Daddy. He hadn't worked in the log woods his whole life to be brought low by a brow log.

Like Harry

Mama stayed in Taos for a long time. With her gone, Sheron and Esther took care of things at the house. I did what I could to help out. For the first time being oldest at home felt heavy with both Mama and Daddy gone. Mary was getting along okay with Daddy hurt. She told me as long as I was there she wasn't too worried. Louie was busy with his own wife so we didn't see much of him.

We talked to Mama on the phone every couple of days. After a couple of weeks I went and picked up Mama so she could see about things and rest. She talked to Louie about her worries over Daddy and called Rubin and Elaine on the neighbor's phone. She told them she was upset with the hospital because they weren't doing much of anything to help Daddy. She was thinking about taking him to a hospital in Santa Fe, but she wasn't sure what to do.

Without Daddy, I didn't drive the truck. We all felt that since I didn't have a driver's license it wasn't a good idea for me to go alone. With neither truck running, we weren't making any money. Mama had to make a deal with the stud mill and give them the truck. I hadn't known they held the papers on it.

People from the church were nice and checked on us and came to ask Mama if she needed anything. Mama said we were all fine. After a few days she went back to Taos, hopeful that something had changed with Daddy while she was gone.

With no work I was able to see Cleta a lot more. She got out of school at four o'clock and her Daddy didn't come in from the ranch until about 5:30. Her mama was at her beauty shop usually until about seven. I would come over if Cleta's little sister, Donna was gone, or she would tell on us. We would go to her house and I would watch TV. The black and white picture was good, but the picture rolled every few seconds. Cleta wouldn't watch it, but it didn't bother me at all.

Right outside her house was a long wire that hung down from a telephone pole that was about chest high. We would sit outside and I would put all the gym tricks I had learned in Alaska to good use. I jumped flat footed and cleared the wire. I did push-ups and handstands. Cleta would cheer me on. She wasn't too sure if her parents would be all right with

Alton and Cleta

me being there while they were gone so I always left before her Daddy came from the ranch. Then I would come back later with them there and spend the evening.

We were on the couch watching TV when Cleta got up and went to the window.

"I hear a car, Alton!"

We looked out and there was Schwartz the ranch foreman bringing Leon home early. I ran from the living room to the kitchen and out the side door. As I jumped, it seemed like I looked Schwartz right in the eye as he sat in the driver's seat of his pickup. I ran along the back porch, dipped under the clothes line and then jumped for the top of the ten foot fence. I grabbed the top with my hands, and swung myself over and made it in one leap.

I was sure Schwartz was already headed inside to tell Cleta's daddy I had been hanging around. I would just have to wait and see what happened the next day.

I drove by the school and talked to Cleta. She told me nothing had happened. We didn't know if Schwartz had not seen me or covered for me.

434

Cleta was nervous about it, so she decided to ask if it was all right if I came over during the day. Her mama told her as long as her grades didn't go down, it was all right, so Cleta started doing her homework right after school. I didn't worry about being caught alone with her at her house anymore. I was going to be eighteen in just a few weeks. She wouldn't be sixteen until the next May but I knew what I wanted.

We were babysitting her brother, Dane, and took him into Polly's bedroom to put him in his crib. We were talking quiet and she was covering up the baby. I looked at her and figured this was a good a time as any. I asked her the question,

"Don't you wish we were like Harry and Sharon?"

"Harry and Sheron, your sister?"

"No! Harry and Sharon Padmore, his wife."

Cleta walked towards the front room and I followed.

"Like them how?" she asked.

"Married, like them. Together. Living in our own house."

The more I was trying to explain, the more I started to feel silly.

"Well, yes, I do wish that." She smiled at me, but her face was kind of red. I didn't feel silly anymore. We sat on the couch in the front room, not watching the TV for a long time.

When I got ready to leave I grinned at her. "So, we'll just plan on that then. We'll go together until you get out of school and then we'll get married."

She nodded, we were both nervous about telling our folks, but I figured I had two years until I had to tell her mother.

Family

"What're y'all up to now?" I asked Mary.

Her and Roger were in the back yard. They had built a fire inside an old tire and had a raw chicken, still half froze, cooking in a pan over the fire.

"Makin' fried chicken," Mary said. Roger stayed silent like normal.

"Don't y'all dare eat that," I said. I went over and plucked it out of the pan.

Mary started to argue, "But we're hungry, Alton."

"Come on in the house," I told the both of them.

When I walked in, I hollered for Sheron. I saw right then that it was easy to lose track of the little kids without Mama around. Just the other day Mary and some of her friends, who were all boys, pulled the streamers down in the gym that had been decorated for Halloween. It had taken both Sheron and Esther to get her out of trouble with the school for that one. I was beginning to think she was getting a little wild.

"Sheron, get in here and fix these kids something to eat," I told her.

"Don't come in here tellin' me what to do, Alton," Sheron talked back to me, but she got out some bread and peanut butter.

"You're probably fixin' to go see that ol' gal you been runnin' around with," Mary said.

"She's not an old gal, Mary," I said.

"Well, I don't like her. You don't have no time for any of us since you been with her." I wanted to argue with Mary, but I could see that she was right. I thought maybe I better try to be around more.

Esther ran in the house.

"I just talked to Mama, she called over at the neighbors," Esther said. "She's says things seem to be gettin' better. She likes the hospital at Santa Fe and says the folk's there treat Daddy real nice, and her too."

Daddy's trouble was all in his intestines, but I didn't really understand what was wrong. Whatever it was it was taking a long time to heal, and Daddy just couldn't get his strength back.

"She thinks he might get to come home soon," Esther said. She got busy cleaning up the sandwich mess we had left.

I ate a couple of the sandwiches that Sheron made and got ready to go to work. I had got a job running the forklift at the stud mill at night. With the money I made from the mill and Louie's help, we were able to keep paying the rent and keep everybody fed. I would go over to Cleta's in the evening and when the house went to bed, I went to work. Wayne worked over there with me too. We got off about two in the morning. Sometimes we went to bed and sometimes we didn't. There wasn't nobody to tell me any different.

Esther, Sheron, Mary and Hoyt

Since I had turned eighteen I figured it was time to get that driver's license the cop was always on me about. Mama and Daddy weren't in town to sign for me, but now I didn't need them to. It was about the only test I ever passed and I walked out of the courthouse with a chauffeur's license. With that I thought I might be able to find me a driving job.

437

The stud mill laid me off and I worried over how I was going to help take care of the family and have a good enough job to get married. One way I could make a living was do what Rubin had done and join the service.

I talked it over with Cleta. If I was in the service it might make waiting for her to get out of school go by faster. Cimarron was too small to have an office so I drove into Raton to see the recruiter at his office. The door was locked, I jerked it back and forth a couple of times and then saw the sign saying he was gone for the day. I left Raton wondering what to do next.

I figured my best bet was to go back to the log woods. They had a new outfit running a logging company nearby so I hired on to skid logs. It was more money than working at the mill, but the work was hard as ever. I had bruises up and down my legs from climbing up and down the mountain. At the dinner break, I would rest, most of the time falling asleep. One fellow, trying to spook me, drove the CAT tractor almost on top of me but I didn't wake up. Leaning up against a stump, with my legs stretched out, I figured I must look just like Daddy did all those times he slept up against a tree or car. I knew now when you were tired, it was real easy to doze off anywhere.

When I got back I learned Daddy was finally getting out of the hospital. I don't know if Santa Fe did a better job or if time had finally healed him. Louie went and picked up him and Mama. The man I saw get out of the car didn't look much like the Daddy I had followed for so many miles. Small and weak and his gray hair thinner, Daddy leaned on Louie heavy, as Louie walked him in. It reminded me of all those years ago when Louie was hurt and needed help. This time it was Louie holding Daddy up.

Pretty soon a house on the west end of town came up for rent and Mama and Daddy moved the family over to it. It

438

had an inside bathroom and would be easier on Daddy since he was still sick. After working in the woods all day, I got back after dark. I walked into the house and saw the kids listening to the radio.

"What's going on? Where's Daddy and Mama?"

Sheron looked at me, "They're at the neighbors watching TV."

"Watchin' TV?" I asked.

Esther hurried to tell me, "Haven't you heard, Alton? President Kennedy's been shot and killed!"

"What!?"

"He was riding in his car in Dallas and a man shot him with a rifle. Mama and Daddy went to see the news about it."

I sat down on the couch with the kids and just listened to the radio. We didn't know what to do but to wait. Wait for Daddy and Mama to come back.

The next day nobody went to work. The whole town just about shut down. The schools were out, stores didn't open. Everywhere you went, that was all anybody could talk about. Daddy never

Alton and Rubin

had been a political man, I'm not even sure he ever voted. But when the president's been shot, it seems like it's everybody's business.

Mama kept wondering what this world was coming too. Daddy listened to all the talk, and shook his head saying

439

it was a shame. We hadn't ever been much for belonging to anything but ourselves, but for that time in Cimarron it seemed like the whole town was part of the same family.

Lincoln

Daddy and his five boys were sitting on the porch. We were letting the sun warm us. Rubin had come for Christmas, along with his wife and baby girl. Harry had made it back from California with his wife, who was expecting a baby in June. Louie was sipping coffee and teasing Hoyt Lynn, who was trying to act old enough to be with us all. At thirteen, he was trying awful hard to be big.

"There's jobs in Lincoln," Rubin said to me. "Maybe you oughta come back with me and Ruth Ann and see about workin' there."

I had been talking to them about needing a better paying job. There wasn't much money in skidding logs, and Cimarron didn't have much more going on.

"Maybe I will, what 'd'ya think, Daddy?" I wanted to know what he thought, but I also knew I'd better talk to Cleta about it.

"You're full grown I guess," Daddy said. "I think you can do whatever you think is best."

I left pretty soon after that to talk to Cleta. I hadn't been over as much as I wanted. She'd caught the Mumps over Christmas and her mama was worried they'd fall. I wasn't sure what that meant, but I could tell it was bad because Cleta had to stay in bed all the time. She was getting better now, but I knew I had to tell her what I was planning. Ever since the Navy office had been closed, I hadn't gone back over to Raton. Maybe that wasn't what I was supposed to do anyway.

I got in the Big White Horse, put her in reverse and started over to Cleta's. The transmission had gone out, the car would only move if it was going backwards. Now that we lived on the same side of town, it was easy to just back the car down the road to get to her house.

Cleta didn't want me to go, but I told her if there was a job there it'd be smart to go. I told her I'd be back, but I needed a job to prove to her folks I was worth marrying. By the end of the week I was riding in Rubin's '63 Ford Station wagon, headed to Nebraska.

Lincoln was about the biggest town I'd ever lived in. Rubin and Ruth Ann lived in a little house in what they called a subdivision. Rubin worked for Bernard Jensen at his co-op which was a service station and garage. He was in charge of servicing and fixing the Ford trucks that went through there. Rubin got me a job driving one of those trucks.

The trucks hauled the mail from the substation to the post office. All I had to do was load the carts into the trailer, drive, then push the carts into the post office. This was a great job considering how little labor I had to do. The more I drove a truck, the more I saw driving took a lot less backbreaking work to make a dollar. Before long, and I had enough money to buy a cute little candy apple red '47 Ford Coupe.

While I lived with Rubin, I hung around with his buddies but I missed Cleta. When I found a typewriter in the house I thought it would be a good idea to write to her. I hand wrote my letter first and then I started typing it onto the paper. The whole thing took over an hour. By the time I pecked out all the words in my letter, it was three lines long, but I mailed it anyway.

Rubin talked to Mama on the phone and she told him Daddy thought we ought to come back. He had a line on some timber and we could go in business together and make a good living. Rubin figured he'd go so he left with his family. I wanted to have some money in my pocket so I worked a few weeks more and then left too.

Things were starting to warm up in Cimarron. It was March, the snow was gone but the wind sure did blow. Mama's house was full with Rubin and his family so I moved in with Harry and Sharon. I spent most of the time I wasn't working at Cleta's now that her folks were used to me. Me and her had a lot of time to make up for while I was in Lincoln. I stayed as late as I could at her house even though the work day started early.

Daddy ran the operation for Miller Brother's Logging but didn't have to do the labor. He found the timber and made the deals. Harry worked the loader and put the logs on the log trucks. We had two, one for Louie to drive and one for Rubin. I hooked the tongs for wages and did what everybody told me to do. There was enough timber that we loaded other trucks too and made money from that.

We were headed to work Monday morning when we heard the news of an earthquake in Alaska. It was a big one. The phone lines were out up there and Mama worried and waited to hear news of Elaine. We saw pictures of how tore up Anchorage was, which was right where Elaine lived. Mama was beside herself worrying about her.

We were eating supper when somebody banged at the door. I got up to go see who it was.

"Y'all the Miller`s, ain't ya?" he asked.

"Yessir."

"Got somebody on my ham radio trying to get ahold of y'all. Name's Elaine Smith."

"Oh my," Mama said. She walked to the door.

Sheron took Mama over to the man's house and she got to talk to Elaine for a few minutes on the two way radio. They were all fine, but it had scared Elaine and she was talking about wanting to come out of Alaska.

Mama prayed more than ever. With the shooting of the president and now this earthquake, she worried that the end of the world might be coming. I felt bad for Mama but I knew for me things were just beginning.

A Good Job

The more I thought about it the more I figured that there just wasn't much reason for me and Cleta to not go ahead and get married. I talked to her and she wanted to. She would be sixteen in May and lots of girls got married at that age. I told her the next time I came over I was going to tell her folks.

When I came in to her house, Cleta was nervous as a cat. She wasn't too sure about how things were going to go and kind of hung back. I sat down at the table with Polly and Leon, looked at them and started talking.

"Cleta and me would like to get married." After I said it, nobody talked right away.

"After she is out of school, we'll see if that's still what y'all want," Polly said as she looked at me over the top of her reading glasses.

"We're thinking about right away."

Leon pushed back from the table and put his arms across his chest.

"Is there a reason you need to get married right away?" Leon arched an eyebrow at me.

I knew what he was getting at.

"No sir. We're just ready to get married."

"No daughter of mine is going to get married before she is even sixteen years old," Polly said like she was chewing on nails. She was getting madder and madder.

Polly got up from the table and went to the kitchen counter and started banging pots and pans and dishes. She

443

was acting like she was washing them, but I wasn't too sure any of them were going to survive.

"Boy, I think you better go," Leon told me. I hated to leave Cleta there to handle the rest of it. She was already starting to cry. I looked at her folks but knew I'd better go.

The next morning I went back over. I hadn't slept all night worrying, and I had to get this settled. Cleta let me in the door and she had a smile on her face.

"It's okay," she said. "They talked to me this morning and they'll let us get married as long as you agree to some things."

"How did that come about?" I asked her.

"Daddy sat down with Mama and told her there wasn't much point to fighting us. That we were probably gonna do what we were gonna do. He said you couldn't stop young kids from doing things no matter what. She could fight us and we were likely to run off and get married anyway. If they didn't fight it, we could all do this together and it would work out better."

"What'd your mama think?"

"She had about the biggest fit I ever saw and I was sent to bed. This morning she said we could get married as long as you had a steady job and could support me."

We walked together into the kitchen. Polly was there drinking coffee and smoking a cigarette.

"Alton, I'll agree to this, but you have to have a good job and show that you can take care of her. I don't like it much, but I expect there isn't much I can say to change things," she said as she blew out smoke into the air.

"I'll always take care of her," I said, but wondered how I would get that done.

I was working for the Miller Brothers and it seemed like it all ought to work, but Louie wouldn't listen to Rubin, Rubin wouldn't listen to Harry, and Harry wouldn't listen to anybody. I kept my mouth shut, knowing I was just the little brother, but in the end it all fell apart and everybody was mad at each other before it was over. Miller Brothers shut down and along with it, my job.

Cleta turned sixteen in May and finished the tenth grade. We knew we would be getting married soon, but hadn't decided on when yet. The motor in my '47 Coupe went out and now I didn't have a car to drive and still didn't have a job that Polly and Leon would call steady. I beat the brush for a job that would support me and Cleta.

I finally got to thinking about Lincoln and the job that Rubin had left. I called Rubin's old boss and talked to him. I told him I needed a job and was willing to do whatever he had. He liked me and told me that if I came back to Lincoln I could have the job Rubin used to have servicing and working on trucks. I finally had a line on a good job, the only trouble was it was seven hundred miles away. That might be another fight with Polly.

The Big Day

I kissed Cleta good bye as I got on the bus in Raton headed to Lincoln. It was June and I was going there to work until we could get married at the end of July. We figured we'd better get married before her folks changed their minds. I planned to work hard, get a car and drive back to Cimarron when it was time to get married. Then Cleta would come back to Lincoln with me.

I'd been so worried about convincing Polly and Leon that Cleta and me should get married, I kind of forgot to talk about it with Mama and Daddy. I figured I'd better tell them before I left for Lincoln again, so I talked to them one evening in the kitchen. Since I was the fifth one to get married, it wasn't a new thing to them. Mama said at least she'd see one

445

of her children get married. Daddy told me to make sure I did right by my girl. I promised I would.

I made it back to Lincoln and got to work. What I had to do at the co-op was easy enough and I worked hard to show Bernard Jensen I was a good hand. I found a car for $200. It was an off-white '54 Ford that was owned by a friend of my boss. He stood good for me since I didn't have all the money and the fellow sold it to me for payments. I told Mr. Jensen I had to go back to Cimarron for a few days at the end of July to get my wife and he let me off. I headed west as soon as I got off on Friday.

I drove straight to Cleta's house and after resting a while on her couch, looked at the things she had got ready for the wedding. She had a dress, the house was decorated with daisies and everything was ready. We were getting married in the living room of Cleta's folk's house. We were getting married on Monday, since that was the day Polly's beauty shop was closed.

I figured I'd better go see Mama and Daddy. Elaine met me at the door to hug my neck. She'd got so upset after the earthquake in Alaska, she had sent Mama a plane ticket to come up and help her drive out. Mama helped load Elaine's things in her car and had driven her and the four grandbabies all the way from Anchorage to Cimarron. Don planned on coming later. Elaine was proud as punch over the trip they had made. Mama didn't seem to think it was all that much.

With a full house I stayed with Harry and his wife again and met their baby girl. Before long it was Monday and time to get married. Harry loaned me his suit. It was dark and fit well enough. It was a little too long and the sleeves went down half way past my hands.

"You look sharp, little brother," Harry said as he fixed my tie. It was the first suit I had had on since Mama had

446

made me wear that green plaid thing up in Alaska. Up against that I was sure I looked great.

Somebody knocked at the door and Harry's wife went to answer it. Harry and me turned to look and see who it was.

It was the Johnny Arnello, the cop, and he was there to see me.

I went to the door to talk to him.

"Alton Miller?" he asked.

"You know who I am, Johnny."

"I'm here to serve you papers and take you to see the judge."

"What for?"

He handed me some papers and I couldn't make heads or tails of them. Harry came to stand beside me.

"What's going on here?" Harry asked.

"I guess I'm going to jail," I answered.

"You got to come with me." Johnny had me get in the car. Harry said I wasn't going anywhere without him and got in beside me. Johnny drove us both to the courthouse. We went inside to see the judge. He didn't look up when he started talking.

"Mr. Miller?"

I didn't answer.

"Mr. Miller!"

I realized he was talking to me. I'd never been called Mister before.

"Yes sir?"

He started reading and I couldn't believe what I was hearing. Old Man Whitton had served papers on me for the $40 he said I owed him for the tires I gotten from him over a year ago. I couldn't believe he had picked now to come after me.

I started to tell all of this to the judge when I heard a door slam behind me. Daddy was walking in from outside. It

447

seemed like Daddy took three steps and he was standing beside me.

"What's goin' on in here?" Daddy asked. He looked straight at the judge and told him, "This boy is supposed to get married today." Daddy told the judge about how I had been treated by Whitton and this wasn't the time for such a small thing. Daddy said he was taking us out of there and he'd deal with all this later. The judge couldn't do much more than agree with Daddy.

"Let's go boys," Daddy told us and turned around and walked out, Harry and me right behind him. Nobody stopped us. It was time to get married.

It was still light outside when the preacher called us man and wife and we kissed. There were handshakes and back slaps, hugging and a lot of tears, mostly from Polly. After cake and punch we ran outside through the

Alton and Cleta on their Wedding Day

door. We were pelted with rice, but we ducked instead of running through it which got a big laugh. We loaded up in the cars to drive through town.

The car was decorated with streamers and good luck was painted on the sides with shoe polish. Cleta and I got in my Ford and my brothers got in their cars to follow us as we paraded through town to show we had gotten married. My

448

buddies drove up beside us and blew their horn and fell in behind as we headed back to Cleta's.

It was pretty late when I got to thinking about where we were going for the night. Leon walked over to me and put something in my hand. It was a room key for the Don Diego Hotel. I made sure I didn't smile at him, but I sure wanted to.

Home

The next morning we went to Polly's and finished loading Cleta's things into the car. Her mama cried and her daddy hugged her as we said good bye. It was time to drive back to Lincoln. We stopped by to see Mama, Daddy and the kids at their house. Mama hugged me and Daddy shook my hand and told me he would take care of the law for me.

I realized I was leaving home for good. For Mama and Daddy, home had always been Louisiana, but it never had been for me. It wasn't any of the houses, shacks, railroad cars or road side camps we had lived. It wasn't a place. Home had been the sound of the saw, the smell of cut timber, the feel of wind in my face as we headed down the highway.

Home was the whisper of my mama's prayers, my daddy's booming voice as he preached, Louie's stories and Elaine's boogie woogie piano. It was headstrong Rubin, Harry's wink, and tomboy Sheron. It was Esther's fast talk and faster walk. Hoyt Lynn who tried so hard to be big like his brothers and Mary's flying red hair. Mama and Daddy were home, wherever we were.

We walked to the car and I looked back at all of them. Daddy had his arm around Mama's shoulders. She waved as we got into the car and took off.

I steered the car around the curve in the road and looked up ahead. With my wife sitting beside me I knew no matter where the road took us, I was home.

449

Louie, Alton, Rubin, Harry
Esther, Wesley, Fonceal, Sheron,
Hoyt Lynn and Mary
1964

LOUISIANA 1993

The rain fell onto the canopy as it shielded the two graves. One had been there for over a decade, the other, a day. I stood with my brothers and sisters as we laid Daddy to rest.

We were here to see him home. Here to Louisiana and home to his place beside Mama. There were only about ten chairs set up and still the seats in the back row were empty. The girls sat in the chairs. Their husbands stood behind them, they weren't going to sit if the Miller boys didn't. Elaine stood up to give Daddy's eulogy. She stepped back and got in the rain. Rubin took her arm and helped her back under the canopy so she didn't get wet.

It had been hard on Daddy to live without Mama. We had all done what we could to make him happy. Only Mama had been able to do that.

Elaine began reading and I thought of our life growing up. Elaine's voice was strong and clear.

"Daddy offered us few material things; rather he gave us the golden sunsets of New Mexico, the magnificent Rockies of Colorado, the evergreens of Oregon, the rich plains of Texas, the diamond sparkles of Arizona, and Alaska's winter beauty, the bountiful bayous of Louisiana and much, much more. One would be mesmerized as he told the fast colorful stories of his life and his reference to himself as 'Ol' Wesley.' Despite some people's belief, I think 'Ole Wesley's bunch' turned out to be the best I need and the best I know."

I kept myself from crying as I looked over at the brothers and sisters I had grown up with. Our faces were lined and a few of us had grey in our hair. It had been many years since we had all been together. As I let a few tears fall, I knew myself to be home.

I guess the life we lived had been quite a story.

Fonceal and RW Miller

I want to thank everyone who contributed to getting these stories down on paper. Not only those who lived it, but those listened over the years and remembered wonderful details.

I especially appreciate the input and advice from Robert Mayer's writing workshop I attended in Santa Fe. His insight, along with the other participants, helped to shape this story into the book it has become.

I want to thank my family, my husband Randy and my children, for all their help. From reading and rereading manuscripts to technical support on the computer, you know I couldn't have done it without you...Sarah.

Special thanks to my mother, Cleta Pigman Miller. As we retraced the miles travelled by Wesley's bunch she documented our travels in photographs. Traipsing through brush, standing in muddy ditches and navigating dusty roads she helped daddy and I tell his American story. We asked much of her and many times the 'RW' came out in us as we demanded she do things our way.

Some things never change.

By the way-
Alton and Cleta have been married for over fifty years.

21796791R00278

Made in the USA
San Bernardino, CA
06 June 2015